Preface

This book is mainly targeted for BCA exam of Computer-oriented Numerical Techniques. It has been introduced in market after seeing the huge demand of ready to grasp material for exams with high level of quality, and its un-availability in market. We the GullyBaba Publishing House took a step ahead to publish the quality material focusing on exams at the same time giving you indepth knowledge about the subject.

GPH Book is the pioneer effort that provides a unique methodology so as to perform better in exams. If your goal is to attain higher grade use this powerful study tool independently or along with your text.

*On the Web : **www.gullybaba.com** is the vital resource for your exams acting as catalyst to boost up your preparation. Gullybaba.com has been Listed **no.1** in www.google.com and www.yahoo.com when you search "IGNOU MCA BCA MBA". Now you can access us on the net through **www.doctorignou.com, www.doeacconline.com, www.gphindia.com, and www.gullybabapublishinghouse.com.***

Feedback about the book can be sent at **cs71writers@gullybaba.com.**

Acknowledgments :

We appreciate the staff and facility support provided by GullyBaba Publishing House. In particular, we appreciate the encouragement and professional advises received from Mr. Ajay Saini, Mr. Tarun Sharma, Mr. Ajay Jain, Mr. Amit Mahajan and many more.

Also we would like to thank typesetting and designing team Mrs. Bhawna Verma, Mr. Shravan Vats, Mr. Mukesh.

We gratefully acknowledges the significant contributions of Mr. Mahesh Chand, Mrs. Bimla Devi, Mrs. Bhawna Verma and our experts in bringing out this publication.

New Delhi ***Publisher***

Feedback is the breakfast of Champions.

Ken Blanchard

You can Help other students.
"Inform any error or mistake in this book."

We and Universe
will reward you for Your Kind act.

Email at : feedback@gullybaba.com
or
WhatsApp on 9350849407

COMPUTER-ORIENTED NUMERICAL TECHNIQUES

CS-71

For

Bachelor of Computer Applications

[BCA]

Dr. A.K. Saini

Vimal Kumar Sharma

Useful For

IGNOU, Nalanda University, Lalit Narayan Mithila University, Andhra University, Pt. Sunderlal Sharma (Open) University (Bilaspur), Annamalai University, Bangalore University, Bharathiar University, Bharathidasan University, HP University, Jamia Millia Islamia, Kakatiya University (Andhra Pradesh), KSOU (Karnataka), KOU (Rajasthan), MPBOU (MP), MDU (Haryana), Punjab University, Tamilnadu Open University, Sri Padmavati Mahila Visvavidyalayam (Andhra Pradesh), Sri Venkateswara University (Andhra Pradesh), UCSDE (Kerala), University of Jammu, YCMOU, Rajasthan University, UPRTOU (UP) and all other Indian Universities.

GULLYBABA PUBLISHING HOUSE (P). LTD

AN ISO 9001:2008 CERTIFIED CO.

Developed and Produced by:

GullyBaba Publishing House (P) Ltd.

Regd. Office:
2525/193, 1st Floor,
Onkar Nagar-A, Tri Nagar,
New Delhi-110035
Landmark: Kanhaiya Nagar Metro Station

Branch Office:
1A/2A, 20, Hari Sadan,
Ansari Road, Daryaganj,
New Delhi-110002
Ph. 011-23289034

E-mail: info@gullybaba.com, Website: GullyBaba.com

Edition: 2013

ISBN: 978-81-89086-17-6

Contents

Question Papers

CHAPTER-1

COMPUTER ARITHMETIC

Everyone come across a wide variety of information in the form of figures, tables, graphs, etc. through newspapers, radio, television and other means of communication. It is therefore essential to know how to extract relevant and exact information from such data statistics. This approach to get relevant information involves formulation of mathematical models of physical situations. It requires development, analysis and use of algorithms. When a calculator or digital computer is used to perform numerical computations, an unavoidable error called round off error must be considered. This error arises because the arithmetic operations performed in a machine involves number with only a finite number of digits, with the result that many calculation are performed with approximate representation of actual number. The computer has the capability to perform only the basic arithmetic operations of addition, subtraction multiplication and division. But when we use the algorithm then all other mathematics operators are reduced to these basic operation. Here we will discuss the various forms of approximation and errors and then sources and how they propagate during the numerical process.

i) Non associative of arithmetic due to round of Error

Non-Associative of arithmetic due to round off error if x* is an approximation to x, then use say that x* approximates x to n significant β digits provided absolute error.

$$|x - x^*| \leq 1/2\ \beta^{s-n+1}$$

with s the largest integer such that $\beta^s \leq |x|$

x* is said to be approximate x correct to n significant β digit if

$$\frac{|x-x^*|}{|x|} \leq 1/2\ \beta^{1-n}$$

ii) Sources of errors while carrying out numerical calculations to solve a problem

We list below the type of errors that are encountered while carrying out numerical calculation to solve a problem:

1) Round off errors arises due to floating point representation of initial data in the machine. Subsequent error in the solution due to this is called propagated error.
2) Due to finite digit arithmetic operations the computer generates in the solution of a problem errors known as generated error or rounding error.
3) Sensitivity of algorithm of the numerical process used for solving a problem affects accuracy of the solution of the problem and is know as instability and the process is said to be unstable.
4) Error due to finite representation of an inherently infinite process. For example, consider the use of a finite number of terms in the infinite series expansion of sinx, cosx or f(x) by Maclaurin's or Taylor's Series expression. Such errors are called truncation errors

iii) Generated Errors

Error arising due to inexact arithmetic operation is called generated error. In exact arithmetic operation results due to finite digit arithmetic operations in the machine. In arithmetic operation is done in infinite digit i.e rational form of simplication then this error would not appear. During an arithmetic operation on two floating point numbers of same length n, we obtain a floating point number of different length m (usually m>n) computer can not store the resulting number exactly since it is working with a length n. So only n digits are stored. This gives rise to error.

(iv) Floating Point representation of a number

The numbers are stored in a computer in two forms : fixed-point and floating-point forms. The fixed point mode is used to represent integers while the floating-point mode is used to represent real numbers.
A floating-point number is of the form

$x = \pm(d_1.d_2.....d_n)\,\beta^n, 0 \leq di < \beta, m \leq e \leq M$

where d_1, d_2 .... d_n are all digits in the base 'β' of the number system used and lie between o and β. The exponent m is such that $M_1 \leq m \leq M_2$, where M_1 and M_2 vary with the computer. The fractional part.d_1d_2 .... d_n is called the mantissa which lies between ± 1 and restricts the size of a number. If a floating-point number has a fixed mantissa of l digits, we say that the word length of the computer is l. For instance, the number 22.74×10^4 is represented as .2274E4 (E4 is used to represent 10^4). Hence the mantissa is .2274 and the exponent is 4. While storing numbers, the leading digit in the mantissa is always made non-zero by suitably shifting it and adjusting the value of the exponent accordingly. This process is called normalization. Therefore the number .003374 in normalized floating point mode would be stored as .3374E-2.Thus the shifting of the mantissa to the left till its most significant digits is non-zero is called normalization.

v) Truncation Error

There are errors caused by using approximate formulas in computations. Such as the one that arises when a function f (x) is evaluated from an infinite series for x after 'truncating' it of a certain stage.

$$S = \sum_{i=0}^{\infty} a_i x^i \text{ is replaced by the finite sum } \sum_{i=0}^{n} a_i x^i$$

The series has been truncated.

For example if $e^x = 1 + x^2/2! + x^3/3! + x^4/4! + \ldots$

is replaced by $1 + x + x^2/2! + x^3/3! + x^4/4! = x'$ (say),

then the truncation error is x-x1. Truncation error is a types of algorithm error.

vi) Instability of algorithm

Algorithm is a step by step process that describe a method for solving any mathematical problem. In numerical Algorithm errors grow in each step of calculation let ε be an initial error and Rn (ε) represents the growth of an error at the nth step after n subsequent operation due to ε. Some time in an algorithm a step is reached when, the alternative is to state that relative error ≥ epsilon', In such case the algorithm is said to be unstable since the solution has to convergence in n iterations.

vii) Round off error

Round off errors arises due to floating point representation of initial data in the machine Sub sequent error in the solution due to this is called propagated error. Due to the finite digit arithmetic operations, the computers generates in the solution of a problem error known as rounding errors.

Let flow be floating point representation of real number x. Then $e^x = x - f(x)$ is called Round off error. This errors occur when a fixed number of digits are use to represent exact number.

viii) Non-Associativity of addition of number

Computer addition of numbers is non-associative which is illustrated by following example.

Let $a = 0.345 \times 10^0$, $b = 0.245 \times 10^{-3}$

and $c = 0.432 \times 10^{-3}$

Now using 3 digit decimal arithmetic with rounding, we have

$b + c = 0.000245 + 0.000432$

$= 0.000677$

$= 0.677 \times 10^{-3}$

Now $a + (b + c) = 0.345 + 0.000677$ (in accumulator)

$= 0.346 \times 10^0$ (in memory) with rounding

$a + b = 0.345 \times 10^0 + 0.245 \times 10^{-3}$

$= 0.345 \times 10^0$ (in memory)

$(a + b) + c = 0.345432$ (in accumulator)

$= 0.345 \times 10^0$ (in memories)

Hence we see that

$(a + b) + c \neq a + (b + c)$

ix) Loss of Significant digits

Any digit is a significant digit except when it is used to fix the decimal point or to fill the places of unknown digits. For example, in the number 0.00154, the significant digits are 1, 5 and 4. The zeroes, on the other hand, are used to fix the decimal point. However, in the number 1234.0567 all digits are significant. Accuracy of a result is dependent upon the number of significant digits needed to express it. In general , if a solution is required to be accurate to n significant digits, we must see that relative error is less than 10^{-n} . In interative calculation, the iterative process stops when the required number of significant digits in the answer is reached. Thus, if a relative error must lie between 0.0001 and 0.001for a four digit normalised floating point number, then to guarantee 3 significant digit accuracy the relative error should be ≤ 0.001.

x) Propagated Errors

Since in a numerical problems, the true value of numbers may not be used exactly i.e. in place of true values of the numbers, some approximate values like floating point numbers are used initially. The error arising in the problem due to these inexact/ approximate values is called propagated error. Let x^* and y^* be approximations to x and y respectively and a be arithmetic operation. Then, The propagated error = $xay - x^*ay^*$

r.p.e. = relative propagated error

$$= \frac{xay - xa^* y^*}{xay}$$

(xi) Rounding of a number

In the round off method, the last retained significant digit is rounded up by 1, if the first discarded digit is larger or equal to 5; other wise the last retained digit is unchanged.

Rules to round off a number to n significant figures:

i) Discard all digits to the right of the nth digit.

ii) if the discarded number is :

a) Less than half a unit in the 17th place, leave the 17th digit unchanged.

b) greater than half a unit in the 17th place, increase the 17th digit by unity.
c) exactly half a unit in the 17th place, increase the 17th digit by unity if it is odd otherwise leave it unchanged.

for example

2.453 to 2.45 3.567 to 3.57
98.865 to 98.9 5.8254 to 5.82
1.4332 to 1.43 28698 to 28700

Also the number = 6.284359, 9.864651, 12.464762
round off to four places of decimal at 6.2844, 9.8646, 12.4648 respectively.

xii) Chopping

In chopping the extra digits are dropped. This is called truncating the number. If fl(x) is chosen as the normalized floating point number between 0 to x and nearest to x. Here $d_{i+1}......d_{i+2}$ etc. are neglected and f 1(x) $=d_1d_2$ etc. are neglected and f 1(x) = $d_1d_{2....}d_n\beta^e$.

Suppose we are using a computer with a fixed word length four digits. Then number like 42.7893 will be stored as 42.78, and the digit 93 will be dropped.

Mathmatical preliminaries:

In this section we state, without proof, certain mathematical results which would be useful in the sequel.

THEOREM: If f(x) is continuous in $a \le x \le b$, and if f(a) and f(b) are of opposite signs, then $f(\xi)=0$ for atleast one number ξ such that a< ξ <b.

THEOREM: Rolle's theorem. if

(i) f (x) is continuous in $a \le x \le b$,

(ii) f'(x) exists in a<x<b, and

(iii) f(a) = f(b) =0, then there exists atleast one value of x, say ξ, such that

$$f'(\xi) = 0, \quad a<\xi<b$$

THEOREM: Generalized Rolle's theorem. Let f(x) be a function which is n times differentiable on [a ,b]. If f(x) vanishes at the (n+1) distinct points $x_{0,}x_{1,..............,}x_n$ in (a ,b), then there exists a number ξ in (a ,b) such that $f^{(n)}(\xi)=0$.

THEOREM : Intermediate value theorem. Let f(x) be continuous in [a,b] and let k be any number between f(a) and f(b). Then there exists a number ξ in (a,b) such that f(ξ) =k.

THEOREM : Mean-value theorem for derivatives. If

(i) f(x) is continuous in [a,b],

and (ii) f'(x) exists in (a,b),

then there exists atleast one value of x, say ξ, between a and b such that

$$f'(\xi)=\frac{f(b)-f(a)}{b-a}, \quad a<\xi<b$$

Setting b = a + h, this theorem takes form

$$f(a+h)=f(a)+hf'(a+\theta h),\ 0<\theta<1.$$

THEOREM : Taylor series for a function of one variable. If f(x) is continuous and possesses continuous derivatives of order n in an interval that includes x = a, then
in that interval

$$f(x)=f(a)+(x-a)f'(a)+\frac{(x-a)^2}{2!}f''(a)$$

$$+..........+\frac{(x-a)^{n-1}}{(n-1)!}f^{n-1}(a)+R_n(x),$$

Where $R_n(x)$, the remainder term , can be expressed in the form

$$R_n(x)=\frac{(x-a)^n}{n!}f^n(\xi), a<\xi<x.$$

THEOREM : Maclaurin's expansion.

$$f(x)=f(0)+xf'(0)+\frac{x^2}{2!}f''(0)+....+\frac{x^n}{n!}f^n(0)+......$$

Q1. Describe/Define the following with one example for each : **[DEC03, Q1]**

(i) Sources of Errors
(ii) Relative Error
(iii) Direct Methods

(i) Sources of Errors

There are some types of errors that are encountered while carrying out numerical calculation to solve a problem.

(1) Round off errors arise due to floating point representation of initial data in the machine. Subsequent error in the solution due to this is called propagated error.

(2) Due to finite digit arithmetic operations, the computer generates in the solution of a problem errors known as generated error or rounding error.

(3) Sensitivity of the algorithm of the numerical process used for solving a problem (as calculation of f(x) from x) affects accuracy of the solution of the problem and is known as instability and the process is said to be unstable.

(4) Errors due to finite representation of an inherently infinite process. For example, consider the use of a finite number of terms in the infinite series expansions of Sinx, Cosx or f(x) by Maclaurian's or Taylor Series expression. Such errors are called truncation errors.

(ii) Relative Error

Relative Error is the ratio of round - off error with real number.

Let f(x) be floating point representation of real number x. Then $e^x = x\text{-}f(x)$ is called round off error and.

$$r_x = \left(\frac{x - f(x)}{x}\right) \text{ or } \left(\frac{e^x}{x}\right)$$

is called the relative error.

(iii) Direct Methods

The Direct Method is a method of computing the value in linear equation in which amount of computation is fixed. This method reduce the given equations to a form from which the solution can be obtained by simple method Gauss Jordan Method is the example of Direct Method.

The Direct Methods are generally used when the Matrix is dense or filled i.e. there are few zero elements, and the order of the matrix is not very large, say $n < 50$.

CHAPTER-2

SOLUTION OF NON-LINEAR EQUATIONS

We will dissuss the must basic problems in numerical analysis. The problem is called a root-finding problem and consists of finding-values of the variables x(real) that satisfy the equation f(x) = 0, for a given function. Numerical computations of the real roots of a given equation.

$$f(x) = 0$$

Which may be algebraic or transcendental. It will be assumed that the function f(x) is continuously differentiable a sufficient number of times. All the methods for numerical solution of equations discussed here will consist of two steps. First step, is the location of the roots, i.e., rough approximate value of the roots and obtained as initial approximation to a root.

Second step, consists of methods,. Which improve the rough value of each roof.

A method of improvements of the value of a root at the second step usually involves a process of successive approximation or iteration. In such a process of successive approximation a sequence $\{x_n\}$ n = 0,1, 2,......is generated by the method used starting with the initial approximation X_0 of the root α obtained in the first steps such that the sequence $\{X_n\}$converges to α as $n \to \infty$. This x_n is called the nth approximation or n^{th} iterate and it gives a sufficiently accurate value of the root α, if n is sufficiently large.

Bisection Method : Bisection Method states that if a function f(x) is continuous between a and b and f(a) and f(b) are of opposite signs, Then there exists at least one root between a and b. Let f(a) be negative and f(b) positive. Then the roots lies between a and b and let its approximate value be given by $X_0 = \frac{a+b}{2}$. If $f(x_0)$ =0, we conlude that x_0 is a root of the equation f(x) = 0. Otherwise, the roots lies either between x_0 and b, or between x_0 and a depending on whether $f(x_0)$ is negative or positive. We designate this new interval as $[a_1, b_1]$ whose length is [b-a]/2. As before, this bisected at x_1 and the new interval will be exactly half the length of the previous one. We repeat this process until the latest interval is as small as desired, say ε. Then we have

$\frac{[b-a]}{2^n} \leq \varepsilon$ for the nth Where $\left[a_{n,} b_n\right]$ new interval.

Fixed point method : Any function in the form of

$$f(x) = 0 \text{ -------------(1)}$$

Can be manipulated such that x is on the left hand side of the equation as shown below:

$$x = g(x) \text{-------------(2)}$$

Equation (1) and (2) are equivalent and therefore a root of Equation (2) is also the root of equation(1). The root of equation (2) is given the point of intersection of the curves y = x and y = g(x). This intersection point in known as the fixed point of g(x)

Regular – Falsi Method : Regular falsi method attempts to speed up bisection method retaining its guaranteed convergence. In this method, we choose two points x_0 and x_1. Such that f (x_0) and f (x_1) are of opposite signs. Since the graph of y=f(x) crosses the x-axis between these two points, a root must lie in between these points.

Now, the equation of the chord joining the two points, $[x_0, f(x_0)]$ and $[x_1, f(x_1)]$ is:

$$y-f(x_0) = \frac{f(x_1)-f(x_0)}{x_1-x_0}(x-x_0)$$

This cut x-axis at the point x_2 given by

$$0-f(x_0) = \frac{f(x_1)-f(x_0)}{x_1-x_0}(x_2-x_0)$$

$$x_2 = \frac{x_0 f(x_1)-x_1 f(x_0)}{f(x_1)-f(x_0)}$$

If $f(x_2)$ and $f(x_0)$ one of the opposite signs, then the roots lies between x_0 and x_2 and we replace x_1 by x_2 and obtain the next approximation, otherwise replace x_0 by x_2 and generate the next approximation.

Newton-Rapson Method : Newton-Rapson is a special example of fixed point. This method is generally used to improve the result obtained by one of the previous methods. Let x_0 be and approximate root of f (x)=0 and let $x_1 = x_0 + h$ be the correct root so that f (x_1)=0.

Expanding f (x_0+h) by Taylor's series then

$$f(x_0)+hf'(x_0)+\frac{h^2}{2!}f''(x_0)+...........=0$$

Neglecting the second and higher order derivatives, we have

$f(x_0) + hf^1(x_0) = 0$

which gives $h=-\dfrac{f(x_0)}{f'(x_0)}$

A better approximation than x_0 in therefore givenby x_1 ,where

$$x_1 = x_0 - \frac{f(x_0)}{f^1(x_0)}$$

Successive approximations are given by $x_2, x_3, ..., x_{n+1}$, Where

$$x_{n+1} = x_n - \frac{f(x_n)}{f'(x_n)}$$

Which is the Newton Raphson Formula

Secant Method : Secant method is a modification of the regular-falsi method and retains the use of second throughout, but dispenses the bracketing of the root. Function f(x) and two given points x_0 and x_1 instead of using Newton Raphson method.

$$x_1 = x_0 - \frac{f(x_0)}{f^1(x_0)}$$

$$f'(x_0) \approx \frac{f(x_1)-f(x_0)}{x_1-x_0}$$

$$x_2 = x_0 - \frac{f(x_0)}{\frac{f(x_1)-f(x_0)}{x_1-x_0}}$$

$$= \frac{x_0 f(x_1) - x_1 f(x_0)}{f(x_1)-f(x_0)}$$

$$\frac{f(x_1)-f(x_0)}{x_1-x_0}$$

Q1. Compare the following treating methods with each other
i) Bisection Method
ii) False position Method
iii) Newton-Rapson Method

iv) Secant Method
v) Fixed point Method

i) Bisection

The Bisection method converges slowly. It is, however the simplest iterative method and is guaranteed to converge. Convergence is slow and steady.

ii) False position

The false position method is guaranteed to converges. It is, however slow as it is first order convergent. The amount of computational effort per iteration is one function evaluation. It is not necessarily a monotonic convergence to the root but most often it will be superior to bisection method.

iii) Newton-Raphson

Newton-Raphson method has the fastest convergence. It is an excellent method if one is already near the root. It is, however, quite sensitively as it may diverge if f^1 (x) is near zero anytime during the iterative cycle.

iv) Secant

Secant method is not guaranted to converge. It, however, converges faster than the false position method. It also computes the given function only once per iteration. It may be considered the most economical method, giving reasonable rapid convergence at low cost.

v) Fixed point Method

Fixed-point method is suitable in some special cases. It is easy to program and is first order convergence. It is not guaranted to converge.

Q2. x_2 = .6071 for the given equation given below, 3x - cosx - 1 = 0
Justify x_2 by
(i) false position (Regula Falsi Method)
(ii) Netwon Raphson method
Solution :

False position Method :- y = f(x) = 3x - cosx-1

let x = .60, f(.60) = -0.025

f(.61) = .010

we tell that root lies in the interval (.60, .61) the successive approximations are

	x	y
First	.60	-.025
approx	.61	.010
difference	.01	.035

$$\therefore h_1 = \frac{.01 \times .025}{0.035} = .007$$

$$x^{(1)} = .60 + .007 = .607$$

second	.607	-.00036
approx	.608	.00321
difference	.001	.00357

$$h_2 = \frac{.001 \times .0036}{.00357} = .0001$$

$$\therefore x^{(2)} = 60.7 + .0001 = .6171$$

Third	.001	.00357
Approx	.6071	.00000
Differ.	.0001	.00035

$$h_3 = \frac{.0001 \times .0000}{.00035} = 0$$

$$x^{(3)} = .6071 + 0 = .6071$$

Since $x^{(2)} = x^{(3)}$ so value of root is .6071

By method of Newton Raphson

$f(x) = 3x - \cos x - 1$

$f^1(x) = 3 + \sin x$

we have $x_{n+1} = x_n - \dfrac{f(x_n)}{f^1(x_n)}$

$$n = 0,\ x_1 = x_0 - \frac{f(x_0)}{f^1(x_0)}$$

$$\text{Let } x_0 = .60, x_1 = .60 - \left\{\frac{3 \times .60 - \cos(.60) - 1}{3 + \sin(.60)}\right\}$$

$$= .60 - \frac{-0.25}{3.56464} = .60701$$

$$\therefore\ x_1 = .60701$$

$$x_2 = x_1 - \frac{f(x_1)}{f^1(x_1)}$$

$$= .60701 - \left\{\frac{3.60707 - \cos(.60701) - 1}{3 + \sin(.60701)}\right\}$$

$$x_2 = .60701$$

Hence by both method we see that x_2 =.60701 Hence root is justified.

Q3. Solve the equation $e^x + x - 2 = 0$ by Newton-Raphson iterative method, staring with value x = 0.4. [DEC03, Q1(i, b)] [6]

Here $f(x) = e^x + x-2$

$f^1(x) = e^x + 1$

Hence equation gives

$$x_{n+1} = x_0 - \frac{f(x_0)}{f^1(x_0)}$$

$x_0 = 0.4$

$f(0.4) = e^{(0.4)} + 0.4 - 2$ where $e^{0.4}$=1.491824698

$= -0.108175$

$f^1(0.4) = 2.491824$

$$x_1 = x_0 - \frac{f(x_0)}{f^1(x_0)}$$

$$= 0.4 - \left(\frac{-0.108175}{2.491824}\right)$$

$= 0.4 - (-0.0434119)$

$= .4434$

$f(x_1) = f(0.4434) = 0.0014139$

$f^1(x_1) = f^1(0.4434) = 2.5580$

$$x_2 = x_1 - \frac{f(x_1)}{f^1(x_1)}$$

$$=0.4434 - \left(\frac{-0.014139}{2.5580}\right)$$

$= 0.4439$

Therefore, the roots of equation, by Newton Raphson method,

(x_1, x_2) are $(0.4434, 0.4439)$

Q4. Using any one of the iterative methods (e.g., bisection, fixed-point, Newton-Raphson etc.) find the real root of the equation $x^3 + 3x^2 + 4x + 12$ starting with value x = 2. [DEC02, Q1(b)] [6]

Here $f(x) = x^3 + 3x^2 + 4x + 12$

$f^1(x) = 3x^2 + 6x + 4$

given $x_0 = 2$

First iteration $x_0 = 2$, $f(x_0) = 40$, $f^1(x_0) = 28$

$$\therefore \; x_1 = x_0 - \frac{f(x_0)}{f^1(x_0)} = 2 - \frac{40}{28}$$

$= 2-1.428$

$= 0.571$

Second iteration $x_0 = 0.571$

$f(x_0) = (0.571)^3 + (0.571)^2 + 4(0.571) + 12$

$= 0.1861694 + 0.978123 + 2.284 + 12$

$= 15.448$

$f^1(x_0) = 3(0.571)^2 + 6(0.571) + 4$

$= 0.978123 + 3.426 + 4$

$= 8.404$

$$\text{Now} \quad x_1 = x_0 - \frac{f(x_0)}{f^1(x_0)}$$

$$= 0.571 - \frac{15.448}{8.404}$$

$= 0.571 - 1.838$

$= -1.267$

Third iteration

$x_0 = -1.267$

$f(x_0) = (-1.267)^3 + 3(-1.267)^2 + 4(-1.267) + 12$

$= -2.034 + 4.816 - 5.068 + 12$

$= -7.102 + 16.816 = 9.714$

$f'(x_0) = 3(-1.267)^2 + 6(-1.267) + 4$

$= 4.816 - 7.602 + 4$

$= 8.816 - 7.602$

$= 1.214$

$$\text{Now } x_1 = x_0 - \frac{f(x_0)}{f^1(x_0)} = -1.267 - \frac{9.714}{1.214}$$

$= -1.267 - 8.0016$

$= -9.268$

Hence, the approximate value of root to three places of decimal is -9.268

Q5. Using Newton-Raophon method, find square root of 11 (eleven) with initial valve of $x_0 = 3$. **[DEC01, Q1(c, i)]**

(1) Using Newton-Raphson method we have

Let $x = \sqrt{11}$ $\quad \therefore x^2 = 11$

$\therefore f(x) = x^2 - 11 = 0$

$f(x) = 2x$

$x_0 = 3$ (given)

Iteration 1

$f(x_0) = f(3) = x^2 - 11 = (3)^2 - 11 = 9 - 11 = -2$

$f'(x_0) = f'(3) = 2x = 2 \times 3 = 6$

$f'(x_0) = f'(3) = 2x = 6$

$$x_1 = x_0 - \frac{f(x_0)}{f'(x_0)} = 3 - \frac{-2}{6}$$

$$= 3 + \frac{1}{3} = \frac{10}{3} = 3.333$$

$\therefore x_1 = 3.33$

Iteration 2

$$x_1 = \frac{10}{3}, \; f(x_1) = \left(\frac{10}{3}\right)^2 = 0.1111$$

=0.11

$$f'\left(\frac{10}{3}\right)=\frac{2\times10}{3}=\frac{20}{3}$$

= 6.6666

$$x_2=x_1-\frac{f(x_1)}{f'(x_1)}$$

$$x_2=3.3333-\frac{0.11}{6.6666}$$

x_2= 3.3333 - 0.0165

x_2 = 3.3168

Iteration 3

we now take $x_2 = 3.3168$

$\therefore f(x_2) = (3.3168)^2 - 11$

$f(x_2)$= 11.001162 - 11

$f(x_2)$= 0.001162

$f'(x_2) = 2x$

$= 2\times 3.3168$

$f'(x_2)$= 6.6336

$$x_3=x_2-\frac{f(x_2)}{f'(x_2)}$$

$$x_3=3.3168-\frac{0.001162}{6.6336}$$

= 3.3168 - 0.001834

= 3.31496

we observe that the values obtained as x_2 and x_3 closed very much.
Hence sequare root of 11 is 3.31682

CHAPTER-3

SOLUTION OF LINEAR ALGEBRAIC EQUATIONS

In this chapter, we will consider two techniques for solving systems of linear algebraic equations. Direct method and Iterative method. These methods are specially suited for computers. Direct methods are those which, in the absence of round-off or other error, yield the exact solution in a finite number of elementary arithmetic operations. In practice, because a computer works with a finite word length, direct method do not yield exact solutions.
Indeed, errors arising from round-off instability and loss of significance may lead to extremely poor or even useless results. The fundamental method used for direct solutions is Gauss elimination.
Iterative methods are those which start with an initial approximations and which, by applying a suitably chosen algorithm, lead to successively better approximations.
The important advantages of iterative methods are the simplicity and uniformity of the operations to be performed and well suited for computers and then relative insensitivity to the growth of round-off errors.

Some basic Definitions

1) Matrix : A matrix is an array of mn element arranged in m rows and n columns. Such a matrix A is usually denoted by :

$$A = \begin{bmatrix} a_{11} & a_{12} \dots a_{1n} \\ a_{21} & a_{22} \dots a_{2n} \\ \dots & \dots \dots \dots \\ a_{m1} & a_{m2} \dots a_{mn} \end{bmatrix} = [a_{ij}]$$

where a_{11}, a_{12}, ..., called its elements and may be either real or complex. The matrix A is said to be f size $(m \times n)$
If m = n, the matrix is said to be square matrix of order n, Thus,

$$B = \begin{bmatrix} b_{11} & a_{12} & \dots & a_{13} \\ b_{21} & a_{22} & \dots & a_{23} \\ b_{31} & b_{32} & \dots & b_{33} \end{bmatrix}$$

is a square matrix of order n. We also have a single row or single column matrix.These are called vectors. Thus, $\left[a_{11,}a_{12,}a_{13,....,}a_{1n}\right]$ is a single row matrix or a row vector, and

$$\begin{bmatrix} a_{11} \\ a_{21} \\ \vdots \\ a_{n1} \end{bmatrix}$$

is a single column matrix or column vector.

2) Diagonal Matrix: A matrix in which all non-diagonal elements vanish, ie $a_{ij} = 0$ for $i \neq j$ is called a diagonal matrix:

$$A = \begin{bmatrix} a_{11} & 0 & 0 \\ 0 & a_{22} & 0 \\ 0 & 0 & a_{33} \end{bmatrix}$$

is a 3 × 3 diagonal matrix.
A Square matrix is said to be upper-triangle.
If $a_{ij} = 0$ for $i > j$ e.g.

$$A = \begin{bmatrix} a_{11} & a_{12} & a_{13} \\ 0 & a_{22} & a_{23} \\ 0 & 0 & a_{33} \end{bmatrix}$$

A square matrix is said to be lower triangular.
If $a_{ij} = 0$ for $i < j$ e.g.

$$A = \begin{bmatrix} a_{11} & 0 & 0 \\ a_{12} & a_{22} & 0 \\ a_{13} & a_{23} & a_{33} \end{bmatrix}$$

Rank of matrix: Consider a square matrix of order n. Of the n rows and n columns, if there are atleast k rows and k columns which must be detected in order to obtain a nonvanishing determinant, then the order of the highest order nonvanishing determinant in A is given by r=n-k, and this number is defined as the rank of A and is written r(A). Hence, the rank of a matrix isequal to the order of the highest ordered nonvanishing determinant in A. It follows, therefore, that for a nonsingular square matrix of order n, the rank is equal to n.

Cramer's Rule : Let $\Delta = \det(A)$ or determinant of matrix A and $b \neq 0$. Then the solutions of the system is obtained as $x_i = \Delta_i/\Delta$, i = 1, 2, ..., n where Δ_i is the determinant of the matrix obtained from A by replacing the ith column of Δ by the column vector of b.

For example

Let $A = \begin{bmatrix} a_{11} & a_{12} \\ a_{21} & a_{22} \end{bmatrix}$ $b = \begin{bmatrix} b_{11} \\ b_{21} \end{bmatrix}$

Let $(D) = \begin{vmatrix} a_{11} & a_{12} \\ a_{21} & a_{22} \end{vmatrix}$, $D_1 = \begin{vmatrix} b_{11} & a_{12} \\ b_{21} & a_{22} \end{vmatrix}$, $D_2 = \begin{vmatrix} a_{11} & b_{11} \\ a_{21} & b_{21} \end{vmatrix}$

$$x = \frac{D_1}{D} = \frac{\begin{vmatrix} b_{11} & a_{12} \\ b_{21} & a_{22} \end{vmatrix}}{\begin{vmatrix} a_{11} & a_{12} \\ a_{21} & a_{22} \end{vmatrix}} \qquad y = \frac{D_2}{D} = \frac{\begin{vmatrix} b_{11} & a_{11} \\ b_{21} & a_{21} \end{vmatrix}}{\begin{vmatrix} a_{11} & a_{12} \\ a_{21} & a_{22} \end{vmatrix}}$$

Gauss Elimination Method : In Gauss's elimination method, one usually finds successively a finite number of linear system and it reduces the system of equations to an equivalent upper triangular system which can be solved by back substitution.

Let the system be

$$a_{11}x_1 + a_{12}x_2 + a_{13}x_3 = b_1$$
$$a_{21}x_1 + a_{22}x_2 + a_{23}x_3 = b_2$$
$$a_{31}x_1 + a_{32}x_2 + a_{33}x_3 = b_3$$

At first form the augmented matrix of the system

$$\begin{bmatrix} a_{11} & a_{12} & a_{13} & b_1 \\ a_{21} & a_{22} & a_{23} & b_2 \\ a_{31} & a_{32} & a_{33} & b_3 \end{bmatrix}$$

To eliminate x_1 from the second equation, we multiply the first equation by $\frac{-a_{21}}{a_{11}}$ and then add it to the second equation. Similarly to eliminate x_1 from the third equation, we multiply the first equation by $\frac{-a_{31}}{a_{11}}$ and add it to the third equation.

Then the new equivalent system becomes

$$-\frac{a'_{32}}{a'_{22}}\begin{bmatrix} a_{11} & a_{12} & a_{13} & b_1 \\ 0 & a'_{22} & a'_{23} & b'_2 \\ 0 & a'_{32} & a''_{33} & b'_3 \end{bmatrix}$$

Now eliminate the x_2 from the third equation. We multiply $\frac{-a_{32}}{a_{22}}$ to second equation and add to it with third equation. Then the system becomes

$$\begin{bmatrix} a_{11} & a_{12} & a_{13} & b_1 \\ 0 & a'_{22} & a'_{23} & b'_2 \\ 0 & 0 & a''_{33} & b''_3 \end{bmatrix}$$

Now we have upper triangular system from which the values of x_1, x_2 and x_3 can be contained by back substitution.

Pivoting Strategies : In the Gauss elimination method, the element a_{ij} when i = j is known as pivot element. Each row is normalised by dividing the coefficients of that row by its pivot element. i.e.

$$a_{kj} = \frac{a_{kj}}{a_{kk}} \quad j = 1, ..., n$$

If $a_{kk} = 0$ k^{th} row cannot be normalised. Therefore, the procedure fails one way overcome this problem is to interchange this row with another row so as to obtain a non-vanishing pivot or to choose one that is largest in magnitude in the column. This is called pivoting strategy.

There are two types of pivoting strategies :-

✓ Partial pivoting, and

✓ Complete pivoting.

(i) Partial Pivoting : Partial Pivoting is also called column pivoting. In the first stage of partial pivoting, the first column of the matrix A ([Alb]) is searched for the largest element in magnitude and this largest element is then brought at the position of the first pivot by interchanging first row with the row having the largest element in the first column. After elimination of x_1, the second column of derived system is searched for the largest element, this largest element is brought at the position of the second pivot by interchanging the second row with row having the largest element in the second column. This process of searching and interchanging is repeated in all the (n - 1) stages of elimination.

(ii) Complete Pivoting : In the complete pivoting, at first we look for the largest element in the magnitude in the entire matrix A first. If the element is a_{pq} , then we interchange first row with p^{th} row and interchange first column with q^{th} column. So that a_{pq} can be used as a first pivot. After eliminating x_1, the process is repeated in the derived system, at n - 1 stages of elimination.

Scaled Partial Pivoting: In scaled pivoting at first scale factor d_i for each row i is defined by

$$d_i = \max_{i \le j \le n} |a_{ij}|$$

If $d_i = 0$ for any i, there is no unique solution and procedure is terminated. In the first stage choose the first integer k such that

$$|a_{k_i}| / d_k = \max_{i \le j \le n} \left| a_{ji} / d_j \right|$$

interchange first row and k^{th} row and terminate x_1. This process is repeated in the derived system leaving aside first row and first column.

✓ **Direct method :** The direct method is a method of compute the value in linear equation in which amount of computation is fixed. This method reduces the given equations to a form from which the solution can be obtained by simple substitution, Gauss elimination method and Cramer's method and Gauss Jordan Method is the example of Direct method.

✓ **Iterative Method :** The iterative methods, which starts from an approximation to the true solution, if convergent, drive a sequence of closes approximations the cycle of computations being repeated till the required accuracy is obtained.

Consider the system of equations

$$Ax = b$$

Where A is n × n non-singular matrix. An iterative method starts with an initial approximation $x^{(o)}$ to the solution x, and generates a sequence of vectors $\{x^{(k)}$ that converges to x, the actual solution vector (when $\max_{1 \le i \le n} \left| x_i^{(k)} - x_i \right| < \varepsilon$ where ε is a given small positive numbers).

✓ **Jacobi Iterative Method :** Jacobi Method is one of the simple iterative method. Jacobi Method consists of solving the ith equation of Ax = b for x_i, to obtain

$$x_i = \sum_{\substack{j=1 \\ j \ne ij}}^{n} \left(\frac{-a_{ij}x_j}{a_{ij}} \right) + \frac{b_i}{a_{ij}} \text{ for } i = 1, 2, ..., n.$$

provided $a_{ij} \ne 0$.

We generates $x^{(k+1)}$ from $x^{(k)}$ for $k \ge 0$ by

$$x^{(k+1)} = \sum_{\substack{j=1 \\ j \ne i}}^{n} \left(-a_{ij}x_j^{(k)} \; b_i \right) \Big/ a_{ij} \quad i = 1, 2, ..., n.$$

✓ **Gauss Seidel Method :** Gauss Seidel Method is an improved version of Jacobi iteration method. In Jacobi method, we begin with initial value x_1^{0}, $x_2^{(0)}$

..., $x_n^{(0)}$ and obtain next approximation.

But the Gauss Seidel method uses the most recent values of x as soon as they become available at any point of iteration process. During the $(k + 1)^{th}$ iteration of Gauss Seidel Method, x_i takes the form

$$x_i^{(k+1)} = \frac{b_i - \left(a_{ij}x_1^{(k+1)} + ... + a_{ii-1}x_{i-1}^{(k+1)} + a_{ii+1}x_{i+1}^{(k)} ... + a_{in}x_n^{(k)}\right)}{b_{ij}}$$

When i = 1, all superscripts in the right-hand side become (k) only. Similarly, when i = n, all become (k + 1).

Both the Directive and Iterative methods have their strengths and weakness and a choice is based on the particular linear system to be solved. We mention a few of those below: -

Direct Method : (1) The Direct Methods are generally used when the matrix A is dense or filled, that is. There are few zero elements, and the order of the matrix is not very large, say $n < 50$.

(2) The rounding error may become quite large for ill conditioned equations (if at any stage during the application of pivoting strategy. It is found that all values of { | a_{mk} 1 | for m = k + 1, to n are less than a pre-assigned small quantity ε, then the equations are ill-conditioned and is useful solution is obtained)

(3) In a Direct method the amount of computation is fixed.

Iterative Method : (1) These methods are generally used when the matrix A is sparse and the order of matrix A is very large say $n > 50$. Sparse matrices have very few non-zero elements.

(2) An important advantage of iteration method is small rounding error. Thus, these methods are good choice for ill-conditioned systems.

(3) However, convergence may be guaranteed only under special conditions. But when convergence is assured this method is better than direct.

(4) In an iterative method, computation depends on the accuracy required.

Q1. Define the following terms: -
(i) Ill-conditioned equations.
(ii) Pivoting
(iii) Gauss Elimination Method
(iv) Gauss Jacobi Iterative Method
(v) Gauss Seidel Method

(i) Ill-conditioned : Not visible conditioned Equation one method of improving the accurate for an ill-conditioned system is by means of working all the calculations to more number of significant digits. But multilength arithmetic is tile consuming and therefore uneconomical. One possible alternative is to improve to accuracy of the approximate solution by an iterative procedure. This is described below.

Let the system be

$$\left.\begin{aligned} a_{11}x_1 + a_{12}x_2 + a_{13}x_3 = b_1 \\ a_{21}x_1 + a_{22}x_2 + a_{23}x_3 = b_2 \\ a_{31}x_1 + a_{32}x_2 + a_{33}x_3 = b_3 \end{aligned}\right\}$$

Let $\bar{x}_1, \bar{x}_2, \bar{x}_3$ be an approximate solution.

Substituting these values on the left hand side, we get new values of b_1, b_2, b_3 say $\bar{b}_1, \bar{b}_2, \bar{b}_3$. Thus, the new system is

$$\begin{aligned} a_{11}\bar{x}_1 + a_{12}\bar{x}_2 + a_{13}\bar{x}_3 = \bar{b}_1 \\ a_{21}\bar{x}_1 + a_{22}\bar{x}_2 + a_{23}\bar{x}_3 = \bar{b}_2 \\ a_{31}\bar{x}_1 + a_{32}\bar{x}_2 + a_{33}\bar{x}_3 = \bar{b}_3 \end{aligned}$$

Subtracting each equation from to corresponding equation we get

$$\left.\begin{aligned} a_{11}e_1 + a_{12}e_2 + a_{13}e_3 = d_1 \\ a_{21}e_1 + a_{22}e_2 + a_{23}e_3 = d_2 \\ a_{31}e_1 + a_{32}e_2 + a_{33}e_3 = d_3 \end{aligned}\right\}$$

Where $e_i = x_i - \bar{x}_i$ and $d_i = b_i + \bar{b}_i$. We now solve the system for e_1, e_2 and e_3. Since $e_i = x_i - x_i$ e obtain $x_i = e_i + \bar{x}_i$

Which is better approximation for x_i. The procedure can be repeated again to improve upon the accuracy.

(ii) Pivoting: If at any stage of the Gauss elimination, one of these pivots say $a_{ij}^{i-1}\left(a_{11}^{0} = a_{11}\right)$ vanishes than we have indicated a modified procedure. But it may also happen that the pivot $a_{ij}^{(i-1)}$, through not zero, may be very small in magnitude compared to the remaining elements (i) in the ith column. Using a small number as divisor may lead to growth of the round-off error. The use of large multiplier likes

$$\frac{-a_{i+1}^{(i-12)}, i}{a_{ij}^{(i-1)}}, \frac{a_{i+2}^{(i-1)}, i}{a_{ij}^{(i-1)}} \text{ etc.}$$

will tend to magnification of errors both during the elimination phase and during the back substitution phase of the solution procedure. This can be avoided by rearranging is remaining rows (from i^{th} row up to n^{th} row) so as to obtain a non-vanishing pivot or to choose one that in largest in magnitude in that column. This is called Pivoting.

(iii) Gauss Elimination Method : In Gauss's elimination method, one usually find successively a finite number of linear systems equivalent to the given one such that the final system is so simple that its solution may be readily computed. In this method matrix A is reduced to the form U (Upper triangular matrix) by using the elementary row operations like

(i) interchanging any two rows

(ii) Multiplying (or dividing) any row by non-zero constant

(iii) adding (or subtracting) a constant multiply of one row or another row.

If any matrix A is transformed to another matrix B by a series of row operations, we say that A and B are equivalent matrices.

(iv) Jacobi Iterative Method : Jacobi Iterative method consists of solving the ith equation of $Ax = b$ for x_i

Suppose $x_1^{(1)}, x_2^{(1)}, \ldots x_n^{(1)}$ are any first approximations to the unknown $x_1, x_2, \ldots, x_n$. Substituting in the right side of the second approximations.

$$\left.\begin{aligned} x_1^{(2)} &= \frac{b_1}{a_{11}} - \frac{a_{12}}{a_{11}} x_2^{(1)} - \ldots - \frac{a_{1n}}{a_{11}} x_n^{(1)}. \\ x_2^{(2)} &= \frac{b_2}{a_{22}} - \frac{a_{21}}{a_{22}} x_1^{(1)} - \ldots - \frac{a_{2n}}{a_{22}} x_n^{(1)}. \\ x_n^{(2)} &= \frac{b_n}{a_{nn}} - \frac{a_{n1}}{a_{nn}} x_1^{(1)} - \ldots - \frac{a_{n,n-1}}{a_{nm}} x_{n-1}^{(1)}. \end{aligned}\right\}$$

Similarly, if$x_1^{(n)}, x_2^{(n)} \ldots x_n^{(n)}$ are a system of nth approximations

$$\left.\begin{aligned} x_1^{(n+1)} &= \frac{b_1}{a_{11}} - \frac{a_{12}}{a_{11}} x_2^{(n)} - \ldots - \frac{a_{1n}}{a_{11}} x_n^{(n)}. \\ x_2^{(n+1)} &= \frac{b_2}{a_{22}} - \frac{a_{21}}{a_{22}} x_1^{(n)} - \ldots - \frac{a_{2n}}{a_{22}} x_n^{(n)}. \\ &\ldots \ldots \ldots \ldots \ldots \ldots \ldots \ldots \ldots \ldots \ldots \ldots \ldots \ldots \\ x_n^{(n+1)} &= \frac{b_n}{a_{nn}} - \frac{a_{n1}}{a_{nn}} x_1^{(n)} - \ldots - \frac{a_{n,n-1}}{a_{nm}} x_{n-1}^{(n)}. \end{aligned}\right\}$$

then the iteration formula may be written as

$x^{(n+1)} = Bx^{(n)} + C$

This method is due to Jacobi. It can be shown that a sufficient condition for the convergence of this method is that

$|| B || < 1$

(v) Gauss Seidel Method : Gauss Seidel method, we have write the iterative scheme of the system of equation

Ax = b as follows: -

$a_{11}x_i^{(k+1)} = -a_{12}x_2^{(k)} - a_{13}x_3^{(k)} - .... - a_n x_n^{k} + b_1$

$a_{21}x_1^{(k+1)} + a_{22}x_2^{(k+1)} = -a_{23}x_3^{(k)} - ... - a_{2n}x_n^{(k)} + b_2$

....

$a_{n1}x_1^{(k+1)} + a_{n2}x_2^{(k+1)} .... + a_{nn}x_n^{(k+1)} = +b_n$

This iteration method is also know as the method of successive displacement. For computation point of view, we rewrite (Ax) as

$$x_i^{(k+1)} = -1/a_{ii} \left[\sum_{j=1}^{i-1} a_{ij}\, x_j^{(k-1)} \sum_{ij=j+1}^{n} a_{ij}\, x_j^{(k)} - b_i \right]$$

i = 1, 2, ... n.

Partial Pivoting : Partial Pivoting is also called column pivoting. In the first stage of partial pivoting, the first column of the matrix A ([Alb]) is searched for the largest element in magnitude and this largest element is then brought at the position of the first pivot by interchanging first row with the row having the largest element in the first column. After elimination of x_1, the second column of derived system is searched for the largest element, this largest element is brought at the position of the second pivot by interchanging the second row with row having the largest element in the second column. This process of searching and interchanging is repeated in all the (x - 1) stages of elimination.

Complete Pivoting: In the complete pivoting, at first we look for the largest element in the magnitude in the entire matrix A first. If the element is apq, then we interchange first row with p^{th} row and interchange first column with q^{th} column. So that a_{pq} can be used as a first pivot. After eliminating x_1, the process is repeated in the derived system, at n - 1 stages of elimination.

Scaled Partial Pivoting : In scaled pivoting at first scale factor di for each row i is defined by

$$di = \max_{i \le j \le n} \left| a_{ij} \right|$$

If di = 0 for any i, there is no unique solution and procedure is terminated. In the first stage choose the first integer k such that

$$\left| ak_i \middle/ d_k \right| = \max_{i \le j \le n} \left| a_{ji} \middle/ d_j \right|$$

interchange first row and kth row and terminate x_1. This process is repeated in the derived system learning aside first row and first column.

$-4x_3 = -6$
Now $x_3 = 3/2$, $x_2 = 3/2$, $x_1 = 0$
Therefore the solutions are
$x_1 = 0$, $x_2 = 3/2$, $x_3 = 3/2$

Q2. Show that the matrices.

$$\mathbf{A} = \begin{bmatrix} \text{Cos}\theta & -\text{Sin}\theta \\ \text{Sin}\theta & \text{Cos}\theta \end{bmatrix}$$

and

$$\mathbf{B} = \begin{bmatrix} -\frac{2}{3} & \frac{1}{3} & \frac{2}{3} \\ \frac{2}{3} & \frac{2}{3} & \frac{1}{3} \\ \frac{1}{3} & -\frac{2}{3} & \frac{2}{3} \end{bmatrix}$$

are orthogonal matrices,

We have

$$A' = \begin{bmatrix} \text{Cos}\theta & \text{Sin}\theta \\ -\text{Sin}\theta & \text{Cos}\theta \end{bmatrix}$$

and therefore

$$AA' = \begin{bmatrix} \text{Cos}\theta & -\text{Sin}\theta \\ \text{Sin}\theta & \text{Cos}\theta \end{bmatrix} \begin{bmatrix} \text{Cos}\theta & \text{Sin}\theta \\ -\text{Sin}\theta & \text{Cos}\theta \end{bmatrix} = \begin{bmatrix} 1 & 0 \\ 0 & 0 \end{bmatrix} = I.$$

The reader should verify that B is also orthogonal.

Q3. Express the matrix

$$A = \begin{bmatrix} 1 & 7 & 8 \\ 6 & 2 & 9 \\ 5 & 4 & 3 \end{bmatrix}$$

as the sum of a symmetric and a skew-symmetric matrix.

In general, we can write A as

$$A = \frac{A+A'}{2} + \frac{A-A'}{2} = C + D, \text{ say}$$

where

$$C=\frac{(A+A')}{2} \text{ and } D = \frac{A-A^1}{2}$$

$$\therefore C' = \left(\frac{A+A'}{2}\right)' = \frac{(A+A')'}{2} = \frac{[A'+(A')']}{2} = \frac{A'+A}{2} = \frac{(A+A')}{2} = c$$

which shows that C is a symmetric matrix.

Again,

$$D = \frac{(A-A)'}{2}$$

$$\therefore D' = \left(\frac{A-A'}{2}\right)' = \frac{A'-(A')'}{2} = \frac{(A'-A)}{2} = -\frac{(A-A')}{2} = -D$$

which shows that D is skew-symmetric.

For the example given above, we have

$$A' = \begin{bmatrix} 1 & 6 & 5 \\ 7 & 2 & 4 \\ 8 & 9 & 3 \end{bmatrix}$$

Hence $\frac{A+A'}{2} = \begin{bmatrix} 1 & 6.5 & 6.5 \\ 6.5 & 2 & 6.5 \\ 6.5 & 6.5 & 3 \end{bmatrix}$, which is a symmetric matrix,

and $\frac{A-A'}{2} = \begin{bmatrix} 0 & 0.5 & 1.5 \\ -0.5 & 0 & 2.5 \\ -1.5 & -2.5 & 0 \end{bmatrix}$, which is a skew-symmetric matrix.

The reader may verify that their sum is equal to A itself.

The Inverse of a Matrix

Let A be a nonsingular square matrix of order n. Let B be another square matrix of the same order such that

BA = I,

Where I is the unit matrix of ordern n. Then B is said to be the inverse of A which is written as A^{-1} so that

$$AA^{-1} = A^{-1}A = I$$

The following ten properties can be shown to hold on the inverse of a square matrix :

(i) A^{-1} exists if and only if $|A| \neq 0$. If $|A| = 0$, is said to be a singular matrix.

(ii) If A^{-1} exists, it is unique.

(iii) If A^{-1} exists, $|A^{-1}| = |A|^{-1} = 1/|A|$.

(iv) $(A^{-1})^{-1} = A$

(v) $(A')^{-1} = (A^{-1})'$

(vi) $(AB)^{-1} = B^{-1}A^{-1}$

(vii) If A is a diagonal matrix with diagonal elements a_{ij}, then A^{-1} is also a diagonal matrix with diagonal elements $1/a_{ij}$. For example, if

$$A = \begin{bmatrix} a_{11} & 0 & 0 \\ 0 & a_{22} & 0 \\ 0 & 0 & a_{33} \end{bmatrix}$$

then
$$A^{-1} = \begin{bmatrix} \frac{1}{a_{11}} & 0 & 0 \\ 0 & \frac{1}{a_{22}} & 0 \\ 0 & 0 & \frac{1}{a_{33}} \end{bmatrix}$$

(viii) $I^{-1} = I$.

(ix) The inverse of an upper triangular matrix is also an upper triangular matrix. For example, if

$$A = \begin{bmatrix} 2 & 3 & 4 \\ 0 & 5 & 6 \\ 0 & 0 & 7 \end{bmatrix}$$

then
$$A^{-1} = 1/70 \begin{bmatrix} 35 & -21 & -2 \\ 0 & 14 & -12 \\ 0 & 0 & 10 \end{bmatrix}$$

Similarly, the inverse of a lower triangular matrix is also a lower triangular matrix.

(x) The inverse A^{-1}, when it exists, can be computed as follows.

$$A^{-1} = \frac{1}{|A|}\begin{bmatrix} A_{11} & A_{21} & \dots & A_{n1} \\ A_{21} & A_{22} & \dots & A_{n2} \\ \dots & \dots & \dots & \dots \\ A_{n1} & A_{n2} & \dots & A_{nm} \end{bmatrix}$$

where A_{11}, A_{12}, ... are the cofactors of a_{11}, a_{12}, .. in the determinant of the transpose A' of A. The matrix on the right side of is called the adjoint of A. This is not an efficient method for the computation of the inverse. A better method is the Guassian elimination method.

For a nonsquare matrix also, it is possible to define an inverse, called the generalized inverse. However, in this book, we shall consider inverses for square matrices only.

Q4.

If $\begin{bmatrix} 3 & -5 \\ -4 & 2 \end{bmatrix}$

Show that A^2- 5A - 14 I = 0

$$A^2 = A \bullet A = \begin{bmatrix} 3 & -5 \\ -4 & 2 \end{bmatrix} . \begin{bmatrix} 3 & -5 \\ -4 & 2 \end{bmatrix}$$

$$= \begin{bmatrix} 29 & -25 \\ -20 & 24 \end{bmatrix}$$

$$\text{Now } A^2 - 5A - 14$$

$$= \begin{bmatrix} 29 & -25 \\ -20 & 24 \end{bmatrix} - 5\begin{bmatrix} 3 & -5 \\ -4 & 2 \end{bmatrix} - 14\begin{bmatrix} 1 & 0 \\ 0 & 1 \end{bmatrix}$$

$$= \begin{bmatrix} 29 - 15 - 14 & -25 + 25 + 0 \\ -20 + 20 + 0 & 24 - 10 - 24 \end{bmatrix}$$

$$= \begin{bmatrix} 0 & 0 \\ 0 & 0 \end{bmatrix}$$

$$= 0 \text{ proved}$$

Q5. Using Gauss elimination method, solve the following system of equations : [DEC03, Q1(d)]

$3x_1 + x_2 + 2x_3 = 3$ **[6]**

$2x_1 - 3x_2 - x_3 = -3$

$x_1 + 2x_2 + x_3 = 4$

Dividing the given equation their respective pivot elements.

$$3x_1 + x_2 + 2x_3 = 3 \Rightarrow x_1 + \frac{x_2}{3} + \frac{2}{3}x_3 = \frac{3}{3}$$

$$\Rightarrow x_1 + \frac{x_2}{3} + \frac{2}{3} \times x_3 = 1 \longrightarrow (1)$$

$$2x_1 - 3x_2 - x_3 = -3 \Rightarrow x_1 - \frac{3}{2}x_2 - \frac{1}{3}x_3 = \frac{-3}{2} \longrightarrow (2)$$

$$x_1 + 2x_2 + x_3 = 4 \Rightarrow x_1 + \frac{2}{1}x_2 + \frac{1}{1}x_3 = \frac{4}{1} \longrightarrow (3)$$

$$from(1)$$

$$x_1 = 1 - \frac{x_2}{3} - \frac{2}{3}x_3 \, putting(2)$$

$\therefore$ from(2)

$$\left(1 - \frac{x_2}{3} - \frac{2}{3}x_3\right) - \frac{3}{2}x_2 - \frac{1}{3}x_3 = \frac{-3}{2} - 1$$

$$\left(\frac{11}{6}\right)x_2 - x_3 = \frac{-5}{2}$$

$$x_2 - \frac{6}{11}x_3 = \frac{-15}{11}$$

$$from(3)$$

$$\left(1 - \frac{x_2}{3} - \frac{2}{3}x_3\right) - 2x_2 + x_3 = 4$$

$$-x_2\left(\frac{1}{3} + 2\right) - x_3\left(\frac{2}{3} - 1\right) = 4 - 1$$

$$-\frac{7}{3}x_2 + \frac{1}{3}x_3 = 3$$

$$x_2 - \frac{1}{7}x_3 = \frac{-9}{7}$$

We can write we have elliminiate x_1 from(2) and (3) using (1), the system of equation becomes.

$$x_1 + \frac{1}{3}x_2 + \frac{2}{3}x_3 = 1 \longrightarrow (4)$$

$$x_2 - \frac{6}{11}x_3 = \frac{-15}{11} \longrightarrow (5)$$

$$x_2 - \frac{1}{7}x_3 = \frac{-9}{7} \longrightarrow (6)$$

$(6)-(5)$

$$x_2 - \frac{1}{7}x_3 = \frac{-9}{7} \longrightarrow (6)$$

$$x_2 - \frac{6}{11}x_3 = \frac{-15}{11} \longrightarrow (5)$$

$$- \quad + \quad +$$

$$\frac{31}{77}x_3 = \frac{6}{77}$$

$$x_3 = \frac{6}{11 \times 31} = \frac{6}{341} = 0.017595 = 0.02$$

put in (3) *value of* x_3

$$x_2 - \frac{6}{11} \times \frac{6}{341} = \frac{-15}{11}$$

$$x_2 = \frac{-15}{11} + \frac{36}{3751}$$

$$= \frac{-5115+36}{3751} = \frac{-5079}{3751}$$

$$= -1.3540$$

$$x_2 = -1.4$$

Putting x_2 and x_3 in (4)

$$x_1 + \frac{1}{3} \times -1.4 + \frac{2}{3} \times 0.02 = 1$$

$$x_1 - \frac{1.4}{3} + 0.04 = 1$$

$$x_1 = 1 + \frac{1.4}{3} + 0.04 = 1.426666$$

$$x_1 = 1.43$$

Hence the solution is x_1=1.43

x_2 = -1.4

x_3 = 0.02

CHAPTER-4

INTERPOLATION

The Interpolation has been defined as the cut of reading between the lines of a table, and in elementary mathematics the term usually denotes the process of computing intermediate values of a function from a set of given values of that function.

If the value of f(x) is to be found at some point y in the internal $[x_1, x_n]$ and y is not one of the tabulate points then the value is estimated by using the known values of f(x) at the surrounding points.

Suppose that the value of the function f(x) is tabulated at discrete set of values of the arguments x at $x_0, x_1, \ldots, x_n$ $x_0 \leq x_1 \leq \ldots.. \leq x_n$. If the value of f(x) is to be found at some point ξ in the internal $[x_0, x_1]$ and ξ is not one of the notes x_i, then value is estimated by using the known values of f(x) at the surrounding points. Such estimates of f(x) can be made using a function that fits the given data.

If the point y is outside the internal $[x_1, x_n]$ then the estimation of f(y) is called extrapolation. Extrapolation assumes that the behavior of f(x) outside the range $[x_1, x_n]$ is identical to the inside the range and this may not always be valid.

We derive forms of the interpolating polynomial. Polynomials are used as the basic means of approximation in nearly all areas of numerical analysis. Let f(n) is a polynomial, the process is called the polynomial interpolation and f(x) is called the interpolating polynomial. Similarly, different types of interpolation arises depending on whether f(x) is a finite or infinite.

In this unit, we will discuss the lagrange from of interpolating polynomial, Newton from of interpolating polynomial and Newton's forward and Backward difference method.

Lagrange's interpolation

The technique of determining an approximate value of f(x) for a non-tabular value of x which lies in the interval is called interpolation.

The universal technique for interpolating is to fit a polynomial through the points surrounding the point 'y' where the value of the function is to be found. This polynomial is an approximation of the function and is used to find f(y). This is called Lagrange's Interpolation.

Let y(x) be continuous and differentiable(n+1) times in the interval (a+b).Given the (n + 1) points $(x_0, y_0), (x_1, y_1), ..., (x_n, y_n)$ where the values of x need not necessarily be equally spaced, we find a polynomial of degree n, day $L_n(x)$. Such that

$L_n(x_i) = y(x_i) = y_i$ $\quad\quad$ i = 0, 1, ..., n.

The equation of a Linear polynomial passing through two points (x_0, y_0) and (x_1, y_1). Then $L_1(x)$ is

$$L_1(x) = \frac{x - x_1}{x_0 - x_1} y_0 + \frac{x - x_0}{x_1 - x_0} y_1$$

$$= L_0(x)y_0 + L_1(x)y_1$$

$$= \sum_{i=0}^{1} L_i(x) y_i$$

Now, the Lagrange polynomial of degree two passing through three points $(x_0, y_0), (x_1, y_1)$ and (x_2, y_2) is written as

$$= \frac{(x - x_1)(x - x_2)}{(x_0 - x_1)(x_0 - x_2)} y_0 + \frac{(x - x_0)(x - x_2)}{(x_1 - x_0)(x_1 - x_2)} y_1 + \frac{(x - x_0)(x - x_1)}{(x_2 - x_0)(x_2 - x_1)} y_2$$

$$= L_0(x) + L_1(x) + L_2(x)$$

$$= \sum_{i=0}^{2} L_1(x)$$

Therefore, we can write $L_n(x)$ for a linear combination of $(x_0, y_0), (x_1, y_1) ... (x_n, y_n)$. Hence we write

$$L_n(x) = \sum_{i=0}^{n} L_i(x) y_i$$

where $L_i(x)$ are polynomials in x of degree n.

Hence $L_n(x)$ may be written as

$$L_n(x) = \frac{(x - x_1)(x - x_2)...(x - x_n)}{(x_0 - x_1)(x_0 - x_2)...(x_0 - x_n)} y_0 + \frac{(x - x_0)(x - x_2)...(x - x_n)}{(x_1 - x_0)(x_1 - x_2)...(x_1 - x_n)} y_1$$

$$+ \frac{(x - x_0)(x - x_1)...(x - x_n)}{(x_2 - x_0)(x_2 - x_1)...(x_2 - x_n)} y_2 .... + \frac{(x - x_0)(x - x_1)...(x - x_{n-1})}{(x_n - x_0)(x_n - x_1)...(x_n - x_{n-1})} y_n$$

or $L_n(x) = L_1(x) + L_2(x) ... + L_n(x)$

$$\text{or } L_n(x) = \sum_{i=0}^{n} L_i(x) y_i$$

Now, This the required Lagrange from the interpolating polynomial. The uniqueness of the interpolating polynomial can be established easily with the help of polynomial equations.

Inverse Interpolation with the help of example.

In inverse interpolation in a table of values of x find y = f(x), one is given a number $\bar{y}$ and wishes to find the point $\bar{x}$ so that $f(\bar{x}) = \bar{y}$, where f(x) is the tabulated function. For this, we naturally assume that the function y = f(x) has unique inverse x = g(y) in the range of table.

Let a given set of value of x and y, the process of finding the value of x for certain value of y is the inverse interpolation when the value of x are at unequal intervals. The most obvious way of performing this process is by interchanging x and y in. Lagrange's method.

This process is called inverse Interpolation for example, Let the value of x and y are

x	4	7	10	12
y	-1	1	2	4

Then the value of x when y = 3 through inverses interpolation.

$$L(y) = \frac{(y-1)\ (y-2)\ (y-4)}{(-2)\ (-3)\ (-5)}(4) + \frac{(y+1)\ (y-2)\ (y-4)}{(2)\ (1)\ (-3)}(7)$$

$$+ \frac{(y+1)\ (y-1)\ (y-4)}{(3)\ (1)\ (-2)}(10) + \frac{(y+1)\ (y-1)\ (y-2)}{(5)\ (3)\ (2)}(12)$$

$$\text{so } P(3) = \frac{(2)\ (1)\ (-1).4}{-15} + \frac{(4)(1)(-1)}{6}.7 + \frac{(4)(2)(-1)}{-6}.10 + \frac{(4)(2)(1)}{30}.(12)$$

$$= \frac{4}{15} - \frac{14}{3} + \frac{40}{3} + \frac{48}{15} = \frac{182}{15} = 12.1333.$$

Newton's Divided Difference method :

The Lagrange interpolation formula has the disadvantages that if another interpolation point were added, then the interpolation coefficients $L_i(n)$ will have to be recomputed. We therefore seek an interpolation polynomial which has the property that a polynomial of higher degree may be derived from it by simply adding new terms. Newton's divided differences method is one such formula for that calculation.

Let $(x_0, y_0), (x_1, y_1) \dots (x_n, y_n)$ be the given (n + 1) points. Then the divided differences of orders 1, 2, ..., n are defined by the relation

$$[x_0, x_1] = \frac{y_1 - y_0}{x_1 - x_0}$$

$$[x_0, x_1, x_2] = \frac{[x_1, x_2] - [x_0, x_1]}{x_2 - x_0}$$

$$[x_0, x_1, \dots x_n] = \frac{[x_1, x_2 \dots x_n] - [x_0, x_1, \dots x_{n-1}]}{x_n - x_0}$$

This is a Newton's Divided Difference formulae or (n + 1) points and unequally splaced differences.

FINITE DIFFERENCES

Assume that we have a table of values (x_i, y_i), i = 0, 1, 2, ..., n of any function y=f(x), the values of x being equally spaced, i.e., $x_i = x_0 + ih$, i=0, 1, 2..., n. Suppose that we are required to recover the values of f(x) for some intermediate values of x, or to obtain the derivative of f(x) for some x in the range $x_0 \le x \le x_n$. The methods for the solution of these problems are based on the concept of the differences of a function which we now proceed to define.

Forward Differences

If $y_0, y_1, y_2, \dots, y_n$ denote a set of values of y, then $y_1-y_0, y_2-y_1, \dots, y_n - y_{n-1}$ are called the differences of y. Denoting these differences by $\Delta y_0, \Delta y_1, \dots, \Delta y_{n-1}$ respectively, we have

$$\Delta y_0 = y_1 - y_0, \Delta y_1 = y_2 - y_1, \dots, \Delta y_{n-1} = y_n - y_{n-1},$$

where Δ is called the forward difference operator and $\Delta y_0, \Delta y_1, \dots$, are called first forward differences. The differences of the first forward differences are called second forward differences and are denoted by $\Delta^2 y_0, \Delta^2 y_1, \dots$ Similarly, one can define third forward differences, fourth forward differences, etc. thus

$$\Delta^2 y_0 = \Delta y_1 - \Delta y_0 = y_2 - y_1 - (y_1 - y_0) = y_2 - 2y_1 + y_0$$

$$\Delta^3 y_0 = \Delta^2 y_1 - \Delta^2 y_0 = y_3 - 2y_2 + y_1 - (y_2 - 2y_1 + y_0)$$

$$= y_3 - 3y_2 + 3y_1 - y_0$$

and $\Delta^4 y_0 = \Delta^3 y_1 - \Delta^3 y_0$

$$= y_4 - 3y_3 + 3y_2 - y_1 - (y_3 - 3y_2 + 3y_1 - y_0)$$

$$= y_4 - 4y_3 + 6y_2 - 4y_1 + y_0$$

It is therefore clear than any higher order difference can easily be expressed in terms of the ordinates, since the coefficients occurring on the right side are the binomial coefficients.

The following table shows how the forward differences of all orders can be formed:

Table Forward Difference Table

x	y	Δ	Δ^2	Δ^3	Δ^4	Δ^5	Δ^6
x_0	y_0						
		Δy_0					
x_1	y_1		$\Delta^2 y_0$				
		Δy_1		$\Delta^3 y_0$			
x_2	y_2		$\Delta^2 y_1$		$\Delta^4 y_0$		
		Δy_2		$\Delta^3 y_1$		$\Delta^5 y_0$	
x_3	y_3		$\Delta^2 y_3$		$\Delta^4 y_1$		$\Delta^6 y_0$
		Δy_3		$\Delta^3 y_2$		$\Delta^5 y_1$	
x_4	y_4		$\Delta^2 y_3$		$\Delta^4 y_2$		
		Δy_4		$\Delta^3 y_3$			
x_5	y_5		$\Delta^2 y_4$				
		Δy_5					
x_6	y_6						

Backward Differences

The differences $y_1 - y_0, y_2 - y_1, ..., y_n - y_{n-1}$ are called first backward differences if they are denoted by $\nabla y_1, \nabla y_2, ..., \nabla y_n$ respectively, so that $\nabla y_1 = y_1 - y_0$, $\nabla y_2 = y_2 - y_1, ..., \nabla y_n = y_n - y_{n-1}$, where ∇ is called the backward difference operator. In a similar way, one can define backward differences of higher orders. Thus we obtain:

$$\nabla^2 y_2 = \nabla y_2 - \nabla y_1 = y_2 - y_1 - (y_1 - y_0) = y_2 - 2y_1 + y_0,$$
$$\nabla^3 y_3 = \nabla^2 y_3 - \nabla^2 y_2 = y_3 - 3y_2 + 3y_1 - y_0.$$

With the same values of x and y as in Table 3.1, a backward difference table can be formed.

Table Backward difference Table

x	y	∇	∇^2	∇^3	∇^4	∇^5	∇^6
x_0	y_0						
x_1	y_1	∇y_1					
x_2	y_2	∇y_2	$\nabla^2 y_2$				
x_3	y_3	∇y_3	$\nabla^2 y_3$	$\nabla^3 y_3$			
x_4	y_4	∇y_4	$\nabla^2 y_4$	$\nabla^3 y_4$	$\nabla^4 y_4$		
x_5	y_5	∇y_5	$\nabla^2 y_5$	$\nabla^3 y_5$	$\nabla^4 y_5$	$\nabla^5 y_5$	
x_6	y_6	∇y_6	$\nabla^2 y_6$	$\nabla^3 y_6$	$\nabla^4 y_6$	$\nabla^5 y_6$	$\nabla^6 y_6$

Central Differences

The central difference operator δ is defined by the relations

$$y_1 - y_0 = \delta y_{1/2},\ y_2 - y_1 = \delta y_{3/2},\ \ldots\ y_n - y_{n-1} = \delta y_{n-1/2}.$$

Similarly, higher order central differences can be defined. With the values of x and y as in the preceeding two tables, a central difference table can be formed thus :

Table Central Difference Table

x	y	δ	δ^2	δ^3	δ^4	δ^5	δ^6
x_0	y_0						
		$\delta y_{1/2}$					
x_1	y_1		$\delta^2 y_1$				
		$\delta y_{3/2}$		$\delta^3 y_{3/2}$			
x_2	y_2		$\delta^2 y_2$		$\delta^4 y_2$		
		$\delta y_{5/2}$		$\delta^3 y_{5/2}$		$\delta^5 y_{5/2}$	
x_3	y_3		$\delta^2 y_3$		$\delta^4 y_3$		$\delta^6 y_3$
		$\delta y_{7/2}$		$\delta^3 y_{7/2}$		$\delta^5 y_{7/2}$	
x_4	y_4		$\delta^2 y_4$		$\delta^4 y_4$		
		$\delta y_{9/2}$		$\delta^3 y_{9/2}$			
x_5	y_5		$\delta^2 y_5$				
		$\delta y_{11/2}$					
x_6	y_6						

It is celar from the three tables that in a definite numerical case, the same numbers occur in the same positions whether we use forward, backward or central differences. Thus we obtain

$$\Delta y_0 = \nabla y_1 = \delta y_{1/2}$$
$$\Delta^3 y_2 = \nabla^3 y_5 = \delta^3 y_{7/2}$$
etc.

Newton's Formulae for Interpolation

Given the set of (n+1) values, viz., $(x_0, y_0), (x_1, y_1), (x_2, y_2), \ldots, (x_n, y_n)$, of x and y, it is required to find $y_n(x)$, a polynomial of the nth degree such that y and $y_n(x)$ agree at the tabulated points. Let the values of x be equidistant, i.e., let

$$x_i = x_0 + ih,\quad i = 0, 1, 2, \ldots, n$$

Since $y_n(x)$ is a polynomial of the nth degree, it may be written as

$$y_n(x) = a_0 + a_1 (x-x_0) + a_2(x-x_0)(x-x_1) + \\ + a_3 (x-x_0)(x-x_1)(x-x_2) + \ldots \\ + a_n(x-x_0)(x-x_1)(x-x_2) \ldots (x-x_{n-1}).$$

Imposing now the condition that y and $y_n(x)$ should agree at the set of tabulated points, we obtain

$$a_0 = y_0;\ a_1 = \frac{y_1 - y_0}{x_1 - x_0} = \frac{\Delta y_0}{h};\ a_2 = \frac{\Delta^2 y_0}{h^2 2!};\ a_3 = \frac{\Delta^3 y_0}{h^3 3!};\ ....;\ a_n = \frac{\Delta^n y_0}{h^n n!};$$

Setting $x = x_0 + ph$ and substituting for $a_0, a_1, ..., a_n$, equation gives

$$y_n(x) = y_0 + p\Delta y_0 + \frac{p(p-1)}{2!}\Delta^2 y_0 + \frac{p(p-1)(p-2)}{3!}\Delta^3 y_0 + ...$$

$$+ \frac{p(p-1)(p-2)...(p-n+1)}{n!}\Delta^n y_0,$$

which is Newton's forward difference interpolation formula and is useful for interpolation near the beginning of a set of tabular values.

To find the error committed in replacing the function y(x) by means of the polynomial $y_n(x)$, we use formula to obtain

$$y(x) - y_n(x) = \frac{(x - x_0)(x - x_1)...(x - x_n)}{(n+1)!} y_{(n+1)}(\xi),$$

$$x_0 < \xi < x_n.$$

As remarked earlier we do not have any informations concerning $y^{(n+1)}(x)$, and therefore formula (11) is useless in practice. Neverthless, if $y^{(n+1)}(x)$ does not vary too rapidly in the interval, a useful estimate of the derivative can be obtained in the following way. Expanding y(x+h) by Talyor's series , we obtain

$$y(x + h) = y(x) + hy'(x) + \frac{h^2}{2!}y''(x) + ...$$

Neglecting the terms containing h^2 and higher powers of h, this gives

$$y'(x) = 1/h\,[y(x+h) - y(x)] = 1/h\ \Delta y(x)$$

Writing y'(x) as Dy(x) where $D = \frac{d}{dx}$, the differentiation operator, the above equation gives the operator relation $D = 1/h\ \Delta$

and so $$D^{n+1} \equiv \frac{1}{h^{n+1}}\Delta^{n+1}\, y(x)$$

Equation (1) can therefore be written as

$$y(x) - y_n(x) = \frac{p(p-1)(p-2)...(p-n)}{(n+1)!}\Delta^{n+1}\, y(\xi)$$

in which form it is suitable for computation.

Instead of assuming $y_n(x)$ as if we choose it in the form

$$y_n(x) = a_0 + a_1(x - x_n) + a_2(x - x_n)(x - x_{n-1})$$
$$+ a_3(x - x_n)(x - x_{n-1})(x - x_{n-2}) + ...$$
$$+ a_n(x - x_n)(x - x_{n-1}) ... (x - x_1).$$

and then impose the condition that y and $y_n(x)$ should agree at the tabulated points $x_n, x_{n-1}, x_2, x_1, x_0$, we obtain (after some simplification)

$$y_n(x) = y_n + p\nabla y_n + \frac{p(p+1)}{2!}\nabla^2 y_n + ...+ \frac{p(p+1)...(p+n-1)}{n!}\nabla^n y_n,$$

where $$p = \frac{x - x_n}{h}.$$

This is Newton's backward difference interpolation formula and it uses tabular values to the left of y_n. This formula is therefore useful for interpolation near the end of the tabular values.

It can be shown that the error in this formula may be written as

$$y(x) - y_n(x) = \frac{p(p+1)(p+2)...(p+n)}{(n+1)!} h^{n+1} y^{(n+1)}(\xi)$$

The following examples illustrate the use of these formulae.

Q1. Find the cubic polynomial which takes the following values
y(0) = 1, y(1) = 0, y(2) = 1 and y(3) = 10
Hence, or otherwise, obtain y(4).

We form the difference table

x	y	Δ	Δ^2	Δ^3
0	1			
		-1		
1	0		2	
		1		6
2	1		8	
		9		
3	10			

Here h = 1. Hence, using the formula $x = x_0 + ph$ and choosing $x_0 = 0$, we obtain p = x. Substituting this value of p in (3.10), we get

$$y(x) = 1 + x(-1) + \frac{x(x-1)}{2}(2) + \frac{x(x-1)(x-2)}{6}(6)$$
$$= x^3 - 2x^2 + 1,$$

which is the polynomial from which we obtained the above tabular values. To compute y(4) we observe that p = 4. Hence formula (3.10) gives

$$y(4) = 1 + 4(-1) + 12 + 24$$
$$= 33$$

which is the same value as that obtained by substituting x = 4 in the cubic polynomial above.

Note : This process of finding the value of y for some value of x outside the given range is called extrapolation and this example demonstrates the fact that if a tabulated function is a polynomial, then interpolation and extrapolation would give exact values.

Q2. The population of a town in the decennial census was as given below. Estimate the population for the year 1895.

Year : x	1891	1901	1911	1921	1931
Population: y (in thousands)	46	66	81	93	101

Putting h = 10, x_0 = 1891, x = 1895 in the formula $x = x_0 + ph$, we obtain p = 2/5 = 0.4. The difference table is

x	y	Δ	Δ^2	Δ^3	Δ^3
1891	46				
		20			
1901	66		-5		
		15		2	
1911	81		-3		-3
		12		-1	
1921	93		-4		
		8			
1931	101				

Hence equation gives

$$y(1895) = 46 + 0.4(20) + \frac{0.4\,(0.4 - 1)}{2}(-5) + \frac{0.4\,(0.4 - 1)\,(0.4 - 2)}{2}(2)$$

$$+ \frac{0.4\,(0.4 - 1)\,(0.4 - 2)\,(0.4 - 3)}{24}(-3)$$

$$= 54.85 \text{ thousands.}$$

Q3. Find the lagrange interpolating polynomial of degree 2 approximating the function y = 1n x defined by the following tables of values. Hence determine the value of 1n 2.7.

x	**2**	**2.5**	**3.0**
y = 1n x	**0.69315**	**0.91629**	**1.09861**

We have $$l_0(x)=\frac{(x-2.5)(x-3.0)}{(-0.5)(-1.0)}=2x^2-11x+15$$

similarly, we find $L_1(x) = (4x^2 - 20x + 24)$
and $L_2(x) = 2x^2 - 9x + 10$
Hence $L_2(x) = (2x^2 - 11x + 15)(0.69315)$
$-(4x^2 - 20x + 24)(0.91629)$
$+(2x^2 - 9x + 10)(1.09861)$
$= -0.08164x^2 + 0.81366x - 0.60761$
which is the required quadratic polynomial.

putting x =2.7 in the above polynomial, we obtain
In 2.7 $\approx$ L2 (2.7) = $-0.08164(2.7)^2 + 0.81366(2.7) - 0.60761$
= 0.9941164
Actual value of In 2.7 = 0.9932518, so that

|Error| = 0.0008646.

Q4. A table of x versus f(x) is given below. Find the value of f(x) at x=2.5 using any interpolation method (e.g. Lagrange's method) [7]
[JAN01, Q2(a)]

x	-1	1.5	4
F(x)	-20	5	16

The Lagrangian Polynomial of degree 2 and passing through 3 points is given by:-

$$f(x) = (-20)\frac{(x-1.5)(x-4)}{(-1-1.5)-1-4)} + 5\frac{(x-(-1))(x-4)}{1.5-(-1(1.5-4)} + 16\frac{(x-(-1))(x-1.5)}{(4-(-1)(4-1.5)}$$

$$= (-20)\frac{(x-1.5)(x-4)}{(4-2.5)(-5)} + 5\frac{(x+1)(x-4)}{(2.5)(-2.5)} + 16\frac{(x+1)(x-1.5)}{(5)(2.5)}$$

$$= (-20)\frac{(x-1.5)(x-4)}{12.5} + (5)\frac{(x+1)(x-4)}{6.25} + (16)\frac{(x+1)(x-1.5)}{12.5}$$

We want to find value of f (x) at x = 2.5. Hence,

$$f(2.5) = (-20)\frac{(2.5-1.5)(2.5-4)}{12.5} + (5)\frac{(2.5-1)(2.5-4)}{6.25}$$

$$+(16)\frac{(2.5-1)(2.5-1.5)}{12.5}$$

$$=(-20)\frac{(1)(-1.5)}{12.5}+(5)\frac{(3.5)(-1.5)}{-6.25}+(16)\frac{(3.5)(1)}{12.5}$$

$$=(-20)\frac{(-1.5)}{12.5}+(5)\frac{(3.5)(-1.5)}{-6.25}+(16)\frac{3.5}{12.5}$$

$$=\frac{20\times 1.5}{12.5}+\frac{5\times 3.5\times 1.5}{6.25}+\frac{16\times 3.5}{12.5} \quad =\frac{4\times 3}{5}+\frac{7\times 3}{5}+\frac{16\times 7}{25}$$

$$=\frac{12}{5}+\frac{21}{5}+\frac{112}{25}$$

$$=\frac{60+105+112}{25}=\frac{277}{25}$$

$\therefore$ f (2.5) =11.8

CHAPTER-5

NUMERICAL INTEGRATION

NUMERICAL INTEGRATION

Numerical Integration :- The process of computing the value of a definite integral from a set of numerical values of the integrand is called Numerical Integration. The problem of Numerical Integration is handled by using the integrand by an interpolation formula and then integrating this within given limits.

To find the value of $\int_a^b y\,dx$, y is replaced by an interpolation formula usually one involving differences, and then integrate this formula between limit a & b where a is called lower limit and b is called upper limit.

Let us consider, $I = \int_a^b y\,dx$

where $y = f(x)$

Let f(x) is defined for certain equidistant values of x say x_0, $x_0 + h$, $x_0 + 2h$, ...

where

$$b - a = nh \quad \text{i.e} \quad h = \frac{b-a}{h}$$

and, let $x_0 = a$, $x_1 = x_0 + h = a + h$, $x_2 = a + 2h$, ...

Let n + 1 ordinate at equal intervals, corresponding to x are, y_0, y_1, ... y_n.

$$I = h\left[ny_0 + \frac{n^2}{2}\Delta y_0 + \left(\frac{n^3}{2} - \frac{n^2}{2}\right)\frac{\Delta^2 y_0}{2!} + \left(\frac{n^4}{4} - n^3 + n^2\right)\frac{\Delta^3 y_0}{3!} + \text{---} + \text{upto}\,(n+1)\text{terms}\right] \qquad \text{...........(1)}$$

The above formula represent general formula for integration this may also known as mother formula. Because, trapezoidal formula, Simpson's $\frac{1}{3}^{rd}$ formula, $\frac{3}{8}^{th}$ formula which are obtained by putting n = 2, 3 and 6 repestively in equation (1) is respectively.

Trapezoidal formull a

put n = 2 in formula 1 and neglect second and higher differences, we get,

$$\int_{x_0}^{x_0+h} ydx = h\left[y_0 + \frac{1}{2}\Delta y_0\right]$$

$$\text{where } I = \int_a^b ydx = \int_{x_0}^{x_0+h} ydx$$

$$(\text{where } a = x_0,\ b = x_0 + h)$$

$$=h\left[y_0 + \frac{1}{2}(y_1 - y_0)\right]$$

$$=h\left[\frac{y_0 + y_1}{2}\right]$$

$$\text{similarly, } \int_{x_0+h}^{x_0+2h} ydx = h\left[\frac{y_{n-1} + y_n}{2}\right]$$

Summing these n integrals, we get

$$\int_{x_0}^{x_{0+nh}} ydx = h\left[\frac{1}{2}(y_0 + y_n) + (y_1 + y_2 + ... + y_{n-1})\right] \quad ....(2)$$

This rule is known as trapezoidal rule

Simpson's $\frac{1}{3}^{rd}$ Rule.....

By putting n=3 in formula 1 we may obtain, formula given below.

$$\int_{x_0}^{x_0+nh} ydx = \frac{h}{3}[(y_0 + y_n) + 4(y_1 + y_3 + y_5 + --- + y_{n-1}) + 2(y_2 + y_4 + -- + y_{n-2})] \quad ------------------(3)$$

This formula is know as simpson's $\frac{1}{3}^{rd}$ rule. we remember that the third and higher order differences should be neglect for derivation of formula.

Simpson $\frac{3}{8}^{th}$ rule :-

Putting n=6 in the formula 1 and neglecting all differences above the third we get, simpson's $\frac{3}{8}^{th}$ the rule, which is given below,

$$\int_{x_0}^{x_0+nh} ydx=\frac{3}{8}h\left[(y_0+y_n)+3(y_1+y_2+y_4+y_5+...y_{n-1})+2(y_3+y_6...y_{n-3})\right] \quad (4)$$

Q1. Compute the approximate value of integral $I=\int_0^6 \frac{dx}{1+x^2}$ by using simpson's Rule **[DEC 2000]**

Decide the range of integration (0, 6) into 6 equal parts for h,

$$h=\frac{6-0}{6}=1$$

the values of y for each point of subdivision are given below :-

x	$y=\frac{1}{1+x^2}$	y
$x_0 = 0$	1.0000000	y_0
$x_0 + h = 1$	.5000000	y_1
$x_0 + 2h = 2$	.2000000	y_2
$x_0 + 3h = 3$	.1000000	y_3
$x_0 + 4h = 4$	.0588235	y_4
$x_0 + 5h = 5$	.0384615	y_5
$x_0 + 6h = 6$	.0270270	y_6

By Using Simpson's $\frac{1}{3}$ rd Rule

$$\int_0^6 \frac{dx}{1+x^2}=\frac{h}{3}\left[(y_0+y_6)+4(y_1+y_3+y_5)+2(y_2+y_4)\right]$$

$$=\frac{1}{3}\left[(1+.0270270)+4(.5+.1+.0384615)+2(.2+.0588235)\right]$$

$$=\frac{1}{3}\left[(1.0270270)+4(.6384615)+2(.2588235)\right]$$

$$=\frac{1}{3}\left[1.0270270+2.5538460+.5176470\right]$$

$$=\frac{1}{3}[4.0985200]$$

$=1.3661733$

$=1.3662$ Answer

CHAPTER-6

CURVE FITTING

CURVE FITTING AND PRINCIPLE OF LEAST SQUARES

Curve Fitting : Let (x_i, y_i) ; i = 1, 2, ...n be a given set of n pairs of values. X being independent variable and Y the dependent variable. The general problem in curve fitting is to find, if possible, an analytic expression of the form y = f(x), for the functional relationship suggested by the given data.

Fitting of curves to a set of numerical data is of considerable importance theoretical as well as practical. Theoretically it is useful in the study of correlation and regression, e.g., lines of regression can be regarded as fitting of linear curves to the given bivariate distribution. In practical statistics it enables us to represent the relationship between two variables by simple algebraic expressions, e.g., polynomials, exponential or logarithmic functions. Moreover, it may be used to estimate the value of one variable which would correspond to the specified values of the other variable.

Fitting of a straight line : Let us consider the fitting of a straight line

$$Y = a + bx \quad \text{..(1)}$$

to a set of n points (x_i, y_i); i = 1, 2, ..., n. Equation (1) represents a family of straight lines for different values of the arbitrary constants 'a' and 'b'. The problem is to determine 'a' and 'b' so that the line is the line of "best fit".

The term 'best fit' is interpreted in accordance with Legender's principle of least squares which consists in minimising the sum of the squares of the deviations of the actual values of y from their estimated values as given by the line of best fit.

Let P_i (x_i, y_i) be any general point in the scatter diagram . Draw $P_iM \perp$ to x-axis meeting the line, in H_i. Abscissa of H_i is x_i and since H_i lies on (1) its ordinate is $a+bx_i$. Hence the co-ordinates of H_i are $(x_i, a + bx_i)$, is called the error of estimate or the residual for y_i.

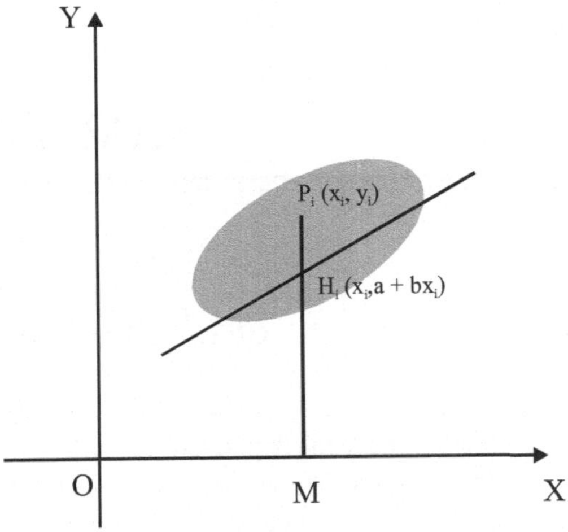

According to the principle of least squares, we have to determine a and b so that

$$E = \sum_{i=1}^{n} P_i H_i^2 = \sum_{i=1}^{n} (y_i - a - bx_i)^2$$

is minimum. From the principle of maxima and minima, the partial derivatives of E, with respect to (w.r.t.) a and b should vanish separately, ie.

$$\frac{\partial E}{\partial a} = 0 = -2 \sum_{i=1}^{n} (y_i - a - bx_i) \text{ and } \frac{\partial E}{\partial a} = 0 = -2 \sum_{i=1}^{n} x_i (y_i - a - bx_i)$$

$$\Rightarrow \sum_{i=1}^{n} y_i = na + b \sum_{i=1}^{n} x_i \text{ and } \sum_{i=1}^{n} x_i y_i = a \sum_{i=1}^{n} x_i + b \sum_{i=1}^{n} x_i^2$$

These equations are known as the normal equations for estimating a and b.

All the quantities $\sum_{i=1}^{n} x_i$, $\sum_{i=1}^{n} x_i^2$, $\sum_{i=1}^{n} y_i$ and $\sum_{i=1}^{n} x_i y_i$, can be obtained from the given set of points (x,y_i); i = 1,2....,n and the equations obtained above can be solved for a and b. With the values of a and b so obtained and the line of best fit to the given set of points (x_i, y_i); i = 1, 2, ...n may be write.

Remark

The equation of the line of best fit of y on x is obtained on eliminating a and b can be expressed in the determinant form as follows :

$$\begin{vmatrix} Y & X & 1 \\ \Sigma y_i & \Sigma x_i & n \\ \Sigma x_i y_i & \Sigma x_i^2 & \Sigma x_i \end{vmatrix} 0$$

Method of least squares

Let $x_0, x_1, x_2, \ldots\ldots, x_{n-1}$ are the values of the independent variables x and $y_0, y_1, y_2, \ldots\ldots, y_{n-1}$ are the values of the dependent y. The scatter diagram for this given data is

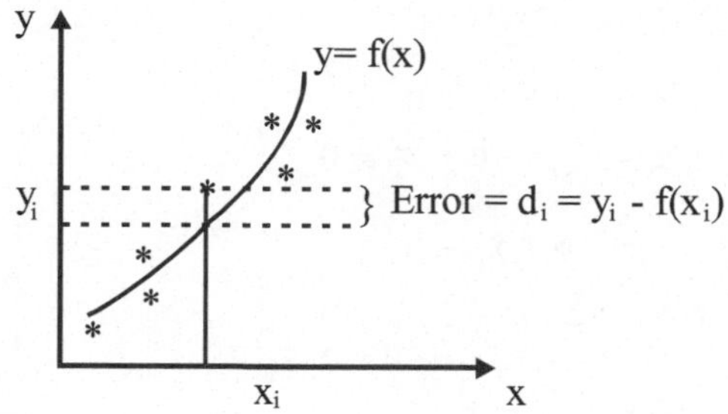

Let us suppose that

$$y = f(x)$$

be an approximation to the function. The errors between y's obtained from the above approximation and the actual tabulated values of y's are

$$d_0 = y_0 - f(x_0)$$
$$d_1 = y_1 - f(x_1)$$
$$d_2 = y_2 - f(x_2)$$
$$\vdots$$
$$d_{n-1} = y_{n-1} - f(x_{n-1})$$

According to least square method, Sum(S)

$$S = d_0^2 + d_1^2 + \ldots\ldots\ldots + d_{n-1}^2$$
$$= \sum_{i=1}^{n} d_i^2$$

Fitting of a straight line :

Let us suppose that in the Biuariate distribution (x_i, y_i), i = 1, 2, 3 ....n, y is dependent and x is the independent variable.

Let the line of regression of y on x be

$$y = a + bx$$

So the estimate line would be,

$$y = a + bx \qquad \text{[where d is difference or deviation]}$$

We have to minimise the sum of squares (SS) of deviation, i.e.,

$$\min_{a,b} \sum d_i^2 \quad \text{or} \quad \min_{a,b} \sum (y_i - a - bx_i)^2$$

We get the following normal equations

$$\begin{cases} \frac{\partial}{\partial a} \Sigma (y_i - a - bx_i)^2 = 0 \\ \frac{\partial}{\partial a} \Sigma (y_i - a - bx_i)^2 = 0 \end{cases}$$

Or $$\begin{cases} 2 \Sigma (y_i - a - bx_i)(-1) = 0 \\ 2 \Sigma (y_i - a - bx_i)(-x_i) = 0 \end{cases}$$

Or $$\begin{cases} \Sigma y_i - na - b \Sigma x_i = 0 \\ \Sigma y_i x_i - a\Sigma x_i - b \Sigma x_i^2 = 0 \end{cases}$$

$$\begin{cases} \Sigma y_i - na - b \Sigma x_i = 0 \\ \Sigma y_i x_i - a\Sigma x_i - b \Sigma x_i^2 = 0 \end{cases}$$

$$a = \frac{1}{n} (\Sigma y - b \Sigma x)$$

$$b = \frac{n\ (\Sigma xy) - (\Sigma x)(\Sigma y)}{n(\Sigma x^2) - (\Sigma x^2)}$$

So, the equation of the estimated regression line is

$$\hat{y} = a + bx$$

where,

$$a = \frac{1}{n} (\Sigma y - b \Sigma x)$$

$$b = \frac{n\ (\Sigma xy) - (\Sigma x)(\Sigma y)}{n(\Sigma x^2) - (\Sigma x^2)}$$

Q1. Fit a second degree parabola to the following data

x :	**0**	**1**	**2**	**3**	**4**
y :	**1**	**5**	**10**	**22**	**38**

Solution : Let the parabola to be fitted is given by $y = a + bx + cx^2$

The normal equations are

$$\left.\begin{aligned} \Sigma y &= na + b\Sigma x + c\Sigma x^2 \\ \Sigma xy &= a\Sigma x + b\Sigma x^2 + c\Sigma x^3 \\ \Sigma x^2 y &= z\Sigma x^2 + b\Sigma x^3 + c\Sigma x^4 \end{aligned}\right\} \quad \text{--------------------------(1)}$$

x	y	x^2	x^3	x^4	xy	x^2y
0	1	0	0	0	0	0
1	5	1	1	1	5	5
2	10	4	8	16	20	40
3	22	9	27	81	66	198
4	38	16	64	256	152	608
10	76	30	100	354	243	851

Substituting the value from table in (1) equation (1) we get

$76 = 51a + 10b + 30c$

$243 = 10a + 30b + 100c$

$851 = 30a + 100b + 354c$

On solving these equations, we get

$a = 1.43$, $b = 0.24$, $c = 2.21$ putting in

$y = 1.43 + 0.24x + 2.21x^2$

Hence, this is our required equation to the second degree parabola.

Feedback is the breakfast of Champions.

Ken Blanchard

You can Help other students.
"Inform any error or mistake in this book."

We and Universe
will reward you for Your Kind act.

Email at : feedback@gullybaba.com
or
WhatsApp on 9350849407

SOLVED PAPERS
CS-71

Wondering who is Gullybaba?

© Gullybaba is a combination of two signi? cant words '**Gully**' & '**Baba**'. The word 'Gully' comes from the ancient game played in Rural India–**Tip cat**. In Hindi, we call it **Gully Danda** (**गुल्ली डंडा**) which is a great **symbol of Focus & Fitness**.

The word 'Baba' stands for **Respect & Honour**. And these are the fundamental parameters for achieving success. **Focus & Fitness** are required to help one go a long way in life. This is all about achieving excellence in education and giving respect & honour to everyone, and thus, the name 'Gullybaba'.

To know more about why name GullyBaba visit: **GullyBaba.com/why-name-gullybaba.html**

CS-71 : COMPUTER ORIENTED NUMERICAL TECHNIQUES
JAN-2001

Note: *Question 1 is* ***compulsory****. Answer any* ***three*** *from the rest.*

Q1(a). Fit a straight line to the data given in the following table : [6]

Independent variable x	**5**	**7**	**8**	**9**
Dependent variable y	**10**	**8**	**11**	**7**

Here, n = 4. To fit the straight line, we use the method of least squares.
Now

x	y	x^2	xy
5	10	25	50
7	8	49	56
8	11	64	88
9	7	81	63
$\Sigma x=29$	$\Sigma y=36$	$\Sigma x^2=219$	$\Sigma xy=257$

The equation of straight line to be fitted is
y=ax+b

$$a=\frac{n\left(\sum xy\right)-\left(\sum x\right)\left(\sum y\right)}{n\left(\sum x^2\right)-\left(\sum x\right)^2}=\frac{4(257)-(29\times 36)}{4(219)-(29)^2}=\frac{1028-1044}{876-841}$$

$$=\frac{-16}{35}$$

$$=-0.457$$

$$b=\frac{1}{n}\left[\sum y-a\sum x\right]=\frac{1}{4}\left[36-\left(\frac{-16}{35}\right)\times 29\right]$$

$$=\frac{1}{4}\left[36+\frac{16\times 29}{35}\right]$$

$$=9+\frac{4\times 29}{35}=9+3.314$$

$$=12.314$$

Thus, the equation of the line would be

$y = a+bx$

$y = 12.314 - 0.457\ x.$

(b) Explain the following concepts with suitable examples: **[6]**

(i) Truncation error in numerical computation

(ii) Mantissa in floating point representation

(iii) Pivoting

(i) Truncation errors : These are errors caused by using approximate formulae in computations — such as the one that arises when a function f(x) is evaluated from an infinite series for x after 'truncating' it at a certain stage. The study of this type of error is usually associated with the problem of convergence. Truncation error in a problem can be evaluated and it is desirable to make it as small as possible.

(ii) Mantissa in floating point representation

In floating point representation the number that is other than exponent which is on the left of E and has the value less than 1 and greater than or equal to .1 is the mantissa e.g. in .4485E8, .4485 is mantissa.

(iii) Pivoting

Refer to DEC01, Q1(a, vi) Page No.-142

(c) Solve the following system of simultaneous linear equations using either Gauss-Elimination method or Gauss-Siedel method : **[6]**

$-3x_1+5x_2+x_3 = 3$

$2x_2 - 5x_3 = -3$

$3x_1 + 5x_2 = 8$

The augmented matrix of coefficients of x, x_2 and x_3 is -

$$\begin{bmatrix} -3 & 5 & 1 & 3 \\ 0 & 2 & -5 & -3 \\ 3 & 5 & 10 & 8 \end{bmatrix}$$

The coefficient of x_1 is already 0 in the 2nd row. To make it zero in 3rd row, we perform following operation:- Add row 1 to row 3, we get

$$\begin{bmatrix} -3 & 5 & 1 & 3 \\ 0 & 2 & -5 & -3 \\ 0 & 10 & 1 & 11 \end{bmatrix}$$

Now, we perform $R_3 \rightarrow R_3$ ¾ $5 \times R_2$ and obtain

$$\begin{bmatrix} -3 & 5 & 1 & 3 \\ 0 & 2 & -5 & -3 \\ 0 & 0 & 26 & 26 \end{bmatrix}$$

Performing back substitution, we write the equation in triangular form as below:-

$- 3x + 5x_2 + x_3 = 3$ ...... (1)

$2x_2 - 5x_3 = - 3$ ...... (2)

$26 x_3 = 26$ ...... (3)

From the equation (3), we get

$26 x_3 = 26$

$x_3 = 1$

Substituting value of x_3 in equation (2), we get

$2x_2 - 5x_3 = -3$

$2x_2 - (5 \times 1) = -3$

i.e. $2x_2 = -3 + 5 = 2$

$\therefore \quad x_2 = 1$

Substituting values of x_3 and x_2 in equation (1), we get

$-3x_1 + 5x_2 + x_3 = 3$

$-3x + (5 \times 1) + 1 = 3$

i.e. $-3x_1 + 5 +1 = 3$

i.e. $-3x_1 = -3$

or $x_1 = \frac{3}{3} 1 \Rightarrow x_1 = 1$

Thus $x_1 = 1, x_2 = 1, x_3 = 1.$

(d) Using any of the iterative method (e.g. Newton-Raphson method), solve the equation **[6]**

$e^{-x} - x = 0$

$f(x) = e^{-x} - x = 0$

We may write the above equation in the form :

$f(x) = xe^x-1 = 0$ .... (1)

$f'(x)=(1+x)e^x$

Let $x_0=1$

$$x_1=x_0-\frac{f(x_0)}{f'(x_0)}$$

$$=1-\frac{1.e^1-1}{(1+1)e^1}$$

$x_1 = 0.6839397$

Now $f(x_1) = 0.3553424$

$f'(x_1) = 3.337012$

So that

$$x_2 = x_1 - \frac{f(x_1)}{f'(x_1)}$$

$$= 0.6839397 - \frac{0.3553424}{3.337012}$$

$= 0.5774545$

processing in this way, we obtain

$x_3=0.5672297$

$x_4=0.5671433$

Since x_3 and x_4 are very much closed in their values so we can say that required root is 0.5671.

(e) Using any method of numerical integration (e.g. Simpson's rule), find the value of the definite integral : [6]

$$\int_1^3 (2x^2 - 3x + 5)dx$$

If required, you may take h = 1.

The given definite integral is

$$I=\int_1^3 (2x^2-3x+5)dx$$

Let $y=2x^2-3x+5$

$$\therefore I=\int_1^3 ydx$$

The range is from 1 to 3.

We take h = 1

The value of x and y are plotted as below:-

x	1	2	3
y	4	7	14
	y_0	y_1	y_2

Simpson's 1/3 rule states that

$$I=\int_1^3 ydx=\frac{h}{3}\left[y_0+4(y_1+y_3+y_5+\text{---}+y_{n-1})+2(y_2+y_4+y_6+\text{---}+y_{n-2})+y_n\right]$$

$h = 1$, $y_0 = 4, y_1 = 7, y_3 = 14$

$I=1/3[(y_0+y_2)+4y_1)$

$$I=\frac{1}{3}\ [4 + 4(7) +14]$$

$$=\frac{1}{3}\ [4 + 28 + 14]$$

$$=\frac{1}{3}\times 46$$

$= 15.33$

The approximate value of given definite integral is 46 / 3.

Q2(a). A table of x versus f(x) is given below. Find the value of f(x) at x=2.5 using any interpolation method (e.g. Lagrange's method) [7]

x	**-1**	**1.5**	**4**
F(x)	**-20**	**5**	**16**

Refer to Study material, Q4, Page No.-42

(b) Using four digit mantissa and two digit exponent, find 4 value of each of the numerical expression:
(i) .5641E5 - .8721E3
(ii) .3125E4*.612E3

(i) .5641E5 - .8721E3
Their exponents are different. Hence we normalize the number 0.8721E3 resulting in 0.80087E5 with 4 digit mantissa.
Hence,

Minu end0.5641E5	
Subtrahend	0.0087E5
Difference	0.5554E5

(ii) .3125E4 * .6121E3
We want to multiply the two numbers.
$\therefore$ 0.3125E4 * 0.6121E3
$= (0.3125 \times 0.6125)$ E (4+3)

= 0.114062E7

After truncating mantissa to 4 digits we get the product as

= 0.1914E7

Q3(a). Using any of iterative methods (e.g. Newton-Raphson method), determine the two smallest roots of the following equation: f(x) = x sinx + cos x = 0, to 3 significant digits.

Using Newton-Raphson Method

Given eq. $f(x) = x \sin x + \cos x = 0$

$$f(x) = x \sin x + \cos x$$

$f'(x) = \sin x + x \cos x - \sin x = x \cos x$

Now, on putting

$x = 0,\ f(0) = 1$ (Positive)

$x=\frac{\pi}{2},\ f(\frac{\pi}{2})=\frac{\pi}{2}\sin\frac{\pi}{2}+\cos\frac{\pi}{2}=\frac{\pi}{2}$ (Positive)

$x=\pi\quad f(\pi)=\pi \sin\pi+\cos\pi=-1$ (Negative)

$\therefore$ Roots lies between $\frac{\pi}{2}$ and π

Take $x_0 = \pi = \frac{22}{7} = 3.142857$

$$f(x_0) = \pi \sin \pi + \cos \pi = -1$$

$$f`(x_0) = \pi \cos \pi = -\pi = -\frac{22}{7}$$

By Newton Raphson's rule

$$x_1 = x_0 - \frac{f(x_0)}{f`(x_0)} = 3.142857 - \frac{-1}{(-22/7)}$$

$$= 3.142857 - \frac{1}{22} \times 7 = 2.824675$$

$f(x_1) = f(2.824675) = 2.824675 \times \sin 2.824675 + \cos 2.824675$

$= -0.069921929$

$f'(x_1) = x \cos x = 2.824675 \times \cos 2.824675$

$= -2.684008221$

$$\therefore \quad x_2 = x_1 - \frac{f(x_1)}{f`(x_1)} = 2.824675 - \frac{-0.069921929}{-2.684008221}$$

=2.798624

Again,

$f(x_2) = -0.00063$

$f`(x_2) = -2.63563$

$x_3 = 2.798386$

Here, x_3 & x_2 are approximately equal.

so, Required Roots are $x_3 = 2.798386$

(b) Compare any two iterative methods of solving the above 4 equation on the basis of

(i) the amount of computational effort per iteration

(ii) the rate of convergence

(i) In case of Newton-Raphson method, computational effort is considerable in computing the values of f(x) and f'(x) . The overall computing time is large though rate of convergence is high. The secant method computes the given function only once per iteration. It is the most economical method with rapid convergence at low cost.

(ii) Newton-Raphson method has the fastest convergence. It converges faster than secant method. It is a good method if the assumed root is near the root. However, it is very sensitive and may diverge if f'(x) is near zero anytime during the iterative process.

The Secant method does not guarantee convergence. It converges faster then False Position method, but much lower then N-R method.

Q4(a). solve the following simultaneous equations by Gauss-Elimination method:

$9x_1 + 6x_2 + 4x_3 = 20$

$x_1 + 10x_2 + 4x_3 = 6$

$2x_1 - 4x_2 + 10x_3 = -15$

Refer to JUNE01, 5(a), Page No.-163

(b) Compare the direct and iterative methods for solving simultaneous linear equations.

Refer to DEC01, Q1(b, ii), Page No.-143

Q5. Find solution of the following differential equation, using any one of the numerical methods for solving differential equation:

dy/dx = 2xy

y(0) - 0.5

and 0=$\leq$ x =$\leq$ 1

given equation is

$$\frac{dy}{dx}=2xy$$

by Euler Method we have

Also y (0) = 0.2

i.e. y = 0 when x = 0.5

also $0 \le x \le 1$

∴ We have,

x_0 0.5 y_0 = 0 let h = 0.2

We prepare following table of values for x and y, for range of x = 0 to 1

x y $\frac{dy}{dx}$=2xy oldy+0.2$\left(\frac{dy}{dx}\right)$=newy

x	y	$\frac{dy}{dx} = 2xy$	oldy + 0.2$\left(\frac{dy}{dx}\right)$ = newy
0.0	1.0	0	1+.2(0)=1
0.2	1.0	0.4	1+.2×.4=108
0.4	1.08	2.4×1.08 = 0.864	1.08+.2×.865 = 1.2528
0.6	1.2528	2×.6×1.2528 = 1.50336	12528+(0.2×1.50336) = 1.5533
0.8	1.5535		
1.0	2.0506	2.0506 2×1×2.0506 = 4.1012	2.0506+(.2×4.1012) = 2.8706

Thus values of x and y are:-

x	0	0.2	0.4	0.6	0.8	1.0
y	1.0	1.0	1.08	1.2528	1.5535	2.0506

Q6. Using any method of numerical integration, find the value of

$$\int_0^1 (5x^3 - 3x^2 + 1)dx$$

With $h^{-1} = 1$, find also the truction/roundoff error in your computation

The given definite integral is

$$I=\int_{-1}^{1} (5x^3-3x^2+2x+1)dx$$

Let $y=5x^3-3x^2+2x+1$

$\therefore I=\int_{-1}^{1} ydx$

	x	y	
x_0	-1	-9	y_0
x_1	0	1	y_1
x_2	1	5	y_2

$I=\frac{h}{3}[(y_0+y_2+4y_1]$

$=\frac{1}{3}[(-9+5)+4\times1]$

$=\frac{1}{3}[-4+4]$

$=0$

By direct integration :

$I=\int_{-1}^{1}(5x^3-3x^2+3x+1)dx$

$=5\int_{-1}^{1}x^3dx-3\int_{-1}^{1}x^2dx+2\int_{-1}^{1}xdx+\int_{-1}^{1}dx$

$5\frac{[x^4]_{-1}^{1}}{4}-3\frac{[x^3]_{-1}^{1}}{3}+2\frac{[x^2]_{-1}^{1}}{2}+[x]_{-1}^{1}$

$\frac{5}{4}[(1)^4-(-1)^4]-[(1)^3-(-1)^3]+[(1)^2-(-1)^2]+[1-(-1)]$

$=\frac{5}{4}[1-1]-[1+1]+[1-1]+[1+1]$

$=0$

We see that the given integration has value zero by Simpson's 1/3rd rule and by direct method of integration, so there is no truncation error.

CS-71 : COMPUTER ORIENTED NUMERICAL TECHNIQUES
JUNE-2001

Note: *Question 1 is **compulsory**. Answer any **three** from the rest.*

Q1(a). Solve the following system of simultaneous linear equations by using Gaussian Elimination method OR Gauss-Seidel iterative method:

$$5x_1 - 2x_2 + 4x_3 = 7$$
$$3x_1 + 5x_2 - 8x_3 = 0$$
$$2x_1 - 4x_3 = -2$$

We use the Gauss Elimination method

Given equations are ¾

$5x_1 - 2x_2 + 4x_3 = 7$

$3x_1 + 5x_2 - 8x_3 = 0$

$2x_1 - 4x_3 = -2$

It coefficient matrix would be

$$\begin{bmatrix} 5 & -2 & 4 & 7 \\ 3 & 5 & -8 & 0 \\ 2 & 0 & -4 & -2 \end{bmatrix}$$

We now reduce coefficient of x_1 to 0 in row 2, by performing

$R_1 - \frac{5}{2} R_2$

$$\begin{bmatrix} 5 & -2 & 4 & 7 \\ 0 & -31/3 & 52/3 & 7 \\ 2 & 0 & -4 & -2 \end{bmatrix}$$

We now make coefficient of x_1 in 3rd row zero, by performing

$R_1 - \frac{5}{2} R_3$

We get,

$$\begin{bmatrix} 5 & -2 & 4 & 7 \\ 0 & -31/3 & 52/3 & 7 \\ 0 & -2 & 14 & 12 \end{bmatrix}$$

We now reduce coefficient of x2 to 0 in third row by performing

$R_2 - \frac{31}{6} R_3$

$$\begin{bmatrix} 5 & -2 & 4 & 7 \\ 0 & -31/3 & 52/3 & 7 \\ 0 & 0 & -55 & -55 \end{bmatrix}$$

Back substituting the x unknowns, we get

$5x_1 - 2x_2 + 4x_3 = 7$ ..... (1)

$-\frac{31}{3}x_2 + \frac{52}{3}x_3 = 7$ .... (2)

$-55x_3 = -55$ ..... (3)

From equation (3),

i.e. $-55x_3 = -55 \Rightarrow x_3 = 1$

Substituting this value in (2), we get

$-\frac{31}{3}x_2 + \frac{52}{3}x_3 = 7$

i.e. $-\frac{31}{3}x_2 + \frac{52}{3} . 1 = 7$

or $-31x_2 = 21 - 52 = -31$

$x_2 = 1$

Substituting value of (x_2) and (x_3) in (1), we get

$5x_1 - 2x_2 + 4x_3 = 7$

i.e. $5x_1 - (2*1) + 1\ (4*1) = 7$

i.e. $5x_1 - 2 + 4 = 7$

or $5x_1 = 7 + 2 - 4 = 5$

i.e. $x_1 = 1$

Therefore,

$x_1 = 1$

$x_2 = 1$

$x_3 = 1$

(b) Explain the following concepts with suitable examples:

(i) Floating point representing of numbers

Refer to DEC01, Q1(a, i), Page No.-140

(ii) Pivoting

Refer to DEC01, Q1(a, vi), Page No.-142

(iii) Rounding (or Round-off) error in computation.

Refer to JUNE02, Q1(a, i), Page No.-124

(iv) Ill-conditional Equation

Refer to DEC02, Q1(a, iv), Page No.-112

(c) Fit a straight line to the data given in the following table:

Independent variable x	**-2**	**0**	**2**	**4**
Dependent variable y	**10**	**7**	**8**	**5**

We are given the following table for value of x and y:¾

Independent variable x	-2	0	2	4
Dependent variable y	10	7	8	5

To fit the straight line use the method of least squares.
Here we have n = 4

X	y	x^2	xy
-2	10	4	-20
0	7	0	0
2	8	4	16
4	5	16	20
$\Sigma x_i=4$	$\Sigma y_i=30$	$\Sigma x^2=24$	$\Sigma xy^2=16$

The equation of straight line to be fitted is $y = b_0 + b_1 x$
Where,

$$b_1 = \frac{n(\sum xy)-(\sum x)(\sum y)}{n(\sum x^2)-(\sum x)^2}$$

$$= \frac{(4\times16)-(4\times30)}{(4\times24)-(4)^2}$$

$$= \frac{(64-120)}{(96-16)} = \frac{-56}{80}$$

$$= \frac{7}{10} = -0.7$$

$$b_0 = \frac{1}{n}\left[\sum y - b_1 \sum x\right]$$

$$= \frac{1}{4}[30\text{-}(\text{-}0.7\times4)]$$

$$= \frac{1}{4}[30 + 2.8] = \frac{32.8}{4} = 8.2$$

Thus, the equation of the line that would fit given data would be

$y = b_0 + b_1 x$

$y = 8.2 - 0.7 x$

(d) Using any of the iterative methods (e.g. Newton-Raphson method), solve the equation:

f(x) = sin x + cos x = 0

f(x) = sin x + cos x = 0

f `(x) = cos x - sin x

(x take in radian) and we know that π = 3.14

and x = 0

f(0) = 1 (Positive)

f(π) = sin π +cos π

f(π) = sin(3.14)+cos(3.14)

= -0.9984061 (-ve value)

we see that f(x) have opposite sign for x=0, x=π

so, we can say Roots lies between 0 and π

Take $x_0 = \pi$

$$x_1 = x_0 - \frac{f(x_0)}{f`(x_0)}$$

$f`(x_0) = \cos x_0 - \sin x_0 = -1.00159$

& $f(x_0) = \sin x_0 + \cos x_0 = -0.9984061$

$$x_1 = 180 - \frac{-0.9984061}{-1.00159} = 179.0032$$

$$x_0 = \pi \Rightarrow x_1 = 179.0032$$

$$x_2 = x_1 - \frac{f(x_1)}{f`(x_1)} = 179.0032 - \frac{32031.138}{358.0064}$$

$x_2 = 89.53232$

$$x_3 = x_2 - \frac{f(x_2)}{f`(x_2)} = 44.82759$$

$$x_4 = x_3 - \frac{f(x_3)}{f`(x_3)} = 22.53649$$

$$x_5 = x_4 - \frac{f(x_4)}{f`(x_4)} = 11.51229$$

$$x_6 = x_5 - \frac{f(x_5)}{f`(x_5)} = 6.233896$$

$$x_7 = x_6 - \frac{f(x_6)}{f`(x_6)} = 3.992221$$

$$x_8 = x_7 - \frac{f(x_7)}{f`(x_7)} = 3.374878$$

$$x_9 = x_8 - \frac{f(x_8)}{f`(x_8)} = 3.3171128$$

$$x_{10} = x_9 - \frac{f(x_9)}{f`(x_9)} = 3.3166$$

we see that x_9 and x_{10} are very much closed so, x_{10} = 3.3166 is our required root.

(e) Using any method of numerical integration (e.g. Simpson's rule), find the value of the definite integral

$$\int_0^2 (5x^2 - 3x+2)dx$$

If required, you may take h = 1.

The given definite integral is

$$\int_0^2 \left(5x^2 - 3x + 2\right)dx$$

The interval used h = 1. x varies from 0 to 2. The values of x and y are plotted below in the table as: -

f (x) = y = $5x^2$ - 3x + 2

x	0	1	2
y	2	4	16
	y_0	y_1	y_2

By the method of Simpson's 1/3 rd Rule : -

Where, h = 1,

$$I=\frac{h}{3}[(y_0+y_2)+4y_1]$$

$$I=\frac{1}{3}[(2+16)+4\times 4]$$

$$=\frac{1}{3}[18+16]$$

$$I=\frac{34}{3}$$

$$\therefore \int_0^2 (5x^2-3x+2)dx=\frac{34}{3}$$

The approximate value of the Definite Integral is 34/3.

Q2(a). A table of x versus f(x) is given below. Find the value of f(x) at x = 4 using any interpolation method (e.g. Lagrange's method).

x	**1**	**3**	**6**
f(x)	**-1**	**2**	**20**

The given table of x versus f (x) is

x	1	3	6
f(x)	-1	2	20

We have to interpolate and find value of f(x) at x = 4.
The Lagrangian polynomial of degree 2 passing through 3 points is given by

$$f(x)=(y_0)\frac{(x-x_1)(x-x_2)}{(x_0-x_1)(x_0-x_2)}+y_1\frac{(x-x_0)(x-x_2)}{(x_1-x_0)(x_1-x_2)}+y_2\frac{(x-x_0)(x-x_1)}{(x_2-x_0)(x_2-x_1)}$$

$$\therefore f(x)=(-1)\frac{(x-3)(x-6)}{(1-3)(1-6)}+(2)\frac{(x-1)(x-6)}{(3-1)(3-6)}+(20)\frac{(x-1)(x-3)}{(6-1)(6-3)}$$

$$=(-1)\frac{(x-3)(x-6)}{-2\times 5}+(2)\frac{(x-x_1)(x-6)}{2\times(-3)}+(20)\frac{(x-1)(x-3)}{5\times 3}$$

$$=\frac{(x-3)(x-6)}{-10}+\frac{(x-1)(x-6)}{-3}+\frac{4}{3}.\frac{(x-1)(x-3)}{}$$

at x=4.

$$f(4) = \frac{(4\text{-}3)(4-6)}{\text{-}10} - \frac{(4\text{-}1)(4-6)}{\text{-}3} + \frac{4}{3}.(4-1)(4-3)$$

$$= \frac{1\times(\text{-}2)}{\text{-}10} - \frac{3\times(-2)}{\text{-}3} + \frac{4}{3}.3\times 1$$

$$= \frac{1}{5} + 2 + 4$$

f(4)=6.5

(b) Using four digit mantissa and two digit exponent, find the value of each of the following numerical expressions:
(i) .3872E4 + .5083E7
(ii) .1111E5 * .1234E2
(i) .3872E4 + .5083E7

We have to add

.3872E4 and .5083E7 using 4 digit mantissa and 2 digit exponent. The exponent differ in both terms. We normalise .3872E4 as .0003872 E 7

Now adding the expressions, we get

.0003872E7
+.5083000E7
.5086872E7

We wish to use 4 digit mantissa. The fifth digit is 8, hence we round off 4th digit 6 to 6 + 1 =7.

Thus the final expression of addition will be .5087 E7.

(ii) .1111E5 * .1234E2

We want to multiply two expressions-

.1111E5 * .1234E2

This will be equal to

= (.1111 * .1234) E (5+2) = 0.0137097E7

= 0.0137E7 using 4 digit mantissa

0.1371E6

Q3(a). Using any of the iterative methods. (e.g. Newton-Raphson's method), determine the root of the equation to x^3 - 4x + 1 = 0 to 3 significant digits.

The given equation is

$x^3 - 4x + 1 = 0.$

We have to find its roots to 3 significant digits.

Let

$$f(x) = x^3 - 4x + 1$$

$$f^1(x) = 3x^2 - 4$$

we get,

$$f(0) = 0^3 - 4 \times 0 + 1 = 0 - 0 + 1 = 1$$

$$f(1) = 1^3 - 4 \times 1 + 1 = 1 - 4 + 1 = -2,$$

$f'(0)=3 \times 0^2 -4 = -4$

Hence, the root lies between x = 0 and 1.

Let $x_0=0$

$$\therefore x_1 = x_0 - \frac{f(x_0)}{f'(x_0)} = 0\text{-}1/4 = 0.25$$

$x_1=0.25$

Now

$$x_2 = x_1 - \frac{f(x_1)}{f'(x_1)}$$

$$x_2 = .25 - \frac{(.25)^3 - 4(.25) + 1}{3(.25)^2 - 4}$$

$$x_2 = .25 - \frac{0.015625}{-3.8125}$$

$x_2=0.24590$

Since, x_1 and x_2 are very much closed to the required root is 0.2459.

(b) Compare any two iterative methods of solving the above equation on the basis of

(i) Rate of convergence

The Newton-Raphson method has the fastest convergence. It converges faster than secant method. It is a good method if the assumed root is near the root. However, it is very sensitive and may diverge if f'(x) is near zero anytime during the iterative process. The Secant method does not guarantee convergence. It converges faster then False Position method, but much slower turn N-R method.

(ii) Amount of computational effort per iteration

In case of Newton-Raphson method, computational effort is considerable in computing the values of f(x) and f'(x). The overall computing time is large though rate of convergence is high. The secant method computes the given function only once per iteration. It is the most economical method with rapid convergence at low cost.

Q4. Find a solution of the following differential equation, using any one of the numerical methods for solving differential equation: dy/dx = - xy, y(0) = 1

The given differential equation is $\frac{dy}{dx} = -xy$

y (0) = 1

i.e. when x = 0, y = 1. We use Euler's method of numerical differentiation and prepare following table ¾

We take interval of h = 0.2 as x varies from 0 to 1. (assumed)

x	y	$\frac{dy}{dx} = -xy$	oldy + $0.2\left(\frac{dy}{dx}\right)$ = newy
0.0	1	0	1+0.2(0) = 1
0.2	1	-0.2	1+0.2(-2)=96
0.4	0.96	-0.384	0.96+0.2(-0.384) = 0.8832
0.6	0.8832	0.5299	0.8832+0.2(-0.5299)=0.772

Thus various values of y for are

x	y
0	1
0.2	1
0.4	0.96
0.6	0.8832
0.8	0.7772
1	0.6528

Q5(a). Solve the following simultaneous equation by Guass elimination method :

$9x_1 + 2x_2 + 4x_3 = 20$ **[JAN 2001, Q4(a)]**

$x_1 + 10x_2 + 4x_3 = 6$

$2x_1 + 4x_2 - 10x_3 = -15$

We write the given equation as: -

$$x_1 = \frac{1}{9}(20 - 2x_2 - 4x_3) \text{ ----- } (1)$$

$$x_2 = \frac{1}{10}(6 - x_1 - 4x_3) \text{ ----- } (2)$$

$x_3 = \frac{1}{10}(-15 - 2x_1 - 4x_2)$ ----- (3)

Initialization,
Let x_2 - 0, $x_3 = 0$ in eq (1)
First iteration
putting $x_2 = 0$, $x_3 = 0$ in eq (1), we get

$x_1 = \frac{1}{9}(20) = 2.22222$

putting $x_1 = 2.22222$ and $x_3 = 0$ in eq (2), we get

$x_2 = \frac{1}{10}(6 - 2.22222 - 4 \times 0) = 0.377777$

putting x1 = 2.22222 and $x_2 = 0.377777$ in eq (3), we get

$x_3 = \frac{1}{10}(-15 - 2 \times 2.22222 + 4 \times 0.377777)$

$\Rightarrow$ x1 = 2.22222, x2 = 0.377777, x3 = - 1.79333
Second iteration

from eq (1) $\quad x_1 = \frac{1}{9}[20 - 2 \times 0.377777 + 4 \times 1.79333]$

= 2.93530

from eq (2) $\quad x_2 = \frac{1}{10}[6 - 2.93530 + 4 \times 1.79333]$

= 1.02380

from eq (3) $\quad x_3 = \frac{1}{10}[-15 - 2 \times 2.93530 + 4 \times 1.79333]$

= - 1.67754

$\Rightarrow x_1 = 2.93530$, $x_2 = 1.02380$, $x_3 = -1.67754$

Similarly from
Third iteration
$x_1 = 2.74028$, $x_2 = 0.99654$, $x_3 = -1.64944$

Fourth iteration
$x_1 = 2.73385$. $x_2 = 0.98575$, $x_3 = -1.65247$

Fifth iteration
$x_1 = 2.72649$, $x_2 = 0.98834$, $x_3 = -1.64996$

6th iteration

$x_1 = 2.736591, x_2 = 0.98639, x_3 = -1.65263$

7th iteration

$x_1 = 2.73753, x_2 = 0.98730, x_3 = -1.65259$

8th iteration

$x_1 = 2.73271, x_2 = 0.98728, x_3 = -1.65259$

9th iteration

$x_1 = 2.73731, x_2 = 0.98731, x_3 = -1.65254$

on Comparing the values of x_1, x_2 x_3 obtained in the eight and ninth iteration, we find that the digits in the first three places of decimals are the same in both these iterations

∴ Solution to three places of decimal is

$x_1 = 2.737, x_2 = 0.987, x_3 = -1.652$

(b) Compare the direct and iterative methods for solving simultaneous linear equations.

Refer to DEC01, Q1(b, ii), Page No.-143

Q6. Evaluate the integral

$$\int_0^1 x^3 e^{x-1} dx$$

Using any one of the following :

(i) Gauss method with 6 points

(ii) Trapezoidal rule with 20 points

(iii) Simpson's rule with 10 points

(iv) Any other numerical integration method

The given definite integral is $\int_0^1 x^3 ex^{x-1} dx$

We use Simpson's rule with 10 points i.e. the interval h = 0.1= 1/10

We have $y = f(x) = x^3 e^{x-1}$

h = 0.1

x_n	$y=x^3 e^{x-1}$	y_n
0.0	0	y_0
0.1	$(0.1)^3 e^{-0.9} = (.1)^3(.4066) = 0.0004$	y_1
0.2	$(0.2)^3 e^{-0.8} = (.2)^3(.4493) = 0.0035$	y_2
0.3	$(0.3)^3 e^{-0.7} = (.3)^3(.4966) = 0.0035$	y_3
0.4	$(0.4)^3 e^{-0.6}$	y_4
0.5	$(0.4)^3 e^{-0.6} = (.5)^3(.5488) = 0.0035$	y_5
0.6	$(0.4)^3 e^{-0.5} = (.6)^3(.6065) = 0.0758$	y_6
0.7	$(0.4)^3 e^{-0.4} = (.7)^3(.6707) = 0.02541$	y_7
0.8	$(0.4)^3 e^{-0.3} = (.8)^3(.8187) = 0.4192$	y_8
0.9	$(0.4)^3 e^{-0.2} = (.9)^3(.9048) = 0.6596$	y_9
1.0	$(1)^3 e^0 = 1\times1=1$	y_{10}

Now by using Simpson 1/3 rule, we have

$$I = \frac{h}{3}[(y_0+y_{10})+4\ (y_1+y_3+----+y_9)+2\ (y_2+y_4+---y_8)]$$

$$= \frac{0.1}{3}\left[\begin{matrix}0+1(0.0004+0.0134+0.0758+0.2541+0.6596 \\ +2(0.0035+0.0351+0.1447+0.04192\end{matrix}\right]$$

$$= \frac{0.1}{3}[1+4(1.0033)+2\ (0.6025)]$$

$$= \frac{0.1}{3}[1+4.0132+1.205]$$

$$= 0.2073$$

CS-71 : COMPUTER ORIENTED NUMERICAL TECHNIQUES
DEC-2001

Note: *Question 1 is* ***compulsory****. Answer any* ***three*** *from the rest.*

Q1(a). Explain the following concepts with one suitable example for each:

(i) Floating point representation of numbers.

The memory of a digital computer has separate cells called 'words'. Each word contains the same number of binary digits called 'bits'. The number of digits which can be stored in a computer is known as its word length.

The numbers are stored in a computer in two forms : fixed-point and floating-point forms. The fixed point mode is used to represent integers while the floating-point mode is used to represent real numbers.

A floating-point number is of the form

$$x = \pm(d_1.d_2.....d_n)\,\beta^n, 0 \leq di < \beta, m \leq e \leq M$$

where d_1, d_2 .... d_n are all digits in the base 'β' of the number system used and lie between o and β. The exponent m is such that $M_1 \leq m \leq M_2$, where M_1 and M_2 vary with the computer. The fractional part.d_1d_2 .... d_n is called the mantissa which lies between ± 1 and restricts the size of a number. If a floating-point number has a fixed mantissa of l digits, we say that the word length of the computer is l. For instance, the number 22.74×10^4 is represented as .2274E4 (E4 is used to represent 10^4). Hence the mantissa is .2274 and the exponent is 4. While storing numbers, the leading digit in the mantissa is always made non-zero by suitably shifting it and adjusting the value of the exponent accordingly. This process is called normalization. Therefore the number .003374 in normalized floating point mode would be stored as .3374E-2.Thus the shifting of the mantissa to the left till its most significant digits is non-zero is called normalization.

(ii) Rounding of a number.

There are numbers with large number of digits e.g.,
22/7 = 3.142857143. In practice, it is desirable to limit such numbers to a manageable number of digits such as 3.14 or 3.142. This process of dropping unwanted digits is called rounding off.

Rule to round off a number to n significant figures :

(i) Discard all digits to the right of the nth digit.

(ii) if the discarded number is :
(a) less than half a unit in the nth place, leave the nth digit unchanged.
(b) greater than half a unit in the nth place, increase the nth digit by unity.
(c) exactly half a unit in the nth place, increase the nth digit by unity if it is odd otherwise leave it unchanged.

For instance, the following numbers rounded off to three significant figures are :

2.453 to 2.45 3.567 to 3.57
98.865 to 98.9 28698 to 28700
1.4332 to 1.43 5.8254 to 5.82

Also the numbers 6.284359, 9.864651, 12.464762 rounded off to four places of decimal at 6.2844, 9.8646, 12.4648 respectively.

(iii) Propagated Error

Since in a numerical problems, the true value of numbers may not be used exactly i.e. in place of true values of the numbers, some approximate values like floating point numbers are used initially. The error arising in the problem due to these inexact/ approximate values is called propagated error. Let x^* and y^* be approximations to x and y respectively and a be arithmetic operation.
Then, The propagated error = $xay - x^*ay^*$
r.p.e. = relative propagated error

$$= \frac{xay - xa^* y^*}{xay}$$

(iv) Loss of significant digits

Any digit is a significant digit except when it is used to fix the decimal point or to fill the places of unknown or discarded digits. For example, in the number 0.00154, the significant digits are 1, 5 and 4. The zeroes, on the other hand, are used to fix the decimal point. However, in the number 1234.0567 all digits are significant. Accuracy of a result is dependent upon the number of significant digits needed to express it. In general , if a solution is required to be accurate to n significant digits, we must see that relative error is less than 10^{-n} . In iterative calculation, the iterative process stops when the required number of significant digits in the answer is reached. Thus, if a relative error must lie between 0.0001 and 0.001 for a four digit normalised floating point number, then to guarantee 3 significant digit accuracy the relative error should be ≤ 0.001.

(v) Instability of an algorithm

Algorithm is a step by step process that describe a method for solving any mathematical problem. Sometimes in an algorithm a step is reached when, the alternative is to state that 'relative error $\geq$ epsilon'. In such case, the algorithm is said to be unstable, since the solution has no convergence in n iterations.

(vi) Pivot

If at any stage of the Gauss elimination, one of these pivots say a_{ii}^{i-1} $(a_{11}^{(0)}=a_{11})$ vanishes then we have indicated a modified procedure. But it may also happen that the pivot $a_{ii}^{(i-1)}$, though not zero, may be very small in magnitude compared to the remaining elements (^{3} i) in the ith column. Using a small number as divisor may lead to growth of the round-off error. The use of large multipliers like

$$\frac{-a_{i+1,i}^{(i-12)}}{a_{ii}^{(i-1)}}, \frac{a_{i+2,i}^{(i-1)}}{a_{ii}^{(i-1)}} \text{ etc.}$$

will lend to magnification of errors both during the elimination phase and during the back substitution phase of the solution procedure. This can be avoided by rearranging the remaining rows (from ith row up to nth row) so as to obtain a non-vanishing pivot or to choose one that is largest in magnitude in that column. This is called pivoting strategy.

(b) Describe the following :

(i) Sources of error in numerical computation.

Errors. In any numerical computation, we come across the following types of errors:

Inherent errors: Such Errors which are already present in the statement of a problem before its output is reached are called inherent errors. Such errors arise either due to the given data being approximate or due to the limitations of mathematical tables, calculators or the digital computer. Inherent errors can be minimized by taking better data for using high precision computing adds.

Rounding errors: It arise from the process of rounding off the numbers during the computations. Such errors are unavoidable in most of the calculations due to the limitations of the computing aids. Rounding errors can, however, be reduced :

(i) by changing the calculation procedure so as to avoid subtraction of nearly equal numbers or division by a small number;

(ii) by retaining at least one more significant figure at each step than that given in the data and rounding off at the last step.

Truncation errors: are caused by using approximate results or on replacing an infinite process by a finite one. If we are using a decimal computer having a fixed word length of 4 digits, rounding off of 13.658 gives 13.66 whereas truncation gives 13.65.

For example, if $e^x = 1+x+\frac{x^2}{2!}+\frac{x^3}{3!}+\frac{x^4}{4!}+....¥$

is replaced by $1+x+\frac{x^2}{2!}+\frac{x^3}{3!}+=X'$(say),

then the truncation error is X-X'. Truncation error is a type of algorithm error.

Absolute, Relative and Percentage errors: If X is the true value of a quantity and X' is its approximate value, then | X- X'| is called the absolute error E_a.

The relative error is defined by $E_r=|\frac{X-X'}{X}|$

and the percentage error is $E_p=100E_r=100|\frac{X-X'}{X}|$.

If $\overline{X}$ be such a number that $|X-X'|\leq\overline{X}$

then $\overline{X}$ is an upper limit on the magnitude of absolute error and measures the absolute accuracy.

digits, rounding off of 13.658 gives 13.66 whereas truncation gives 13.65.

For example, if $e^x=1+x+\frac{x^2}{2!}+\frac{x^3}{3!}+\frac{x^4}{4!}+....\infty$

is replaced by $1+x+\frac{x^2}{2!}+\frac{x^3}{3!}+=X'$(say),

then the truncation error is X-X'.

(ii) Relative merits/demerits of direct methods and iterative methods for solving a system of linear equations.

Both direct and iterative methods have their strengths and weaknesses and a choice is based on the particualr linear system to be solved.

Direct Method: -

(i) The direct methods are generally used when the matrix A is dense or filled, that is, there are few zero elements, and the order of the matrix is not very large, say n < 50.

(ii) The rounding errors may becomes quite large for ill conditioned equations (If at any stage during the application of pivoting strategy, it is found that all values of $\{|a_m k_1|$ for m = k + 1, to n are less than a pre-assigned small quantity $\in$, then the equations are ill conditioned and no useful solution is obtained)

Iterative Methods : -

(1) These methods are generally used when the matrix A is sparse and the order of the matrix A is very large say n > 50. Sparse matrices have very few non-zero elements

(2) An important advantage of the iterative methods is the small rounding error. Thus, these methods are good choice for ill-conditioned systems.

(3) However, Convergence may be guaranteed only under special conditions. But when Convergence is assured, this method is better than direct

(c) Do as directed:

(i) Using Newton-Raphson method, find square root of 11 (eleven) with initial valve of x_0 = 3.

Refer to Study material, Q5, Page No.-15

(ii) Solve the following system of linear equations using Gauss elimination method:

$16x_1 + 22x_2 + 4x_3 = -2$

$4x_1 - 3x_2 + 2x_3 = 9$

$12x_1 + 25x_2 + 2x_3 = -11$

Also comment on the nature of the solution.

The given system of linear equations are: -

$16x_1 + 22x_2 + 4x_3 = -2$ - (1)

$4x_1 - 3x_2 + 2x_3 = 9$ - (2)

$12x_1 + 25x_2 + 2x_3 = -11$ - (3)

We use the Gauss-Elimination Method to solve the above equations -

$$[A|b] = \left[\begin{array}{ccc|c} 16 & 22 & 4 & -2 \\ 4 & -3 & 2 & 9 \\ 12 & 25 & 2 & 11 \end{array}\right]$$

$$= \left[\begin{array}{ccc|c} 1 & 11/8 & 1/4 & -1/8 \\ 0 & -17/2 & 1 & 19/2 \\ 0 & 17/2 & -1 & -19/2 \end{array}\right] \quad (\because \frac{R1}{16}, R2-\frac{4}{16}, R3-\frac{12}{16}R1)$$

$$= \left[\begin{array}{ccc|c} 1 & 11/8 & 1/4 & -1/8 \\ 0 & 1 & 2/17 & -19/2 \\ 0 & 0 & 0 & 0 \end{array}\right]$$

Hence, the solution of the given set of equations does not exist. As we cannot obtain x_3. This system has infinitely many solutions

Q2(a)(i). Is the computer addition of numbers associative? Justify your answer.

The computer addition of number is not necessarily associative.

for example: - $(a + b) - c \neq (a - c) + b$

(ii) Is computer multiplication distributive of addition? Justify your answer.

The computer multiplication is not necessarily distributive of addition.

for example: - $a(b - c) \neq (ab - ac)$

(b) The function $f(x) = e^x$ is to be evaluated for x, $0 = \leq x = \leq 50$, correct to at least 6 significant digits. What digit arithmetic should be used to get the required accuracy?

Has for be change

Let $f(x) = e^{x.}$

$$|y_{f(x)}| |r_x| \left|\frac{xf'(x^x)}{f(x)}\right|$$

$$= |r_x| \left|\frac{x.^{ex}}{e^x}\right|$$

$$= |r_x| |x|$$

Let n digit arithmetic be used, then

$$|x| < \frac{1}{2} 10^{1-n}$$

This is possible, if

$$\Rightarrow |x| |r_x| \leq \frac{1}{2} 10^{1-6}$$

$$\Rightarrow \text{or } 50.\frac{1}{2} 10^{1-6} \leq \frac{1}{2} 10^{1-6}$$

$$=> \frac{1}{2}\ 10^{1-n} \leq \left(\frac{1}{100}\right).10^{1-6}$$

$$=> 10^{1-n} \leq 2.10^{1-8}$$

$$=> \text{or } 10^{-n} \leq 10^{1-8}.2$$

$$=> -n \leq -8 + \log_{10}{}^{2}$$

$$=> 8- \log_{10}{}^{2} \leq n$$

$$=> \text{or } 8 -0.3 \leq n$$

This is $n \geq 8$ hence arithmetic may be used.

Q3(a). Solve the quadratic equation $2x^2 + 18.7x - 1.8 = 0$, using two decimal digits floating arithmetic with rounding.

Quadratic equation is $2x^2 + 18.7x - 1.8 = 0$

we want to solve the above equation using two decimal digit floating arithmetic with rounding.

The roots are $x_{1,2} = \dfrac{b \pm \sqrt{b^2 - 4ac}}{2a}$

$$= \frac{-18.7 \pm \sqrt{(18.7)^2 - 4 \times 2 \times (-1.8)}}{2 \times 2}$$

$$= \frac{-18.7 \pm \sqrt{349.69 + 14.4}}{4} = \frac{-18.7 \pm 19.081142}{4}$$

$$= -4.675 \pm 4.7702855$$

The two solutions are

$x_1 = 0.0952855$

and $x_2 = 9.4452855$

Rounding off two decimal digit floating arithmetic, we get

$x_1 = 0.0953$, $x_2 = -9.4453$

with rounding up to 4 significant places.

(b) For the equation $2x^3 - 2x - 1 = 0$ find a positive root by fixed point method.

We observe that for

x = 0 LHS = - 1

x = 1 LHS = - 1

x = 2 LHS = 11

The sign changes from - ve to + ve. Hence, we take two

initial values of x as a = 1
and b = 2

Ist approximation

$$x_1 = a - \frac{(b-a)f(a)}{f(b)-f(a)}$$

$$= 1 - \frac{(2-1)(-1)}{11-(-1)}$$

$$= 1 - \frac{-1}{11+1} = 1 + \frac{1}{12} = 1.0833$$

f (1.0833) = 2 $(1.0833)^3$ - 2 (1.0833) - 1
= 2.5428 - 2.1666 - 1
= - 0.6238 < 0
Since f (1.0833) and f (2) have different signs, the root lies between 1.0833 and 2
a = 1.0833 and b = 2

2st approximation

$$x_2 = a - \frac{(b-a)f(a)}{f(b)-f(a)}$$

= 1.0833 - (2- 1.0833) (- 0.6238)
= 11- (-0.6238)

$$= 1.0833 + \frac{0.5718}{11 - (0.6238)} = 1.0833 + 0.0492$$

= 1.1325
f (x_2) = f (1.1325)
= 2 $(1.1325)^3$ - 2 (1.1325) - 1
= 2.9049 - 2.265 - 1
= - 0.3 601
< 0
Since f (1.1325) and f (2) have opposite signs the root lies between 1.1325 and 2.

3rd approximation

∴ a = 1.1325, b = 2

$$x_3 = a - \frac{(b-a)f(a)}{f(b)-f(a)}$$

$=1.1325-\frac{(-0.8675)(-0.3600)}{11-(-0.36)}$

$=1.1325+\frac{0.3123}{11.36} = 1.1325 + 0.0275$

$= 1.1600$

$f(x_3) = f(1.16)$

$= 2(1.16)^3 - 2(1.16) - 1$

$= 3.1217 - 2.32 - 1$

$= 0.1983$

> 0

Sincef $(x_2) < 0$

and f $(x_3) > 0$

The approximate root is x_3 1.16

Q4(a). Solve the system of equations given below using Gauss Elimination method with partial (maximal column) pivoting:

$x_1 + x_2 + x_3 = 6$

$3x_1 + 3x_2 + 4x_3 = 20$

$2x_1 + x_2 + 3x_3 = 13$

OR

(a) Instead of Gauss Elimination method with partial pivoting, solve the above system of equations, using Gauss-Seidal Iteration method. You may take the initial solution as

$X^0 = [1.5, 1.5, 1.5]$

The given equations are

$x_1 + x_2 + x_3 = 6$.......................(1)

$3x_1 + 3x_2 + 4x_3 = 20$....................... (2)

$2x_1 + x_2 + 3x_3 = 13$............................ (3)

We use Gauss Elimination Method with partial (maximal column) pivoting- Multiplying (1) by 3 and subtracting (2) from 1 AND multiplying (1) by 2 and subtracting (3) from 1, we get

$x_1 + x_2 + x_3 = 6$......................1(a)

$0 + 0 - x_3 = -2$.......................2(a)

$0 + x_2 - x_3 = -1$......................3(a)

From 2(a) , we have $-x_3 = -2$

$x_3 = 2$

i.e.

From3(a), putting value of $x_3 = 2$, we get

$x_2 - x_3 = -1$

$x_2 - 2 = -1$

$x_2 = 1$

Now from 1(a), putting values of x_3 and x_2, we get

$$x_1 + x_2 + x_3 = 6$$
$$x_1 + 1 + 2 = 6$$
$$x_1 = 1$$

Hence, $x_1 = 3, x_2 = 1, x_3 = 2$

Pivotation was not found necessary to solve the equations.

(b) Write a short note on pivoting (partial, complete, scaled)

Suppose we are given a system of equations

$a_{11}x_1 + a_{12} x_2 + a_{13} x_3 = b_1$
$a_{21}x_1 + a_{22} x_2 + a_{23} x_3 = b_2$
$a_{31}x_1 + a_{32} x_2 + a_{33} x_3 = b_3$

To solve these equations by Gauss elimination method, we reduce them to a triangular form as shown below

$a_{11}x_1 + a_{12} x_2 + a_{13} x_3 = k_1$
$a_{22} x_2 + a_{23} x_3 = k_2$
$a_{33} x_3 = k_3$

It is seen that all elements except a_{11} is called the pivot element. After a_{21} and a_{31} are eliminated the next step in triangularisation is to eliminate all the terms below a_{22} in second row(in this a_{32} only). The pivot here is a_{22}.
In elimination process the pivot should not be zero or too small. For maximum precision below in its column. Thus a_{11} should be selected as the maximum of $a_{11,}$ a_{21} and $a_{31.}$ The element a_{22} should be greater then a_r. In general the pivot element a11 should be the largest of
(|a|) for m = k + 1, n

$x_1 + x_2 + 3x_3 = 2$ - (i)

$5x_2 + 4x_3 = 5$ - (ii)

$-9 x_2 + 3x_3 = 8$ - (iii)

then as |-9|>5,

∴ eq (ii) & (iii) should be interchanged to yield

$x_1 + x_2 + 3x_3 = 2$ - (4)

$-9x_2 + 3x_3 = 8$ - (5)

$-5x_2 + 4x_3 = 5$ - (6)

Interchange of equations has no affect on solution. The algorithm for picking the largest element as the pivot and interchange the equation is called pivotal condensation

Thus during the Gauss elimination procedure |a| should be searched and the equation with the maximum value of $|a_m|$ should be interchanged with the current equation. For example, if during elimination we have the following situation:

Q5(a). Using the following table of values, find EITHER Newton's form of interpolating polynomial OR Lagrange's form of interpolating polynomial that approximates f(x)

	x_0	x_1	x_2	x_3	x_4
x	-1	0	3	6	7
f(x)	3	-6	39	822	1611
	$f(x_0)$	$f(x_1)$	$f(x_2)$	$f(x_3)$	$f(x_4)$

Also, find the approximate value of f(x) at x = 2

The given table of values is

	x_0	x_1	x_2	x_3	x_4
x	-1	0	3	6	7
f(x)	3	-6	39	822	1611
	$f(x_0)$	$f(x_1)$	$f(x_2)$	$f(x_3)$	$f(x_4)$

So by Lagranges form of interpolating Polynomial, using the above values of y = f (x) and x, we have

$$f(x) = \frac{(x-x_1)(x-x_2)(x-x_3)(x-x_4)}{(x_0-x_1)(x_0-x_2)(x_0-x_3)(x_0-x_4)} f(x_0)$$

$$+\frac{(x-x_0)(x-x_2)(x-x_3)(x-x_4)}{(x_1-x_0)(x_1-x_2)(x_1-x_3)(x_1-x_4)} f(x_1)$$

$$+\frac{(x-x_0)(x-x_1)(x-x_3)(x-x_4)}{(x_2-x_0)(x_2-x_1)(x_2-x_3)(x_2-x_4)} f(x_2)$$

$$+\frac{(x-x_0)(x-x_1)(x-x_2)(x-x_4)}{(x_3-x_0)(x_3-x_1)(x_3-x_2)(x_3-x_4)} f(x_3)$$

$$+\frac{(x-x_0)(x-x_1)(x-x_2)(x-x_3)}{(x_4-x_0)(x_4-x_1)(x_4-x_2)(x_4-x_3)}f(x_4)$$

$$=\frac{(x-0)(x-3)(x-6)(x-7)(3)}{(-1)(-4)(-7)(-8)}+\frac{(x+1)(x-3)(x-6)(x-7)(-6)}{(1)(-3)(-6)(-7)}$$

$$=\frac{(x+1)(x)(x-6)(x-7)(39)}{(4)(3)(-3)(-4)}+\frac{(x+1)(x)(x-3)(x-7)(822)}{(7)(6)(3)(-1)}$$

$$=\frac{(x+1)(x)(x-3)(x-6)(1611)}{(8)(7)(4)(1)}$$

$\therefore$ At x = 2

$$f(2)=\frac{(2)(-1)(-4)(-5)(3)}{(-1)(-1)(-7)(-8)}+\frac{(3)(-1)(-4)(-5)(-6)}{1(-3)(-6)(-7)}$$

$$+\frac{(3)(2)(-4)(-5)(39)}{(4)(3)(-3)(-4)}+\frac{(3)(2)(-1)(-5)(822)}{(7)(6)(3)(-1)}+\frac{(3)(2)(-1)(-4)(1611)}{(8)(7)(4)(1)}$$

= -0.5-2.9+3.25-195.7+172.6
= 6

(b) Find Newton's backward difference form of interpolating polynomial for the data.

x	-3	5	7	9
f(x)	11	29	57	100

Hence interpolate f(8).

Newton's backward difference form is given by (x values are equally spaced)
Backward difference table :

i	x_i	y_i	∇y_i	$\nabla^2 y_i$	$\nabla_3 y_i$
1	3	11			
2	5	29	∇y_2 = 29-11 = 18		$\nabla^3 y_4$ = 15-10 = 5
3	7	57	∇y_3 = 57-29 = 28	$\nabla^2 y_3$ = 28-18 = 10	
4	9	100	∇y_4 = 100-57 = 43	$\nabla^2 y_4$ = 43-28 = 15	

h = 2
f(8) = ?

x = 8 lies between 3rd and 4th point, therefore we consider the backward differences at the fourth point. The Newton's backward difference interpolating polynomial for above case is

$$f(x) = y(x)\ y_4 + \nabla y_4 m +$$

$$= + \frac{\nabla^2 y_4}{2}\mu(4+1) + \frac{\nabla^2 y_4}{6}\mu(\mu+1)(\mu+2)$$

$$\text{Now } \mu = \frac{x - x_4}{h} = \frac{8-9}{2} = \frac{-1}{2}$$

= -0.5

Therefore,

$$f(8) = 100 + 43 \times (-0.5) + \frac{15}{2} \times (-0.5)(-0.5+1)$$

$$+ \frac{-1}{2} \times \frac{1}{2} \times \frac{3}{2} + \frac{1}{6} \times 5 \times (-0.5)(-0.5+1)(-0.5+2)$$

$$f(8) = 100 - 21.5 - \frac{15}{8} + \left(\frac{5}{6} \times \frac{-3}{8}\right)$$

= 100 - 21.5 - 1.8750 - 0.3125 = 100 - 23.6875

= 76.3125 = 76.31

Truncated to two decimal places.

Q6(a). Determine an approximate root of the equation. cos x - x e^x = 0 Using Secant Method with two initial values as x_0 = 0 and x_1 = 1. Perform two iterations.

Here f(x) = Cos x - xe^x

X_0 = 0, and x_1 = 1'

f(x0) = f(0) = Cos 0 - Oxe^0

= 1

f(x1) = f(1) = Cos^1 - 1 xe^1 = Cos 1 - e. 2.1780

$$\text{Now } x^2 = \frac{x_0\ f(x_1) - x_1\ f(x_0)}{f(x_1) - f(x_0)} = \frac{0 \times 2.1780 - 1 \times 1}{2.1780}$$

$$= \frac{-1}{1.178} = 0.8488$$

$$x_3 = \frac{x_1 f(x_2) - x_2 f(x_1)}{f(x_2) - f(x_1)}$$

$$= \frac{0.5 \times 2.1780 - 1 \times 0.0532}{2.1780 - 0.0532}$$

$= 0.5178$

Now $f(x_3) = f(0.5178) = \cos(0.5178) - 0.5178 \times e^{0.5178} = 0.000$

After third iteration, the function f(x) is zero.

Thus x = 0.5178 is the required solution.

(b) Obtain the smallest positive root of the equation $x^3 - 5x + 1$, by using 3 iterations of the bisection method.

The given equation is

$x^3 - 5x + 1 = 0$

If x = 0 the L.H.S. = 1

If x = 1 the L.H.S. = - 3

Hence, a small positive root lies between x = 0 and x = 1

because $f(0) \times f(1)$

$= 1 \times (-3)$

$= -3$

< 3

Iteration 1 :

Therefore , starting with $x_1 = 0$ and $x_2 = 1$

$f(x_1) = f(0) = 0^3 - 5 \times 0 + 1 = 1$

$f(x_2) = f(1) = 1^3 - 5 \times 1 + 1 = -3$

$$x^3 = \frac{0+1}{2} = \frac{1}{2} = 0.5$$

$f(x_3) = f(.5)^3 - 5 \times (.5) + 1$

$= 0.125 - 0.250 + 1$

$= 0.875$

Since $f(x_1) \times f(x_3)$

$= (1) \times (0.875)$

> 0

We replace x_1 by x_3

The new search interval is (0.5.0.1)

Iteration 2 :

Here we take $x_1 = 0.5 =$ and $x_2 = 1$

$f(x_1) = f(0.5) = (0.5)^3 - 5. \times 5 + 1$

$= 0.875$

$f(x_2) = f(1) = 1^3 - 5 \times 1 + 1 = -3$

$$x_3 = \frac{0.875+1}{2} = 0.9375$$

$f(x_3) = (.9375)^3 - 5.\times 0.9375 + 1$

0.0824 - 4.6875 + 1

= - 3.6051

Since $f(x_1) \times f(x_3)$

$= 0.875 \times (-3.6051)$

< 0

replace $x_2 \times$ by x_3.

The new search interval becomes (0.5, 0.9375)

Iteration 3 :

Now, let

$x_1 = 0.5$

$x_{2\,-.}9375$

$\therefore\ f(x_1) = (0.5)^3 - 5\,(.5) + 1$

= 0.125 - 0.250 + 1

= 0.875

$f(x_2) = (0.9375)^3 - 5\,(0.9375) + 1$

= - 3.6051

$$x_3 = \frac{x_1 + x_2}{2}$$

and $= \dfrac{0.5 + 0.9375}{2}$

= 0.71875

and $f(x_3) = (0.71875)^3 - 5 \times (0.71875) + 1$

= 0.3713 - 0.3594 +1 = 1.0119

Here 6 The smallest positive root is 0.71875.

CS-71 : COMPUTER ORIENTED NUMERICAL TECHNIQUES
JUNE-2002

Note: *Question 1 is* ***compulsory****. Answer any* ***three*** *from the rest.*

Q1(a). Describe/define the following with one example for each : [12]

(i) Round-off error

Round off errors arise due to floating point representation of initial data in the machine. Subsequent error in the solution sue to this is called propagated error. Due to the finite digit arithmetic operations, the computer generates in the solution of a problem error known as rounding errors.

(ii) Non-associativity of (computer) addition of numbers.

Computer addition of numbers is non-associative which is illustrated by following example.

Let $a = 0.345 \times 10^0$, $b = 0.245 \times 10^{-3}$

and $c = 0.432 \times 10^{-3}$

Now using 3 digit decimal arithmetic with rounding, we have

$b + c = 0.000245 + 0.000432$

$= 0.000677$

$= 0.677 \times 10^{-3}$

Now $a + (b + c) = 0.345 + 0.000677$ (in accumulator)

$= 0.346 \times 10^0$ (in memory) with rounding

$a + b = 0.345 \times 10^0 + 0.245 \times 10^{-3}$

$= 0.345 \times 10^0$ (in memory)

$(a + b) + c = 0.345432$ (in accumulator)

$= 0.345 \times 10^0$ (in memories)

Hence we see that

$(a + b) + c \neq a + (b + c)$

(iii) Loss of significant digits : Any digit is a significant digit except when it is used to fix the decimal point or to fill the places of unknown or discarded digits. For example, in the number 0.00154, the significant digits are 1, 5 and 4. The zeroes, on the other hand, are used to fix the decimal point. However, in the number 1234.0567 all digits are significant. Accuracy of a result is dependent upon the number of significant digits needed to express it. In general , if a solution is required to be accurate to n significant digits, we must see that relative error is less than 10^{-n} . In iterative calculation, the iterative process stops when the required number of significant digits in the answer is reached. Thus, if a relative error must lie between 0.0001 and 0.001 for a four digit normalised floating point number, then to guarantee 3 significant digit accuracy the relative error should be ≤ 0.001.

(iv) Instability of algorithms

Refer to DEC02, Q1(a, iii), Page No.-111

(b) Using any one of the Iterative methods (e.g., bisection, fixed-point, Newton-Raphson etc.) find the real cube root of 47, starting with initial value x_0 = 3.45. **[6]**

Let $x = \sqrt[3]{47}$

or $x^3 = 47$

$\therefore$ $f(x) = x^3 - 47$ Now by newton-Raphson method, we have

$f^1(x) = 3x^2$

$x_0 = 3.45$

$$x_1 = x_0 - \frac{f(x_0)}{f^1(x_0)}$$

$f(x_0) = 3.45^3 - 47$

$= 41.06 - 47 = -5.9$

$f^1(x_0) = 3 \times 3.45^2$

$= 3 \times 11.90 = 35.70$

$$= 3.45 - \left(-\frac{5.9}{35.70}\right)$$

$= 3.61$

$f(x_1) = 3.61^3 - 47$

$f(x_1) = 47.04 - 47$

$= 0.045$

$f^1(x_1) = 3 \times 3.61^2$

$= 39.09$

$$x_2 = x_1 - \frac{f(x_1)}{f^1(x_1)}$$

$$x_2 = 3.61 - \left(\frac{0.045}{39.09}\right)$$

$= 3.608$

(c) Solve the following system of linear equations using either Gauss elimination method or Gauss-Seidel method : [6]

$3x + 5y = -2$

$5x + 2y = 3$

Given equations are

$3x + 5y = -2$ ----------(1)

$5x + 2y = 3$ -----------(2)

Eliminating x from equation (2) by subtracting it from

$3x + 5y = -2$

$3x - \frac{19}{3}y = \frac{19}{3}$

$\frac{34}{3}y = \frac{-25}{3}$

$y = \frac{-25}{3} \times \frac{3}{34}$

$y = \frac{-25}{34}$

Now substitute value of y in equation (1)

$3x + 5\left(\frac{-25}{34}\right) = -2 \quad 3x - \frac{-125}{34} = -2$

$3x = -2 + \frac{-125}{34}$

$3x = \frac{-68 + (-125)}{34}$

$x = \frac{57}{34 \times 3} \quad x = \frac{19}{34}$

$\frac{34}{3}y = \frac{-25}{3}$

$y = \frac{-25}{3} \times \frac{3}{34} \quad y = \frac{-25}{34}$

$\therefore\ x = \frac{19}{34},\ y = \frac{-25}{34}$

(d) A table of x versus f(x) is given below. Find the value of f(x) at x = 5, using Lagrange's interpolation method. [6]

x	1.5	3	6
f(x)	-0.25	2	20

Given

x	1.5	3	6
f(x)	-0.25	2	20

We have $x_0 = 1.5, x_1 = 3, x_2 = 6$
$f_0 = -0.25, f_1 = 2, f_2 = 20$

The Lagrange's interpolating polynomial f(x) is given by
$f(x) = L_0(x)f_0 + L_1(x)f_1 + L_2(x)f_2$

$$= \frac{(x-3)(x-6)(-0.25)}{(1.5-3)(1.5-6)} + \frac{(x-1.5)(x-6)\times 2}{(3-1.5)(3-6)} + \frac{(x-1.5)(x-3)\times 20}{(6-1.5)(6-3)}$$

$$\text{at } x=5\ f(5) = \frac{(5-3)(5-6)(-0.25)}{(-1.5)(-4.5)} + \frac{(5-1.5)(5-6)\times 2}{(1.5)(-3)} + \frac{(5-1.5)(5-3)\times(20)}{4.5\times 3}$$

$$= \frac{(2)(-1)(-0.25)}{6.75} + \frac{3.5\times(-1)(2)}{-4.5} + \frac{(3.5)(2)(20)}{13.5}$$

$$= \frac{0.5}{6.75} + \frac{7}{4.5} + \frac{140}{13.5}$$

$= 0.074 + 1.555 + 10.370 = 11.999 \approx 12$

Q2(a). Let $f(x) = x^{1/10}$ and x_0 approximates x correct to n significant digits. Prove that $f(x_0)$ approximates f(x) correct to (n + 1) significant digits. [6]

Let $f(x) = x^{1/10},\ f'(x) = \frac{1}{10}x^{\frac{9}{10}}$

Since $r_{f(x)} = r_x \dfrac{xf'(x_0)}{f(x)}$

$\because\ f'(x_0) = \frac{1}{10}x_0^{-9/10}$

$$\therefore r_{f(x)} = r_x \frac{x\frac{1}{10}x^{-\frac{9}{10}}}{x^{\frac{1}{10}}} = r_x(1/10)$$

$\therefore \left|r_{f(x)}\right| = \frac{1}{10}\left|r_x\right|$

We have given that x_0 approximates x correct to n significant digits.

Therefore, $\left|r_{f(x)}\right| = \frac{1}{10}\frac{1}{2}10^{1-n} = \frac{1}{2}10^{1-(n+1)}$

Therefore, $f(x_0)$ approximates f(x) correct to (n+1) significant digits.

(b) How many bits of significance will be lost in the following subtraction? 37.593621 – 37.584216 **[5]**

37.593621 - 37.584216

is $(0.37593621)\ 10^2 - (0.37584216)\ 10^2$

Here $x^* = (0.37593621)\ 10^2, (0.37584216)\ 10^2$ and assume each to be an approximation to x and y, respectively, correct to seven significant digits. Then, in eight-digit floating-point arithmetic,

$= (0.0009405)\ 10^2$

$z^* = x^* - y^* = (0.94050000)\ 10^{-2}$ is the exact difference between x* and y*. But as an approximation to z = x - y, z* is good only to three digits, since the fourth significant digit of z* is derived from the eight digits of x* and y*, and both possibly in error, Here while the error in z* as an approximation to z = x - y is almost the sum of the errors in x* and y*, the relative error in z* is possibly 10,000 times the relative error in x* or y* loss of significant digits is, therefore, dangerous only if we wish to keep the relative error small.

Given $|r_x|, |r_y| < 1/2\ 10^{1-7}$

$z^* = x^* - y^* = (0.94050000)10^{-2}$

is correct to there significant digits.

Max $\left|r_z\right| = \frac{1}{2}\ 10^{1-3} = 10{,}000 \cdot \frac{1}{2}\ 10^{-6} \geq 10{,}000\left|r_z\right|,\ 10{,}000\left|x_y\right|$

(c) Using computer arithmetic, tell whether **[4]**
a(b – c) = ab – ac
where a = 0.5555 x 10, b = 0.4545 x 10, c = 0.4535 x 10

Let $a = 0.5555 \times 10^1$

$b = 0.4545 \times 10^1$

$c = 0.4535 \times 10^1$

Now $b - c = 0.0010 \times 10^1 = 0.1000 \times 10^{-1}$

$a\ (b - c) = (0.5555 \times 10^1) \times (0.1000 \times 10^{-1})$

$= 0.5550 \times 10^{-1}$

$ab = (0.5555 \times 10^1)(0.4545 \times 10^1)$

$= (0.2524 \times 10^2)$

$ac = (0.5555 \times 10^1)(0.4535 \times 10^1)$

$= (0.2519 \times 10^2)$

and $ab - ac = 0.2524 \times 10^2 - 0.2519 \times 10^2$

$= 0.0005 \times 10^2$

$= 0.5000 \times 10^{-1}$

Hence $a(b - c) \neq ab - ac$

Q3(a). The equation $2x^3 + 5x^2 + 5x + 3 = 0$ has a root in the interval [-2, -1]. Starting with $x_0 = -2.0$ and $x_1 = -1.0$ as initial approximations, perform two iterations of the Regula-falsi method. **[8]**

Here $f(x) = 2x^3 + 5x^2 + 5x + 3$

$f(-2) = -16 + 20 - 10 + 3 = -3$

$f(-1) = -2 + 5 - 5 + 3 = 1$

$f(-2)\, f(-1) < 0$

Now $$x_2 = \frac{x_0\, f(x_1) - x_1\, f(x_0)}{f(x_1) - f(x_0)}$$

$$= \frac{-2 \times 1 - (-1)\,(-3)}{1 - (-3)} = \frac{-5}{4}, \text{ i.e}$$

$x^2 = -1.25$ (First iteration)

$$f(x_2) = \frac{-125}{32} + 5 \times \frac{25}{16} + 5 \times \left(\frac{-5}{4}\right) + 3 = \frac{21}{32}$$

The root lies in (x_0, x_2)

$x_3 = -1.384$ or -1.39 (Second iteration)

Since

$$x_3 = \frac{-2 \times \frac{21}{32} - \left(\frac{-5}{4}\right) \times (-3)}{\frac{21}{32} - (-3)}, = \frac{\frac{-42}{32} - \frac{5}{4}}{\frac{21}{32} + 3} = \frac{\frac{-42 - 120}{32}}{\frac{21 + 96}{32}}$$

$$= \frac{-162}{117} = -1.384$$

$= -1.39$

(b) Determine an approximate root of **[7]**
cos x – x e^x = 0 using Secant method or Newton-Raphson method.

Taking the initial approximations as $x_0 = 0$, $x_1 = 1$, we have for the secant method

$f(0) = 1$, $f(1) = \cos 1 - e = -2.177979523$

$$x_2 = \frac{x_0 f(x_1) - x_1 f(x_0)}{f(x_1) - f(x_0)} = 0.3146653378$$

$f(.3146653378) = 0.519871175$

Similarly, $x_3 = 0.4467281466$

The computed results are tabulated in Table.

Similarly other iterative values are found out using the above formula. Briefly they are given in the following table.

Iteration	i = 1	i = 2	i = 3	i = 4	i = 5
x_0	0	1	0.3147	0.4468	0.5317
f_0	1	-2.1780	0.5199	0.2035	-0.0429
x_1	1	0.3147	0.4468	0.5317	0.5169
f_1	-2.1780	0.5199	0.2035	-0.0429	0.0026
x_2	0.3147	0.4468	0.5317	0.5169	0.5173
f_2	0.5199	0.2035	-0.0429	0.0026	0.0014

Hence an approximate root of $f(x) = 0$ is $x = 0.5173$.

By Newton Raphson method :

For the given f(x), $f'(x) = -\sin x - e^x (1+x)$

And for initial value x_0.

$$x_1 = x_0 - \frac{f(x_0)}{f'(x_0)}$$

Various iteration value are tabulated as below. ($x_0 = 0$)

Iteration	X_0	X_1	$f(x_0)$	$f'(x_0)$	$\left\lvert\frac{x_1 - x_0}{x_1}\right\rvert$
0	0	1	1	-1	1
1	1	0.6531	-2.178	-6.2780	0.5312
2	0.6531	0.5314	-0.4606	-3.7839	0.2291
3	0.5314	0.5448	-0.0419	-3.1120	0.0247
4	0.5448	0.5183	-0.0843	-3.1821	0.0511
5	0.5183	0.5177	-0.0017	-3.0449	0.0011
6	0.5177	0.5178	0.0002	-3.0418	0.0001

Hence approximate root of f(x) = 0 is x = 0.5178
Hence the approximate root of f(x) is = 0.5173

Q4(a). Solve the system of linear equations with Gaussian Elimination method with complete pivoting : [9]

$$\mathbf{x_1 - x_2 + 3x_3 = 3}$$
$$\mathbf{2x_1 + x_2 + 4x_3 = 7}$$
$$\mathbf{3x_1 + 5x_2 - 2x_3 = 6}$$

The given equations are: -

$x_1 - x_2 + 3x_3 = 3$
$2x_1 + x_2 + 4x_3 = 7$
$3x_1 + 5x_2 - 2x_3 = 6$

By Gauss elimination method with complete pivoting. Since $|a_{32}|$ is maximum, we rewrite the system as: -

$$\left[\begin{array}{ccc|c} 5 & 3 & -2 & 6 \\ 1 & 2 & 4 & 7 \\ -1 & 1 & 3 & 3 \end{array}\right]$$ by iterchanging R1 and R3 and C1 and C2

$(R2 - \frac{1}{5}R1, R3 + \frac{1}{5}R1 \text{ gives})$

$$\rightarrow \left[\begin{array}{ccc|c} 5 & 3 & -2 & 6 \\ 0 & 7/5 & 22/5 & 29/5 \\ 0 & 8/5 & 13/5 & 21/5 \end{array}\right]$$

Now changing C_2 and C_3

$$\rightarrow \left[\begin{array}{ccc|c} 5 & -2 & 3 & 6 \\ 0 & 22/5 & 7/5 & 29/5 \\ 0 & 13/5 & 8/5 & 21/5 \end{array}\right]$$

Since, $|a_{23}|$ is maximum.

By applying $R_3 - \frac{5}{12} \times \frac{13}{15} R_2$, we have

$$\rightarrow \left[\begin{array}{ccc|c} 5 & -2 & 3 & 6 \\ 0 & 22/5 & 7/5 & 29/5 \\ 0 & 0 & 17/22 & 43/5 \end{array}\right]$$

Now $5x_2 - 3x_1 - 2x_3 = 6$

$$\frac{22}{5}x_3 + \frac{7}{5}x_2 = \frac{29}{5}$$

$$\frac{17}{22}x_2 = \frac{17}{22}$$

We have $x_2 = 1$, $\frac{22}{5}x_3 = \frac{29}{5} - \frac{7}{5}$

or $\frac{22}{5}x_3 = \frac{22}{5}$

$\Rightarrow x_3 = 1$

also $3x_1 = 6 - 5 + 2$

$\Rightarrow x_1 = 1$

$\therefore x_1 = 1, x_2 = 1, x_3 = 1$ are the required solutions.

(b) Compare the strengths and weaknesses of Direct methods vis-a-vis Iterative methods. [6]

Both direct and iterative methods have their strengths and weaknesses and a choice is based on the particular linear system to be solved.

Direct Method : -

(1) The direct methods are generally used when the matrix A is dense or filled, that is, there are few zero elements, and the order of the matrix is not very large, say $n < 50$.

(2) The rounding errors may becomes quite large for ill conditioned equations (If at any stage during the application of pivoting strategy, it is found that all values of $\{|a_m k_1|$ for $m = k + 1$, to n are less than a pre-assigned small quantity $\in$, then the equations are ill conditioned and no useful solution is obtained)

Iterative Methods : -

(1) These methods are generally used when the matrix A is sparse and the order of the matrix A is very large say $n > 50$. Sparse matrices have very few non-zero elements

(2) An important advantage of the iterative methods is the small rounding error. Thus, these methods are good choice for ill-conditioned systems.

(3) However, Convergence may be guaranteed only under special conditions. But when Convergence is assured, this method is better than direct

Q5(a). Using either Jacobi's method or Gauss-Seidel method, perform four iterations for solving the following system of equations : [8]

$$\begin{bmatrix} 2 & -1 & 0 & 0 \\ -1 & 2 & -1 & 0 \\ 0 & -1 & 2 & -1 \\ 0 & 0 & -1 & 2 \end{bmatrix}\begin{bmatrix} x_1 \\ x_2 \\ x_3 \\ x_4 \end{bmatrix} = \begin{bmatrix} -1 \\ 0 \\ 0 \\ 0 \end{bmatrix}$$

with $x^{(0)} = (0.5, 0.5, 0.5, 0.5)^T$
Here $x = (1, 1, 1, 1)^T$
By Jacobi method, we have
Using $x^{(o)} = [0.5, 0.5, 0.5, 0.5]^T$,
we have
$x^{(1)} = [0.75, 0.5, 0.5, 0.75]^T$
$x^{(2)} = [0.75, 0.625, 0.625, 0.75]^T$
$x^{(3)} = [0.8125, 0.6875, 0.6875, 0.8125]^T$
$x^{(4)} = [0.8438, 0.75, 0.75, 0.8438]^T$

By Gauss-Seidal Method :
Initial solution is $x^{(0)} = (0.5, 0.5, 0.5, 0.5)$
$x^{(1)} = (-0.75, -0.125, 0.1875, 0.0938)$
$x^{(2)} = (-1.0625, -0.4375, -0.1719, -0.0859)$
$x^{(3)} = (-1.2188, -0.6953, -0.3906, -0.1953)$
$x^{(4)} = (-1.3477, -0.8691, -0.5322, -0.2661)$

(b) Apply bisection method to find an approximation to the positive root of the equation, [7]
$2x - 3 \sin x - 5 = 0$
rounded off to three decimal places.
Bisection Method :
Here $f(x) = 2x - 3\sin x - 5 = 0$, Let x = 2, and x = 3 (initially)
at x = 2 $\quad$ f(2) = -3.7279
at x = 3 $\quad$ f(3) = 0.5766
∵ f(2) and f(3) are of opp. signs, therefore, we say that root lies between 2 and 3.

1st approximation :
∴ The root of f(x) lies between 2.5 and 3.

$$x_o = \frac{2+3}{2} = 2.5$$

∴ f(2.5) = 2 x 2.5 - 3 sin 2.5-5 = -5.3862 (-ve value)
Again, let x = 2.75

$\therefore$ f(2.75) = -0.6450

$\therefore$ The root of f(x) lies between 2.75 and 3.

IInd approximation

$$x_1 = \frac{2.75+3}{2} = 2.875$$

f(2.875) = -0.0403 (-ve)

f(3) = 0.5766 (+ve)

IIIrd approximation

$$x_2 = \frac{2.875+3}{2} = 2.9375$$

f(2.9375) = 0.2670 (+ve)

f(3) = 0.5766 (+ve)

$\because$ f(2.9375) and f(3) are of same signs to so we conclude the root of f(x) lies between 2.875 and 2.9375

IVth approximation

$$x_3 = \frac{2.875+2.9375}{2} = 2.9063$$

f(2.9063) = 0.1132

f(2.9375) = 0.2670

$\therefore$ The root lies between 2.875 and 2.9063

We see that f(2.9375) and f(2.9063) are of same sign and 2.9063 and 2.9375 are very close to each other so we conclude that the possible real root is 2.9063

Q6(a). Using the following table of values, find EITHER Newton's form of interpolating polynomial
OR Lagrange's form of interpolating polynomial that approximates f(x). [8]

x	1	2	4	6
f(x)	1	8	63	200

Using this polynomial, find the approximate value of f(3).

By Lagrange's form of interpolating polynomial

we have

$f(x) = L_0(x)f_0 + L_1(x)f_1 + L_2(x)f_2 + L_3(x)f_3$

Where

$x_0 = 1, x_1 = 2, x_2 = 4, x_3 = 6$

$f_0 = 1, f_1 = 8, f_2 = 63, f_3 = 200.$

$$\text{Now } f(x) = \frac{(x-2)(x-4)(x-6) \times 1}{(1-2)(1-4)(1-6)} + \frac{(x-1)(x-4)(x-6) \times 8}{(2-1)(2-4)(2-6)}$$

$$+ \frac{(x-1)(x-2)(x-6) \times 63}{(4-1)(4-2)(4-6)} + \frac{(x-1)(x-2)(x-4) \times 200}{(6-1)(6-2)(6-4)}$$

$$= \frac{x^3 - 6x^2 + 8 - 6x^2 + 12x - 48}{-15} + \frac{8\left[x^3 - 5x^2 + 4x - 6x^2 + 30x + 24\right]}{8}$$

$$+ \frac{\left(x^3 - 3x^2 + 2x - 6x^2 + 18x - 12\right)63}{-12} + \frac{\left(x^3 - 3x^2 + 2x - 4x^2 + 12x - 8\right)200}{40}$$

$$= \frac{x^3 - 12x^2 + 20x - 48}{-15} + \frac{\left[x^3 - 11x^2 + 34x + 24\right]}{1}$$

$$+ \frac{\left(x^3 - 9x^2 + 20x - 12\right)63}{-12} + \frac{\left(x^3 - 7x^2\ 14x - 8\right)200}{40}$$

$$= \frac{-x^3}{15} + \frac{12x^2}{15} - \frac{20x}{15} + \frac{48}{15} + x^3 - 11x^2 + 34x + 24$$

$$+ \left(\frac{-x^3}{12} + \frac{9}{12}x^2 - \frac{20}{12}x + 1\right)63 + 5x^3 - 35x^2 + 70x - 40$$

$$= \frac{-x^3}{15} + \frac{4}{5}x^2 - \frac{4}{5}x + \frac{16}{5} + 6x^3 - 46x^2 + 104x - 16 - \frac{63x^3}{12}$$

$$+ \frac{63 \times 9}{12}x^2 - \frac{63 \times 20}{12}x + 63$$

$$= \frac{-x^3}{15} + \frac{4}{5}x^2 - \frac{4}{5}x + \frac{16}{5} + 6x^3 - 46x^2 + 104x - 16 - \frac{21x^3}{4} + \frac{189}{4}x^2 - 105x + 63$$

$$= \left(\frac{-x^3}{15} + \frac{6}{1}x^3 - \frac{21}{4}x^3\right) + \left(\frac{4}{5}x^2 - 46x^2 - \frac{189}{4}x^2\right)$$

$$+ \left(\frac{-4}{5}x - 104x - 105x\right) + \left(\frac{16}{5} - 16 + 63\right)$$

$$= \left(\frac{-4x^3 + 360x^3 - 315x^3}{60}\right) + \left(\frac{16x^2 - 920x^2 - 945x^2}{20}\right) + \left(\frac{-4x + 520x - 525x}{5}\right)$$

$$+ \left(\frac{16 - 80 + 315}{5}\right)$$

$$= \left(\frac{360x^3 - 319x^3}{60}\right) + \left(\frac{961x^2 - 920x^2}{20}\right) + \left(\frac{-529x - 520x}{5}\right)\left(\frac{331 - 80}{5}\right)$$

$$= \frac{41x^3}{60} + \frac{41x^2}{20} - \frac{9x}{5} + \frac{251}{5}$$

(b) Find the Newton's forward-difference interpolating polynomial which agrees with the table of values given below. Hence obtain the value of f(x) at x = 2.5. **[7]**

x	1	2	3	4	5	6
f(x)	9	20	39	81	157	302

<u>Newton's Forward Difference Interpolation Formula</u> :

Let function y(x) is tabulated at (n+1) equally spaced points having interval size h.

Suppose n^{th} order polynomial in x is :

$y = f(x) = a_1 + a_2 (x - x_1) + a_3(x - x_1)(x - x_2) + ...+a_n(x - x_1)(x - x_2)......(x - x_n)$ ....(1)

Let

At $x = x_1 \Rightarrow y_1 = a_1$

At $x = x_2 \Rightarrow y_2 = a_1 + a_2 (x - x_1)$

At $x = x_3 \Rightarrow y_3 = a_1 + a_2(x - x_1) + a_3(x - x_1) (x - x_2)$

and so on.

We have $h = x_{i+h} - x_i$ (interval)

and

$x_{i+m} - x_i = mh$

then we can express the function value y_i's in terms of interval values as

$y_1 = a_1$

$y_2 = a_1 + a_2h$

$y_3 = a_1 + a_2(2h) + a_3(2h)h$

similarly,

$y_{n+1} = a_1 + a_2(nh) + a_3(nh)(n - 1)h + ...+ a_{n-1}(nh)(n - 1)h$

Now solving for $a_1, a_2, a_3, ..., a_{n+1}$ we get

$a_1 = y_1$

$$a_2 = \frac{y_2 - a_1}{h}$$

$$= \frac{y_2 - y_1}{h}$$

$$a_3 = \frac{y_3 - a_2(2h) - a_1}{2h^2}$$

$$= \frac{\left[y_3 - \frac{y_2 - y_1}{h} 2h - y_1\right]}{2h^2}$$

$$= \frac{y_3 - 2y_2 + 2y_1 - y_1}{2h^2}$$

$$= \frac{y_3 - 2y_2 + y_1}{2!h^2}$$

$\vdots \qquad \vdots \qquad \vdots$

$$a_{n+1} = \frac{y_{n+1} - ny_n + ... + y_1}{n!h^n}$$

From forward difference table, we get

$a_1 = y_1$

$$a_2 = \frac{\Delta y_1}{h}$$

$$a_3 = \frac{\Delta^2 y_1}{2!h^2}$$

$\vdots$

$$a_{n+1} = \frac{\Delta^n y_1}{n!h^n}$$

Now substituting these values of a_1, a_2, a_3.........a_{n+1} in eq(1)

y(x) =

$$y_1 + \frac{\Delta y_1}{h}(x - x_1) + \frac{\Delta^2 y_1}{2!h^2}(x - x_1)(x - x_2) + ... + \frac{\Delta^n y_1}{n!h^n}(x - x_1)(x - x_2)..(x - x_n)........(2)$$

If we use $\frac{x - x_1}{h} = u$

then $x - x_1 = hu$

$$x - x_2 = x - (x_1 + h) = hu - h = h(u - 1)$$
$$x - x_3 = x - (x_2 + h) = h(u - h) - h = h(u - 2)$$
$$\vdots$$
$$x - x_n = h(u - (n - 1))$$

Substituting these values in eq. (2)

y = f(x) =

$$y_1 + \frac{\Delta y_1}{h} hu + \frac{\Delta^2 y_1}{2!h^2} hu \times h(u - 1) + ... + \frac{\Delta^n y_1}{n!h^n} hu \times h(u - 1) \times .... \times h(u - (n - 1))$$

After simplication, we get

$$y = f(x) = y_1 + \Delta y_1 u + \frac{\Delta^2 y_1}{2!} u(u - 1) + ... + \frac{\Delta^n y_1}{n!} u(u - 1)....(u - (n - 1))$$

This is called the Newton's forward difference interpolation formula and is particularly suitable if one wants to interpolate near the top of the table.

FORWARD DIFFERENCE TABLE

x	f(x)	$\Delta f(x)$	$\Delta^2 f(x)$	$\Delta^3 f$	$\Delta^4 f$	$\Delta^5 f$
$x_0=1$	9					
		$11 = \Delta f_0$	$8 = \Delta^2 f_0$			
$x_1=2$	20			$15 = \Delta^3 f_0$		
		19			$-4 = \Delta^4 f_0$	
$x_2=3$	39		23			$28 = \Delta^5 f_0$
		42		11		
$x_3=4$	81		34		24	
				35		
$x_4=5$	157		69			
		145				
$x_5=6$	302					

Newton's forward difference polynomial is :

f(x) =

$$f(x_o)+(x-1)\Delta f(x_o)+\frac{(x-1)(x-2)}{2!}\Delta^2 f(x_o)+\frac{(x-1)(x-2)(x-3)}{3!}\Delta^3 f(x_o)$$

$$+\frac{(x-1)(x-2)(x-3)(x-4)}{4!}\Delta^4 f(x_o)+\frac{(x-1)(x-2)(x-3)(x-4)(x-5)}{5!}\Delta^5 f(x_o)$$

$$= 9 + 11(x-1) + 4(x-1)(x-2) + \frac{5}{2}(x-1)(x-2)(x-3) - \frac{1}{6}(x-1)(x-2)(x-3)(x-4) + \frac{7}{30}(x-1)(x-2)(x-3)(x-4)(x-5)$$

On simplification it gives

$$f(x) = \frac{7}{30}x^5 - \frac{11}{3}x^4 + 24x^3 - \frac{208}{3}x^2 + \frac{2963}{30}x - 41$$

$\therefore$ for x = 2.5

$$f(2.5) = \frac{7}{30}(2.5)^5 - \frac{11}{3}(2.5)^4 + 24(2.5)^3 - \frac{208}{3} + (2.5)^2 + \frac{2963}{30}(2.5) - 41$$

$$= 27.1406$$

CS-71 : COMPUTER ORIENTED NUMERICAL TECHNIQUES
DEC-2002

Note: *Question 1 is* ***compulsory****. Answer any* ***three*** *from the rest.*

Q1(a). Describe/define the following with one example for each (any four only). **[12]**

(i) Floating point representation of a number : The numbers are stored in a computer in two forms : fixed-point and floating-point forms. The fixed point mode is used to represent integers while the floating-point mode is used to represent real numbers.

A floating-point number is of the form

$x = \pm(d_1.d_2.....d_n)\,\beta^n, 0 \leq di < \beta, m \leq e \leq M$

where d_1, d_2 .... d_n are all digits in the base 'β' of the number system used and lie between o and β. The exponent m is such that $M_1 \leq m \leq M_2$, where M_1 and M_2 vary with the computer. The fractional part.d_1d_2 .... d_n is called the mantissa which lies between ± 1 and restricts the size of a number. If a floating-point number has a fixed mantissa of l digits, we say that the word length of the computer is l. For instance, the number 22.74×10^4 is represented as .2274E4 (E4 is used to represent 10^4). Hence the mantissa is .2274 and the exponent is 4. While storing numbers, the leading digit in the mantissa is always made non-zero by suitably shifting it and adjusting the value of the exponent accordingly. This process is called normalization. Therefore the number .003374 in normalized floating point mode would be stored as .3374E-2.Thus the shifting of the mantissa to the left till its most significant digits is non-zero is called normalization.

(ii) Truncation error : Errors due to finite representation of an inherently infinite process. For example, consider the use of a finite number of terms in the infinite series expansion of Sinx, Cosx or f(x) by Maclaurian's or Taylor series expression. Such errors are called truncation errors.

(iii) Instability of algorithms : Algorithm is a step by step process that describe a method for solving any mathematical problem. Sometimes in an algorithm a step is reached when, the alternative is to state that 'relative error ≥ epsilon'. In such case, the algorithm is said to be unstable, since the solution has no convergence in n iterations.

(iv) Illconditioned equations :

Not visible conditioned Equation One method of improving the accuracy for an ill-conditioned system is by means of working all the calculations to more number of significant digits. But multilength arithmetic is time-consuming and therefore uneconomical. One possible alternative is to improve the accuracy of the approximate solution by an iterative procedure. This is described below. Let the system be

Let $\tilde{x}_1, \tilde{x}_2, \tilde{x}_3$ be an approximate solution. Substituting these values on the left hand side, we get new values of b1, b2, b3, say, $\tilde{b}_1, \tilde{b}_2, \tilde{b}_3$. Thus the new system is

$$\left.\begin{aligned} a_{11}\tilde{x}_1 + a_{12}\tilde{x}_2 + a_{13}\tilde{x}_3 &= \bar{b}_1 \\ a_{21}\tilde{x}_1 + a_{22}\tilde{x}_2 + a_{23}\tilde{x}_3 &= \bar{b}_2 \\ a_{31}\tilde{x}_1 + a_{32}\tilde{x}_2 + a_{33}\tilde{x}_3 &= \bar{b}_3 \end{aligned}\right\}$$

Subtracting each equation from the corresponding equation we get

$$\left.\begin{aligned} a_{11}e_1 + a_{12}e_2 + a_{13}e_3 &= d_1 \\ a_{21}e_1 + a_{22}e_2 + a_{23}e_3 &= d_2 \\ a_{31}e_1 + a_{32}e_2 + a_{33}e_3 &= d_3 \end{aligned}\right\}$$

Where $e_i = x_i - \tilde{x}_i$ and $d_i = b_i - \tilde{b}_i$. We now solve the system for e_1, e_2 and e_3. Since $e_i = x_i - x_i$ -,e obtain

$x_i = e_i + \tilde{x}_i$

Which is a better approximation for x_i. The procedure can be repeated again to improve upon the accuracy.

(v) Pivot : If at any stage of the Gauss elimination, one of these pivots say $a_{ii}^{i-1}(a_{11}^{(0)} = a_{11})$ vanishes then we have indicated a modified procedure. But it may also

happen that the pivot $a_{ii}^{(i-1)}$, though not zero, may be very small in magnitude compared to the remaining elements (³ i) in the ith column. Using a small number as divisor may lead to growth of the round-off error. The use of large multipliers like

$$\frac{-a_{i+1,i}^{(i-12)}}{a_{ii}^{(i-1)}}, \frac{a_{i+2,i}^{(i-1)}}{a_{ii}^{(i-1)}} \text{ etc.}$$

will lend to magnification of errors both during the elimination phase and during the back substitution phase of the solution procedure. This can be avoided by rearranging the remaining rows (from ith row up to nth row) so as to obtain a non-vanishing pivot or to choose one that is largest in magnitude in that column. This is called pivoting strategy.

(b) Using any one of the iterative methods (e.g., bisection, fixed-point, Newton-Raphson etc.) find the real root of the equation $x^3 + 3x^2 + 4x + 12$ starting with value x = 2. **[6]**

Refer to Study material, Q4, Page No.-14

(c) Solve the following system of linear equations using either Gauss elimination method or Gauss-Seidel interaction method: **[6]**

8x - 5y = 18

2x + 3y = - 4

Given equations are :-

8x - 5y = 18 ------(i)

2x + 3y = -4 ------(ii)

first eliminate x from e.g. (2) by multiplying it with 4 & subtracting it from e.g.(1)

$$\begin{array}{rrl} 8x & -5y & = 18 \\ 8x & +12y & = -16 \\ - & - & \quad + \\ \hline & -17y & = 34 \end{array}$$

y = 34/ -17

y = -2

Now substitute value Y in e.g. (i)

8x-5(-2) = 18

8x + 10 = 18

8x = 18-10

8x = 8

x = 8/8 = 1

x =1, y = -2 are the required solutions

(d) A table of y = f(x) versus x is given below. Find value of y at x = 8, using Lagrange's [6]

x	6.5	9	11	11
y	-7	-2	2	8

Here

$x_0 = 6.5,\quad x_1 = 9,\quad x_2 = 11,\quad x_3 = 14$

$f_o = -7,\quad f_1 = -2,\quad f_2 = 2,\quad f_3 = 8$

The Lagrange's interpolating polynomial $P_3(x)$ is given by $P_3(x) = L_o(x)\, f_o + L_1(x) + f_1 + L_2(x)f_2 + L_3(x)\, f_3$ ______________(1)

$$\text{Where } L_0(x) = \frac{(x-9)(x-11)(x-14)}{(6.5-9)(6.5-11)(6.5-14)} * (-7) = (-18 / -84.375)*(-7) = -1.493$$

$$L_1(x) = \frac{(x-6.5)(x-11)(x-14)}{(9-6.5)(9-11)(9-14)} * (-2) = (27 / 25) * (-2) = -2.16$$

$$L_2(x) = \frac{(x-6.5)(x-9)(x-14)}{(11-6.5)(11-9)(11-14)} * (2) = (9 / -27) * (2) = -0.666$$

$$\text{and}\quad L_3(x) = \frac{(x-6.5)(x-9)(x-11)}{(14-6.5)(14-9)(14-11)} *(8) = (4.5 / 112.5) * (8) = 0.32$$

substituting all of them in eg. (i)

$= (-1.493 -2.16 -0.666 + 0.32)$

$=-3.999$

Q2(a). Calculate the value z = (x² - y²) / (x + y) with x = 0.4800, using normalized floating point arithmetic. Compare it with value of (x - y). Determine the relative error of z. [8]

$$Z = \frac{(x^2-y^2)}{x+y}$$

$$= \frac{(x-y)\,(x+y)}{x+y}$$

$z = x-y$

$x = 0.4845,\ y = 0.4800$

$\therefore z = 0.4845 - 0.4800$

$= 0.0045$

Relative error in $Z = 0.0045 \times 100$

= 0.45

(b) The function $f(x^*) = e^x$ is to be evaluated for any x, $0 \le x \le 50$, correct to at least 6 significant digits. What digit arithmetic should be used to get the required accuracy? [7]

$$|rf_{(x)}| = |r_x| \left| \frac{xf^1(x^x)}{f_{(x)}} \right|$$

$$|r_x| \left| \frac{x.ex^*}{e^x} \right|$$

$= |r_x|\ |x|$

let n digit arithmetic be used, then

$$|r_x| < \frac{1}{2} 10^{1-n}$$

This is possible, if $|x||r_x| \le \frac{1}{2} 10^{1-6}$

$$\Rightarrow 50.\frac{1}{2}\ 10^{1-n} \le \frac{1}{2}\ 10^{1-6}$$

$$\Rightarrow \frac{1}{2}\ 10^{1-n} \le (\frac{1}{100}).10^{1-6}$$

$$\Rightarrow 10^{1-n} \le 2.10^{1-8}$$

OR $\quad 10^{-n} \le 10^{-8}.2$

$$\Rightarrow -n \le -8 + \log_{10}^{2}$$

$$\Rightarrow -8 - \log_{10}^{2} \le \text{nor } 8\text{-}3 \le n$$

$$\Rightarrow -8 - \log_{10}^{2} \le \text{nor } 8\text{-}3 \le n$$

Hence $n \ge 8$ digit arithmetic must be used.

Q3(a). Solve the quadratic equation $x^2 + 8.7x - 1.5$, using two-decimal digit floating arithmetic with rounding. [8]

given equation is

$x^2 + 8.7x - 1.5 = 0$

solving the quadratic equation, we have

a=1, b=8.7, c= -1.5

$$x = \frac{-b \pm \sqrt{b^2 - 4ac}}{2a}$$

Put the value a, b & c

$$x = \frac{-8.7 + \sqrt{(8.7)^2 - 4(1)(-1.5)}}{2 \times 1}$$

$$= \frac{-8.7 + \sqrt{(8.7)^2 - 4(1)(-1.5)}}{2 \times 1}$$

$$= \frac{-8.7 + \sqrt{756.9 + 6}}{2}$$

$$= \frac{-8.7 + \sqrt{762.9}}{2} = \frac{-8.7 + 27.6206}{2}$$

$= 9.46$

While the true solutions are -10 and 0.1. Now, if we rationalize the expression

$$x = \frac{-b + \sqrt{b^2 - 4ac}}{2a}$$

$$= \frac{-4ac}{2a\left(b + \sqrt{b^2 - 4ac}\right)}$$

$$= \frac{-2c}{b + \sqrt{b^2 - 4ac}} = \frac{+2}{8.7 + 27.6206}$$

$$= \frac{2}{36.3206} = 0.055065$$

Which is one of the true solutions

f(c) $x^3 + x = 6$

$x_0 = 1, x_1 = 2$

by Secant Method :

$$x_{n+1} = \frac{x_{x-1} f(x_n) - x_n f(x_{n-1})}{f(x_n) - f(x_{n-1})}$$

for n = 1

$$x_{n+1} = \frac{x_{x-1}\ f(x_n) - x_n\ f(x_{n-1})}{f(x_n) - f(x_{n-1})}$$

$$= \frac{1\times 4 - 2\times(-4)}{4-(-4)}$$

$$= \frac{4+8}{8}$$

$$= \frac{12^3}{8^2} = \frac{3}{2} = 1.5$$

For n = 2

$$x_3 = \frac{x_1\ f(x_2) - x_2\ f(x_1)}{f(x_2) - f(x_1)}$$

$$= \frac{2\times(-1.125) - 1.5\times 4}{-1.125 - 4}$$

$$= 1.609 = 1.61$$

For n = 3

$$x_4 = \frac{x_2 f(x_3) - x_3 f(x_2)}{f(x_3) - f(x_2)}$$

$$= \frac{1.5(-0.2167) - 1.61(-1.125)}{-(0.2167) + 1.125}$$

$$= \frac{-0.3250785 + 1.81125}{0.9083}$$

$$= \frac{1.4861715}{0.9083} = 1.636 = 1.64$$

(b) Let $x^* = 0.3454$ and $y^* = 0.3443$ be approximations to x and y respectively correct to 3 significant digits. Further, let $z^* = x^* - y^*$ be the approximation to (x - y), then show that the relative error in z^* as an approximation to x - y can be as large as 100 times the relative error in x or y. **[7]**

$Z^* = X^* - Y^* = 0.3454 - 0.3443$

$= 0.0011$
$= 0.11 \times 10^{-2}$

This is correct to one significant digit since last digits 4 in x* and 3 in Y* are not reliable and second significant digit of i * is derived from the fourth digits of x* and Y*.

$$\text{Max } |r_z| = \frac{1}{2}\ 10^{1-1} = \frac{1}{2} = 100.\frac{1}{2}.10^{-2}$$

$\geq 100|r_x|, 100\ |r_y|$

Q4(a). Solve the system of linear equations with Gaussian Elimination method with complete pivoting: [8]

$$\mathbf{3x_1 - 2x_2 + 3x_3 = 8}$$
$$\mathbf{2x_1 + 3x_2 + x_3 = 0}$$
$$\mathbf{2x_1 + 5x_2 + x_3 = -2}$$

given equations are :-

$3x_1 - 2x_2 + 3x_3 = 8$
$2x_1 + 3x_2 + x_3 = 0$
$2x_1 + 5x_2 + x_3 = -2$

Since $|a_{32}|$ is maximum, we write the system as by interchanging R_1 and R_3 and C_1 & C_2

$$\left[\begin{array}{ccc|c} 5 & 2 & 1 & -2 \\ 3 & 2 & 1 & 0 \\ -2 & 3 & 3 & 8 \end{array}\right]$$

Now $R_2 \to R_2$-3/5 R_1, $R_3 \to R_3$ + 2/5 R_1 gives

$$\left[\begin{array}{ccc|c} 5 & 2 & 1 & -2 \\ 0 & 4/5 & 2/5 & 6/5 \\ 0 & 19/5 & 17/5 & 36/5 \end{array}\right]$$

By interchanging C_2 and C_3, we have

$$\left[\begin{array}{ccc|c} 5 & 2 & 1 & -2 \\ 0 & 4/5 & 2/5 & 6/5 \\ 0 & 19/5 & 17/5 & 36/5 \end{array}\right]$$

Since $|a_{23}|$ is maximum

so by $R_3 \to (R_3 \div \frac{17}{5}) - \frac{5}{2}R_{2,}$ We have

$$\left[\begin{array}{ccc|c} 5 & 1 & 2 & -2 \\ 0 & 2/5 & 4/5 & 6/5 \\ 0 & 0 & -15/17 & -15/17 \end{array}\right]$$

Now we have

$5\ x_2 + 2x_1 - x_3 = -2$

$$\frac{2}{5}x_3 + \frac{4}{5}x_2 = \frac{6}{5}$$

$$\frac{-15}{17}x_2 = \frac{-15}{17} \quad x_2 = \frac{-15}{17} \times \frac{-17}{-15} = 1$$

$x_2 = 1$

$$or \quad \frac{2}{5}x_3 + \frac{4}{5} = \frac{6}{5} \quad or \quad \frac{2}{5}x_3 = \frac{6}{5} - \frac{4}{5} \quad \frac{2}{5}x_3 = \frac{2}{5}$$

$x_3 = 1$

or $5 \times 1 + 2x_1 - 1 = -2$

$5 + 2x_1 = -2 + 1 - 5$

$x_1 = -6/2 \quad = -3$

$\therefore\ x_1 = -3,\ x_2 = 1,\ x_3 = 1$

(b) Using either Jacobi's or Gauss-Seidel iteration method, perform four iterations for solving the following system of equations: [7]

$$\begin{bmatrix} -8 & 1 & 1 \\ 1 & -5 & -1 \\ 1 & 1 & -4 \end{bmatrix} \begin{bmatrix} x_1 \\ x_2 \\ x_3 \end{bmatrix} = \begin{bmatrix} 1 \\ 16 \\ 7 \end{bmatrix}$$

with $x^{(0)} = (0, 0, 0)^T$.

Jacobi method, we have

$x^{(i)} = [-0.125, -3.2, -1.75]^T$

$x^{(2)} = [-0.7438, -3.5750, -2.5813]^T$

$x^{(3)} = [-0.8945, -3.8650, -2.8297\ ]^T$

$x^{(4)} = [-0.9618, -3.9448, -2.9399]$

Where as by Gauss-Seidel method, we have

$x^{(i)} = [-0.125, -3.225, -2.5875]^T$

$x^{(2)} = [-0.8516, -3.8878, -2.9349]^T$

$x^{(3)} = [-0.9778, -3.9825, -2.9901\ ]^T$

$x^{(4)} = [-0.9966, -3.9973, -2.9985]^T$

Q5(a). The equation $2x^3 + 5x^2 + 5x + 3$ has a root in the interval [-2, -1]. Starting with $x_0 = -2.0$ and $x_1 = -1.0$ as initial approximation, perform three iterations of the Regula-falsi method. [8]

$f(x) = 2x^3 + 5x^2 + 5x + 3 = 0$

now $f(-2) = -16 + 20 - 10 + 3 = -3$

$f(-1) = -2 + 5 - 5 + 3 = 1$

and $f(-2)\, f(-1) < 0$

$$x_2 = \frac{x_0\, f(x_1) - x_1 f(x_0)}{f(x_1) - f(x_0)}$$

$$\frac{-2 \times 1 - (-1)(-3)}{1 - (-3)} = \frac{-5}{4}, \text{ie.,}$$

$x_2 = -1.25$ (First iteration)

$$f(x_2) = -\frac{125}{32} + 5\times\frac{25}{16} + 5\times\frac{-5}{4} + 3 = \frac{21}{32}$$

$\therefore$ The root lies in (x_0, x_2)

$x_3 = -1.384$ or 1.39 (second iteration) since,

$$x_3 = \frac{-2\times\frac{21}{32} - (-\frac{5}{4})\times(-3)}{\frac{21}{32} - (-3)} \rightarrow$$

$$= \frac{\frac{-42}{32} - \frac{5}{4}}{\frac{21}{32} + 3} \quad = \frac{\frac{-42-120}{32}}{\frac{21+96}{32}} \quad = \frac{-162}{117} = -1.384$$

$= -1.39$

(b) Do three iterations of the Newton-Raphson method or Secant method to solve the equation [7]

$x^3 + x - 6 = 0$

Starting with $x_0 = 1$ and $x_1 = 2$.

The given equation is

$$x^3 + x - 6 = 0$$

Now by **Newton Raphson method**, we have.

$f(x)\ x^3 + x - 6 = 0.$

we have $f(1) = -4$ (negative)

$f(2) = 4$ (positive)

Hence the root lies between $x = 1$ & $x = 2$

Ist approximation

Here we use $x_1 = 0.5$ as value of the root

Also $f'(x) = 3x^2+1$

Now second approximation would be: -

$x_2 = x_1 - f(x_1) / f^1(x_1)$

$x_2 = 1- (-4) / (4) = 2$

Similarly $x_3 = x_2 - \frac{f(x_2)}{f'(x_2)}$

$f(x_2)= 8+2-6 = 4$

$f'(x_2) = 12+1 =13$

$x3 = 2- (4/13) = 1.69$

by Secant Method :

we have, $x_0=1$, $x_1=2$

$$x_2=\frac{x_0 f(x_1)-x_1 f(x_0)}{f(x_1)-f(x_0)}$$

$$x_2=\frac{1(4)-2(-4)}{4-(-4)}=1.5$$

$x_2=1.5$

Table showing other iterations :

Iteration	i = 1	i = 2	i = 3	i = 4
x_0	1	2	1.5	1.6098
f_0	-4	4	-1.125	-0.2188
x_1	2	1.5	1.6098	1.6362
f_1	4	-1.125	-0.2188	0.0166
x_2	1.5	1.6098	1.6362	1.6348
f_2	-1.125	-0.2188	0.0166	0.004

Q6(a). If f(1) = -3, f(3) = 9, f(4) = 30 and f(6) = 132, find the Lagrange's interpolation polynomial of f(x). Also find the value of f(5). **[7]**

We have

$X_0 = 1$, $X_1 = 3$, $X_2 = 4$, $X_3 = 6$ and

$f_0 = -3$, $f_1 = 9$, $f_2 = 30$, $f_3 = 132$

The Lagrange's interpolating polynomial f_3 (x) is given by $f(x) = L_0(x)\, f_0 + L_1(x)\, f_1 + L_2(x)\, f_2 + L_3(x)\, f_3$ ....(i)
where

$$L_0(x) = \frac{(x-3)(x-4)(x-6)}{(1-3)(1-4)(1-6)} = \frac{-1}{30}(x^3 - 13x^2 + 54x - 72)$$

$$L_1(x) = \frac{(x-1)(x-4)(x-6)}{(3-1)(3-4)(3-6)} = \frac{1}{6}(x^3 - 11x^2 + 34x - 24)$$

$$L_2(x) = \frac{(x-1)(x-3)(x-6)}{(4-1)(4-3)(4-6)} = \frac{-1}{6}(x^3 - 10x^2 + 27x - 18)$$

substituting these is equation (1), we have

$$f(x) = \frac{-1}{30}(x^3 - 13x^2 + 54x - 72)(-3) + \frac{1}{6}(x^3 - 11x^2 + 34x - 24)(9)$$

$$-\frac{1}{6}(x^3 - 10x^2 + 27x - 18)(30) + \frac{1}{30}(x^3 - 8x^2 + 19x - 12)(132)$$

Which on simplification gives :
$f(x) = x^3 - 3x^2 + 5x - 6$
$f(5) = P_3(5) = (5)^3 - 3(5)^2 + 5x5 - 6$
= 215-75+25-6
= 69

(b) Using Newton's forward differences, show that the following data represents a second degree polynomial: [8]

x	-1	0	1	2	3	4
f(x)	6	1	0	3	10	21

Find the data for 2.5.
Forward Difference table:-
Since there and higher order differences are Zeros, f(x) represents a second order polynomial

$$f(x) = f_2(x) = f_0 + \frac{(x-x_0)}{h}\Delta f_0 + \frac{(x-x_0)(x-x_1)}{2!h^2}\Delta^2 f_0$$

x	f(x)	Δf	$\Delta^2 f$	$\Delta^3 f$
–1	6			
0	1	–5		
1	0	–1	4	0
2	3	3	4	0
3	10	7	4	0
4	21	11	4	0

$$f(x) = 6 + (x+1)(-5) + \frac{(x+1)(x-0)}{2}(4)$$

$$= 2x^2 - 3x + 1$$

$$\text{at } x = 2.5, f(2.5) = 2\times2.5\times2.5 - 3\times2.5 + 1$$

$$f(2.5) = 12.5 - 7.5 + 1$$

$$f(2.5) = 6$$

CS-71 : COMPUTER ORIENTED NUMERICAL TECHNIQUES
JULY-2003

Note: *Question 1 is* ***compulsory****. Answer any* ***three*** *from the rest.*

Q1(a). Describe/define the following with one examples each (any four only): [12]

(i) Non-associativity of Arithmetics due to round off errors

(ii) Linear convergence of the fixed point method

(iii) Backward difference

(iv) Instability of algorithms

(v) Sources of errors while carrying out numerical calculations to solve a problem.

(i) Non-associativity of Arithmetics due to round off errors

Non-Associative of arithmetic due to round off error if x* is an approximation to x, then use say that x* approximates x to n significant β digits provided absolute error.

$$| x - x^*| \le 1/2\ \beta^{s-n+1}$$

with s the largest integer such that $\beta^s \le |x|$

x* is said to be approximate x correct to n significant β digit if

$$\frac{|x-x^*|}{|x|} \le 1/2\ \beta^{1-n}$$

(ii) Linear convergence of the fixed point method

In the non-linear equation, the iteration function g(x) can be formulated in different forms. Convergence of the iteration process depends on the nature of g(x).

If g'(x) is continuous in some neighborhood of the fixed point.

ξ of g, then the fixed method converges linearly. Provided $g'(\xi) \neq 0$.

If g"(x) is continuous in some neighborhood of the fixed point. ξ of g then the fixed point conueges quadratically provided $g'(\xi) = 0$ and $g''(\xi) \neq 0$.

(iii) Backward difference

Suppose that we have a table of values (x_i,y_i), i = 0, 1, 2, ...n of any function y = f(x) the value of x being equally spaced, i.e., $x_i = x_0 + ih$, i = 0,1, 2...... n. The differences y_1-y_0, y_2 - y_1, ... y_n - y_{n-1} are called first backward differences, they are denoted by ∇y_1, ∇y_2,∇y_n, respectively so that $\nabla y_1 = y_1 - y_0$, $\nabla y_2 = y_2 - y_1$,.......$\nabla y_n = y_n - y_{n-1}$, where ∇ is called the backward difference operator. In similar way. We can define backward difference of highest orders. Thus we obtain

$\nabla^2 y_2 = \nabla y_2 - \nabla y_1, \nabla^3 y_3 = \nabla^2 y_3 - \nabla^2 y_2$ etc. With the some value of x and y as in table, a backward difference table can be formed.

Backward Difference Table

x	y	∇	∇^2	∇^3	....	∇^n
x_0	y_0	∇y_1	$\nabla^2 y_2$			
x_1	y_1	∇y_2	$\nabla^2 y_3$	$\nabla^3 y_3$		
x_2	y_2	:	:	$\nabla^3 y_4$	.....	$\nabla^n y_n$
x_3	y_3	:	:	:		
:	:	:	:	:		
x_n	y_n	∇y_n	∇y^2_n	$\nabla^3 y_n$		

Backward Difference Table show the differences of y values up to n points.

(iv) Instability of algorithms

Algorithm is a step by step process that describe a method for solving any mathematical problem. In numerical Algorithm errors grow in each step of calculation let ε be an initial error and Rn (ε) represents the growth of an error at the nth step after n subsequent operation due to ε. Some time in an algorithm a step is reached when, the alternative is to state that relative error ≥ epsilon', In such case the algorithm is said to be unstable since the solution has to convergence in n iterations.

(v) Sources of errors while carrying out numerical calculations to solve a problem.

We list below the type of errors that are encountered while carrying out numerical calculation to solve a problem:

1) Round off errors arises due to floating point representation of initial data in the machine. Subsequent error in the solution due to this is called propagated error.

2) Due to finite digit arithmetic operations the computer generates in the solution of a problem errors known as generated error or rounding error.

3) Sensitivity of algorithm of the numerical process used for solving a problem affects accuracy of the solution of the problem and is know as instability and the process in said to be unstable.

4) Error due to finite representation of an inherently infinite process. For example, consider the use of a finite number of terms in the infinite series expansion of sinx, cosx or f(x) by Maclaurin's or Taylor's Series expression. Such error are called truncation error.

(b) Find the interval in which smallest positive root of the equation $x^3 - x - 4 = 0$ lies. Determine this root correct to two decimals using the Bisection method. **[6]**

Let $f(x) = x^3 - x - 4 = 0$

Then $f(1) = -4$, $f(2) = 2$

Hence root lies between 1 and 2 then we have

$$X_0 = \frac{1+2}{2} = 1.5$$

Now we give the iteration into following table:

n	a(-ve)	b(+ve)	x_0	$f(x_0)$
1	1	2	1.5	-2.125
2	1.5	2	1.75	-0.390625
3	1.75	2	1.875	0.716796
4	1.75	1.875	1.8125	.0.141845
5	1.75	1.8125	1.78125	-0.129608
6	1.78125	1.8125	1.796875	0.0048027

Now n = 6 and

$$\frac{b_n - \alpha_n}{2^n} = \frac{1.8125 - 1.78125}{2^6} = 0.000488$$

i.e. less than the value of ε

So that roots of the equation are

$X_1 = 1.78$ $x_2 = 1.81$

(c) Solve the following system of equations using either Gauss elimination or Gauss-Seidel iteration method : **[6]**

$$4x_1 + x_2 + x_3 = 4$$
$$x_1 + 4x_2 - 2x_3 = 4$$
$$3x_1 + 2x_2 - 4x_3 = 6$$

Refer to JUNE04, Q1(c), Page No.-74

(d) The pressure of a gas measured at various temperatures is given below:

Temperature (x)	0	5	20	30
Pressure (y)	6	7	11	19

Using Lagrange's interpolation method, find the pressure at the temperature value 25.

According to Lagrange's interpolation method :

$$f(x) = \frac{(x-x_1)(x-x_2)(x-x_3)}{(x_0-x_1)(x_0-x_2)(x_0-x_3)} \times f(x_0) +$$

$$\frac{(x-x_0)(x-x_2)(x-x_3)}{(x_1-x_0)(x_1-x_2)(x_1-x_3)} \times f(x_1) +$$

$$\frac{(x-x_0)(x-x_1)(x-x_3)}{(x_2-x_0)(x_2-x_1)(x_2-x_3)} \times f(x_2) +$$

$$\frac{(x-x_0)(x-x_1)(x-x_2)}{(x_3-x_0)(x_3-x_1)(x_3-x_2)} \times f(x_3)$$

$$f(x) = \frac{(x-5)(x-20)(x-30)}{(0-5)(0-20)(0-30)} \times 6 + \frac{(x-0)(x-20)(x-30)}{(5-0)(5-20)(5-30)} \times 7$$

$$+ \frac{(x-0)(x-5)(x-30)}{(20-0)(20-5)(20-30)} \times 11 + \frac{(x-0)(x-5)(x-20)}{(30-0)(30-5)(30-20)} \times 19$$

$$f(x) = \frac{-x^3 + 55x^2 - 850x + 1300}{500} + \frac{7x^3 - 350x^2 + 4200x}{1875}$$

$$- \frac{11x^3 + 385x^2 - 1650x}{3000} + \frac{19x^3 - 475x^2 + 1900x}{7500}$$

$$f(x) = \frac{9x^3 - 175x^2 + 3650x + 90000}{15000}$$

The value of pressure at the temperature value = 25 is

$$\text{f(25)} = \frac{9(25)^3 - 175(25)^2 + 3650(25) + 90000}{15000} = \frac{212500}{15000}$$

=14.167

Therefore, the pressure is 14.167

Q2(a). Use the Newton-Raphson method for finding $N^{1/3}$, where N = 18. Obtain the result correct to two decimals.

(a) Let x be the cube root of N = 18 then as $(8)^{\frac{1}{3}} = 2$ and $(27)^{\frac{1}{3}} = 3$, we may say root lies between 2 and 3.

we may take initially approximate value of the Newton Rapshon formula for obtaining cube root is

$$x_{n+1} = \frac{1}{3}\left[2x_n + \frac{N}{x_n}\right]$$

N = 18,

x_1 = First approximation

$$= \frac{1}{3}\left[2\times 2.5 + \frac{18}{(2.5)2}\right] = \frac{1}{3}\left[5 + \frac{18}{6.25}\right] = 2.62 = 2.6$$

x_2 = Second approximation

$$= \frac{1}{3}\left[2\times 2.6 + \frac{18}{(2.6)^2}\right] = \frac{1}{3} = 2.62$$

$$x^3 = \frac{1}{3}\left[2\times 2.62 + \frac{18}{(2.62)^2}\right] = 2.62130$$

Hence, desired cube root is 2.62130

(b) Perform three iterations of the Regula-falsi method to find the root of the equation x^4 - x - 10 = 0 in the interval [1, 2]. Assume suitable initial approximations.

Let f(x) = x^4 -x -10

$f(x_0)$ = f(1) = 1^4 -1-10 = -10

$f(x_1)$ = f(2) = 2^4-2 -10 = 4

$$x_2 = \frac{x_0 f(x_1) - x_1 f(x_0)}{f(x_1) - f(x_0)}$$

$$x_2 = \frac{1\times 4 - 2\times(-10)}{4-(-10)} = \frac{24}{14}$$

x_2 = 1.714

$f(x_2)$ = f(1.714) = -3.0834

Value of function -ve on 1.714

So that, the value lies between (x_2,x_1) and value of x0 and $f(x_0)$ will be changed to find next iteration

$$x_3 = \frac{1.714\times 4 - 2\times(-3.0834)}{4-(-3.0834)} = \frac{13.0228}{7.0834}$$

= 1.838 (approx)

$f(x_3)$ = f(1.838) = -0.425

Value of function at 1.838 is -ve

So that, x_1 the value lies between (x_3, x_1) and value of x_2 and $f(x_2)$ will be changed to find next iteration.

$$x_4 = \frac{1.838\times 4 - 2\times(-0.425)}{4-(-0.425)} = \frac{8.202}{4.425}$$

Therefore, the iterations of equation are (x_2, x_3 x_4) i.e. (1.714, 1.838, 1.845).

Q3(a). Consider the following system of equations :

4x - y + z = 7

4x - 8y + z = - 21

-2x + y + 5z = 15

Perform only four iterations of Jacobi iteration or Gauss-Seidel iteration method for solving the equations. Assume, to start with (x_0, y_0, z_0) = (1, 2, 2). **[8]**

According to Guass- jacobi Method

$x = (7 + y^{(n)} - Z^{(n)})/4$

$y = (-21-4x^{(n)} - z^{(n)})/-8 = (21 + 4x^{(n)} + z^{(n)})/8$

$z = (15 + 2x^{(n)} - y^{(n)})/5$

Now (x_0, y_0, z_0) = (1, 2, 2)

According Jacobi Method

(x_1, y_1, z_1) = (1.75, 3.375, 3)

(x_2, y_2, z_2) = (1.844, 3.875, 3.025)

(x_3, y_3, z_3) = (1.9625, 3.925, 3.1326)

(x_4, y_4, z_4) = (1.9481, 3.997, 3)

(b) Solve the following system of linear equations with Gaussian elimination method with partial pivoting: **[7]**

$2x_1 - 2x_2 + 5x_3 = 6$

$2x_1 + 3x_2 + x_3 = 13$

$-x_1 + 4x_2 - 4x_3 = 3$

The coefficient matrix is

$$\left[\begin{array}{ccc|c} 2 & -2 & 5 & 6 \\ 2 & 3 & 1 & 13 \\ -1 & 4 & -4 & 3 \end{array}\right]$$

Interchange C_1 and C_3 then

$$\left[\begin{array}{ccc|c} 5 & -2 & 2 & 6 \\ 1 & 3 & 2 & 13 \\ -4 & 4 & -1 & 3 \end{array}\right]$$

Now Reduce x_1 coefficient from 2nd and 3rd row to zero by performing operation

$R_2 \to R_2 - R_1/5$, $R_3 \to R_3 + R_1 \times 4/5$

$$\left[\begin{array}{ccc|c} 5 & -2 & 2 & 6 \\ 0 & 17/5 & 8/5 & 59/5 \\ 0 & 12/5 & 3/5 & 39/5 \end{array}\right]$$

Now $R_3 \rightarrow R_3 - R_2 \times 12/17$

$$\left[\begin{array}{ccc|c} 5 & -2 & 2 & 6 \\ 0 & 17/5 & 8/5 & 59/5 \\ 0 & 0 & -9/17 & -9/17 \end{array}\right]$$

By performing Back substitution on the equations

$5x_3 - 2x_2 + 2x_1 = 6$

$\frac{17}{5}x_2 + \frac{8}{5}x_1 = \frac{59}{5}$

$\frac{-9}{17}x_1 = \frac{-9}{17}$

$x_1 = 1, x_2 = 3, x_3 = 2$

Therefore, the solutions of the equations

$x_1 = 1, x_2 = 3, x_3 = 2.$

Q4(a). Find the Newton's forward difference interpolating polynomial which agrees with the table of values given below. Using the polynomial obtain the value of f(x) at x = 0.25 and x = 0.35.

X	0.1	0.2	0.3	0.4	0.5
f(X)	1.40	1.56	1.76	2.00	2.28

x	$f(x)$	Δf	$\Delta^2 f$	$\Delta^3 f$	$\Delta^4 f$
0.1	1.40	0.16			
0.2	1.56	0.20	0.04	0	
0.3	1.76	0.24	0.04	0	0
0.4	2.00	0.28	0.04		
0.5	2.28				

Since third and higher degree values are zero, so that given data represents a second degree polynomial.

$$f(x_1) = f_0(x) + \frac{(x-x_0)\Delta f_0}{1! \quad h} + \frac{(x-x_0)(x-x_1)}{2!}\frac{\Delta^2 f_0}{h^2}$$

h = 0.1 difference between two x values.

$$f(x_1) = 1.40 + (x-0.1)\times\frac{0.16}{0.1} + \frac{(x-0.1)(x-0.2)}{2!}\times\frac{0.04}{0.1^2}$$

$f(x_1) = 1.40 + 1.6x - 0.16 + 2x^2 - 0.6x + 0.04$

$f(x_1) = f(x) = 2x^2 + x + 1.28$

Value of f(x) at x = 0.25 and x = 0.35

$f(0.25) = 2(0.25)^2 + 0.25 + 1.28 = 1.655$

$f(0.35) = 2(0.35)^2 + 0.35 + 1.28 = 1.875$

(b) Find Lagrange's interpolating polynomial for the following data. Also obtain the value of f(2) using the polynomial. [8]

X	0	1	4	5
f(X)	8	11	68	123

Given:

$$x_0 = 0, x_1 = 1, x_2 = 4, x_3 = 5$$
$$y_0 = 8, y_1 = 11, y_2 = 68, y_3 = 123 \quad \text{and } X=2$$

$$l_0(x) = \frac{(x-x_1)(x-x_2)(x-x_3)}{(x_0-x_1)(x_0-x_2)(x_0-x_3)}$$

$$= \frac{(2-1)(2-4)(2-5)}{(0-1)(0-4)(0-5)} = -\frac{6}{20} = -0.3$$

$$l_1(x) = \frac{(x-x_0)(x-x_2)(x-x_3)}{(x_1-x_0)(x_1-x_2)(x_1-x_3)}$$

$$= \frac{(2-0)(2-4)(2-5)}{(1-0)(1-4)(1-5)} = \frac{12}{12} = 1$$

$$l_2(x) = \frac{(x-x_0)(x-x_1)(x-x_3)}{(x_2-x_0)(x_2-x_1)(x_2-x_3)}$$

$$= \frac{(2-0)(2-1)(2-5)}{(4-0)(4-1)(4-5)} = \frac{6}{12} = 0.5$$

$$l_3(x) = \frac{(x-x_0)(x-x_1)(x-x_2)}{(x_3-x_0)(x_3-x_1)(x_3-x_2)}$$

$$= \frac{(2-0)(2-1)(2-4)}{(5-0)(5-1)(5-4)} = -\frac{4}{20} = -0.2$$

$$f(x) = l_0(x).y_0 + l_1(x).y_1 + l_2(x).y_2 + l_3(x).y_3$$

$$= (-0.3\times 8) + (1\times 11) + (0.5\times 68) + (-0.2\times 123)$$

$$= -2.4 + 11 + 34 - 24.6$$

$$= 18$$

Q5(a). Solve the quadratic equation $2x^2 + 9.5x - 2.9 = 0$ using two-decimal digit floating point arithmetic with rounding. [8]

Solving the quadratic equation :

$$2x^2 + 9.5x - 2.9 = 0$$

$$x = \frac{-b \pm \sqrt{b^2 - 4ac}}{2a} = \frac{-9.5 \pm \sqrt{(9.5)^2 - 4\times 2\times(-2.9)}}{2\times 2}$$

$$= \frac{-9.5 \pm \sqrt{90.25 + 23.2}}{4}$$

$$= \frac{-9.5 \pm 10.65}{4} = 0.2875, -5.037$$

Solution of quadratic equations are

$x_1 = 0.2875$ $x_2 = -5.037$

Rounding of two decimal digit of n_1 and x_2

Thus the Result is $x_1 = 0.29$, $x_2 = -5.04$.

(b) What is the relative error in the computation of X - Y, where X = 0.3274148693 and Y = 0.3273214371 with five decimal digit accuracy? [7]

With five decimal digit accuracy

$x^* = 0.37214\times 10^0$ $y = 0.37202\times 10^0$

$x^*-y^* = 0.00012$ while $x-y = 0.0001234322$

$$\frac{|(x-y) - (x^*-y^*)|}{|x-y|} = \frac{0.0000034322}{0.0001234322} = 3\times 10^{-2}.$$

The magnitude of this relative error is quite large when compared with the relative error of x* and y*.

Q6(a). Compare and contrast giving an example each: [8]
(i) Round off errors versus Truncation errors versus Generated errors.
(ii) Direct method versus Iterative methods for solving linear algebraic equations.

(i) Round off errors versus Truncation errors versus Generated errors.

Round off error : Round off error occur when a fixed number of digits are used to represent exact numbers.
Let fl(x) be floating point representation of real number x. Then $e_x = x - fl(x)$ is called round off error.
For exp: 23.479 is a floating point number. After round off two digit it become 23.48. Now round - off error is 23.480 - 23.479 = 0.001.

Truncation Error : Truncation error arises due to finite representation of an inherently infinite process. If arises from using an approximation in place of an exact mathematical procedure. It is an error resulting from the truncation of the numerical process.
For Example: Consider the use of a finite number of terms in the infinite series expansion of Sinx, cosx or f(x) by Maclarian's or Taylor series expansion.

Generated Error : Generated error arising due to inexact arithmetic operation is called generated error. Inexact arithmetic operation due to finite digit arithmetic operations in the machine. If arithmetic form of simplification then this error would not appear.

(ii) Direct method versus Iterative methods for solving linear algebraic equations.
Both the Directive and Iterative methods have their strengths and weakness and a choice is based on the particular linear system to be solved. We mention a few of those below: -

Direct Method :
(1) The Direct Methods are generally used when the matrix A is dense or filled, that is. There are few zero elements, and the order of the matrix is not very large, say n < 50.
(2) The rounding error may become quite large for ill conditioned equations (if at any stage during the application of pivoting strategy. It is found that all

values of { | a_{mk} 1 | for m = k + 1, to n are less than a pre-assigned small quantity ε, then the equations are ill-conditioned and is useful solution is obtained)
(3) In a Direct method the amount of computation is fixed.

Iterative Method :
(1) These methods are generally used when the matrix A is sparse and the order of matrix A is very large say n > 50. Sparse matrices have very few non-zero elements.
(2) An important advantage of iteration method is small rounding error. Thus, these methods are good choice for ill-conditioned systems.
(3) However, convergence may be guaranteed only under special conditions. But when convergence is assured this method is better than direct.
(4) In an iterative method, computation depends on the accuracy required.

(b) The quadratic equation $x^4 - 4x^2 + 4 = 0$ has a double root at √2. Starting with $x_0 = 1.5$, compute three successive approximations to the root by Newton-Raphson method. Do this with

$$g_1(x) = x - \frac{f(x)}{f'(x)} \text{ and } g_2(x) = x\ \frac{2\,f(x)}{f'(x)}$$

Comment on the order of convergence on the results so obtained. [7]

Let $f(x) = x^4 - 4x^2 + 4$
$f'(x) = 4x^3 - 8x$
$f(x) = f(1.5) = 0.0625$
$f'(x_0) = f'(1.5) = 1.5$

$$g_1(x_1) = 1.5 - \frac{(0.0625)}{1.5} \quad \text{and } g_2(x_1) = 1.5\frac{-2\times(0.0625)}{1.5}$$

$g_1(x_1) = 1.458$ $g_2(x_1) = 1.41667$

$f(x_1) = f(1.458) = 0.0158$ $f(x_2) = f(1.417) = 0.000062236$
$f'(x_1) = f'(1.458) = 0.7334$ $f'(x_2) = f'(1.417) = 0.044715$

$$g_1(x_2) = 1.458 - \frac{0.0158}{0.7334} \quad \text{and} \quad g_2(x_2) = 1.417\frac{-2\times 0.000062236}{0.044715}$$

$g_1(x_2) = 1.436$ $g_2(x_2) = 1.4142$

$f(x_2) = f(1.436) = 0.00386$ $f(x_2) = f(1.4142) = 0.0000001$
$f'(x_2) = f(1.436) = 0.35668$ $f'(x_2) = f'(1.4142) = -0.000216$

$g_1(x_3) = 1.436 - \frac{0.00386}{0.35668}$ and $g_2(x_3) = 1.4142 - \frac{0.0000001}{(-0.000216)}$

$g_1(x_3) = 1.4252$ (approx) $\qquad g_2(x_3) = 1.4142$

Now, the successive approximation by $g_1(x) = x - \frac{f(x)}{f'(x)}$ are (1.458, 1.436, 1.4252) and by $g_2(x) = x - \frac{2f(x)}{f'(x)}$ are (1.41667, 1.4142, 1.4142).

The order of convergence in this equation is 2.

CS-71 : COMPUTER ORIENTED NUMERICAL TECHNIQUES
DEC-2003

Note: *Question 1 is* ***compulsory****. Answer any* ***three*** *from the rest.*

Q1(a). Describe/Define the following with one example for each:
(i) Sources of Errors
(ii) Relative Error
(iii) Direct Methods
Refer to Study material, Q1, Page No.-6

(b) Solve the equation $e^x + x - 2 = 0$ by Newton-Raphson iterative method, staring with value x = 0.4. **[6]**
Refer to Study material, Q3, Page No.-13

(c) Solve the equations by Cramer's rule: **[6]**
$3x + 2y - z = 4$
$2x - y + 2z = 10$
$x - 3y - 4z = 5$
Refer to JUNE04, Q1(e), Page No.-77

(d) Using Gauss elimination method, solve the following system of equations:

$$3x_1 + x_2 + 2x_3 = 3$$ **[6]**

$$2x_1 - 3x_2 - x_3 = -3$$

$$x_1 + 2x_2 + x_3 = 4$$

Refer to Study material, Q5, Page No.-30

(e) Find a root of the equation $x^3 - 4x - 9 = 0$, using the bisection method in four stages. **[6]**

$x^3 - 4x - 9 = 0$

Let $f(x) = x^3 - 4x - 9$

then $f(2) = 23 - (4 \times 2) - 9$

$= 8 - 8 - 9$

$= -9$ (negative)

$f(3) = 33 - (4 \times 3) - 9$

= 29 -12 -9

= +6 (positive)

Since f(x) is positive at x=3 and f(x) is negative at x=2. Hence a root lies between 2 and 3 and we take

$$x_0 = \frac{2+3}{2} = \frac{5}{2} = 2.5$$

Since $f(x_0) = 2.5^3 - (4 \times 2.5) - 9$

= 15.625 -10 -9

= -3.375

Since $f(x_0)$ = -3.375, we choose [2.5,3] as the new interval then.

$$x_1 = \frac{2.5+3}{2} = \frac{5.5}{2} = 2.75$$

$$f(2.75) = 2.75^3 - (4 \times 2.75) - 9$$

= 20.7968 -11-9

= 0.796875

Proceeding in this way, the following table is obtained.

n	a(-ve)	b(+ve)	x	f(x)
1	2	3	2.5	-3.375
2	2.5	3	2.75	+0.7968
3	2.5	2.75	2.325	-1.4121
4	2.625	2.75	2.6875	-0.3391
5	2.6875	2.75	2.7187	+0.22.9
6	2.6875	2.7187	2.7031	-0.0610
7.	2.7031	2.7187	2.7109	+0.0794
8.	2.7031	2.7109	2.7070	+0.0904
9.	2.7031	2.7070	2.7050	-0.02604
10.	2.7050	2.7070	2.7060	-0.00850
11.	2.7060	2.7070		

So that the root lies between

x_1 = 2.7060, x_2 = 2.7070

Q2(a). Given the table of values

x	6	7.2	9	13
f(x)	0.8011	-0.8224	-0.7392	0.9948

Use Lagrangian interpolation to find the value of f(8). **[7]**

Given :

x	Value	f(x)	Value
x_0	6	$f(x_0)$	0.8011
x_1	7.2	$f(x_1)$	-0.8224
x_2	9	$f(x_2)$	-0.7392
x_3	13	$f(x_3)$	-0.9948

The Lagrange's interpolation polynomial is given by

$$f(x)=\frac{(x-x_1)(x-x_2)(x-x_3)}{(x_0-x_1)(x_0-x_2)(x_0-x_3)}f(x_0)+\frac{(x-x_0)(x-x_2)(x-x_3)}{(x_1-x_0)(x_1-x_2)(x_1-x_3)}f(x_1)+$$
$$\frac{(x-x_0)(x-x_1)(x-x_3)}{(x_2-x_0)(x_2-x_1)(x_2-x_3)}f(x_2)+\frac{(x-x_0)(x-x_1)(x-x_2)}{(x_3-x_0)(x_3-x_1)(x_3-x_2)}f(x_3) \quad \text{...... ....(1)}$$

here x=8,

Putting the values from table given in equation (1) we get

$$\mathrm{f}(8)=\frac{(8-7.2)(8-9)(8-13)}{25.2}\times 0.8011+\frac{(8-6)(8-9)(8-13)}{12.528}\times(-0.8224)$$

$$+\frac{(8-6)(8-7.2)(8-13)}{-21.6}\times -0.7392+\frac{(8-6)(8-7.2)(8-9)}{162.4}\times 0.9948$$

$$\mathrm{f}(8)=\frac{3.2044}{25.2}-\frac{8.224}{12.528}-\frac{5.9136}{21.6}-\frac{1.59168}{162.4}$$

f(8) = -0.81287 (approx)

(b) The equation $2x^3 - 7x^2 - x + 12 = 0$ has a root near to x = 1.5. Use the Newton-Raphson method to find the root decimal places. [8]

Let $f(x) = 2x^3 - 7x^2 - x + 12$

$$\mathrm{f}^1(x)=6x^2-14x-1$$

At x = 1.5

$$\mathrm{f}(1.5)=2\times 1.5^3-7\times 1.5^2-1.5+12$$
$$=6.75-15.75-1.5+12=1.5$$
$$f^1(1.5)=6\times 1.5^2-14\times 1.5-1$$
$$=13.5-21-1=-8.5$$

According to newton Raphson method

$$x_{n+1} = x_n - \frac{f(x_n)}{f'(x_n)}$$

$$x_1 = x_0 - \frac{f(x_0)}{f`(x_0)}$$

$$= 1.5 - \frac{1.5}{(-8.5)} = 1.5 + \frac{1.5}{8.5}$$

$x_1 = 1.67647$

f (1.67647) = 0.07328 , f'(1.67647) = -7.60727, $x_2 = x_1 - \frac{f(x_1)}{f`(x_1)}$

$$x_2 = 1.67647 - \frac{0.07328}{(-7.60727)} = 1.67647 + \frac{0.07328}{7.60727}$$

$x_2 = 1.68610289$

Therefore, root of equation at four decimal places are $x_1 = 1.6765$, $x_2 = 1.6861$

Q3(a). Consider the following system of equations:

$$2x_1 + x_2 + x_3 = 5$$
$$x_1 + 3x_2 + 2x_3 = 1$$
$$3x_1 - 2x_2 - 4x_3 = -4$$

Perform only four iterations of Jacobi or Gauss-Seidel iteration method for solving the equations. Assume to start with $x^{(0)} = (0, 0, 0)^T$. [7]

Gauss-Seidel method, we consider the given equation

$2x_1 + x_2 + x_3 + = 5$
$x_1 + 3x_2 + 2x_3 = 1$
$3x_1 + 2x_2 + 4x_3 = -4$

To solve these equations by iterative methods, we write them as follows:-

$2x_1 = 5 - x_2 - x_3$
$3x_2 = 1 - x_1 - 2x_3$
$4x_3 = 4 + 3x_1 - 2x_2$
$x_1 = 2.5 - 0.5x_2 - 0.5x_3$
$x_2 = 0.33 - 0.33x_1 - 0.66x_3$
$x_3 = 1 + 0.75x_1 - 0.5x_2$

It can be verified that these equations satisfy the conditional given in :

$$\left[\sum_{j=i}^{n} \frac{a_{ij}}{a_{ii}} \le 1, (i = 1, 2, 3, ---, n)\right]$$

The results are given in the tables below :

x	x_1	x_2	x_3
1	2.5	-0.5	3.125
2	1.1875	-2.1458	2.9635
3	2.09115	-2.3394	3.7381
4	1.8007	-2.7590	3.730025

(b) Staring with the interval (1.0, 1.8), apply bisection method, for finding an approximation root of the equation $e^x - 2 - x = 0$ to two places of decimal. [8]

Let $f(x) = e^x - 2 - x$

starting intervals (1.0, 1.8)

$f(1.0) = -ve, \quad f(1.8) = +ve$

So that,

$$\frac{1.0+1.8}{2} = 1.4$$

Now, we give the iterations in following tabular form :

n	a(-ve)	b(+ve)	x	f(x)
1	1	1.8	1.4	0.6552
2	1	1.4	1.2	0.120
3	1	1.2	1.1	-0.0958
4	1.1	1.2	1.15	0.0082
5	1.1	1.15	1.125	-0.0448

Check the iterations by

$$\left|\frac{b_n - a_n}{2^n}\right| \le \varepsilon$$

$$\left|\frac{1.15 - 1.125}{2^5}\right| \le \varepsilon = 0.00078$$

So that, the solutions are

$a = 1.125, \quad b = 1.15$

Q4(a). Determine an approximate root of the equation:

$\cos x - x e^x = 0$

using secant method or regula-falsi method, starting with the two initial approximations as $x_0 = 0$ and $x_1 = 1$.

Secant Method :

Refer to JUNE02, Q3(b), Page No.-130

Regula-falsi method :

Let $f(x) = \cos x - xe^x$

$x_0 = 0$

$f(x_0) = \cos 0 - 0e^0$

$= 1 - 0$

$f(x_0) = 1$

$x_1 = 1$

$f(x_1) = \cos 1 - 1e^1$

$= -1.7184$

$$x_2 = x_0 - \frac{f(x_0)}{f(x_1) - f(x_0)}(x_1 - x_0)$$

$$= 0 - \frac{1}{-1.7184 - 1}(1 - 0)$$

$$= 0 - \frac{1}{-2.7184} \times 1 = 0 - (-0.3679) = 0.3679$$

$= 0 - (-.3679)$

$= 0.3679$

$f(x_2) = 0.9999 - 0.5315$

$= 0.4684$

$f(x_0) = 0.4684$, $x_0 = 0.3679$, $x_1 = 1$, $f(x_1) = -1.7184$

$$x_3 = 0.3679 - \frac{0.4684}{-1.7184 - 0.4684}(1 - 0.3679)$$

$$= = 0.3679 - \left[\frac{0.4684}{-2.1868} \times 0.6321\right]$$

x3 = 0.5032

$f(x_3) = 0.9999 - 0.8322$

$= 0.1677$

$x_0 = 0.5032$, $f(x_0) = 0$

Repeating the process.

(b) Using Newton-Raphson method find the real root of x $\log_{10}$ x = 1.2 correct to four decimal places, starting with value x = 2. **[8]**

$f(x) = x\log_{10}x - 1.2$

$f'(x) = 1 + \log_{10}x$

$x_0=2$,

$f'(2) = 1+\log_{10}2 = 1+0.3010 = 1.3010$

By Newton Raphson method,

$$x_{n+1} = x_n - \frac{f(x)}{f'(x)}$$

$$x_1=x_0-\frac{f(x0)}{f'(x0)}=2-\frac{f(2)}{f'(2)}$$

$$= 2-\frac{(-0.5979)}{(1.3010)}$$

$x_1 = 2.4595695$ i.e. $x_1=2.4596$

$f(x_1) = 2.4596\log(2.4596)-1.2=0.0101243$

$f'(x_1) = 1+ \log_{10}(0.0101243) = 1.455644$

$$x_2=x_1-\frac{f(x_1)}{f'(x_1)}=2.4596-\frac{0.101243}{1.455644}$$

$x_2 = 2.546932$ i.e. $x_2=2.5469$

Q5(a). Find the cube root of 41, using Newton-Raphson method. Obtain the result correct to two decimals. [7]

Let $x = \sqrt[3]{41}$

$x^3 = 41$

$f(x) = x^3 - 41=0$

$f'(x) = 3x^2$

Now by Newton - Raphson method, we have

$$x_{n+1} = x_n - \frac{f(x)}{f'(x)}$$

For n = 0, 1, 2, ------

Starting from $x_0 = 0,1$

$$x_1 = 1-\frac{(-40)}{3} = x_1 = 14.333$$

$f(x_1) = f(14.3333) = 2903.68$

$f'(x_1) = f'(14.3333) = 616.3305$

$$x_2 = 14.333-\frac{2903.68}{616.33}$$

$x_2 = 9.62$

$f(x_2) = f(9.62) = 849.28$

$f'(x_2) = f'(9.62) = 277.63$

$$x_3 = 9.62 - \frac{849.28}{277.63}$$

$x_3 = 6.56$

$f(x_3) = f(6.56) = 241.30$

$f'(x_3) = f'(6.56) = 129.10$

$$x_4 = 6.56 - \frac{241.30}{129.10}$$

$x_4 = 4.69$

So that, the real cube root of 41 are

(x_1, x_2, x_3 or x_4) i.e. (14.33, 9.62, 6.56, 4.69)

(b) Find a real root of the equation x^3 - 2x - 5 = 0 by the regula-falsi method correct to three decimal places. **[8]**

$f(x) = x^3 - 2x - 5$

We abserve that

f(2)= -1 and f(3) = 16

And hence a root lies between 2 and 3.

Equation(1) gives

$$x_2 = x_0 - \frac{f(x_0)}{f(x_1) - f(x_0)} \times (x_1 - x_0) \text{ ------------eq(1)}$$

$x_0 = 2$, $f(x_0) = -1$, $x_1 = 3$, $f(x_1) = 16$

$$x_2 = 2 + \frac{1}{17}(1) = 2.059$$

Now $f(x_2) = -0.386$

Hence the root lies between 2.059 and 3.0 using the equation no.1 once again, we obtain.

$$x_3 = 2.059 + \frac{0.386}{16.386}(3 - 2.059)$$

$= 2.0812$

Repeating the process, we obtain successively:

$x_4 = 2.0904$

$x_5 = 2.0934$, etc.

Therefore, the approximate roots of the equations are

(x_0, x_1, x_2, x_3, x_4, x_5) i.e (2, 3, 2.059, 2.0812, 2.0904, 2.0934).

Q6(a). Apply Newton's forward difference formula, to the data below, to obtain a cubic polynomial in x. Hence evaluate f(4), using the polynomial obtained. [7]

x	0	1	2	3
f(x)	1	2	1	10

x	f(x)	Δf	$\Delta^2 f$	$\Delta^3 f$
0	1			
1	2	1		
2	1	−1	−2	12
3	10	9	10	

h = 1 difference between x values.

$$f(x) = f_0(x) + (x - x_0)\frac{\Delta f_0}{h} + \frac{(x-x_0)(x-x_1)}{2!}\frac{\Delta^2 f_0}{h_2} + \frac{(x-x_0)(x-x_1)(x-x_2)}{3!}\cdot\frac{\Delta^3 f_0}{h^3}$$

$$= 1 + (x-0).1 + \frac{(x-0)(x-1)}{2!}\times(-2) + \frac{(x-0)(x-1)(x-2)}{3!}.12$$

$= 1 + x + x^2 - x + (x^3 - 3x^2 + 2x) . 2$

$= 1 + x^2 + 2x^3 - 6x^2 + 4x$

$f(x) = 2x^3 - 5x^2 + 4x + 1$

Value of f(4) is

$f(4) = 2(4)^3 - 5(4)^2 + 4(4) + 1$

$= 128 - 80 + 16 + 1 = 65$

Therefore, the value f(x) at x = 4 is 65.

(b) From the following table, evaluate f(3.8) using Newton's backward interpolation formula: [8]

x	0	1	2	3	4
f(x)	1.00	1.50	2.20	3.10	4.60

x	f(x)	∇f	$\nabla^2 f$	$\nabla^3 f$	$\nabla^4 f$
0	1.00				
1	1.50	0.50			
2	2.20	0.70	0.20	0	0.40
3	3.10	0.90	0.20	0.40	
4	4.60	1.50	0.60		

Here h = 1

$$f(x) = f(x_n) + (x - x_n)\nabla f + \frac{(x - x_n)(x - x_{n-1}).\ \nabla^2 f}{2!} \ldots\ldots\ldots$$

$$= 4.60 + (x-4)\times 1.50 + \frac{(x-4)(x-3)}{2}\times 0.60 + \frac{(x-4)(x-3)(x-2)}{3!}\times 0.40$$

$$+\frac{(x-4)(x-3)(x-2)(x-1)\times 0.40}{4!}$$

$$f(x) = \frac{4.60 + 1.50x - 6 + 0.3x^2 - 2.1 + 3.6 + 0.2x^3 - 1.8x^2 + 5.2x - 4.8}{3} +$$

$$\frac{0.5x^4 - 4x^3 + 17.5x^2 - 25x + 12}{3}$$

$$f(x) = \frac{0.5x^4 - 4.3x^3 + 16.6x^2 - 21.6x + 13.8}{3}$$

Now the value of f(x) at x = 3.8 f (3.8) = 39.7312

CS-71 : COMPUTER ORIENTED NUMERICAL TECHNIQUES
JUNE-2004

Note: *Question 1 is* ***compulsory****. Answer any* ***three*** *from the rest.*

Q1(a). Using Newton-Raphson method, find the root between 0 and 1 of the $x^3-6x+4=0$ equation correct four decimal places.

<u>Solution by Newton Raphson Method</u>

f(x) = $x^3-6x+4=0$ ....(1)

we have find out root up to 4 places of decimal while interval is 0 to 1 differentiating (1) w.r.t. x

$f'(x)=3x^2-6$

<u>we have</u> : $x_{n+1}=x_n-\dfrac{f(x_n)}{f'(x_n)}$

$$\therefore x_{n+1}=x_n-\frac{x_n^3-7x_n+4}{3x_n^2-6} \quad ....(2)$$

We have given that $x0$ lies between interval (0, 1). Starting this interval by observing the sign of f(x) = $x^3- 6x + 4 = 0$ for x = 0.1, 0.2, 0.3, 0.4, 0.5, 0.6, 0.7, 0.8, 0.9 etc. we see that f(x) is -ve for x = 0.8 and +ve for x = 0.7 $\therefore$ we may start by taking $x_0 = 0.7$ so that from (1)

Let n = 0

$$x_1 = x_0 - \frac{x_0^3-6x_0+4}{3x_0^2-6}$$

$$= 0.7-\frac{(0.7)^3-6(0.7)+4}{3(0.7)^2-6}$$

$$= 0.7 - \frac{.143}{-4.53}$$

= 0.7 + .031567328

$x_1 = .73157$

i.e. $x_0 = 0.7 \Rightarrow x_1 = .73157$

$$x_2 = x_1 - \frac{x_1^3 - 6x_1 + 4}{3x_1^2 - 6}$$

$$= .73157 - \frac{(.73157)^3 - 6 \times .73157 + 4}{3(.73157)^2 - 6}$$

= .73157 - (- .0004807)
= .7320507
x_2 = .73210
$\therefore x_2$ = .73210

$$x_3 = x_2 - \frac{x_2^3 - 6x_2 + 4}{3x_2 - 6} = .7321 - \frac{(.7321)^3 - 6(.7321) + 4}{3(.7321)^2 - 6}$$

$$= .7321 - \frac{.00042}{4.3921}$$

= .7321 - .000096
x_3 = .7321
$\therefore x_3$ = .7321

$$x_4 = x_3 - \frac{x_3^2 - 6x_3 + 4}{3x_3^2 - 6} = .7320 - \frac{(.7320)^3 - 6(.7320) + 4}{3(.7320)^2 - 6}$$

= .7320 - (-.00005007) = .7320 + .00005
= .73205
= .7321
As we see that $x_3 = x_4$ = .7321
$\therefore$ exact value of f(x) = x^3 - 6x + 4 = 0 is 0.7321

(b) Determine the root between 2 and 3, of the equation $x \sin x + \cos x = 0$ **using the bisection method.**

Bisection Method

f(x) = xSinx + cosx = 0

Trying $x = \Pi, \frac{3\Pi}{2}, \ldots\ldots$

$f(\Pi) = \Pi \text{Sin}\,\Pi + \text{Cos}\,\Pi = 2.14(+ve)$

$$f(\frac{3\Pi}{2}) = \frac{3\Pi}{2} Sin \frac{3\Pi}{2} + Cos \frac{3\Pi}{2} = -1(-ve)$$

i.e $f(\Pi)$ and $f\left(\frac{3\Pi}{2}\right)$ are of opposite sings and so we conclude that at least one root of the given equation lies between x = Π and $\frac{3\Pi}{2}$

For Ist approximation,

$$x_0 = \frac{\Pi + \frac{3\Pi}{2}}{2} = \frac{5\Pi}{4}$$

Again $f\left(\frac{5\Pi}{4}\right) = \frac{5\Pi}{4} Sin\left(\frac{5\Pi}{4}\right) + \cos\left(\frac{5\Pi}{4}\right)$

$$= \frac{1}{\sqrt{2}}\left[\frac{5\Pi}{4} - 1\right](+ve)$$

Now

$f\left(\frac{3\Pi}{2}\right) = -ve$ and so we conclude that the root lies between $x = \frac{3\Pi}{2}$ and

$$x = \frac{5\Pi}{4}$$

For second approximation,

$$x_1 = \frac{\frac{3\Pi}{2} + \frac{5\Pi}{4}}{2} = \frac{11}{8}\Pi$$

$$\therefore f\left(\frac{11\Pi}{8}\right) = \frac{11\Pi}{8}\sin\left(\frac{11\Pi}{8}\right) + \cos\left(\frac{11\Pi}{8}\right)$$

$$= -4.3714 \qquad (-ve)$$

$\therefore f\left(\frac{11\Pi}{8}\right) = -ve \; and \; f\left(\frac{5\Pi}{4}\right) = +ve$ so we conclude that the root lies between

$$x = \frac{11}{8}\Pi \; and \; x = \frac{5\Pi}{4}$$

For IIIrd approximation,

$$x_2 = \frac{\frac{11\Pi}{8} + \frac{5\Pi}{4}}{2} = \frac{21\Pi}{16} \quad and$$

$$f(x_2) = f\left(\frac{21\Pi}{16}\right) = \frac{21}{16}\Pi\sin\frac{21}{16}\Pi + \cos\frac{21}{16}\Pi = +ve$$

$\therefore$ root lies between $\frac{11}{8}\Pi$ *and* $x = \frac{21\Pi}{16}$

$$\therefore x_3 = \frac{\frac{11}{8}\Pi + \frac{21}{16}\Pi}{2} = \frac{43}{32}\Pi$$

$$\therefore x_3 = \frac{43}{32}\Pi = \frac{43}{32} \times 3.14 = 4.219375$$

$x_3 = 4.22$ which is the required real root of the given equation.

Note:- Student may further repeat this process upto reaching their desired values of root.

(c) Using the Gauss elimination method, solve the following system of equations:

$$4x_1 + x_2 + x_3 = 4$$
$$x_1 + 4x_2 - 2x = 4$$
$$3x_1 + 2x_2 - 4x_3 = 6$$

By Gauss Elimination Method :

The coefficient matrix is

$$\left[\begin{array}{ccc|c} 4 & 1 & 1 & 4 \\ 1 & 4 & -2 & 4 \\ 3 & 2 & -4 & 6 \end{array}\right]$$

Reduce the coefficient of x_1 from 2nd or 3rd equation to zero by performing the operation.

$R_2 \rightarrow R_2 - R_1/4,\ R_3 \rightarrow R_3 - R_1 \times 3/4$

$$\left[\begin{array}{ccc|c} 4 & 1 & 1 & 4 \\ 0 & 15/4 & -9/4 & 3 \\ 0 & 5/4 & -19/4 & 3 \end{array}\right]$$

Now Reduce the x_2 coefficient to zero by performing the operation i.e.

$R_3 \rightarrow R_3 - R_2 \times 1/3$

$$\left[\begin{array}{ccc|c} 4 & 1 & 1 & 4 \\ 0 & 15/4 & -9/4 & 3 \\ 0 & 0 & -4 & 3 \end{array}\right]$$

By performing Back Substitution Method on equation

$4x_1 + x_2 + x_3 = 4$

$\frac{15}{4}x_2 - \frac{9}{4}x_3 = 3$

$-4x_3 = 2$

$x_3 = -½, x_2 = ½, x_1 = 1$

Now the solution are

$x_1 = 1, x_2 = ½, x_3 = -½$

By Gauss-Seidel method, if

$$4x_1 + x_2 + x_3 = 4$$
$$x_1 + 4x_2 - 2x_3 = 4$$
$$3x_1 + 2x_2 - 4x_3 = 6$$

$$4x_1 = 4 - x_2 - x_3$$
$$4x_2 = 4 - x_1 + 2x_3$$
$$4x_3 = -6 + 3x_1 + 2x_2$$

$$x_1 = 1 - 0.25x_2 - 0.25x_3$$
$$x_2 = 1 - 0.25x_1 + 0.5x_3$$
$$x_3 = -1.5 + 0.75x_1 + 0.5x_2$$

It can be verified that these equation satisfy the condition given in.

$$\left[\sum_{j=1}^{n}\frac{a_{ij}}{a_{ii}} \leq 1, (i = 1, 2, 3, ---, n)\right]$$

The results are given in the tables below:-

n	x_1	x_2	x_3
1	1	0.75	-0.375
2	0.9062	0.5859	-0.5273
3	0.9854	0.49	-0.5159
4	1.0073	0.4902	-0.4995

(d) Evaluate $f(x)=x^3-6x^2+3x-0.149$ at $x=4.71$, using three-digit arithmetic.

$f(x)=x^3-6x^2+3x-0.149 \longrightarrow (1)$

we have to find value of root starting with $x_0 = 4.71$

$$x_1 = 4.71 - \frac{(4.71)^3 - 6\times(4.71)^2 + 3\times 4.71 - 0.149}{3\times(4.71)^2 - 12\times 4.71 + 3}$$

(by $x_1 = x_0 - \dfrac{f(x_0)}{f^1(x_0)}$ using Newton Raphson method)

$x_1 = 5.833$

$$x_2 = 5.83 - \frac{(5.83)^2 - 6(5.83)^2 + 3\times 5.83 - 0.149}{3\times(5.83)^2 - 12\times 5.83 + 3}$$

$= 5.49$ (By $x_2 = x_1 - \dfrac{f(x_1)}{f_1(x_1)}$)

$\therefore x_2 = 5.49$

$$x_3 = 5.49 - \frac{(5.49)^3 - 6(5.49)^2 + 3\times 5.49 - 0.149}{3(5.49)^2 - 12\times 5.49 + 3}$$

$= 5.47$

$\therefore x_3 = 5.473$

$\because x_2$ *and* x_3 are very much closed so $x_3 = 5.473$ may be solution for the given polynomial.

at $x = 4.71$

$f(x) = x^3 - 6(x^2) + 3x - 0.149$

$= (4.71)^3 - 6(4.7)^2 + 3\times 4.71 - 0.419$

$= 104.48715 - 133.1046 + 14.13 - 0.419$

$f(x) = -14.90645 = -14.906$

Hence we conclude that value of f(x) is = -14.906 at x = 4.71 and real root is 5.473 upto three places of decimal.

(e) Solve the following equations by Cramer's rule:

3x+2y-z=4

2x-y+2z=10

x-3y-4z=5

Now, the augmented matrix is

$$|D| = \begin{bmatrix} 3 & 2 & -1 \\ 2 & -1 & 2 \\ 1 & -3 & -4 \end{bmatrix} \quad D_1 = \begin{bmatrix} 4 & 2 & -1 \\ 10 & -1 & 2 \\ 5 & -3 & -4 \end{bmatrix}$$

$$D_2 = \begin{bmatrix} 3 & 4 & -1 \\ 2 & 10 & 2 \\ 1 & 5 & -4 \end{bmatrix} \quad D_3 = \begin{bmatrix} 3 & 2 & 4 \\ 2 & -1 & 10 \\ 1 & -3 & 5 \end{bmatrix}$$

$|D| = 3(4+6)-2(-8-2)-1(-6+1)$

$=30+20+5$

$=55$

$D_1 = 4(4+6) -2(-40-10) -1(-30+5)$

$= 40 + 100 + 25$

$= 165$

$D_2 = 3(-40-10) -4(-8-2) -1(10-10)$

$= -150 + 40$

$=-110$

$D_3 = 3(-5+30) -2(10-10) + 4(-6+1)$

$75 - 20 = 55$

Now.

$$x = \frac{D_1}{D}, \quad y = \frac{D_2}{D} \quad Z = \frac{D_3}{D}$$

$$x = \frac{165}{55} = 3, \quad y = \frac{-110}{55} = -2 \quad Z = \frac{55}{55} = 1$$

Therefore, the solutions of equations are

$x = 3, \quad y = -2, \quad z = 1$

(f) Evaluate $\int_0^1 \frac{dx}{1+x}$ using the trapezoidal rule with 4 subintervals.

divide the range of integration (0, 1) into four equal parts each of width $\frac{1-0}{4} = \frac{1}{4}$

$\therefore h = \frac{1}{4}$ the value of y for each point of sub division are given below

x	$y = \frac{1}{1+x}$	
$x_0 = 0$	1	y_0
$x_0 + h = \frac{1}{4}$	$\frac{4}{5}$	y_1
$x_0 + 2h = \frac{1}{2}$	$\frac{2}{3}$	y_2
$x_0 + 3h = \frac{3}{4}$	$\frac{4}{7}$	y_3
$x_0 + 4h = 1$	$\frac{1}{2}$	y_4

using trapezoidal rule

$$\int_0^1 \frac{dx}{1+x} = h\left[\frac{1}{2}(y_0 + y_4) + (y_1 + y_2 + y_3)\right]$$

$$= \frac{1}{4}\left[\frac{1}{2}\left(1 + \frac{1}{2}\right) + \left(\frac{4}{5} + \frac{2}{3} + \frac{4}{7}\right)\right]$$

$$= \frac{1}{4}\left[\frac{3}{6} + \frac{214}{105}\right]$$

$$= \frac{1}{4}\left[\frac{533}{210}\right]$$

$$= \frac{533}{840}$$

$$= .63452$$

Q2(a). For the given table of values, use Lagrange's interpolation to find the value of f(2.5).

x	1	2	3	4
f(x)	1	8	27	64

Here $x_0 = 1$, $x_1 = 2$, $x_2 = 3$, $x_3 = 4$, $x = 2.5$ Lagrange's Formula for interpolation is given as

$$f_{(x)} = \frac{(x-x_1)(x-x_2)(x-x_3)}{(x_0-x_1)(x_0-x_2)(x_0-x_3)} f(x_0) + \frac{(x-x_0)(x-x_2)(x-x_3)}{(x_1-x_0)(x_1-x_2)(x_1-x_3)} f(x_1)$$

$$+ \frac{(x-x_0)(x-x_1)(x-x_3)}{(x_2-x_0)(x_2-x_1)(x_2-x_3)} f(x_2) + \frac{(x-x_0)(x-x_1)(x-x_2)}{(x_3-x_0)(x_3-x_1)(x_3-x_2)} f(x_3)$$

$$f(2.5\ ) = \frac{(2.5-2)(2.5-3)(2.5-4)}{(1-2)(1-3)(1-4)}\times 1+\frac{(2.5-1)(2.5-3)(2.5-4)}{(2-1)(2-3)(2-4)}\times 8+$$

$$\frac{(2.5-1)(2.5-2)(2.5-4)}{(3-1)(3-2)(3-4)}\times 27+\frac{(2.5-1)(2.5-2)(2.5-3)}{(4-1)(4-2)(4-3)}\times 64$$

$$=\frac{.5\times(-.5)\times(-1.5)}{(-1)(-2)(-3)}+\frac{1.5\times(-.5)(-1.5)}{1\times -1\times -2}\times 8+\frac{1.5\times .5\times -1.5}{2\times 2\times -1}\times 27+\frac{1.5\times .5\times -.5}{3\times 2\times 1}\times 64$$

$$=-\frac{0.375}{6}+\frac{1.125}{2}\times 8+\frac{1.125}{2}\times 27-\frac{.375}{6}\times 64$$

$$=-0.0625+\frac{9}{2}+\frac{30.375}{2}-\frac{24}{6}$$

$$=-0.0625+19.6875-4$$

$$=15.625=15.6(\textit{Nearly})$$

hence for x = 2.5, f(x) = 15.6

(b) Find the root of e^x-4x=0, which lies between 2 and 3, by Newton-Raphson Method, correct to three places of decimals.

$$f_{(x)} = e^x - 4x = 0$$

$$f^1{}_{(x)} = e^x - 4$$

we have $x_{n+1} = x_n - \dfrac{f(x_n)}{f'(x_n)}$.....................(1)

Let x = 0, $f_{(x)}$ = 1(+ve)

x = 1, $f_{(1)}$ = -1.28(-ve)

We observe that $f_{(x)}$ is -ve for x = 1, and +ve for x = 0, so that x_o lies in interval (0,1) shortening this interval by observing the sign of $f_{(x)} = e^x - 4x = 0$ for x = 0.1, 0.2, 0.3, ...etc.

at x = 0.3, f(0.3) = 0.149 (+ve)

at x = 0.4, f(0.4) = -0.18017 (-ve)

We may start by taking x_0 = 0.3

from (1) by Newton Raphson Method :

$$x_1 = x_0 - \frac{f(x_0)}{f'(x_0)}$$

$$=0.3-\frac{f(0.3)}{f'(0.3)}=0.3-\frac{e^{0.3}-4\times0.3}{e^{0.3}-4}=0.3565$$

$x_1 = 0.357$

$x_0 = 0.3 \Rightarrow x_1 = 0.357$

$$x_2 = x_1-\frac{f(x_1)}{f'(x_1)}=0.357-\frac{e^{0.357}-4\times0.357}{e^{0.357}-4}=2.0245$$

$x_2 = 2.0245$

$$x_3 = x_2-\frac{f(x_2)}{f'(x_2)}=2.0245-\frac{e^{(2.0245)}-4\times2.0245}{e^{(2.0245)}-4}=8.3572572$$

$x_3 = 8.3572$

Student may respect this process further to get their own satisfaction for x_4, x_5, x_6 ......

$\therefore$ Hence required root is 8.3572 upto four place of decimal.

Q3(a). Consider the following system of equations:

$$\mathbf{4x+y+2z=4}$$
$$\mathbf{3x+5y+z=7}$$
$$\mathbf{x+y+3z=3}$$

Perform the Gauss-Seidel scheme for the solution starting with $x^{(0)}=(0,0,0)^T$.

$4x + y + 2z = 4$ ....(1)

$3x + 5y + z = 7$ ....(2)

$x + y + 3z = 3$ ....(3)

In first equation the largest coefficient 4 is of x so from this equation x is expressed in terms of y and z.

i.e. $x = \frac{1}{4}(4-y-2z)$ ....(4)

Similarly from (2) and (3)

$y = \frac{1}{5}(7-3x-z)$ ....(5)

$z = \frac{1}{3}(3-x-y)$ ....(6)

Now $x^{(1)}$ is to be obtained from equation (4) by choosing some values of y and z to start with. For convenience, let us choose y = 0, z = 0 (Note we can also proceed with some other values) so choosing y = 0, z = 0, from (4),

$$x = x^{(1)} = \frac{4}{4} = 1 \text{ (first approximation)}$$

Now put x = 1, z = 0 in (5) so that

$$y = y^{(1)} = \frac{1}{5}(7-3) = \frac{4}{15} = 0.2666 = 0.27 \,(\textit{first appro.})$$

Again put x = 1, y = 0.27 in (6), we get

$$z = z^{(1)} = \frac{1}{3}(3-1-0.27) = 0.5766 = 0.577 (\textit{first approx.})$$

i.e. $(x^{(1)}, y^{(1)}, z^{(1)}) = (1, 0.27, 0.577)$

with these values of $x^{(1)}$, $y^{(1)}$, $z^{(1)}$ we proceed to obtain second approximating as :

$$x^{(2)} = \frac{1}{4}[4 - y^{(1)} - 2z^{(1)}] = \frac{1}{4}[4 - 0.27 - 2\times 0.577] = 0.644 = 0.64$$

$$y^{(2)} = \frac{1}{5}[7 - 3x^{(2)} - z^{(1)}] = \frac{1}{5}[7 - 3\times 0.64 - 0.577] = 0.9006 = 0.9$$

$$z^{(2)} = \frac{1}{3}[3 - x^{(2)} - y^{(2)}] = \frac{1}{3}[3 - 0.64 - 0.9] = 0.48666 = 0.49$$

$$\therefore [x^{(2)}, y^{(2)}, z^{(2)}] = [0.64, 0.9, 0.49]$$

With these values of $x^{(2)}$, $y^{(2)}$, $z^{(2)}$ we proceed to obtain third approximations as :

$$x^{(3)} = \frac{1}{4}[4 - y^{(2)} - 2z^{(2)}] = \frac{1}{4}[4 - 0.9 - 2\times 0.49] = 0.53$$

$$y^{(3)} = \frac{1}{5}[7 - 3x^{(3)} - z^{(3)}] = \frac{1}{5}[7 - 3\times 0.53 - 0.49] = 0.984$$

$$z^{(3)} = \frac{1}{3}[3 - x^{(3)} - y^{(3)}] = \frac{1}{3}[3 - 0.53 - 0.984] = 0.495$$

$$\therefore [x^{(3)}, y^{(3)}, z^{(3)}] = [0.53, 0.984, 0.495]$$

These values $x^{(3)}$, $y^{(3)}$, $z^{(3)}$ being sufficiently close to $x^{(2)}$, $y^{(2)}$, $z^{(3)}$ can be considered as most appropriate solution of the given system of equations, hence the solution is :

x = 0.53
y = 0.984
z = 0.495

(b) Starting with the interval [1, 2], solve the equation x^3-4x+1=0 for its root using the bisection method, correct upto three decimal places.

Bisection Method :

$f_{(x)} = x^3 - 4x + 1 = 0$

we have given interval [1, 2] so we conclude that at least one root of the given equation lies between x = 1 and x = 2

For First approximation, $x_0 = \frac{1+2}{2} = 1.5$

$x_0 = \frac{3}{2} = 1.5$

Again $f\left(\frac{3}{2}\right) = \left(\frac{3}{2}\right)^2 - 4 \times \frac{3}{2} + 1 = \frac{-13}{8} (-ve)[from\,(1)]$

$f_{(2)} = (2)^3 - 4 \times 2 + 1 = +1(+ve)$

so we conclude that root lies between

$x = \frac{3}{2}\, and\; x = 2$

For second approximation, $x_1 = \frac{1.5+2}{2} = 1.75$

$f(1.75) = (1.75)^3 - 4 \times 1.75 + 1 = -0.64(-ve\, value)[from\, 1]$

$\therefore f(1.75) = -ve\, and\; f(2) = +ve\, and\; so\; we\; conclude\; that\; the\; root\; lies$
$between\; x = 1.75\; and\; x = 2$

For third approximation, $x_2 = \frac{1.75+2}{2} = 1.875$

$f(1.875) = (1.875)3 - 4 \times 1.875 + 1 = 0.09179(+ve)$

$\therefore$ root lies between 1.875 and 1.75

$\therefore\; x_3 = \frac{1.875+1.75}{2} = 1.8125 = 1.813$ (three places of decimal)

student may repeat this process further for desired accuracy.

$x_3 = 1.813$ Which is our required real root of the given equation.

Q4(a). Find the root of the equation $x^3 + x - 1 = 0$ between 0 and 1, using the Regula-Falsi Method.

Regula Falsi Method:-

$f(x) = x^3 + x - 1 = 0$

inveral is 0 and 1 i.e (0, 1)

The approximation are given below:-

Ist approx difference

	x	y
	0	−1
	1	1
difference	1	2

$$h_1 = \frac{(1-0)1-11}{|-1|+|1|} = \frac{1}{2} = 0.5$$

$$x^{(1)} = 0 + 0.5 = 0.5$$

II approx difference

	0.5	−0.375
	0.6	−0.184
difference	0.1	+0.191

$$h_2 = \frac{0.1 \times 0.375}{0.191} = 0.196$$

$$x^{(2)} = 0.5 + 0.196$$
$$= 0.696$$

III approx difference

	0.695	.0307
	0.696	.0332
difference	.001	.0025

$$h_3 = \frac{.001 \times .0307}{.0025} = 0.0123$$

$$x^{(3)} = 0.695 + 0.0123$$
$$= 0.7073$$

Hence the required value of the root is 0.7013

(b) Using Newton's forward difference formula, find the value of f(1.6), using the given data table

x	1	1.4	1.8	2.2
f(x)	3.49	4.82	5.96	6.5

The table of finite differences for forward differences is given below:-

x	f(x)	Δ f(x)	Δ^2 f(x)	Δ^3f(x)
1	3.49			
		1.33		
1.4	4.82		-0.19	
		1.14		-0.41
1.8	5.96		-0.6	
		0.54		
2.2	6.5			

Newton's formula for forward interpolation is

$$f(a+mh) \equiv f(a)+m\Delta f(a)+\frac{m(m-1)}{2!}\Delta^2 f(a)+\frac{m(m-1)(m-2)}{3!}\Delta^3 f(a) \longrightarrow (1)$$

we have to interpolate f(1.6)
Hence a+mh = 1.6 where a being I term a = 1, h = .4

$$m=\frac{1.6-a}{h}=\frac{1.6-1}{4}$$

$$=\frac{.6}{4}$$

$$m=\frac{6}{40}=\frac{3}{20}$$

Hence from (1), putting $m=\frac{3}{20}$, and taking upto third differences as the fourth and onwards differences are zero, we get

$$f(1.6)=f(1)+\frac{3}{20}\Delta f(1)+\frac{\frac{3}{2}\left(\frac{3}{2}-1\right)}{2!}\Delta^2 f(1)+\frac{\frac{3}{2}\left(\frac{3}{2}-1\right)\left(\frac{3}{2}-2\right)}{3!}\Delta^3 f(1)$$

$$=3.49+\frac{3}{20}\times 1.33+\frac{3}{2}\times\frac{1}{2}\times\frac{1}{2}\times -0.19+\frac{3}{2}\times\frac{1}{2}\times\frac{-1}{2}\times\frac{1}{6}\times -0.41$$

$$=3.49+0.1995-0.07125+0.025625$$

$$=3.643875$$

or

$f(1.6)=3.64$ (rounded up values)

Q5(a). Find the first derivative of f(x) at x = 1.1 from the following tabulated values.

x	f(x)
1.0	0.0000
1.2	0.1280
1.4	0.5440
1.6	1.2960
1.8	2.4320
2.0	4.0000

We have to find out $\frac{dy}{dx} at\, x = 1.1$ from table given in question the difference table is →

x	f(x)=y	Δ	Δ^2	Δ^3	Δ^4	Δ^5
1.0	0.0000					
		0.1280				
1.2	0.1280		0.288			
		0.4160		0.048		
1.4	0.5440		0.336		0.00	
		0.7520		0.048		0.00
1.6	1.2960		0.384		0.00	
		1.36		0.048		
1.8	2.4320		0.432			
		1.568				
2.0	4.0000					

we have formula for Function tabulated as equal Interval is given below:-

$x_0 = 1.1, h = 0.2$

$$\left[\frac{dy}{dx}\right]_{atx=x0} = \frac{1}{h}\left[\Delta y_0 - \frac{1}{2}\Delta^2 y_0 + \frac{1}{3}\Delta^3 y_0 \frac{-1}{4}\Delta^4 y_0 + ...\right] \longrightarrow (1)$$

$$= \frac{1}{0.2}\left[0.128 - \frac{1}{2}\times 0.288 + \frac{1}{3}\times 0.048 - \frac{1}{4}\times 0\right]$$

$$= \frac{1}{0.2}[0.128 - 0.144 + 0.016]$$

$= 0.000$

(b) Find the square root of 18 using Newton-Raphson method upto two correct decimal places.

Newton Raphson method

Let $x = \sqrt{18}$

$\therefore x^2 = 18$

$so\,that\, f(x) = x^2 - 18$

$f^1(x) = 2x$

$f(4) = 16 - 18 - 2(-ve)$

$f(5) = 25 - 18 = 7(+ve)$

So the root lies between x = 4 and x = 5 let $x_0 = 5$ we have by Newton. Raphson Formula

$$x_{n+1} = x_n - \frac{f(x_n)}{f^1(x_n)}\, giving\, x_1 = x_0 - \frac{f(x_0)}{f^1(x_0)}$$

For x = 5, i.e $x_0 = 5$

$$x_1 = 5 - \frac{7}{10} = 4.3$$

Again applying formula for $x_1 = 4.3$
we have

$$x_2 = x_1 - \frac{f(x_1)}{f(x_1)} = 4.3 - \frac{(4.3)^2 - 18}{2 \times 4.3}$$

$$x_2 = 4.3 - \frac{.49}{8.6}$$

$x_2 = 4.3 - 0.0569767$

$x_2 = 4.2430$

$x_2 = 4.24$ (upto two correct decimal places)

Q6(a). Find the smallest positive root of the equation $x^3 - 3x^2 + x + 1 = 0$ using the secant method.

$f_{(x)} = x^3 - 3x^2 + x + 1 = 0$

$Let\, x_0 = 0, \quad x_1 = 2$, $f(x_0) = +1$

$\because f(x_1) = -1$

We have secant formula for root is as:-

$$x_{n+1} = \frac{x_{n-1} f_{(Xn)} - x_n\, f_{(Xn-1)}}{f_{(Xn)} - f_{(Xn-1)}}\, where\, n = 0, 1, 2...$$

$n = 1,$

$$\therefore x_2 = \frac{x_0 f_{(x)} - x_1 f(x_0)}{f(x_1) - f(x_0)}$$

$$= \frac{0 \times -1 - 2 \times 1}{-1 - 1} = \frac{-2}{-2} = 1$$

$x_2 = 1$

$f(x_2) = 1^3 - 3(1)^2 + 1 + 1 = 0$

$n = 2,$

$$(x_3) = \frac{x_1 f(x_1) - x_2 f(x_1)}{f(x_2) - f(x_1)}$$

$$= \frac{2 \times -1 - 1 \times -1}{0 - (-1)}$$

$$= \frac{-2 + 1}{-1} = 1$$

$x_3 = 1$ since roots are x = 0, x = 2, x = 1 smallest positive root is $x_3 = 1$. Because zero may never be a root of any equation.

(b) Apply Newton's backward difference formula to the data below, to obtain a polynomial in x.

x	1	2	3	4	5
f(x)	1	-1	1	-1	1

The table of finite difference is given below:-

x	y=f(x)	∇	∇²	∇³	∇⁴
1	1				
		-2			
2	-1		4		
		2		-8	
3	1		-4		16
		-2		8	
4	-1		4		
		2			
5	1				

$$h=1, b=5\, m=\frac{x-b}{h}=\frac{x-5}{1}=m=x-5$$

$$f_{(x)}=f_{(b)}+m\nabla f_{(b)}+\frac{m(m-5)}{2!}\nabla^2 f(b)+\frac{m(m-1)(m-2)(m-3)}{4!}\nabla^4 f(b)$$

$$=1+(x-5)2+\frac{(x-5)(x-6)}{2}\times 4+\frac{(x-5)(x-6)(x-7)}{6}\times 8+$$
$$\frac{(x-5)(x-6)(x-7)(x-8)}{24}\times 16$$

$$=1+(x-5)\left\{2+2(x-6)+\frac{4}{3}(x-6)(x-7)+\frac{2}{3}(x-6)(x-7)(x-8)\right\}$$

$$=1+(x-5)\left\{2+2x-12+\frac{4}{3}x^2-\frac{52}{3}x+42+\frac{2}{3}(x^2-13x+42)(x-8)\right\}$$

$$=1+(x-5)\left\{2x-10+\frac{4}{3}x^2-\frac{52}{3}x+42+\frac{2}{3}(x^3-13x^2+42x-8x^2+104x-336)\right\}$$

$$=1+(x-5)\left[\frac{2}{3}x^3+x^2\left\{\frac{4}{3}-\frac{42}{3}\right\}+x\left\{2-\frac{52}{3}+\frac{292}{3}\right\}+(-10+42-224)\right]$$

$$=1+(x-5)\left[\frac{2}{3}x^3-\frac{38}{3}x^2-78x-192\right]$$

$$=1+\frac{2}{3}x^4-\frac{38}{3}x^3-78x^2-192x-\frac{10}{3}x^3+\frac{190}{3}+390x+960$$

$$=\frac{2}{3}x^4-\frac{48}{3}x^3-78x^2+198x+\frac{3073}{3}$$

$$=\frac{2}{3}x^4-16x^3-78x^2+198x+1024$$

CS-71 : COMPUTER ORIENTED NUMERICAL TECHNIQUES
DEC-2004

Note: *Question 1 is* ***compulsory****. Answer any* ***three*** *from the rest.*

Q1(a). Find the least positive root of the equation
$f(x) = x^3 + 4x^2 - 10 = 0$, using the Bisection Method. **[6]**

$f(x)=x^3+4x^2-10=0,$ $\quad$ $f(1)=1+4-10=-5(-ve)$

$f(z)=8+16-10=16(+ve)$

$\because$ f(1) is -ve and f(2) is +ve, a root lies between 1 and 2 and therefore, we take.

$$x_0=\frac{1+2}{2}=\frac{3}{2}=1.5$$

$$f(x_0)=\frac{27}{8}+4\times\frac{9}{4}-10=\frac{27-8}{27}=\frac{19}{27}(+\text{ve value})$$

$$f(x_0)=\frac{19}{27}(+\text{ve}),$$

Hence root lies between 1 and 1.5 and we obtain $x_1=\frac{1+1.5}{2}=1.25$

$$f(x_1)=(1.25)^3+4(1.25)^2-10$$

$=1.953125+4\times1.5625-10$

$=1.953125+6.25-10$

$=-1.81875$

$=-1.82(-ve)$

We therefore conclude that the root lies between 1.25 and 1.5.

$$\therefore x_2=\frac{1.25+1.5}{2}=1.375$$

$f(x_3)=(1.375)^3+4\times(1.375)^2-10$

$=2.599609+4\times1.890625-10$

$=2.59609+7.5625-10$

$=0.162109$

$=0.162\ (+ve)$

Now root lies between 1.25 and 1.375

$$x_3 = \frac{1.25+1.375}{2} = 1.3125$$

Hence roots are $x_1=1.5$

$x_2=1.375$

$x_3=1.3125$

(b) Perform three iterations of the Newton-Raphson method to find an approximate value of $\sqrt{\frac{1}{15}}$ starting with the initial approximation x_0 = 0.02. **[5]**

Newton's iterative formula for obtaining sq root of $f_{(x)}$ is

$f(x) = x^2 - b$

$$Xn+1 = \frac{1}{2}\left(Xn + \frac{b}{Xn}\right) --(1)$$

Let

$$X = \sqrt{\frac{1}{15}} \Rightarrow X^2 = \frac{1}{15}$$

$$f_{(x)} = X^2 - \frac{1}{15}$$

As $f(0.02) = (0.02)^2 - \frac{1}{15} = .0004 - .0666 = -0.0666$ (-ve)

and $f(1) = 1^2 - .0666 = .9334(+ve)$

$\therefore$ The root lies between .02 and 1.0 where b = 1/15 = .0666 taking $X_0 = 1.0$ from(1)

$$X_1 = \frac{1}{2}\left(X_0 + \frac{b}{X_0}\right) = \frac{1}{2}\left(1 + \frac{.0666}{1}\right) = \frac{1.0666}{2}$$

$= 0.5333$

Again Taking app. root as 0.5333 and repeating Newton's formula (1), we get

$$X_2 = \frac{1}{2}\left(X_1 + \frac{b}{X_1}\right) = \frac{1}{2}\left(0.5333 + \frac{.0666}{.5333}\right)$$

$$= \frac{1}{2}(0.5333 + .12488)$$

$X_2 = 0.32909$

$$X_3 = \frac{1}{2}\left(X_2 + \frac{b}{X_2}\right) = \frac{1}{2}\left(0.32909 + \frac{.06666}{.26582}\right)$$

$X_3 = .26582$

and

$$X_4 = \frac{1}{2}\left(X_3 + \frac{b}{X_3}\right) = \frac{1}{2}\left(.26582 + \frac{.06666}{.26582}\right)$$

$X_4 = 0.25829$ Ans

(c) Integrate $\int_0^1 \frac{1}{1+x}dx$ by Simpson's rule with $h = \frac{1}{8}$. **[4]**

Simpson's $\frac{1}{3}$ rule

Divide the range (0.1) into eight equal parts of width $\frac{1-0}{8} = \frac{1}{8}$, $\therefore h = \frac{1}{8}$, n=8

The value of y for each point of subdivision are given below:

	x	$y = \frac{1}{1+x}$		
1	$x_0 = 0$	$y = \frac{1}{1+0} = 1$	= 1.0000000	y_0
2	$x_0 + h = 1/8$	$y = \frac{1}{1+1/8} = 8/9$	= 0.8888888	y_1
3	$x_0 + 2h = 2/8 = 1/4$	$y = \frac{1}{1+1/4} = 4/5$	= 0.8000000	y_2
4	$x_0 + 3h = 3/8$	$y = \frac{1}{1+3/8} = 8/11$	= 0.7272727	y_3
5	$x_0 + 4h = 4/8 = 1/2$	$y = \frac{1}{1+1/2} = 2/3$	= 0.6666666	y_4
6	$x_0 + 5h = 5/8$	$y = \frac{1}{1+5/8} = 8/13$	= 0.6153846	y_5
7	$x_0 + 6h = 6/8 = 3/4$	$y = \frac{1}{1+3/4} = 4/7$	= 0.5714285	y_6
8	$x_0 + 7h = 7/8$	$y = \frac{1}{1+7/8} = 8/15$	= 0.5333333	y_7
9	$x_0 + 8h = 8/8 = 1$	$y = \frac{1}{1+1} = 1/2$	= 0.5000000	y_8

$$\int_0^1 \frac{dx}{1+x} = \frac{h}{3}[(y_0+y_8)+4(y_1+y_3+y_5+y_7)+2(y_2+y_4+y_6)]$$

$$= \frac{1}{8} \times \frac{1}{3}\begin{bmatrix}(1+.5)+4(.8888888+.7272727+.6153846+5333333+3)+2 \\ (.8+.6666666+.5714285)\end{bmatrix}$$

$=\frac{1}{24}[1.5+4\times2.7648794+2\times2.0380951]$

$=\frac{1}{24}[1.5+11.059517+4.0761902]$

$=\frac{1}{24}[16.635707]$

$=0.6931544$

(d) List any three sources of errors. **[3]**

There is the types of errors that are encountered while carrying out numerical calculation to solve a problem.

(1) Round off errors arise due to floating point representation of initial data in the machine. Subsequent error in the solution due to this is called propagated error.

(2) Due to finite digit arithmetic operations, the computer generates in the solution of a problem errors known as generated error or rounding error.

(3) Sensitivity of the algorithm of the numerical process used for solving a problem (as calculation of f(x) from x) affects accuracy of the solution of the problem and is known as instability and the process is said to be unstable.

(4) Errors due to finite representation of an inherently infinite process. For example, consider the use of a finite number of terms in the infinite series expansions of Sinx, Cosx or f(x) by Maclaurian's or Taylor Series expression. Such errors are called truncation errors.

(e) Solve the following set of linear equations using Cramer's rule :[6]

$$\mathbf{x_1+2x_2-x_3=2}$$
$$\mathbf{3x_1+6x_2+x_3=1}$$
$$\mathbf{3x_1+3x_2+2x_3=3}$$

Cramer's Rule :-

$x_1+2x_2-x_3=2$

$3x_1+6x_2+x_3=1$

$3x_1+3x_2+2x_3=3$

$$\begin{bmatrix} 1 & 2 & -1 \\ 3 & 6 & 1 \\ 3 & 3 & 2 \end{bmatrix} \begin{bmatrix} x_1 \\ x_2 \\ x_3 \end{bmatrix} = \begin{bmatrix} 2 \\ 1 \\ 3 \end{bmatrix}$$

$\leftarrow A \rightarrow \quad \leftarrow x \rightarrow \quad \leftarrow B \rightarrow$

I step

$$|A| = \begin{vmatrix} 1 & 2 & -1 \\ 3 & 6 & 1 \\ 3 & 3 & 2 \end{vmatrix}$$

$= 1\ (12-3)-\ 2\ (6-3)-1(9-18)$

$= 9 - 6 + 9$

$=12\ (\neq 0)$

$\because |A| \neq 0 \therefore$ the system of equation is consistent and has a unique solution

$$\therefore D_1 = \begin{vmatrix} 2 & 2 & -1 \\ 1 & 6 & 1 \\ 3 & 3 & 2 \end{vmatrix}$$

$=2(12-3)-2(2-3)-1(3-18)$

$=2\times9+2+15$

$=35$

$$D_2 = \begin{vmatrix} 1 & 2 & -1 \\ 3 & 1 & 1 \\ 3 & 3 & 2 \end{vmatrix}$$

$D_2 = 1(2-3) -2(6-3) -1(9-3)$

$= -1 -6 -6$

$D_2 = -13$

$$D_3 = \begin{vmatrix} 1 & 2 & 2 \\ 3 & 6 & 1 \\ 3 & 3 & 3 \end{vmatrix}$$

$= 1(18-3) -2\ (9-3)+2\ (9-18)$

$= 15-12-18$

$D_3 = -15$

Hence By Cramer's Rule

$$x_1 = \frac{D1}{|A|} = \frac{35}{12}$$

$$x_2 = \frac{D2}{|A|} = \frac{-13}{12}$$

$$x_3 = \frac{D_3}{|A|} = \frac{-15}{12}$$

(f) Find the interpolating using Newton's backward difference for the data below : [6]

x	4	6	8	10
f(x)	19	40	79	142

Hence interpolate f(9).

Derivation of Newton's backward difference formula

Let y = f(x) be the given function which can be represented by polynomial of nth degree in x and expressing it in fractional notation, we suppose,

$$f(x)=A_0+A_1[x-(a+nh)]^{(1)}+A_2[x-(a+nh)]^{(2)}+.....+An[x-(a+nh)]^{(n)}.........(1)$$

Where A_0, A_1, A_2....A_n are constants :

$$f(x)=A_0+A_1[x-(a+nh)]+A_2[x-(a+nh)][a-a+(n-1)h]+....+A_n[x-(a+nh)]...[a-(a+h)]$$

put,

$$x = a + nh \Rightarrow f(a+nh) = A_0$$

or $A_0 = f(a+nh)$ similarly

$$A_1 = \frac{f(a+nh)-f(a+nh-h)}{h} = \frac{\nabla f(a+nh)}{h}$$

$$A_2 = \frac{\nabla^2 f(a+nh)}{2!h^2}$$ and so on,

Thus $A_n = \dfrac{\nabla^n f(a+nh)}{n!h^n}$

Putting A_0, A_1, A_2....A_n in (1)

$$f_{(x)}=f(a+nh)+\frac{\nabla f(a+nh)}{h}[x-(a+nh)]+...+...\frac{\nabla^n f(a+nh)}{x_1 h^n}$$

$$[x-(a+nh)][x-\{a+(n-1)h\}]...[x-(a+h)]......(2)$$

Let $\frac{x-(a+nh)}{h} = m \therefore x = a+nh+mh$ then

$$f(a+nh+mh) = f(a+nh) + m\nabla f(a+nh) + \frac{m(m+1)}{2!}\nabla^2 f(a+nh) + ...$$

$$+\frac{m(m+1)...(m+n-1)}{n!}\nabla^n f(a+nh)$$

Which is our required relation

Now, **solution** for f(9) by given table

x	4	6	8	10
$f(x_1)$	19	40	79	142

x	$f(x_1)$	$\nabla f(x_1)$	$\nabla^2 f(x_1)$	$\nabla^3 f(x_1)$
4	19			
		- 21		
6	40		18	
		- 39		-6
8	79		24	
		- 63		
10	142			

a = 4, h = 2, n = 4

f (a+ nh+ mh)= f (9)

a+nh+mh=9

4+4×2+m×2=9

4+8+2m=9

2m=9-12=-3

$m=\frac{-3}{2}$

$$\therefore f(x)=19+\left(\frac{-3}{2}\right)(21)+\left(\frac{-3}{2}\right)\left(\frac{-3}{2}+1\right)\frac{1}{21}\times 18+\frac{\left(\frac{-3}{2}\right)\left(\frac{-3}{2}+1\right)\left(\frac{-3}{2}+2\right)}{3!}(-6)$$

$$f(9)=19+\left(\frac{-3}{2}\right)\times -21+\left(\frac{-3}{2}\right)\left(\frac{-3}{2}+1\right)\times\frac{1}{21}\times 18+\frac{\left(\frac{-3}{2}\right)\left(\frac{-3}{2}+1\right)\left(\frac{-3}{2}+2\right)\times -6}{3!}$$

$$=19+\frac{63}{2}+\frac{3}{4}\times\frac{1}{\cancel{2}}\times\cancel{18}^{9}-\frac{3}{2}\times\frac{1}{2}\times\frac{1}{2}\times\cancel{6}\times\frac{1}{\cancel{3}\times\cancel{2}}$$

$19 + 31.5 + \frac{27}{4} - \frac{3}{8}$

$= 19+31.5+6.75-.375$

$= 56.875$

Q2(a). Using the Secant method,solve the equation $x^3 + x - 6 = 0$, starting with $x_0 = 1$ and $x_1 = 2$. **[8]**

$f(x)=x^3+x-6=0,\ x_0=1,\ x_1=2$

$f(x_0)=1+1-6=-4$

$f(x_1)=8+2-6=4$

$$x_2 = x_1 - \frac{x_1 - x_0}{f_{(x1)} - f_{(x0)}} f_{(x)} = 2 - \frac{2-1}{4-(-4)} \times 4 = 2-(1/2) = 3/2$$

$$x_2 = \frac{3}{2} = 1.5 \quad \therefore f(x_2) = \frac{27}{8} + \frac{3}{2} - \frac{6}{1} = \frac{27+12-48}{8} = \frac{-9}{8}$$

$$x_3 = x_2 - \frac{x_2 - x_1}{f(x_2) - f(x_1)} f(x_2) = \frac{3}{2} - \left[\frac{\frac{3}{2} - 2}{\frac{-9}{8} - 4}\right] \times \frac{-9}{8}$$

$$= \frac{3}{2} - \left[\frac{\frac{-1}{2}}{\frac{-41}{8}}\right] \times \frac{-9}{8} = \frac{3}{2} + \frac{9}{82}$$

$$\frac{123+9}{82} = \frac{66}{41}$$

$x_3 = 1.609756$

Roots are

$x_0=1$

$x_1=2$

$x_2=1.5$

$x_3=1.609756$

(b) Find the Lagrange's interpolating polynomial for the following data:

x	$\frac{1}{4}$	$\frac{1}{4}$	1
f(x)	-1	2	7

[7]

Also find f(1/2) and f′(1/2)

	x_0	x_1	x_2
x	1/4	1/3	1
f(x)	-1	2	7
	$f(x_0)$	$f(x_1)$	$f(x_2)$

Lagrange's Interpolation Formula:

$$f(x)=\frac{(x-x_1)(x-x_2)}{(x_0-x_1)(x_0-x_2)}f(x_0)+\frac{(x-x_0)(x-x_2)}{(x_1-x_0)(x_1-x_2)}f(x_1)+\frac{(x-x_0)(x-x_1)}{(x_2-x_0)(x_2-x_1)}f(x_2)$$

$$f(x)=\frac{\left(x-\frac{1}{3}\right)(x-1)}{\left(1-\frac{1}{3}\right)\left(\frac{1}{4}-1\right)}x\text{-}1+\frac{\left(x-\frac{1}{4}\right)(x-1)}{\left(\frac{1}{3}-\frac{1}{4}\right)\left(\frac{1}{3}-1\right)}\times 2+\frac{\left(x-\frac{1}{4}\right)\left(x-\frac{1}{3}\right)}{\left(1-\frac{1}{4}\right)\left(1-\frac{1}{3}\right)}\times 7$$

$$=\frac{(3x-1)(x-1)}{\cancel{3}x\frac{-1}{12}\times\frac{-3}{4}}\times\text{-}1-\frac{(4x-1)(x-1)\cancel{2}}{\cancel{4}\times\frac{1}{\cancel{12}_3}\times\frac{-\cancel{2}}{3}}+\frac{(4x-1)(3x-1)}{\cancel{12}\times\frac{3}{\cancel{4}}\times\frac{2}{\cancel{3}}}\times 7$$

$$=\frac{-16(3x-1)(x-1)}{3}=9(4x-1)(x-1)+\frac{7}{6}(4x-1)(3x-1)$$

$$=\frac{-16}{3}\{3x^2-3x-x+1\}-9(4x^2-4x-x+1)+\frac{7}{6}(12x^2-4x-3x+1)$$

$$=\frac{-16}{3}(3x^2-4x+1)-9(4x^2-5x+1)+\frac{7}{6}(12x^2-7x+1)$$

$$=x^2\left\{\frac{-16}{3}\times 3-36+\frac{7}{6}\times 12\right\}+x\left\{\frac{-16}{3}\times 4-9\times 5+\frac{7}{6}\times -7\right\}+\left\{\frac{-16}{3}\times 1-9\times 1+\frac{7}{6}\times 1\right\}$$

$$x^2\{-16-36+14\}+x\left\{\frac{64}{3}+45-\frac{49}{6}\right\}+\left\{\frac{-16}{3}-9+\frac{7}{6}\right\}$$

$=x^2\{-48\}+\frac{1047}{18}x-237$

$=f(x)=-48x^2+\frac{1047}{18}x-237$

$=f\left(\frac{1}{2}\right)=-48\times\frac{1}{4}+\frac{1047}{18}\frac{-1}{2}-237$

$=-12+29.083333-237$

$=-219.91667$

$f'(x) = -96x + (1047/18)$

$\therefore f'(1/2) = -96\times(1/2) + (1047/18)$

$= -48+(1047/18)$

$= 10.17$

Q3(a). Solve the following system of equations using the Gauss-elimination method with partial pivoting : [8]

$x_1+x_2-x_3=6$

$3x_1+3x_2+4x_3=20$

$2x_1+x_2+3x_3=13$

Gauss-elimination Method with Partial Pivoting

$x_1+x_2+x_3=6$ -----(1)

$3x_1+3x_2+4x_3=20$ -----(2)

$2x_1+x_2+3x_3=13$ -----(3)

<u>using partical pivoting</u>

(1)×3 - (2)×1

$3x_1+3x_2+3x_3=18$

$3x_1+3x_2+4x_3=20$

$-x_3=-2 \qquad \therefore x_3=2$

(1)×2 - (3)

$2x_1+2x_2+2x_3=12$

$-2x_1\pm x_2+3x_3=13$

$x_2-x_3=-1 \qquad \therefore x_3=2$

$x_2-2=-1$

$x_2=1$

putting values of x_2 and x_3 in (1)

$x_1+1+2=6 \qquad \therefore x_1=3$

Hence $x_1 = 3, x_2=1, x_3=2$

pivotation was not found necessary to solve the equations.

(b) Solve the equation $x^3 + 7x^2 + 9 = 0$ using the regula-falsi method with initial approximation $x_0 = -8$ and $x_1 = -7$. **[7]**

The successive approximate are given below:-

$$\text{first Approx} \quad \begin{array}{cc} x & y \\ \underline{-8} & \underline{1} \\ \underline{-7} & \underline{2} \\ 1 & 64 \end{array}, \; h1 = \frac{\{-7(-8)\}\times -55}{|-55|+|9|}$$

$$=\frac{1\times -55}{64}=\frac{-55}{64}$$

h_1=-.859375=-859

$x^{(1)}$=-8+.859375=-7.140629

=-714

$$\text{Second Approx} \quad \begin{array}{cc} x & y \\ \underline{-7.140} & \underline{1.87} \\ \underline{-7.15} & \underline{1.36} \\ .01 & 3.23 \end{array}, \; h_2 = \frac{\{-7.15-(-7014)\}\times 1.87}{3.23}$$

$$=\frac{-.01\times 1.87}{3.23}$$

$$=\frac{-.0187}{3.23}$$

=-0.00578

=-0.006

$x^{(2)}$=-7.15+(-.006)

$x^{(2)}$=-7.1506

Hence the value of the root is -7.1506

=-7.151

Q4(a). Find $f'(x)$ at x = 0.1 from the following table of values: **[7]**

x	0.1	0.2	0.3	0.4
f(x)	1.10517	1.22140	1.34986	1.49182

We use lagrange's Interpolation formula

Here $x_0 = 0.1$, $x_1 = 0.2$, $x_2 = 0.3$, $x_4 = 0.4$

$$f_{(x)}=\frac{(x-x_1)(x-x_2)...(x-x_n)}{(x_0-x_1)(x_0-x_2)....(x_0-x_n)}f(x_0)+....$$

$$=\frac{(x-0.2)(x-0.3)(x-0.4)}{(0.1-0.2)(0.1-0.3)(0.1-0.4)}\times 1.10517+$$

$$+\frac{(x-0.1)(x-0.3)(x-0.4)}{(0.2-0.1)(0.2-0.3)(0.2-0.4)}\times 1.22140+\frac{(x-0.1)(x-0.1)(x-0.3)}{(0.3-0.1)(0.3-0.2)(0.3-0.4)}\times 1.34986+$$

$$\frac{(x-0.1)(x-0.2)(x-0.4)}{(0.4-0.1)(0.4-0.2)(0.4-0.3)}\times 1.49182$$

$$=\frac{(x^2-0.5+.06)(x-0.4)}{-.1\times -.2\times -.3}\times 1.10517+\frac{(x^2-0.4+.03)(x-0.4)}{+.1\times -.1\times -.2}\times 1.22140+$$

$$+\frac{(x^2-0.2x+.01)(x-0.3)}{.2\times .1\times -.1}\times 1.34986+\frac{(x^2-0.3+.02)(x-0.4)}{.3\times .3\times .1}\times 1.49182$$

$$=(x-0.4)\left\{\frac{x^2-0.5x+.06}{-.00600}\times 1.10517+\frac{x^2-.4x+.03}{.00200}\times 1.22140+\frac{x^2-0.3+.02}{.00600}\times 1.49182\right\}+$$

$$+\frac{(x^2-0.2x+.01)}{-.002000}\times(x-0.3)\times 1.348986$$

$$=(x-.4)\left\{(x^2-0.5x+.06)\left(\frac{-110517}{600}\right)+(x^2-4x+.03)\left(\frac{12214}{20}\right)+(x^2-0.3x+.02)\left(\frac{149182}{600}\right)\right\}+$$

$$+(x^2-0.2x+.0)(x-0.3)\times\frac{1348986}{2000}$$

$$=(x-0.4)\left[\begin{array}{l}x^2\{-184.195+610.7+248.64\}+x(-0.5\times 184.195-.4\times 610.7-0.3\times\\ 248.64)+(0.06\times 184.195+0.03\times 610.7+0.02\times 248.67)\end{array}\right]+$$

$$+\left(\frac{x^3-0.2x2+.01x-.003}{-0.3x2+.06x}\right)674.5$$

$$f_{(x)}=(x-0.4)[675.5x^2-410.95x+1128.9]-67435x^3-.5\times 674.5x^2-674.5\times .07x-.003\times 674.5$$

$$=675.2x^3-410.95x^2-1128.9x\ \ -0.4\times 675.2x^2-0.4\times 410.95x-0.4\times 1128.9$$

$$-674.5x^3-0.5\times 674.5x^2-674.5\times .07x-0.003\times 674.5$$

$f(x)=0.7x^3-1018.3x^2-1340.5x-453.6$

$\therefore f^1(x)=.7\times 3x^2-1018.3\times 2x-1340.5-0$

$f^1(x)=2.1x^2-2036.6x-1340.5$

$f'(x=0.1)=2.1(0.1)^3-2036.6\times 0.1-1340.5$

$=.0021-203.66-1340.5$

$= -1544.2$

(b) Perform four iterations using the Gauss-Seidel method for the following system of equations : [8]

$-8x_1+x_2+x_3=1$

$x_1-5x_2-x_3=16$

$x_1+x_2-4x_3=7$

with $x^{(o)} = (0,0,0)^T$.

<u>Guass-Seidal Method For System of Equals</u>

$-8x_1+x_2+x_3=1$

$x_1-5x_2-x_3=16$

$x_1+x_2-4x_3=7$

With $x^{(0)}=(0, 0, 0)^T$

with $x^{(0)} = (0, 0, 0)^T$

Using Gauss-seidal method,

We have,

$x^{(1)} = [-0.125, -3.225, -2.5875]T$

$x^{(2)} = [-0.9778, -3.9825, -2.9901]^T$

$x^{(3)} = [-0.9778, -.3.9825, -2.9901]^T$

$x^{(4)} = [-0.9966, -3.9973, -2.9984]^T$

Q5(a). Determine an approximate positive root of the equation 2x-3 sin x-5 =0 rounded off to 3 decimal places, using the bisection method. [8]

$f(x)=2x-3\sin x-5=0$ trying $x=0,1,2....$

Let $x=a$, $f_{(0)}=2\times 0-3\times \sin 0-5$

$=0-0-5$

$f_{(0)}=-5$ $\qquad \because \text{Sin}1=.8414$

$x=1, f(1)=2\times 1-3\sin 1-5$

$=2-3\times.8414-5$

$=2-2.5242-5=-5.5242$

$f(.3) = 2\times.3-3\times\sin(.3)-5$

$=.6-3\times.1381-5$

$=.6-.4143-5$

$=.6-5.4183$

$=-4.8183$ $\quad\quad Sin3 = .1409$

$f(3) = 2\times 3 - 3\times \sin 3 - 5$

$= 6 - 3\times\sin 3 - 5$

$= 1 - 3\times.1409$

$= 1 - .4227$

$= .5773$

We so that f(1) and f(3) are of opposite sign and show that at least one root of the given equation lies between x=0, and x=3.

First approximation, $x_0 = \dfrac{0+3}{2} = 1.5$

(b) If $f(x) = \dfrac{1}{x}$, show that $f[a, b, c, d] = -\dfrac{1}{abcd}$. [7]

<u>By Intermediate value theorem :-</u>

f(x) =1/x, f(x) is continious in [a, c] and let b be any no. between f(a) and f(c) , then $\exists$ a no. ξ in (a, c) such that, $f(\xi) = b$.

Similarly again let C be any no., between f(b) and f(d) then $\exists$ a no. ξ^1 in (b, d) such that $f(\xi^1) = c$

So we can say that $f[a, b, c, d] = -\dfrac{1}{abcd}$

Hence showed.

Q6(a). Find the Newton's forward- difference interpolating polynomial which agrees with the table of values given below. Hence obtain the value of f(x) at x =2.5 [8]

x	1	2	3	4	5	6
f(x)	10	19	40	79	142	235

<u>Newton's Forward Different:-</u>

The different table is given below:-

x	1	2	3	4	5	6
$f(x_1)$	10	19	40	79	142	235

x	$f(x_1)$	$\Delta f(x_1)$	$\Delta^2 f(x_1)$	$\Delta^3 f(x_1)$	$\Delta^4 f(x_1)$	$\Delta^5 f(x_1)$
1	10					
		9				
2	19		12			
		21		6		
3	40		18		0	
		39		6		0
4	79		24		0	
		63		6		
5	142		30			
		93				
6	235					

Newton's Forward Different Formula for interpolation x = 2.5

$$f(a+mh)=f(a)+m\Delta f(a)+\frac{m(m-1)}{2!}s^2f(a),+\frac{m(m-1)(m-2)}{3!}\Delta^3f(a)+....$$

$$a=1, h=1, =m=\frac{2.5-1}{1}=1.5$$

$$f(2.5)=f(1)+1.5\times9+\frac{1.5(1.5-1)}{2}\times12+\frac{1.5(1.5-1)(1.5-2)}{6}\times6+0+0$$

$$=10+13.5+\frac{.75}{2}\times6+1.5\times.5\times-.5$$

$$=10+13.5+4.5-.375$$

$$=28-.375$$

$$=27.625=27.6$$

$$f(2.5)=27.6$$

(b) Find the positive root of the equation x^3-x-1=0 by the fixedpoint method **[7]**

$$f(x)=X^3-X-1=0$$

let

$$X=0,\ f_{(x)}=0-0-1=-1$$

$$x=2,\ f_{(1)}=1-1-1=-1$$

$$x=2, f_{(2)}=8-2-1=5$$

we see that sign changes from -ve to +ve Hence we take 2 initial values of x as a =1, b = 2

I approximation

$$x_1 = a - \frac{(b-a)f(a)}{f(b)-f(a)}$$

$$X_1 = 1 - \frac{(2-1)}{5-(-1)} \times -1 = 1 + \frac{1}{6} = \frac{7}{6} = 1.16666 = 1.27$$

$$\therefore f\left(\frac{7}{6} = 1.27\right) = \left(\frac{7}{6}\right)^3 - \left(\frac{7}{6}\right) - 1 = \frac{343}{216} - \frac{7}{6} - 1 = \frac{343-1512-1296}{216 \times 6}$$

$$= -\frac{2465}{1296} = -1.90$$

$$f(1.27) = -1.90$$

Since f(1.27) and f(2) have different signs, the root lies between 1.27 and 2

a = 1.27, b = 2

II approximation

$$X_2 = a - \frac{(b-a)f(a)}{f(b)-f(a)} = 1.27 - \frac{(2-1.27)}{5-(-1.9)} \times -1.9$$

$$= 1.27 - \frac{.73}{6.9} \times -1.9$$

$$= 1.27 + \frac{.73 \times 19}{19} = 1.27 + \frac{13.87}{69} = 1.27 + .2010$$

$$= 1.27 + 2.010101 = 3.28$$

$$= 3.28$$

$$f(x_2) = (3.28)^3 - 3.28 - 1 = 35.29 - 4.28 = 31.007552$$

$$f(x_2) = 31.01 > 0$$

$\therefore$ approximate root is 3.28

IMPORTANT QUESTIONS

Q1. Evaluate the sum $S = \sqrt{3} + \sqrt{5} + \sqrt{7}$ to 4 significant digits and find its absolute and relative errors.

Given :

$$\sqrt{3} = 1.732, \quad \sqrt{5} = 2.236 \text{ and } \sqrt{7}=2.646$$

Hence S = 6.614

and

$$E_A = 0.0005 + 0.0005 + 0.0005$$
$$= 0.0015$$

The total absolute error shows that the sum is correct to 3 significant figures only. Hence we take S = 6.61 and then $E_R = \frac{0.0015}{6.61} = 0.0002.$

Q2. Find the root of the equation 2x = cos x + 3 correct to three decimal places.

After rewriting the equation in the form

$$x = \frac{1}{2}(\cos x + 3)$$

so that

$$\phi(x) = \frac{1}{2}(\cos x + 3),$$

and

$$|\phi`(x)| = \left|\frac{\sin x}{2}\right| < 1$$

Hence the iteration method can be applied to the eq. (i) and we start with $x_0 = \frac{\pi}{2}$. The successive iterates are

$x_1 = 1.5,$ $x_2 = 1.535,$ $x_3 = 1.518,$
$x_4 = 1.526,$ $x_5 = 1.522,$ $x_6 = 1.524,$
$x_7 = 1.523,$ $x_8 = 1.524$

Hence we take the solution as 1.524 correct to three decimal places.

Q3. Find a double root of the equation
$f(x) = x_3 - x_2 - x + 1 = 0,$

Choosing $x_0 = 0.8$

We have $f'(x) = 3x^2 - 2x - 1,$

and $f''(x) = 6x - 2.$

With $x_0 = 0.8$, we obtain

$$x_0 - 2 \cdot \frac{f(x_0)}{f'(x_0)} = 0.8 - 2 \cdot \frac{0.072}{-(0.68)} = 1.012,$$

and
$$x_0 - \frac{f'(x_0)}{f''(x_0)} = 0.8 - \frac{(-0.68)}{2.8} = 1.043.$$

The closeness of these values indicates that there is a double root near unity. For the next approximation we choose $x_1 = 1.01$ and obtain

$$x_1 - 2\frac{f(x_1)}{f'(x_1)} = 1.01 - 0.0099 = 1.0001,$$

and
$$x_1 - \frac{f'(x_1)}{f''(x_1)} = 1.01 - 0.0099 = 1.0001.$$

We conclude that there is a double root at x = 1.0001 which is sufficiently close to the actual root unity.

On the other hand, if we apply Netwon-Raphson method with $x_0 = 0.8$, we get

$$x_1 = 0.8 + 0.106 = 0.91,$$

and
$$x_2 = 0.91 + 0.046 = 0.96.$$

It is clear that the generalized Newton's method converges more rapidly than the Newton-Raphson method.

Q4. Certain experimental values of x and y are given in the table below:

x	0	2	5	7
y	-1	5	12	20

If $y=a_0 + a_1x$, find approximate values of a_0 and a_1.

After making the following table of values (Table)

Table

x	y	x^2	xy
0	-1	0	0
2	5	4	10
5	12	25	60
7	20	49	140
14	36	78	210

Formulae give the two equations

$$4a_0 + 14a_1 = 36$$

and

$$14a_0 + 78a_1 = 210$$

Solving the above two equations, we obtain

$$a_0 = -1.1381 \text{ and } a_1 = 2.8966$$

Using these values we obtain y(5) = 13.3449.

It may be noted that the given table is obtained from the relation y = -1.0334 + 2.6222 x so that the correct value of y(5) is 12.0776.

Q5. Fit a function of the form

$$y=a_1e^{\lambda_1 x}+A_2e^{\lambda_2 x}$$

to the data given by

x	1.0	1.1	1.2	1.3	1.4	1.5	1.6	1.7	1.8
y	1.54	1.67	1.81	1.97	2.15	2.35	2.58	2.83	3.11

Choosing x_1 = 1.0, 1.2 and x_2 = 1.4, equation gives

$$0.07 = a_1\left[-\int_{1.0}^{1.2} y(x)dx + \int_{1.2}^{1.4} y(x)dx\right]$$

$$+ a_2\left[-\int_{1.0}^{1.2} (1.0 - t)\, y(t)\, dt + \int_{1.2}^{1.4} (1.4 - t)\, y(t)\, dt\right]$$

Evaluating the integrals by Simpson's rule and simplifying, the above equation becomes

$$1.81a_1 + 2.180a_2 = 2.10 \qquad \text{(ii)}$$

Again, choosing $x_1 = 1.4$, $a = 1.6$ and $x_2 = 1.8$, and evaluating the integrals in as before, we obtain the equations

$$2.88a_1 + 3.104a_2 = 3.00 \qquad \text{(iii)}$$

Solving (ii) and (iii) we obtain

$$a_1 = 0.03204 \text{ and } a_2 = 0.9364$$

Equation now gives

$$\lambda^2 - 0.03204\lambda - 0.9364 = 0$$

from which we obtain

$$\lambda_1 = 0.988 = 0.99$$

and

$$\lambda_2 = -0.96$$

Using the method of least squares, we obtain

$$A_1 = 0.499 \quad \text{and } A_2 = 0.491$$

The above data was actually constructed from the function y = cosh x so that $A_1 = A_2 = \frac{1}{2}$, $\lambda_1 = 1.0$ and $\lambda_2 = -1.0$.

Q6. Apply trapezoidal and Simpson's rules to the integral

$$\mathbf{I} = \int_0^1 \sqrt{1 - x^2}\, dx$$

continually having the interval h for better accuracy.

Using 10, 20, 30, 40 and 50 subintervals successively, an electronic computer, with a nine decimal precision, produced the results given in Table. The true value of the integral is $\frac{\pi}{4} = 0.785398163$.

Table

No. of subintervals	Trapezoidal rule	Simpson's rule
10	0.776 129582	0.781 752 040
20	0.782 116220	0.784 111 766
30	0.783 610789	0.784 698 434
40	0.784 236934	0.784 943 838
50	0.784 567 128	0.785 073 144

Q7. Solve the equations

$$3x + y + 2z = 3$$
$$2x - 3y - z = -3$$
$$x + 2y + z = 4.$$

Matrices of Coefficients are as

$$A = \begin{bmatrix} 3 & 1 & 2 \\ 2 & -3 & -1 \\ 1 & 2 & 1 \end{bmatrix}, \quad B = \begin{bmatrix} 3 \\ -3 \\ 4 \end{bmatrix}$$

Here $$|A| = \begin{vmatrix} 3 & 1 & 2 \\ 2 & -3 & -1 \\ 1 & 2 & 1 \end{vmatrix} = 8$$

Also $$A` = \begin{vmatrix} 3 & 2 & 1 \\ 1 & -3 & 2 \\ 2 & -1 & 1 \end{vmatrix}$$

Hence $$A^{-1} = \frac{1}{8}\begin{vmatrix} -1 & 3 & 5 \\ -3 & 1 & 7 \\ 7 & -5 & -11 \end{vmatrix}$$

Now, as a result

$$X = \begin{vmatrix} x \\ y \\ z \end{vmatrix} = A^{-1}B = \frac{1}{8}\begin{bmatrix} -1 & 3 & 5 \\ -3 & 1 & 7 \\ 7 & -5 & -11 \end{bmatrix}\begin{bmatrix} 3 \\ -3 \\ 4 \end{bmatrix}$$

$$= \frac{1}{8}\begin{bmatrix} 8 \\ 16 \\ -8 \end{bmatrix} = \begin{bmatrix} 1 \\ 2 \\ 1 \end{bmatrix}$$

which gives x = 1, y = 2 and z = -1.

This method is obviously unsuitable for solving large systems, since the computation of A^{-1} by cofactors will then become increasingly difficult, and one should therefore adopt methods which do not require the computation of the cofactors.

Q8. Solve the following system

$$\mathbf{2x + y + z = 10}$$
$$\mathbf{3x + 2y + 3z = 18}$$
$$\mathbf{x + 4y + 9z = 16}$$

(a) Gauss Method. In the first stage, the multipliers are -3/2 and -1/2. We multiply the first equation successively by -3/2 and -1/2 and add it to the second and third equations respectively to obtain the equations.

$$\frac{1}{2}y + \frac{3}{2}z = 3$$

and
$$\frac{7}{2}y + \frac{17}{2}z = 11$$

The augmented matrix therefore becomes

$$\begin{bmatrix} 2 & 1 & 1 & 10 \\ 0 & \frac{1}{2} & \frac{3}{2} & 3 \\ 0 & \frac{7}{2} & \frac{17}{2} & 11 \end{bmatrix}$$

At the second stage, we eliminate y from the third equation by multiplying the second equation by -7 and adding it to the third. The resulting system will be upper triangular

$$2x + y + z = 10$$
$$\frac{1}{2}y + \frac{3}{2}z = 3$$
$$-2z = -10$$

Back substitution gives the solution :

$$x = 7,\ y = -9 \text{ and } z = 5.$$

(b) Gauss-Jordan Method. At the end of the first stage, we have as in (a) above

$$\begin{bmatrix} 2 & 1 & 1 & 10 \\ 0 & \frac{1}{2} & \frac{3}{2} & 3 \\ 0 & \frac{7}{2} & \frac{17}{2} & 11 \end{bmatrix}$$

Now, instead of eliminating y from the third equation only, we shall eliminate it from the first equation also. This reduces the system to

$$-7x + 0y + 5z = -24$$

$$\frac{1}{2}y + \frac{3}{2}z = 3$$

$$-2z = -10.$$

The elimination is now trivial and gives the same result as before.

Q9. Find the Lagrange's Interpolating Polynomial for the following data and hence find the value of f(6).

x	2	4	7	11	13
f(x)	7	11.5	16.5	25.5	30

The given data is

$x_0 = 2$	$f(x_0) = 7$
$x_1 = 4$	$f(x_1) = 11.5$
$x_2 = 7$	$f(x_2) = 16.5$
$x_3 = 11$	$f(x_3) = 25.5$
$x_4 = 13$	$f(x_4) = 30$

Lagrange's Interpolating Polynomial is

$$f(x) = \frac{(x - x_1)(x - x_2)(x - x_3)(x - x_4)}{(x_0 - x_1)(x_0 - x_2)(x_0 - x_3)(x_0 - x_4)} f(x_0)$$

$$+ \frac{(x - x_0)(x - x_2)(x - x_3)(x - x_4)}{(x_1 - x_0)(x_1 - x_2)(x_1 - x_3)(x_1 - x_4)} f(x_1)$$

$$+ \frac{(x - x_0)(x - x_1)(x - x_3)(x - x_4)}{(x_2 - x_0)(x_2 - x_2)(x_2 - x_3)(x_2 - x_4)} f(x_2)$$

$$+ \frac{(x - x_0)(x - x_1)(x - x_2)(x - x_4)}{(x_3 - x_0)(x_3 - x_1)(x_3 - x_2)(x_3 - x_4)} f(x_3)$$

$$+ \frac{(x - x_0)(x - x_1)(x - x_2)(x - x_3)}{(x_4 - x_0)(x_4 - x_1)(x_4 - x_2)(x_4 - x_3)} f(x_4)$$

$$= \frac{(x - 4)(x - 7)(x - 11)(x - 13)}{(-2)(-5)(-9)(-11)}(7) \frac{(x - 2)(x - 7)(x - 11)(x - 13)}{(2)(-3)(-7)(-9)}(11.5)$$

$$+ \frac{(x - 2)(x - 4)(x - 11)(x - 13)}{(5)(3)(-5)(-6)}(16.5) + \frac{(x - 2)(x - 4)(x - 7)(x - 13)}{(9)(7)(4)(-2)}(25.5)$$

$$+ \frac{(x - 2)(x - 4)(x - 7)(x - 11)}{(11)(9)(6)(2)}(30)$$

On simplification,

$f(x) = -0.0120x^4 + 0.3659x^3 - 3.6621x^2 + 15.4205x - 11.9274$

therefore $f(6) = -0.0120(6)^4 + 0.3659(6)^3 - 3.6621(6)^2 + 15.4205(6) - 11.9274$

$= 12.2424$ (approximately)

Q10. To the following points

X	0	1	2	3	4	5	6	7	8	9
Y	11.0	3.33	2.20	1.52	1.00	0.91	0.82	0.66	0.56	0.49

Fit the following curves

(i) a straight line

(ii) a curve of the form $\frac{1}{a + bx}$

X	Y	xy	Y = 1/y
0	11.0	0	0.09
1	3.33	3.33	0.30
2	2.20	4.4	0.45
3	1.52	4.56	0.66
4	1.00	4	1.00
5	0.91	4.55	1.10
6	0.82	4.92	1.22
7	0.66	4.62	1.52
8	0.56	4.48	1.79
9	0.49	4.41	2.04

(i) for a straight line normal equations are :

$\Sigma y = na + b\Sigma x$

$\Sigma xy = a\Sigma x + b\Sigma x^2$

here $\Sigma y = 22.49$ $\Sigma x = 45$ $\Sigma x^2 = 285$ & $\Sigma xy = 39.27$

therefore the equations become

$22.49 = 10a + 45b$

$39.37 = 45a + 285b$

solving the equations we get

$b = 0.75, a = 562$

fitted line is $y = 5.62 - 0.75\ x$

(ii) The curve is $y = \frac{1}{a + bx}$

let $y = 1/y$ therefore $Y = 1/y$

hence we have to fit

$Y = a + bx$

therefore the normal equations are

$\Sigma Y = na + b\Sigma x^2$

$\Sigma xY = a\Sigma x^2 + b\Sigma x^2$

there $\Sigma Y = 10.16, \Sigma xY = 10$

hence the equations are

$10.16 = 10a + 45b$

$10 = 45a + 285$

solving them we get $\hat{a} = 2.95$ $\hat{b} = -0.43$

the fitted curve is

$$y = \frac{1}{2.95 + (-0.42)x}$$

Q11. Compare Fixed point method, Newton's Rapson method, Secent method, Bisection method and Regula falsi method.

Method	**order of convergence**	**Comparision of order of convergence**	**Amount of computational effort**	**Sensitivity of the method to the starting value & the intermediate value**
1.Fixed Point Method	order of convergence is generally 1 i.e., linear convergence or 1st order convergence	Smallest	Easy to program	
2. Newton's Rapson method	order of convergence is 2 i.e., conerges quadratically	Faster than secent method	Computational effort to compute f(x) and f` (x) is considerable. It is time consuming	It may diverse if f(x) is near zero anytime during the iterative cycle.
3. Secent Method	Order of Convergence is 1.618 ≈1.62	Faster than fixed point method Second is not guaranted converge		
4. Bisection method	Guranteed to converge	but convergence is slow		
5. Regula falsi	Order to Convergence is 1	Guaranted to converge but it is slow		

CS-71 : COMPUTER ORIENTED NUMERICAL TECHNIQUES
JUNE 2005

Note : *Question no. 1 is* **compulsory.** *Answer any* **three** *from the rest.*

Q1(a). Find, by the bisection method, the interval of length 0.125 in which the positive root of the equation $2^x - x - 3 = 0$ lies. [4]

Let $f(x) = 2^x - x - 3 = 0$

$$f(2) = -1, f(3) = 2$$
$$f(2) \times f(3) < 0$$
$$f(2.4) = -0.122, f(2.5) = 0.157$$
$$f(2.4) \times f(2.5) < 0$$

∴ The smallest interval is [2.4, 2.5], in which the root of f(x) lies.

a = 2.4, b = 2.5

a	f(a)	b	f(b)	$m = \frac{a+b}{2}$	f(m)
2.4	-	2.5	+	2.45	+
2.4	-	2.45	+	2.425	-
2.425	-	2.45	+	2.4375	-
2.4375	-	2.45	+	2.44375	-
2.44375	-	2.45	+	2.446875	-

∴ The least positive root of f(x) is 2.446875, which lies in the interval [2.44375, 2.45]

(b) Given that one of the roots of the equation $x^3 - 2x - 5 = 0$ lies between 1.75 and 2.50, show one iteration of the Regula – Falsi method and mention the interval in which the root lies. [3]

Let $f(x) = x^3 - 2x - 5 = 0$

$$f(1.75) = -3.141$$
$$f(2.5) = 5.625$$
$$f(1.75) \times f(2.5) < 0$$

$\therefore$ The root of f(x) lies in the interval [1.75, 2.50]

$$x_0 = 1.75, x_1 = 2.5$$

The Regula-Falsi iteration Scheme is

$$x_{n+1} = \frac{x_{n-1}f(x_n) - x_n f(x_{n-1})}{f(x_n) - f(x_{n-1})}, \qquad x = 1, 2, 3, ...$$

$$x_1 = \frac{x_0 f(x_1) - x_1 f(x_0)}{f(x_1) - f(x_0)}$$

$$= \frac{1.75(-3.141) - 2.5(5.625)}{-3.141 - -5.625}$$

$$x_1 = 2.231$$

Hence the root of f(x) = $= x^3 - 2x - 5 = 0$ lies in the interval [1.75, 2.50] and the approximate root is 2.231.

(c) Find the values of the function f(x) = cos x – x² – x at x = 0 and x = 1. Taking x_0 = 0.5, compute by Newton – Raphson's method the next estimate x_1 for the zero of the function. [3]

$f(x) = \cos x - x^2 - x$ at x = *0* and *x* = *1*. Taking $x_0 = 0.5$, compute the Newton-Raphson's method the next estimate x_1 for the zero the function.

$$f(x)\cos x^2 - x = 0$$

$$x_0 = 0.5$$

the Newton- Raphson's iterative Scheme is

$$x_{n+1} = x_n - \frac{f(x_n)}{f'(x_n)'} \qquad b = 0, 1, 2., 3, ...$$

$$f'(x) = \textit{-sinx - 2x - 1}$$

$$x_1 = x_0 - \frac{f(x_0)}{f'(x_0)}$$

$$= 0.5 - \frac{f(0.5)}{f'(0.5)}$$

$$= 0.5 - \frac{Cos(0.5) - (0.5)^2 - (0.5)}{-Sin'(0.5) - 2 \times 0.5 - 1}$$

$$= 0.5 - \frac{0.128}{(-2.479)}$$

$$x_1 = 0.552$$

Hence, the value of x_1 is 0.552 up to 3 decimal digits.

(d) (i) Prove $\Delta - \nabla = \Delta\nabla$

$\Delta - \nabla = \Delta\nabla$

L.H.S. $\Delta - \nabla = (E - 1) - \left(1 - E^{-1}\right)$

$(E - 1)\left(1 - E^{-1}\right)$

$\Delta\nabla = \text{R. H. S.}$

(ii) Find $\Delta^2 x^2$ taking h = 1. **[4]**

Find $\Delta^2 x^2$ taking $h = 15$

$$f[x_{k1}, \ldots\ldots, x_{k+n}] = \frac{1}{n!h^n}\Delta^n f_k$$

$$= \frac{1}{2!(1)}\Delta^2$$

(e) Using Newton's forward difference formula, find the lowest degree polynomial passing through the points (0, 1), (2, 7), (4, 21) and (6, 43).[3]

(0, 1) (2, 7) (4, 21) and (6, 43)

x	f(x)	Δf	$\Delta^2 f$	$\Delta^3 f$
$x_0 = 0$	1			
		6		
$x_1 = 2$	7		8	
		14		0
$x_2 = 4$	21		8	
		22		
$x_3 = 6$	43			

$$p(x) = f(x) + \frac{(x - x_0)\Delta f(x)}{1!h} + \frac{(x - x_0)(x - x_1)\Delta^2 f(x)}{2!h^2}$$

$$= 1 + \frac{(x-0)6}{2} + \frac{(x-0)(x-2)8}{2 \times 2^2} + 0$$

$$= 1 + 3(x) + x(x - 2)$$

$$= 1 + 3(x) + x^2 - 2x$$

$$p(x) = x^2 + x + 1$$

Hence, $p(x) = x^2 + x + 1$ represent a second degree polynomial.

(f) Compute $\sqrt{5}$ by Lagrange's method from the following data : [4]

x	1	4	9
$\sqrt{x}$	1	2	3

xf(x) = $\sqrt{x}$

$x_0 = 1$ 1

$x_1 = 4$ 2

$x_2 = 9$ 3

$$p(x) = \frac{(x-x_1)(x-x_2)}{(x_0-x_1)(x_0-x_2)} f(x_0) + \frac{(x-x_0)(x-x_1)}{(x_1-x_0)(x_1-x_2)} f(x_1) + ----$$

$$p(x) = \frac{(5-4)(5-9)}{(1-4)(1-9)} \times 1 + \frac{(5-1)(5-9)}{(4-1)(4-9)} \times 2 + \frac{(5-1)(5-4)}{(9-1)(9-4)} \times 3$$

$$= \frac{(1)(-4)(1)}{(-3)(-8)} + \frac{(4)(-4)(2)}{(3)(-5)} + \frac{(4)(1)(3)}{(8)(5)}$$

$$= \frac{-1}{6} + \frac{32}{15} + \frac{3}{10} = 2.267$$

Hence, P(5) = 2.267 approximately.

(g) Solve the following system of equations by the Gaussian Elimination method: [3]

2x + y + z = 10
3x + 2y + 3z = 18
x + 4y + 9z = 16

Let $A = \begin{bmatrix} 2 & 1 & 1 \\ 3 & 2 & 3 \\ 1 & 4 & 9 \end{bmatrix}$. $B = \begin{bmatrix} 10 \\ 18 \\ 16 \end{bmatrix}$

$$[A|B] = \begin{bmatrix} 2 & 1 & 1|10 \\ 3 & 2 & 3|18 \\ 1 & 4 & 9|16 \end{bmatrix}$$

Operating $R_2 \to R_3 - 7R_2$

$$=\begin{bmatrix} 2 & 1 & 1 & | 10 \\ 0 & 1/2 & 3/2 & | 3 \\ 0 & 7/2 & 17/2 & | 11 \end{bmatrix}$$

Operating $R_3 \to R_3 - 7R_2$

$$=\begin{bmatrix} 2 & 1 & 1 & | 10 \\ 0 & 1/2 & 3/2 & | 3 \\ 0 & 0 & -2 & | -10 \end{bmatrix}$$

Using Backward Substitution,

$$-2z = -10 \Rightarrow z = 5$$

$$1/2y + 3/2z = 3 \Rightarrow y + 3z = 6$$

$$\Rightarrow y = 6 - 3(5)$$

y = - 9

y = - 9

2x + y + z = 10

$$\Rightarrow 2x = 10 + 9 - 5$$

$$\Rightarrow 2x = 14$$

$$\Rightarrow x = 7$$

Hence, x = 7, y - -9, z = 5

(h) Show only three iterations of the Gauss - Seidel method for solving the equations

2x + y + z = 5

3x + 5y + 2z = 15

2x + y + 4z = 8 **[6]**

Using Gauss - Seidal iteration Scheme

$$x = \frac{5 - y - z}{2}$$

$$y = \frac{15 - 3x - 2z}{5}$$

$$z = \frac{8 - 2x - y}{4}$$

initially, we take $X^0 = \begin{bmatrix} 0 \\ 0 \\ 0 \end{bmatrix}$

First Iteration

$$x = \frac{5 - 0 - 0}{2} 2.5$$

$$y = \frac{15 - 3(2.5) - 2(0)}{5} = 1.5$$

$$z = \frac{8 - 2(2.5) - 1.5}{4} = 0.375$$

$$\therefore x' = \begin{bmatrix} 2.5 \\ 1.5 \\ 0.375 \end{bmatrix}$$

Second Iteration

$$x = \frac{5 - 1.5 - 0.375}{2} = 1.5625$$

$$y = \frac{15 - 3(1.5625) - 2(0.375)}{5} = 1.9125$$

$$z = \frac{8 - 2(1.5625) - 1.9125}{4} = 0.7406$$

$$\therefore X^2 = \begin{bmatrix} 1.5625 \\ 1.9125 \\ 0.7406 \end{bmatrix}$$

Third Iteration

$$x = \frac{5 - 1.9125 - 0.7406}{2} = 1.1735$$

$$y = \frac{15 - 3(1.1735) - 2(0.7406)}{5} = 1.9997$$

$$z = \frac{8 - 2(1.1735) - 1.9997}{4} = 0.9133$$

$$\therefore X^3 = \begin{bmatrix} 1.1735 \\ 1.9997 \\ 0.9133 \end{bmatrix}$$

Hence, the values after three iterations are

x = 1.1735, y = 1.9997, z = 0,9133

Q2(a). The root of the equation $x^3 + x^2 - 1 = 0$ lies between 0.5 and 1.0. Show that by choosing $x = \frac{1}{\sqrt{1+x}}$, the method of successive iterations

will converge. Hence compute the root correct upto 3 significant digits. **[7]**

$f(x) = x^3 + x^2 - 1 = 0$

Let $g(x) = x = \dfrac{1}{\sqrt{1+x}}$

$g^1(x) = \dfrac{1}{2(1+x)^{3/2}}$ $g'(x)_{at\ x=0.5} \left|\dfrac{-1}{2(1+0.5)^{3/2}}\right| = 0.272 < 1$

$\therefore$ by choosing $x = \dfrac{1}{\sqrt{1+x}}$, the method of successive iterations will converge.

$\therefore x_{n+1} = \dfrac{1}{\sqrt{1+x_n}}, n = 0,1,2,3,......$

and $x_0 = 0.5$

if n = 0, $x_1 = \dfrac{1}{\sqrt{1+x_0}} = \dfrac{1}{\sqrt{1+0.5}} = 0.816$

if n = 1, $x_2 = \dfrac{1}{\sqrt{1+x_1}} = \dfrac{1}{\sqrt{1+0.816}} = 0.742$

if n = 2, $x_3 = \dfrac{1}{\sqrt{1+x_2}} = \dfrac{1}{\sqrt{1+0.742}} = 0.758$

(b) Compute y(2.35) from the following table (use upto third differences only) : **[8]**

x	2.00	2.25	2.50	2.75	3.00
y	9.00	10.06	11.25	12.56	14.00

x	f(x)	Δf	$\Delta^2 f$	$\Delta^3 f$	$\Delta^4 f$
2	9				
		1.06			
2.25	10.06		0.13		
		1.19		-0.01	
2.5	11.25		0.12		0.02
		1.31		0.01	
2.75	12.56		0.13		
		1.44			
3	14				

$$P(x)=f(x)+\frac{(x-x_0)}{1!h}\Delta f(x)+\frac{(x-x_0)(x-x_1)}{2!h^2}\Delta^2 f(x)+$$

$$\frac{(x-x_0)(x-x_1)(x-x_2)}{3!h^3}\Delta^3 f(x)+\frac{(x-x_0)(x-x_1)(x-x_2)(x-x_3)\Delta^4 f(x)}{4!h^4}$$

$$P(2.35)=9+\frac{(2.35-2)1.06}{1\times 0.25}+\frac{(2.35-2)(2.35-2.25)0.13}{2\times(0.25)^2}$$

$$+\frac{(2.35-2)(2.35-2.25)(2-2.5)(-0.01)}{6\times(0.25)^3}$$

= 9 + 1.484 + 0.0364 + 0.0018667
= 10.5222
Hence P(2.35) = y (2.35) = 10.52 (approx.)

Q3(a). Construct divided difference table and find the polynomial satisfying the following data : [8]

x	**0**	**1**	**4**	**5**
y	**8**	**11**	**68**	**123**

Using the polynomial, find the value of y at x = 2.

Hence f[..] = $\frac{11-8}{1-0}=3$

x	f(x)	f[..]	f[...]	f[....]
$x_0=0$	8			
$x_1=1$	11	$\frac{11-8}{1-0}=3$		
$x_2=4$	68	$\frac{68-11}{4-1}=19$	$\frac{19-3}{4-0}=4$	
$x_3=5$	123	$\frac{123-68}{5-4}=55$	$\frac{55-19}{5-1}=9$	$\frac{9-4}{5-0}=1$

$$P(x)=f[.]+(x-x_0)f[..]+(x-x_0)(x-x_1)f[...]+(x-x_0)(x-x_1)(x-x_2)f[....]$$

$$= 8+(x\text{-}0)(3)+(x\text{-}0)(x\text{-}1)(4)+(x\text{-}0)(x\text{-}1)(x\text{-}4)(1)$$

$$= 8+3x+4x^2\text{-}4x+x^3 - 5x^2 + 4x = x^3 - x^2 + 3x + 8$$

Hence, the polynomial obtained is $P(X) = x^3 - x^2 + 3x + 8$ and P (2) $= 2^3 = 2^2 + 3(2) + 8 = 18$

(b) Find the cube-root of 10 by Newton - Raphson's method, correct upto three places of decimal. **[7]**

Let x = $\sqrt[3]{10}$

$$x^3 = 10$$

$$f(x) = x^3 - 10 = 0, f'(x) = 3x^2$$

$$\because f(2) = -2(-ve)$$

$$f(2.10 = .648(+ve)$$

$\therefore$ We conclude that root lies between 2 and 2.1

$$x_0 = \frac{2+2.1}{2} = \frac{4.1}{2} = 2.05$$

$$\therefore x_1 = x_0 - \frac{f(x_0)}{f(x_0)} = 2.05 - \frac{(2.05)^3 - 10}{3(2.5)^2} = 2.5 - \frac{.8615125 - 10}{12.6075}$$

$$= 2.05 - \frac{15.6250}{18.750} = 2.05 - \frac{(-1.384875)}{12.6075}$$

$$= 2.05 + 1.098 = 2.1598 = 2.16$$

$$= \boxed{x_3 = 2.16}$$

$$x_2 = x_1 - \frac{f(x_1)}{f(x_1)} = 2.16 - \frac{(2.16)^3 - 10}{3 \times (2.16)^2}$$

$$x_2 = 2.16 - \frac{0.077696}{13.9968}$$

$$= 2.16 - 0.00555$$

$$= 2.15444$$

$$\boxed{x_2 = 2.154}$$

$$x3 = x2 - \frac{f(x_2)}{f(x_2)} = 2.154 - \frac{(2.154)^3 - 10}{3 \times (2.154)^2}$$

$$= 2.154 - \frac{(-00605174)}{f(13.919148)}$$

$$= 2.154 + .000434778$$
$$= 2.153565222$$

$\boxed{x_3 = 2.154}$ (on rounding)

we see that x_2 and x_3 are just near to each other.

$\therefore$ 2.154 be the cube root of 10 upto three decimal places.
Hence, the exact root of f(x) upto 3 decimal digits is 2.154.

Q4(a). From the following data estimate the number of students getting marks between 20 and 25. **[7]**

Marks Below	No. of Students
10	20
20	45
30	115
40	210
50	325

x	f(x)	∇f	$\nabla^2 f$	$\nabla^3 f$	$\nabla^4 f$
10	20				
		25			
20	45		45		
		70		-20	
30	115		25		15
		95		-5	
40	210		20		
		115			
50	325				

Using Newton's Backward interpolation,

$P(x) = P(xn + hu) = f(x) + u\nabla f(x) +$

$$\frac{u(u+1)}{2!}\nabla^2 f(x)+\frac{u(u+1)(u+2)}{3!}\nabla^3 f(x)+\frac{4(u+1)(u+2)(u+3)}{4!}\nabla^4 f(x)$$

here h = 10

x = xn + hu

20 = 50 + 10u

and 25 = 50 + 10u

u = -3 u = -2.5

$$P(20) = 325 + (-3)(115) + \frac{(-3)(-3+1)(20)}{2} +$$

$$\frac{(-3)(-3+1)(-3+2)(-5)}{6}+\frac{(-3)(-3+1)(-3+2)(-3+3)(15)}{24}$$

= 325 - 345 + 60 + 5 + 0

P(20) = 45

P(25) = 325 + (-2.5)(115) +

$$\frac{(-2.5)(-2.5+1)(20)}{2}+\frac{(-2.5)(-2.5+1)(-2.5+2)(-5)}{24}$$

= 325 - 287.5 + 37.5 + 1.5625 - 0.5859376

= 75.97656250

P(Marks between 20 and 25) $= P(20 \le x \le 25) = P(25) - P(20)$

= 75.97656250-45

= 30.97656250.

= 30.976 $\cong 30$

Hence, the number of students getting marks between 20 and 25 is 30.

(b) Integrate $\int_0^1 \frac{1}{1+x^2}$ dx by Simpson's rule, with $h = \frac{1}{6}$. **[5]**

$\int_0^1 \frac{1}{1x^2}$ dx $x_0 = a = 0, b = 1$

$$h=\frac{b-a}{n}=\frac{1=0}{5}=0.2$$

i	x_i	$y_1 = \frac{1}{1+x_1^2}$
0	$x_0 = 0$	$y_0 = \frac{1}{1+0^2} = 1$
1.	$x_1 = x_0 + h = 0 + 0.2 = 0.2$	$y_1 = \frac{1}{1+(0.2)^2} = 0.9615$
2.	$x_2 = x_0 + 2h = 0.4$	$y_2 = \frac{1}{1+(0.4)^2} = 0.8621$

3. $x_3 = x_0 + 3h = 0.6$ $\qquad y_3 = \dfrac{1}{1+(0.6)^2} = 0.7353$

4. $x_4 = x_0 \; 4h = 0.8$ $\qquad y_4 = \dfrac{1}{1+(0.8)^2} = 0.6098$

5. $x_5 = x_0 + 5h = 1$ $\qquad y_5 = \dfrac{1}{1+1^2} = 0.5$

By Simpson's's Rule,

$$\int_a^b f(x)\,dx = \frac{h}{3}\left[(y_0 + y_n) + 4(y_1 + y_3 + y_5......) + 2(y_2 + y_4 + ...)\right]$$

$$\cdot\int_a^b \frac{1dx}{1+x^2} = \frac{h}{3}\left[(y_0 + y_5) + 4(y_1 + y_3) + 2(y_2 + y_4)\right]$$

$$= \frac{1}{5\times 3}\left[(1+0.5) + 4(0.9615 + 0.7353) + 2(0.6098)\right]$$

$$= \frac{1}{15}[11.23] = 0.74873$$

hence $\displaystyle\int_0^1 \frac{1}{1+x^2}dx = 0.74873$

(c) If a = 0.36, b = 0.41 and c = 0.70, using two decimal digit arithmetic with rounding check whether $\dfrac{a - b}{c} = \dfrac{a}{c} - \dfrac{b}{c}$ or not. [3]

a = 0.36 b = 0.41 c = 0.70

L.H.S. $\dfrac{a-b}{c} = \dfrac{0.36-0.41}{0.70} = \dfrac{-0.05}{0.70} = -0.07$

R.H.S $\dfrac{a}{c} - \dfrac{b}{c} = \dfrac{0.36}{0.70} - \dfrac{0.41}{0.70}$

= 0.51- 0.59 = -0.08

Hence $\dfrac{a-b}{c} \neq \dfrac{a}{c} - \dfrac{b}{c}$

Q5(a). Solve the following equation by the Gauss - Jacobi method, upto 3 decimal places : [7]

$2x_1 - 3x_2 + 20x_3 = 25$

$20x_1 - x_2 + 2x_3 = 17$

$3x_1 - 20x_2 - x_3 = -18$

$2x_1 - 3x_2 - 20x_3 = 25$
$20x_1 + x_2 - 2x_3 = 17$
$3x_1 + 20x_2 - 2x_3 = -18$

Now we eliminate x_1, x_2 and x_3 from above three equations respectively.

First, $\dfrac{25 + 3x_2 - 20x_3}{2}$

$$x_2 = 17 - 20x_1 + 2x$$
$$x_3 = 18 + 3x_1 + 20x_2$$

Initially

$$X^0 = \begin{bmatrix} 0 \\ 0 \\ 0 \end{bmatrix}$$

Using Gauss-Jacobi method:

First iteration

$$x_1 = \frac{25 + 3(0) - 20(0)}{2} = 12.5$$
$$x_1 = 17 - 20(0) + 2(0) = 17$$
$$x_2 = 18 + 3(0) + 20(0) = 18$$

$$\therefore X^1 = \begin{bmatrix} 12.5 \\ 17 \\ 18 \end{bmatrix}$$

Second iteration

$$x_1 = \frac{25 + 3(17) + -20(18)}{2} = -142$$
$$x_2 = 17 - 2\ (12.5) + 2\ (18) = -197$$
$$x_3 = 18 + 3(12.5) + 20(17) = 395.5$$

$$\therefore X^2 = \begin{bmatrix} -142 \\ -197 \\ 395.5 \end{bmatrix}$$

Third Iteration

$$x_1 = \frac{25 + 3(-197) - 20(395.5)}{2} = -4238$$
$$x_2 = 7 - 20(-142) + 2(395.5) = 3648$$
$$x_3 = 18 + 3(-142) + 20(-197) = 4348$$

$$\therefore X^3 = \begin{bmatrix} -4238 \\ 3648 \\ -4348 \end{bmatrix}$$

(b) Find f' (x) at x = 0.1 from the following table of values :

x	0.1	0.2	0.3	0.4	0.5
f(x)	10	19	40	79	142

Also find the value of f''(0.1). **[6]**

x	f(x)	Δf	$\Delta^2 f$	$\Delta^3 f$	$\Delta^4 f$
0.1	10				
		9			
0.2	19		12		
		21		6	
0.3	40		18		0
		39		6	
0.4	79		24		
		63			
0.5	142				

$x = x_0 + uh, \qquad x_0 = 0.1, x = 0.1$

$0.1 = 0.1 + u(0.1)$

$\Rightarrow u = 0$

$$f'(x) = \frac{1}{h}\left[\Delta f(x) + \frac{2u-1}{2!}\Delta^2 f(x) + \frac{(3u^2 - 6u + 2)}{3!}\Delta^3 f(x) + 0\right]$$

$$= \frac{1}{0.1}\left[9 + \frac{(-1)}{2}\times 12 + \frac{2}{6}\times 6\right]$$

$$f'(x) = \frac{1}{0.1}[9 - 6 + 2] = 50$$

$$f''(x) = \frac{1}{h}\left[\Delta^2 f(x) + (u-1)\Delta^3 f(x)\right]$$

$$= \frac{1}{0.1}\left[12 + (-1)6\right] = \frac{6}{0.1} = 60$$

Hence f'(0.1) = 50
and f' (0.1) = 60

(c) List any two sources of errors. [2]

Sources of errors: We are listing below the types of errors that are encountered while carrying out numerical calculation to solve a problem:

1. Round off errors arise due to floating point representation of initial data in the machine. Subsequent errors in the solution of problem due to floating point representation of data are called propagated error.

2. Due to finite digit arithmetic operation, the computer generates in the solution of a problem, and that errors are known as generated error or rounding error.

3. Sensitivity of algorithm of the numerical process used for solving a problem affects accuracy of the solution of the problem and is know as instability and the process is said to be unstable.

4. Error due to finite representation of an inherently infinite process. For example, consider the use of a finite number of terms in an infinite series expansion of sinx, cosx, or f(x) y Maclaurin's or Taylor's Series expansion. Such errors are called truncation error.

CS-71 : COMPUTER ORIENTED NUMERICAL TECHNIQUES
DEC - 2005

Note : *Question no. 1 is* **compulsory.** *Answer any* **three** *from the rest.*

Q1(a). Write down the Newton-Raphson formula to find $\sqrt{10}$. Starting from the initial value x_0 = 3, find the next two estimates. Compute upto two decimals. **[3]**

Let us take x = $\sqrt{10}$ so that $x^2 - 10 = 0$

From this it is clear that $x^2 - 10$ becomes -ve for x = 3 whereas it is +ve for x = 3.2

Hence the root of $x^2 - 10 = 0$ lies in the interval (3, 3.2). Further let f(x) = $x^2 - 10$, so that the given equation f(x) = 0. Again $f'(x) = 2x$. Now by Newton - Raphson Method, we have :

$$x_{n+1} = x_n - \frac{f(x_n)}{f'(x_n)} \Rightarrow x_1 = x_o - \frac{f(x_o)}{f'(x_o)}$$

$$= 3 - \frac{f(3)}{f'(3)} \text{ where } x_o = 3$$

$$= 3 - \frac{(3^2 - 10)}{2 \times 3}$$

$$= 3 - \left(\frac{-1}{6}\right)$$

$$= 3 + \frac{1}{6} = \frac{19}{6} = 3.16666$$

$$x_1 = 3.1666$$

Again we have :

$$x_2 = x_1 - \frac{f(x_1)}{f'(x_1)} = 3.1666 - \frac{(x_1^2 - 10)}{2x_1}$$

$$x_2 = 3.1666 - \frac{\{(3.1666)^2 - 10\}}{2 \times 3.1666}$$

$$x_2 = 3.1666 - \frac{0.02735556}{6.3332}$$

$$x_2 = 3.1709$$

$$x_3 = x_2 - \frac{f(x_2)}{f'(x_2)} = 3.1709 - \frac{\left(x_2^2 - 10\right)}{2x_2}$$

$$= 3.1709 - \frac{\left((3.1709)^2 - 10\right)}{2 \times 3.1709}$$

$$x_3 = 3.1623$$

$\therefore$ x_1 *and* x_3 are very similar, so $\sqrt{10}$ =3.16 (Upto 2 places of decimal)

(b) Show that a root of the equation $x^3 + x - 6 = 0$ lies between 1 and 2. Perform the next two iterations of Regula - Falsi method towards computing the root. Compute upto two decimal places. [5]

Let $y = x^3 + x - 6 = 0$

<u>For first approximation</u>

at $x_1 = 1, \quad y_1 = -4$

at $x_2 = 2, \quad y_2 = 4$

$$\therefore x^{(1)} = x_1 + \frac{\left|(x_2 - x_1)\right| . \left|y_1\right|}{\left|y_1\right| + \left|y_2\right|} = 1 + \frac{(2-1)\left|1-4\right|}{\left|-4\right| + \left|4\right|}$$

$$1 + \frac{1 \times 4}{4+4} = 1 + \frac{4}{8} = 1 + \frac{1}{2} = \frac{3}{2} = 1.5$$

<u>For second approximation, we have</u>

$x_1 = 1.5, \ y_1 = (1.5)^3 + (1.5) - 6 = -1.125$

$x_2 = 1.6, \ y_2 = (1.6)^3 + (1.6) - 6 = -304$

$$x^{(2)} = 1.5 + \frac{0.1 \times 1.125}{1.125 \times 304} = 1.5 + \frac{0.1125}{0.342}$$

$x^{(2)} = 1.828 \cong 1.83$

<u>Again for IIIrd approximation</u> :

$x_1 = 1.83, \ y_1 = (1.83)^3 + 1.83 - 6 = 1.96$

$x_2 = 1.84,\ y_2 = (1.84)^3 + 1.83 - 6 = 2.06$

$$x^{(3)} = 1.83 + \frac{(1.84-1.83).(1.96)}{1.96+2.06} = 1.83 + \frac{0.0196}{4.03}$$

$x^{(3)} = 1.834 \cong 1.83$

$\Rightarrow that\, the\, root\, is\, 1.83$ which lies between 1 and 2 hence showed.

(c) If f(x) = $\frac{1}{X}$, find Δ^3 f(x). **[3]**

$$\Delta^3\left(\frac{1}{x}\right) = \Delta^2\left\{\Delta\left(\frac{1}{x}\right)\right\}$$

$$= \Delta^2\left\{\frac{1}{x+1} - \frac{1}{x}\right\}$$

$$= \Delta^2\left\{\frac{x-x-1}{x(x+1)}\right\}$$

$$= \Delta^2\left\{\frac{-1}{x^2+x}\right\} = \Delta\left\{\Delta\left(-\frac{1}{x^2+x}\right)\right\}$$

$$= -\Delta\left\{\frac{1}{(x+1)^2+(x+1)} - \frac{1}{x^2+x}\right\}$$

$$= -\Delta\left\{\frac{1}{(x+1)(x+1+1)} - \frac{1}{x(x+1)}\right\}$$

$$= -\Delta\left\{\frac{1}{(x+1)(x+2)} - \frac{1}{x(x+1)}\right\}$$

$$= -\Delta\left\{\frac{x-(x+2)}{x(x+1)(x+2)}\right\}$$

$$= \Delta\left\{\frac{2}{x(x+1)(x+2)}\right\}$$

$$= 2\left\{\frac{1}{(x+1)(x+2)(x+3)} - \frac{1}{x(x+1)(x+2)}\right\}$$

$$= 2\left\{\frac{x-(x-3)}{x(x+1)(x+2)(x+3)}\right\}$$

$$= \left\{ \frac{-6}{x(x+1)(x+2)(x+3)} \right\}$$

$$= \left\{ \frac{-6}{(x^2+1)(x^2+5x+6)} \right\}$$

(d) Show, by the divided difference table that a polynomial of degree three may be made to pass through the points (0, 1) (1, 1), (3, 25), (4, 61) and (6, 211). You do not need to find the actual polynomial. [3]

We have given that the points are (0, 1), (1, 1), 3, 25), (4, 61) and (6, 211) which may be understand as :

x = 0, 1, 3, 4, and 6

f(x) = 1, 1, 25, 61, 211

and we have to construct the divided difference table for the given set of values for thee degree polynomial divided difference table :

x	f(x)	Δ f(x)	Δ^2 f(x)	Δ^3 f(x)
0	1	$\frac{1-1}{1-0}=0$		
1	1	$\frac{25-1}{3-2}=24$	$\frac{24-0}{3-1}=12$	$\frac{4-12}{4-0}=-2$
3	25	$\frac{61-25}{4-3}=36$	$\frac{36-24}{4-1}=4$	
4	61	$\frac{211-61}{6-4}=75$	$\frac{75-36}{6-3}=13$	$\frac{13-4}{6-1}=1.4$
6	211			

(e) Find the cube root of 20 by Lagrange's method from the following data: [3]

x	x	8	27	64
y	$\sqrt[3]{x}$	2	3	4

We have to find cube root of 20

Let y = U_x then we are given that a = 8, b = 27, c = 64 and $U_a = 2, U_b = 3, U_c = 4$ and we have to find U_{20} i.e. U_x when x = 20. Now the Lagrange's formula is :

$$\frac{U_x}{(x-a)(x-b)..........(x-m)}=\frac{U_a}{(a-b)(a-c).......(a-m)(x-a)}+........................$$

$\therefore$ Here we have

$$\frac{U_{20}}{(20-8)(20-27)(20-64)}=\frac{2}{(8-27)(8-64)(20-8)}+\frac{3}{(27-8)(27-64)(20-27)}+\frac{4}{(64-8)(64-27)(20-64)}$$

$$\frac{U_{20}}{12\times -7\times -44}=\frac{2}{-19\times -56\times 12}+\frac{3}{19\times -37\times -7}+\frac{4}{56\times 37\times -44}$$

$$\frac{U_{20}}{12\times 7\times 44}=\frac{2}{19\times 56\times 12}+\frac{3}{19\times 37\times 7}-\frac{4}{56\times 37\times 44}$$

$$\frac{U_{20}}{12\times 44}=\frac{2}{19\times 8\times 12}+\frac{3}{19\times 37}-\frac{4}{8\times 37\times 44}$$

$$U_{20}=\frac{2\times 12\times 44}{19\times 8\times 12}+\frac{3\times 12\times 44}{19\times 37}-\frac{4\times 12\times 44}{8\times 37\times 44}$$

$$=\frac{11}{19}+\frac{1584}{703}-\frac{6}{37}$$

$= 0.57895 + 2.253201 - 0.162162162$

$= 2.669989 \cong 2.7$

$U_{20} = 2.7$ (approx.)

Therefore, cube root of 20 is 2.7 (approx.)

(f) Show only three iterations of Gauss - Jacobi method for solving the equation, [6]

3x + 5y + 2z = 15,

2x + y + 4z = 8,

5x + 2y + z = 10.

Ans.

The simultaneous equations are :

8x + 5y + 2z = 15 ....(i)

2x + y + 4z = 8 ....(ii)

5x + 2y + z = 10 ....(iii)

Solution **from (i)**

$$x = \frac{1}{8}(15-5y-2z)$$

from **(ii)** y = (8 - 2x - 4z)

from **(iii)** z = (10 - 5x - 2y)

starting with $x^{(0)}=(0,0,0)^T$

$$\therefore x=x^{(1)}=\frac{15}{8},\ y=y^{(1)}=8,\ z=z^{(1)}=10$$

$$\therefore x^{(1)}=\left[\frac{15}{8},8,10\right]=[1.875,8,10]$$

$$x^{(2)}=-45,\ y^{(2)}=\frac{94}{8},z^{(2)}=-\frac{128}{8}$$

$$x^{(2)}=\left[-45,-\frac{94}{8},-\frac{123}{8}\right]\ or$$

Similarly $x^{(2)}=[-45,-11.75,-2.875]$

$$x^{(3)}=[-6.8195,109.5,258.5] \qquad Ans.$$

(g) Evaluate the integral $\int_{-\pi/2}^{\pi/2}\cos x\,dx$

$$I=\int_{-\pi/2}^{\pi/2}\cos x\,dx=2\int_{0}^{\pi/2}\cos x\,dx$$

Now divide the range of integration into 4 equal parts taking $h=\frac{\pi}{8}$ and then compute the value of the function f(x) = cos x for each point of subdivision. These computed values are as follows:

x	y = cosx	
$x_0=0$	1	y_0
$x_0+h=\frac{II}{8}$	0.99998	y_1
$x_0+2h=\frac{II}{8}\times 2=\frac{II}{4}$	0.707106	y_2
$x_0+3h=\frac{3II}{8}$	0.9998	y_3

(i) by Trapezoidal Rule.

(i) <u>Trapezoidal Rule</u>

$$\int_{-\pi/2}^{\pi/2} \cos x\, dx = 2\int_{0}^{\pi/2} \cos x\, dx$$

$$= 2\left[\frac{h}{2}\{(y_0 + y_3) + 2(y_1 + y_2)\}\right]$$

$$= h\ [(1+.9998)+2(0.9999+0.707106)]$$

$$= \frac{\pi}{8}[1.9998+3.414012]$$

$$= \frac{3.14\times 5.413812}{8}$$

$$= \frac{16.99936968}{8}$$

$= 2.12492121$

$= 2.1$ (which is little greater than actual value (2)) Ans.

(ii) by Simpson's $\frac{1}{3}$ Rule.

Divide the interval into four equal subintervals. **[4]**

$$\int_{-\pi/2}^{\pi/2} \cos x\, dx = 2\int_{0}^{\pi/2} \cos x\, dx$$

$$=2\left[\frac{h}{3}\{(y_0 + y_3)+4(y_1 + y_2)\}\right] \qquad \left(\because h = \pi/8\right)$$

$$= 2\left[\frac{\pi}{24}\{(1+.9998)+4(0.9999+0.707106)\}\right]$$

$$= \frac{\pi}{12}[1.9998+6.828024]$$

$$= \frac{3.14}{12}\times 8.827824$$

$$= \frac{27.71936736}{12}$$

$= 2.30$ (which is some greater than actual value that is 2)

(h) Given $\frac{dy}{dx}$ = x + y, y(0) = 1. Find, by Euler's method, y(0.2) and y(0.6), taking h = 0.2. **[3]**

The given differential equation is

$$\frac{dy}{dx}=x+y=f(x,y)\ Say$$

Initial condition is $x_0=0, y_0=1$, h = 0.2

This gives $f(x_0,y_0)=\left(\frac{dy}{dx}\right)_0=0+1=1$

Now, $y_1^{(1)}=y_0+f(x_0,y_0)\times h=1+1\times 0.2=1.2$

$$f\left(x_1,y_1^{(1)}\right)=\left(\frac{dy}{dx}\right)_1^{(1)}=f\left(x_1,y_1^{(1)}\right)=\left(x_1+y_1^{(1)}\right)$$

$(x_1=0.2)$

$= 0.2 + 1.2 = 1.4$

$$y_1^{(2)}=y_0+\frac{\left(\frac{dy}{dx}\right)_0+\left(\frac{dy}{dx}\right)_1^{(1)}}{2}h=1+\frac{1+1.4}{2}\times 0.2=1.24$$

$$\left(\frac{dy}{dx}\right)_1^{(2)}=f(x_1,y_1^{(2)})$$

$= x_1+y_1^{(2)}$

$= .2 + 1.24 = 1.44$

$$=1+\frac{2.44}{2}\times\frac{2}{10}=1.244$$

$$y.^{(3)}=y_0+\frac{\left(\frac{dy}{dx}\right)_0+\left(\frac{dy}{dx}\right)^2}{2}.h$$

$$=1+\frac{1+1.44}{2}\times 0.2$$

$$=1+\frac{2.44}{2}\times 0.2$$

$= 1.244$

$$\left(\frac{dy}{dx}\right)_1^{(3)}=f(x_1,y_1^{(3)})=x_1+y_1^{(3)}$$

$= 0.2 + 1.244 = 1.444 = 1.44$

$$y_1^{(4)} = y_o + \frac{\left(\frac{dy}{dx}\right)_0 + \left(\frac{dy}{dx}\right)_1^{(3)}}{2} h = 1 + \frac{1+1.44}{2} \times 0.2 = 1.244$$

$y_1^{(4)} = 1.244$

It is obvious that $y_1^{(3)} = y_1^{(4)}$ (nearly) so we stop here and say that

$y_1^{(3)} = y_1^{(4)} = 1.44$

Q2(a). Find the root of the equation f(x) = x² - In x - 2 = 0 by Newton - Raphson's method correct upto two places of decimals only taking x_0 = 1.5. [5]

Which may be written as

$$f(x) = x^2 - \log x - 2 = 0$$

and $f'(x) = 2x - \frac{1}{x} = \frac{2x^2 - 1}{x}$

$x_0 = 1.5$

$$x_1 = x_0 - \frac{f(x_0)}{f'(x_0)} = 1.5 - \frac{(1.5)^2 - \log 1.5 - 2}{\frac{2(1.5)^2 - 1}{1.5}}$$

$$= 1.5 - \frac{0.11085}{3.50}$$

$$= 1.468 \cong 1.47$$

$$x_2 = x_1 - \frac{f(x_1)}{f'(x_1)} = 1.47 - \frac{(1.47)^2 - \log(1.47) - 2}{\frac{2(1.47)^2 - 1}{1.47}}$$

$$= 1.47 - \frac{(2.161 - .1673 - 2)}{2 \times 2.161 - 1} \times 1.47$$

$$= 1.47 - \frac{(.161 - .1673)}{4.322 - 1} \times 1.47$$

$$= 1.47 - \frac{(-.0063)}{3.22} \times 1.47$$

$= 1.47 + \frac{.0063}{3.22} \times 1.47$
$= 1.472876$
$= 1.47$

$\therefore x_2$ *and* x_1 are quite same, therefore root is 1.47 Ans.

(b) From the following data, compute f(5) and F(9) using Newton's forward and backward difference formulae, respectively: [5]

x	4	6	8	10
f(x)	19	40	79	142

We have to find f(5) and f(9) so the table takes new shape as below:

x	4	5	6	8	9	10
f(x)	19	?	40	79	?	142

Forward difference method :

x	f(x)	$\Delta f(x)$	$\Delta^2 f(x)$	$\Delta^3 f(x)$
4	19			
6	40	21	18	
8	79	39	24	6
10	142	63		

a = 4, h = 2, $u = \frac{x-a}{h} = \frac{x-4}{2}$

$$f(x) = f(a) + u\Delta f(a) + \frac{u(u-1)}{2!}\Delta^2 f(a) + \frac{u(u-1)(u-2)}{3!}\Delta^3 f(a) + \dots\dots\dots$$

$$= f(4) + \frac{(x-4)}{2}.\Delta f(4) + \frac{u(u-1)}{2}.\Delta^2 f(4) + \frac{u(u-1)(u-2)}{6}\Delta^3 f(4)$$

$$= 19 + \frac{(x-4)}{2}.21 + \frac{\left(\frac{x-4}{2}\right)\left(\frac{x-4}{2}-1\right)}{2}.18 + \frac{\left(\frac{x-4}{2}\right)\left(\frac{x-4}{2}-1\right)\left(\frac{x-4}{2}-2\right)}{6}6$$

$$= 19 + \frac{(x-4)21}{2} + \frac{(x-4)(x-6)}{4} \times 9 + \frac{(x-4)(x-6(x-8)}{8}$$

$$=\frac{152+21x-84+9x^2-90x+324+x^3-16x^2+84x-144}{8}$$

$$=\frac{x^3-7x^2+15x+248}{8}$$

Let x = 5

$$\therefore f(5)=\frac{125-175+75+248}{8}=\frac{273}{8}$$

f(5) = 34.125

Let x = 9

$$\therefore f(9)=\frac{9^3-7(9)^2+15\times9+248}{8}$$

$$=\frac{729-567+135+248}{8}=\frac{545}{8}$$

f(9) = 68.125

Newton's backward difference method :

x	f(x)	$\Delta f(x)$	$\Delta^2 f(x)$	$\Delta^3 f(x)$
4	19			
6	40	21	18	
8	79	39	24	6
10	142	63		

a = 4, h = 2, a+nh = 10, a+nh+uh = 5

First of all we would find f(5) here a = 4, h = 2, a + x h = 10

$10 + u \times 2 = 5$

$2u = 5 - 10 = -5$

u = -5/2 ....(i) and f (a + nh + uh) = 5

$$f(a+nh+uh)=f(a+nh)+\frac{u}{1!}\nabla f(a+nh)+\frac{u(u+1)}{2!}\nabla^2 f(a+nh)+\frac{u(u+1)(u+2)}{3!}\nabla^3 f(a+nh)$$

$$f(5)=142+\left(-\frac{5}{2}\right)63+\frac{\left(-\frac{5}{2}\right)\left(-\frac{5}{2}+1\right)}{2!}24+\frac{-\frac{5}{2}\left(-\frac{5}{2}+1\right)\left(-\frac{5}{2}+2\right)}{6}\times 6$$

= 142 - 157.5 + 45 - 1.875 = 187 - 159.375 = 27.625

f(5) = 27.625

<u>IInd part</u> Now we would find f(9)

$\therefore a + nh = 10,$ a + nh + hu = 9

$10 + 2u = 9 \therefore u = -\frac{1}{2}$

$$\therefore f(a+nh+hu) = f(a+nh) + \frac{u}{1!}\nabla f(a+nh) + \frac{u(u+1)}{2!}\nabla^2 f(a+nh) + \frac{u(u+1)(u+2)}{3!}\nabla^3 f(a+nh)$$

$$f(9) = 142 + \left(-\frac{1}{2}\right)63 + \frac{\left(-\frac{1}{2}\right)\left(-\frac{1}{2}+1\right)}{2}24 + \frac{\left(-\frac{1}{2}\right)\left(-\frac{1}{2}+1\right)\left(-\frac{1}{2}+2\right)}{6}\times 6$$

$$= 142 - 31.5 - 3 - \frac{3}{8}$$

= 142 - 34.5 - 0.375
= 142 - 34.875
= 107.125

(c) The distance of a car at different times is given below: **[5]**

t	2	4	6
S(t)	18	12	16

Using Newton's forward formula find the time when

(i) $\frac{ds}{dt} = 0, \frac{d^2s}{dt^2} = 0.$

We are given

t	2	4	6
s(t)	18)	12	16

Newton's interpolating polynomial is given by

$$S(t) = S_0 + \frac{(t-t_0)}{1!}\frac{\Delta S_0}{h} + \frac{(t-t_0)(t-t_1)}{2!}\frac{\Delta^2 S_0}{h^2}$$

t	S(t)	ΔS	Δ^2S
2	**18**		
		-6	
4	**12**		**10**
		4	
6	**16**		

$$S(t) = 18 + (t-2)\frac{(-6)}{2} + \frac{(t-2)(t-4)}{2}\frac{10}{2^2}$$

$$= 18 - 3(t-2) + \frac{5}{4}(t-2)(t-4)$$

$$= 18 - 3(t-2) + \frac{5}{4}(t^2 - 6t + 8)$$

$$= \frac{1}{4}[72 - 12t + 24 + 5t^2 - 30t + 40]$$

$$S(t) = \frac{1}{4}[5t^2 - 42t + 136]$$

$$\frac{ds}{dt} = \frac{1}{4}[10t - 42] \qquad (1)$$

$$\frac{d^2s}{dt^2} = \frac{10}{4} = \frac{5}{2} \qquad (2)$$

We have to find the time when $\frac{ds}{dt} = 0$ and $\frac{d^2s}{dt^2} = 0$

Putting $\frac{ds}{dt} = 0$ we get

$$\frac{1}{4}[10t - 42] = 0$$

10t-42=0

$$t = \frac{42}{10} = 4.2 \quad \frac{ds}{dt} = 0 \text{ and } \frac{d^2s}{dt^2} = 0$$

Q3(a). Solve the following simultaneous equations by Gaussian elimination method : [5]

$$x_1 + 2x_2 + 3x_3 = 14$$
$$3x_1 + x_2 + 5x_3 = 20$$
$$2x_1 + 5x_2 + 2x_3 = 18$$

$x_1 + 2x_2 + 3x_3 = 14$ ....(i)

$3x_1 + x_2 + 5x_3 = 20$...............(ii) .... **(1)**

$2x_1 + 5x_2 + 2x_3 = 18$..............(iii)

Ist Step We eliminate x_1 from IInd and IIIrd equations by

(ii) - (i) $\times 3$ and (iii) - (i) $\times 2$

$$\begin{aligned} x_1 + 2x_2 + 3x_3 &= 14 \\ -5x_2 - 4x_3 &= -22 \\ x_2 - 4x_3 &= -10 \end{aligned} \quad \text{............ (2)}$$

II Step we eliminate x_2 from III equation $(By\,(ii) + (iii) \times 5)$

$x_1 + 2x_2 + 3x_3 = 14 \ldots\ldots\ldots\ldots\ldots\ldots(iv)$

$-5x_2 - 4x_3 = -22 \ldots\ldots\ldots\ldots\ldots\ldots(v)$

$-24x_3 = -72 \ldots\ldots\ldots\ldots\ldots\ldots(vi)$

from (vi) $x_3 = 3$

from (ii) $-5x_2 - 4 \times 3 = -22$

$-5x_2 = -10$

$x_2 = 2$

putting x_2, x_3 in (i)

$x_1 + 2 \times 2 + 3 \times 3 = 14$

$x_1 = -15$

Hence $x_1 = -15$, $x_2 = 2$, $x_3 = 3$

(b) Find, by the bisection method, the interval of length 0.125 in which the least positive root of the equation x³ - 4x- 0 = lies. [5]

The given polynomial is $f(x) = x^3 - 4x - 9 = 0$

Let x = 1, f(1) = -12 (-ve), f(2.8) = 1.75 (+ve)

Since f(1) is -ve and f(2.8) is +ve, then root lies between 1 and 2.8 so

$$x_0 = \frac{1 + 2.8}{2} = \frac{3.8}{2} = 1.9$$

$f(x_0) = (1.9)^3 - 4(1.9) - 9 = -9.471(-ve)$

Hence root lies between 2.8 and 1.9

$$\therefore x_1 = \frac{2.8 + 1.9}{2} = 2.4 \qquad \text{(nearly)}$$

$f(x_1) = (2.4)^3 - 4(2.4) - 9 = -4.776(-ve)$

$\therefore$ root lies between 1.9 and 2.4

$$x_2 = \frac{1.9+2.4}{2} = 2.2 \qquad \text{(nearly)}$$

$$f(x_2) = (2.2)^3 - 4(2.2) - 9 = -7.152 \,(-ve)$$

$\therefore$ route lies between 2.4 and 2.2

$$\therefore\; x_3 = \frac{2.2+2.4}{2} = \frac{4.6}{2} = 2.3$$

Hence the roots are :

$$x_1 = 2.4$$
$$x_2 = 2.2$$
$$x_3 = 2.3$$

(c) Evaluate $\frac{\Delta^2}{E}(x^2)$. **[5]**

$$\frac{\Delta^2}{E}(x^2) = \Delta^2 E^{-1}(x^2) = \Delta^2 (x-1)^2 = \Delta\left\{\Delta\left(x-1\right)^2\right\}$$

$$= \Delta\left\{(x+1-1)^2 - (x-1)^2\right\} \qquad \textit{where } h = 1$$

$$= \Delta x^2 - \Delta(x-1)^2$$

$$= (x+1)^2 - x^2 - \left\{\left(x+1-1\right)^2 - (x-1)^2\right\}$$

$$= x^2 + 1 + 2x - x^2 - x^2 + (x-1)^2$$

$$= 1 + 2x - x^2 + x^2 + 1 - 2x$$

$$= 2$$

Q4(a). Solve the following simultaneous equations by the Gauss- Seidel method nearest to a whole number:

$2x_1 + 10x_2 + x_3 = 51$

$x_1 + 2x_2 + 10x_3 = 61$

$10x_1 + x_2 + 2x_3 = 44$

Simultaneous equations are :

$$2x_1 + 10x_2 + x_3 = 51 \ldots\ldots\ldots\ldots\ldots\ldots (i)$$

$$x_1 + 2x_2 + 10x_3 = 61 \ldots\ldots\ldots\ldots\ldots\ldots (ii)$$

$$10x_1 + x_2 + 2x_3 = 44 \ldots\ldots\ldots\ldots\ldots\ldots (iii)$$

We solve each equation of the system for the unknown with the largest coefficient in terms of remaining unknowns :

$x_1 = \frac{1}{2}(51 - 10x_2 - x_3)$ *from (i)*

$x_2 = \frac{1}{2}(61 - x_1 - 10x_3)$ *from (ii)*

$x_3 = \frac{1}{2}(44 - 10x_1 - x_2)$ *from (iii)*

Starting with $x_2 = 1, x_3 = 0, x_1 = x^{(1)} = \frac{1}{2}(51 - 10) = 20.5$

Now putting

$x_1 = 20.5,\ x_3 = 0, x_2 = x^{(1)} = \frac{1}{2}(61 - 20.5) = 20.25$ *first approximation*

Again putting $x_1 = 20.5, x_2 = 20.25$ *in (iii), we get*

$$x_3 = x_3^{(1)} = \frac{1}{2}(44 - 10 \times 20.5 - 20.25) = -90.625 \textit{ first approx.}$$

Now we proceed to obtain the second approx.

$$x_1^{(2)} = \frac{1}{2}\left(51 - 6x_2^{(1)} - x_3^{(1)}\right) = \frac{1}{2}(51 - 6 \times 20.25 - (-90.625))$$

$$x_1^{(2)} = \frac{1}{2}(51 - 121.55 + 90.625) = 10.0375 = 10.04$$

$$x_2^{(2)} = \frac{1}{2}\left(61 - x_1^{(1)} - 10x_3^{(1)}\right) = \frac{1}{2}(61 - 20.5 - 10 \times -90.625)$$

$$x_2^{(2)} = \frac{1}{2}(61 - 20.5 + 906.25) = \frac{1}{2}473.375 = 473.4$$

$$x_3^{(2)} = \frac{1}{2}(44 - 10 \times 20.5 - (-90.625)) = \frac{1}{2}(44 - 205.0 + 90.625) = -35.1875 = -35.2$$

Similarly

$$x_3^{(3)} = \frac{1}{2}(44 - 10 \times 10.4 - 473.4) = \frac{1}{2}(44 - 104.0 + 473.4) = \frac{1}{2}(-533.4) = -226.7$$

Hence the solution is :

$x^{(1)}$ $20.5, 20.25, -90.625$

$x^{(2)}$ $10.4, 473.4, -35.2$

$x^{(3)}$ $-23626.9, 43.08, -266.7$

(b) Find the magnitude of the maximum error in computing $\int_2^4 \log_e x\, dx$ *by*

$$I=\int_{2}^{4}\log_e^x\,dx,\quad h=0.5$$

In this case divide the range of integration into equal parts by taking h = 0.5 and then the value of function y = log x is computed for each points of subdivision.

	x	$\log x = \log x \times 2.30258$
x_0	2	$0.3010 \times 2.30258 = 0.6931$
x_0+h	2.5	$0.3010 \times 2.30258 = 0.6931$
x_0+2h	3.0	$0.4771 \times 2.30258 = 1.09860$
x_0+3h	3.5	$0.5440 \times 2.30258 = 1.125276$
x_0+4h	4.0	$0.6020 \times 2.30258 = 1.38629$

(i) Trapezoidal Rule

By Trapezoidal Rule

$$\int_{2}^{4}\log x\,dx=\int_{2}^{2+4\times0.5}\log x\,dx$$

$$=\left(\frac{0.5}{2}\right)[0.6931+1.38629)+2(0.91628+1.09860)]$$

$$=\left(\frac{0.5}{2}\right)[2.07939+2(2.01488)]$$

$$= 1.5272875$$

(ii) Simpson's Rule
where h = 0.5.

By Simpson's $\frac{1}{3}^{rd}$ Rule

$$\int_{2}^{4}\log_e^x\,dx=\frac{0.5}{3}[0.6931+1.38629+4(0.91628+1.09860)]$$

$$=\frac{0.5}{3}[2.07939+4(2.01488)]$$

$$= 1.689818$$

Now we again take :

$$\int_2^4 \log_e^x \, dx = 2.30258 \int_2^4 \log_{10}^x \, dx$$

$$= 2.30258\left[\frac{1}{x}\right]_2^4$$

$$= 2.30258\left[\frac{1}{4}-\frac{1}{2}\right]$$

$$= \frac{2.30250}{2} \qquad \text{(leave -ve sign)}$$

$$= 1.15129$$

Error from Trapezoidal Rule = 1.5272875 - 1.15129 = 0.3759975
Error from Simphson's Rule = 1.689818 - 1.15129 = 0.538528

(c) Prove that the convergence of Newton - Raphson's method is quadratic. [5]

The methods that do not require the derivatives should be emphasized and among these Regula Falsi and Muller's Methods deserve first mention. If we wish to attain reasonably fast convergence, the starting values are not very far.

Q5(a). Given $\frac{dy}{dx}$ = x + y where y(0) = 1, compute y at x = 0.1 and x = 0.2 by Runge - Kutta fourth order method. Take h = 0.1. Compute upto two decimal places only. [8]

Given, $x_0 = 0,\ y_0 = 1,\ h = 0.1$

f(x, y) = x+y

$$k_1 = 0.1[0+1] = .1\times 1 = .1 \Rightarrow k = .1$$

$$k_2 = (0.1)\left[\left(0+\frac{0.1}{2}\right)+1+\left(\frac{1}{2}\right)\right]$$

$$k_2 = (0.1)[0.05+1+.05]$$

$$k_2 = 0.1\times 1.1$$

$$k_2 = 0.11$$

$$k_3 = (0.1)\left[0+\frac{0.1}{2}+1+\frac{0.11}{2}\right]$$

$k_3 = (0.1)[0 + 0.5 + 1 + 0.55]$

$k_3 = 0.1105$

$k_4 = (0.1)[0 + 0.1 + 1 + 0.1105]$

$k_4 = (0.1)[0 + 1.2105]$

$k_4 = 0.12105$

$$k = \frac{1}{6}[(k_1 + k_4) + 2(k_2 + k_3)]$$

$$k = \frac{1}{6}[(0.10 + 0.12105) + 2(0.11 + 0.1105)]$$

$$k = \frac{1}{6}[0.662050]$$

k = 0.1103

$\therefore y = y_0 + k = 1 + 0.1103 = 1.1103$

y = 1.1103

We have take above informations by taking x = 0, Now students have put x = 0.1 and x = 0.2 and find y in both cases.

(b) Find the condition number of

(i) f(x) = $\frac{1}{1-x}$

(ii) f(x) = $\frac{1}{\sqrt{x.}}$

Further, are these functions ill-conditioned ? Give reasons for your answer.

The word condition is used to describe the sensitivity of the function value f(x) to changes in the argument x. The informal formula for condition of f at x.

$$= \left| \frac{f^1(x),(x)}{f(x)} \right|$$

The larger the condition, the more ill-conditioned the function is said to be.

(i) $f(x)\frac{1}{1-x}$

The condition of f is approximately

$$\left|\frac{f^1(x).(x)}{f(x)}\right| = \left|\frac{\frac{-1}{(1-x)^2}.x}{\frac{1}{1-x}}\right|\frac{x}{1-x}$$

The number can be very large when x is near 1 signalling that the function is quite ill-conditioned.

(ii) $f(x)=\frac{1}{\sqrt{x}}$

The condition of f is approximately

$$\left|\frac{f'(x).(x)}{f(x)}\right| = \left|\frac{\frac{-1}{2x.\sqrt{x}}.x}{\frac{1}{\sqrt{x}}}\right| = \frac{1}{2}$$

The indicates that taking square root is a well conditioned process.

(c) If f(x) = ax² + bx + c (a, b, c, ∈ R) then show that f[1, 2, 3] = a. **3**

$$f(x) = ax^2 + bx + c$$

To Show *f[1, 2, 3] = a*

x	f(x)	f[..]	f[...]
1	a+b+c		
2	4a+2b+c	$\frac{(4a+2b+c)-(a+b+c)}{2-1} = 3a+b$	
3	9a+3b+c	$\frac{(9a+3b+c)-(4a+2b+c)}{3-2} = 5a+b$	$\frac{(5a+b)-(3a+b)}{3-1} = \frac{2a}{2} = a$

Hence f[...] = f[]1, 2, 3] = a.

CS-71 : COMPUTER ORIENTED NUMERICAL TECHNIQUES
JUNE - 2006

Note : *Question no. 1 is* ***compulsory.*** *Answer any* ***three*** *from the rest.*

Q1(a). The equation $9x^3 + 3x^2 - 5x + 1 = 0$ has a double root near 0.3. Obtain one approximation to the root using the Newton-Raphson method, upto three decimal places.

$f(x)=9x^3 + 3x^2 - 5x + 1=0$ x = 0.3

$$f(x)=27x^2 + 6x - 5$$

Then

$$X_{n+1} = x_n - \frac{f(xn)}{f'(xn)} = x_n - \frac{9x_n^3 + 3x_n^2 - 5x_n + 1}{27x_n^2 + 6x_n - 5}$$

$$= \frac{27x_n^3 + 6x_n^2 - 5x_n - 9x_n^3 - 3x_n^2 + 5x_n - 1}{27x_n^2 + 6x_n - 5}$$

$$= \frac{18x_n^3 + 3x_n^2 - 1}{27x_n^2 + 6x_n - 5}$$

$$\therefore \textit{First approximation } (x_1) = \frac{18(.3)^3 + 3(.3)^2 - 1}{27(.3)^2 + 6(.3)^2 - 5}$$

$$= \frac{-0.244}{2.03} = 0.12019704$$

$$= 0.120$$

(b) Find the relative error in the computation of x - y, where x = 0.572133869, y = 0.572021437 with five decimal digit accuracy.

We have given that x = 0.572133869 and y = 0.572021437

x - y = 0.000112432 = 0.00011

x* = 0.57213

y* = 0.57202

x*-y* =0.00011

$$\therefore \textit{relative error} = \frac{x^* - y^*}{x - y}$$

$$=\frac{0.00011}{0.00011}=1$$

(c) If f(x) = $\frac{1}{x}$, find the third divided difference $f[x_0, x_1, x_2]$.

$$f(x)=\frac{1}{x}$$

x	f(x)	f[. .]	f[. . .]
(1)	$\frac{1}{x_0}$		
2	$\frac{1}{x_1}$	$\frac{\frac{1}{x_1} - \frac{1}{x_0}}{2-1}$ $=\frac{x_0 - x_1}{x_0 x_2}$	
3	$\frac{1}{x_2}$	$\frac{\frac{1}{x_2} - \frac{1}{x_1}}{3-2}$ $=\frac{x_0 - x_2}{x_1 x_2}$	$\frac{\frac{x_1 - x_2}{x_1 x_2} - \frac{x_0 - x1}{x_0 x_1}}{3-1}$ $=\frac{(x_1 - x_2)x_0 - x_2(x_0 - x1)}{2x_0 x_1 x_2}$ $=\frac{x_1 x_0 - x_2 x_0 - x_2 x_0 + x_1 x_2}{2x_0 x_1 x_2}$ $\frac{x_1 x_0 - 2x_0 x_2 + x_1 x_2}{2x_0 x_1 x_2}$

Hence $f[x_0, x_1, x_2]=\frac{x_1 x_0 - x_0 x_2 + x_1 x_2}{2x_0 x_1 x_2}$

(d) Using the Newton's backward difference formula, obtain an approximation to f(4.5) from the data of values.

x	1	2	3	4	5
f(x)	8	21	46	89	156

The difference table is as under for Newton's backward difference formula :

x	f(x)	$\Delta f(x)$	$\Delta^2 f(x)$	$\Delta^3 f(x)$	$\Delta^4 f(x)$
1	8	13			
2	21	25	6		
3	46	43	6	0	
4	89	67			
5	156				

Newton - Gregory Formula for equal intervals, gives :

$f(a+mh)=f(a)+{}^{m}c_1\Delta f(a)+{}^{m}c_2\Delta^2 f(a)+{}^{m}c_3\Delta^3 f(a)+{}^{m}c_4\Delta^4 f(a)+$..........(1)

Here we want to interpolate f(4.5)

Hence a + mh = 4.5, a = 1, h = 1

$\therefore 1+m\times 1=4.5$

m = 3.5

$$\therefore\ f(4.5)=f(1)+{}^{3.5}c_1\Delta f(1)+{}^{3.5}c_2\Delta^2 f(1)+{}^{3.5}c_3\Delta^3 f(1)+\ldots\ldots\ldots\ldots$$

$$=8+3.5\times 13+\frac{3.5(3.5-1)}{2!}\times 12+\frac{3.5(3.5-1)(3.5-2)}{3!}\times 6$$

$$= 8 + 45.5 + 52.5 + 13.1 = 119.1$$

(e) Evaluate $\int_0^1 xe^{-x^2}dx$ using the Simpson's rule with n = 4 subintervals. Compare the result with the exact solution.

$\left(Given: e^{-1/16}=0.9394, e^{-1/4}=0.7788, e^{-9/16}=0.5698, e^{-1}=0.3679\right)$

Simpson's $\frac{1}{3}$ rule :

Let us divide the whole range of integration into 4 equal intervals,

$$h=\frac{1-0}{4}=\frac{1}{4}=0.25$$

x	$\frac{1}{4}$	$\frac{1}{2}$	$\frac{3}{4}$	$\frac{4}{4}=1$
xe^{-x^2} $f(x)=xe^{-x^2}$	$4e^{\frac{-1}{16}}=\frac{0.9394}{4}$ $=0.23485$	$\frac{1}{2}e^{-\frac{1}{4}}=\frac{0.7788}{2}$ $=0.3894$	$\frac{3}{4}e^{-\frac{9}{16}}=\frac{3\times 0.5698}{4}$ $=\frac{1.7094}{4}$ $=0.42735$ $=0.4274$	e^{-1} $=0.3679$
	y_0	y_1	y_2	y_3

$$\int_0^1 xe^{-x2}dx=\frac{h}{3}\left[(y_o+y_n)+4(y_1+y_2+y_3+........y_{n-1})\right]$$

$$=\frac{1}{4\times 3}\left[(y_o+y_3)+4(y_1+y_2)\right]$$

$$=\frac{1}{12}\left[(0.24585+0.3679)+4(0.3894+0.4274)\right]$$

$$=\frac{1}{12}\left[0.60275+4(0.8168)\right]$$

$$=\frac{1}{12}\left[0.60275+3.2672\right]$$

$$=\frac{3.8700}{12}=0.33091$$

$$=0.331..............................(1)$$

General way of integration is:

$$I=\int_0^1 xe^{-x2}dx$$

Let $x^2 = t$,

$2x\ dx = dt$, $x\ dx = \frac{dt}{2}$ Limits when

$$x = 0, t = 0$$

$$I = \frac{1}{2}\int_0^1 e^{-t} dt \qquad x = 1, t = 1$$

$$= \frac{-1}{2}\left[e^{-t} dt\right]_0^1$$

$$= \frac{-1}{2}\left[e^{-t} - e^0\right]$$

$$= \frac{-1}{2}[0.3679 - 1]$$

$$= \frac{-1}{2} \times -0.6321$$

$$= \frac{0.6321}{2}$$

$$\int_0^1 xe^{-x2} dx = 0.316 \text{ ....(2)}$$

Difference from (1) and (2) = 0.331 - 0.316 = 0.015

(f) Obtain the truncation error of the Heun's method for the solution of the initial value problem y = f(t, y), $y(t_0) = y_0$

Initial value problem, truncation error of Heun's method.

$(I \vee P)$ Y= f (t, y)

we start from the given point,

$Y_0 = Y(t_0)$

$t_1 = t_0 + h$

$t_2 = t_0 + 2h$

$t_3 = t_0 + 3h$, - - -

where the step size h, is a fixed no.,

$$y(t+h) = y(t) + h\, y(t) + \frac{h^2}{2} y^4 (t) + \text{- - - - -}$$

Now, for a small value of h, the higher powers h^2, h^3 - - -

are very small

$$y(1+h) \approx y(t) + hy'(t)$$

$$= y(t) + ht + (t_1 y)$$

(with the right side obtained from the given differential equation) and the following iteration process.

In the **first step**, we compute,

$$y_1 = y_0 + h\,f(t_0, y_0)$$

which approximates,

$$y(t_1) = y(t_0 + h),$$

in the **second step**, we compute

$$y_2 = y_1 + hf\,(t_{1,} y_1)$$

which approximates,

$y(t_2) = y(t_0 + 2h)$, etc.----------

and in general,

$$y_{n+1} = y_n + hf\,(t_n, y_n)$$

$$(\,- - -\; n = 0, 1, - --\,)$$

This is called the Euler method

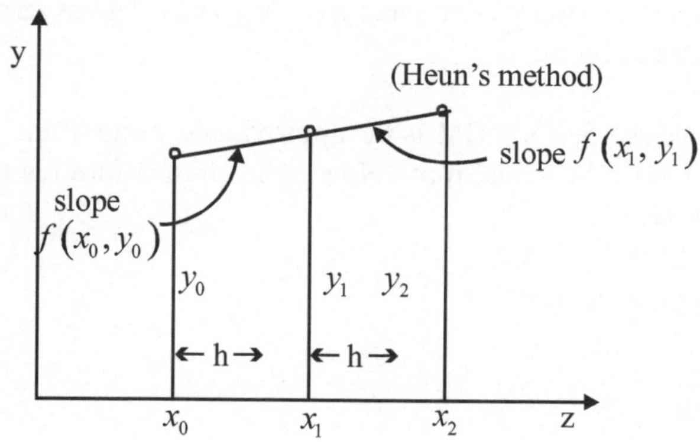

Taylor's formula with remainder has the form,

$$y(t+h) = y(t) + hy^1(t) + \frac{1}{2}h^2 y^4(\xi)$$

(where $(t \le \xi^4 \le t+h)$. It shows,

that in the Heun's method, the truncation error, in each step or local truncation error is proportional to h_2.

(g) Explain what 'instability of an algorithm' is. Support your explanation with appropriate examples.

Ans. Instability of algorithms

Algorithm is a step by step process that describe a method for solving any mathematical problem. In numerical Algorithm errors grow in each step of calculation let e be an initial error and Rn (e) represents the growth of an error at the nth step after n subsequent operation due to e. Some time in an algorithm a step is reached when, the alternative is to state that relative error ³ epsilon', In such case the algorithm is said to be unstable since the solution has to convergence in n iterations.

Q2(a). Derive the regula-falsi method for finding a simple root of the equation f(x) = 0

Regula Falsi Method : This is the oldest method of finding the real root of a numerical equation f(x) = 0. To find it, we find a sufficiently small interval $x = x_1$ to $x = x_2$ in which root of the equation lies. So the graph of the curve y = f(x) will surely cross the x-axis somewhere between $x = x_1$ and $x = x_2$ which will imply that $f(x_1)$ and $f(x_2)$ are opposite in sign.

The basic fact in this way is that growth of the function in the small interval (x_1, x_2) is supposed a straight line joining (x_1, y_1), (x_2, y_2) gives an approximate value of the desired root.

From figure we see that x = OM is the approximate value of the desired root whereas x = ON is the actual root. Now let us draw a formula to determine the root. We have :

$OM = OA + AM = x_1 + AM$

$$\because \triangle DAM \sim \triangle DPC$$

$$\therefore \frac{DA}{AM} = \frac{DP}{CP}$$

$$AM = \frac{DA.CP}{DP}$$

$$= \frac{(x_2 - x_1)DA}{DA + AP}$$

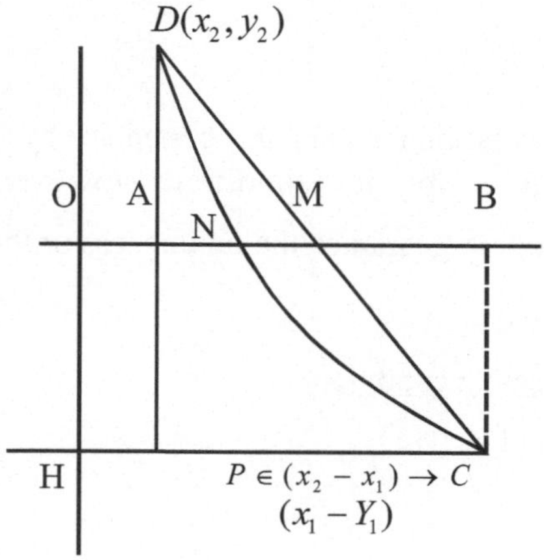

$$=\frac{(x_2 - x_1)|y_1|}{|y_1| + |y_2|}$$

$\therefore OM - OA$

$$=\frac{(x_2 - x_1)|y_1|}{|y_1| + |y_2|}$$

$$\therefore OM = x_1 + = \frac{(x_2 - x_1)|y_1|}{|y_1| + |y_2|} = \text{required value of root.}$$

This approximate value of root may be denoted by $x^{(1)}$. Then to find the better approximation we calculate $y^{(1)}$ from, $y^{(1)} = f(x^{(1)})$.

(b) State the Lipschitz condition. Further, check whether the IVP $y^1 = 1 + y^2, y(0) = 1$ can be solved using this condition,

Lipschitz condition is given by Rudolf Lipschitz (1832 -1903)
German mathematician, professor at Born . By the mean value theorem of differential calculus, we have

Condition (1)

$$f(x_1y_2) - f(x_1y_1) = (y_2 - y_1)\frac{\partial f}{\partial y} \qquad y = \tilde{y}$$

where (x_1y_1) and (x_1y_2) are assumed to be **in R,** and $\tilde{y}$ is a suitable value between y_1 and y_2 from this, it follows that **.**

Condition 2

$f(x_1\ y_2) - f(x_1 y_1)\Big| \leq M1y_2 - y_1\Big|$

It can be shown that condition no. (1) may be replace by the weaker condition (2) which is known as lipschitz condition. However, the continuity of $f(x_1\ y)$ is not enough to guarantee the uniqueness of the solution.

$\boxed{I \vee P}$ $Y^1 = 1+y^2$, $y(o) = 1$

can be solved by <u>lipschitz condition</u>

initial value problem $(I \vee P)$

$y^1 = 1+y^2, y(o) = 1$

and take R: $|x| < 5$, $|y| > 3$,

then a = 5 , b = 3 and

$|f| = |1+y^2| \leq K=10,$

$|\partial f|\partial y| = 2|y| \leq M=6,$

$$\alpha = \frac{b}{k} = 0.3 < a$$

there is no continuous solution valid in the entire interval.

$|x| < 5,$

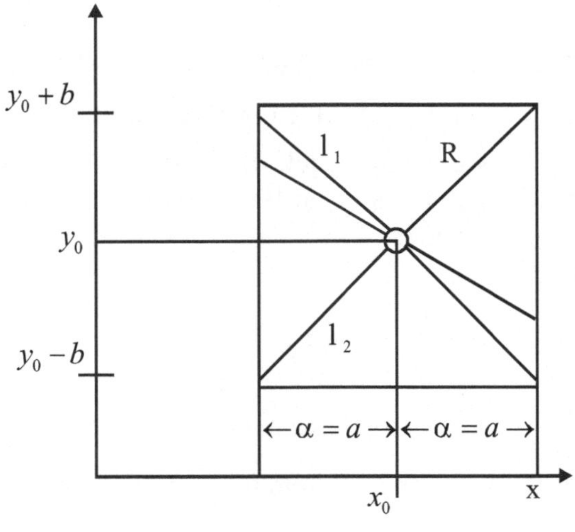

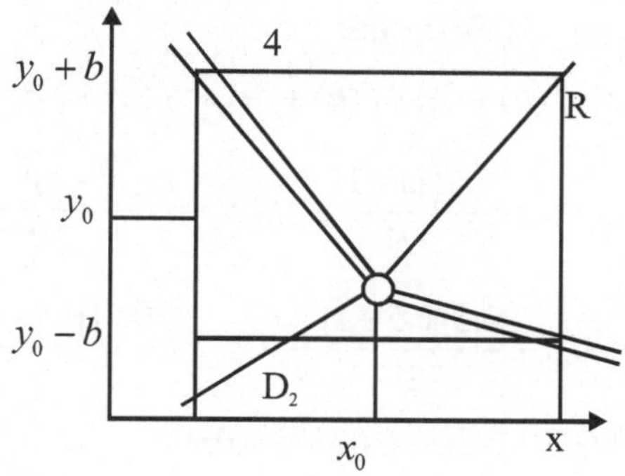

(c) From the following data, approximate f(2.5) using Newton's difference formula:

x	2	3	4	5
f(x)	0.698	1.098	1.386	1.609

We have been given :

x	2	2.5	3	4	5
f(x)	0.698	?	1.098	1.386	1.609

Here a = 2, h = 3 - 2 = 1
a + mh = 2.5

$$\therefore m = \frac{2.5-0}{h} = \frac{2.5-2}{1} = 0.5$$

For the given data we make the following difference table:

x	y = f(x)	$\Delta f(x)$	$\Delta^2 f(x)$	$\Delta^3 f(x)$
2	0.698			
3	1.098	.400	-.222	
4	1.386	.288	-.065	.157
5	1.609	.223		

From Newton Gregory's Formula:

$$f(a+mh)=f(a)+{}^{m}c_1\Delta f(a)+{}^{m}c_2\Delta^2 f(a)+{}^{m}c_3\Delta^3 f(a)$$

$$f(2.5)=0.698+m\Delta f(a)+\frac{m(m-1)}{2!}\Delta^2 f(a)+\frac{m(m-1)(m-2)}{3!}\Delta^3 f(a)$$

$$=0.698+0.5\times 0.4+\frac{0.5(0.5-1)}{2!}-0.222+\frac{0.5(0.5-1)(0.5-2)}{3!}\times 0.157$$

$$=0.698+0.20+0.02775+0.981$$

$$=1.02385$$

$$=1.024$$

Q3(a). For $f(x)-x^2-3x+1=0$, find the smallest positive root by the fixed point iteration method, using three iterations. Find the minimum number of iterations required so that the error in the approximation is $\leq 5\times 10^{-1}$.

We have $f(x)=x^2-3x+1=0$ ....(i)

f(2) = -1, f(3) = 1

We see that the root of (1) lies between 2 and 3 since f(2) if -ve and f(3) is +ve. Let root be

$$\therefore x_0=x^{(0)}=\frac{5}{2}=2.5 \text{ ....(ii)}$$

Again, we have $f(x)=x^2-3x+1=0$, which may be re-written as

$x^2=3x-1 \, or \, (3x-1)^2=\varphi(x)$ i.e. $\varphi(x)=(3x-1)^{1/2}$ and

$$\varphi'(x)=\frac{1\times 3}{2\sqrt{3x-1}}=\frac{3}{2\sqrt{3x-1}}$$

$$\therefore \varphi'(2.5)=\frac{3}{2\sqrt{3\times\frac{5}{2}-1}}=\frac{3}{2\sqrt{\frac{15}{2}-1}}$$

$$=\frac{1.5\times\sqrt{2}}{\sqrt{13}}=\frac{1.5\times 1.414}{3.7}=0.058<1$$

$\therefore$ Interaction formula is -

$$x^{(i+1)} = \left[3\left\{x^{i}\right\} - 1\right]^{1/2} \text{.......................(iii)}$$

put i = 0, $x^{(1)} = \left[3\left(x^{(0)} - 1\right)\right]^{1/2} = \left[3\left(\frac{5}{2}\right) - 1\right]^{1/2} = (6.5)^{1/2} = 2.54$ ....(iv)

put i = 1, $x^{(2)} = \left[3\left(x^{(i)} - 1\right)\right]^{1/2} = \left[3(2.54) - 1\right]^{1/2} = (6.2)^{1/2} = 2.53$..............(v)

put i = 2, $x^{(3)} = \left[3\left(x^{(2)} - 1\right)\right]^{1/2} = \left[3(2.53) - 1\right]^{1/2} = (6.59)^{1/2} = 2.54$ ....(vi)

from (iv) and (vi) we conclude that the real rout is x = 2.54 We see that the real root of equation (i) is 2.54

(b) Solve the following system of equations by Gauss elimination with partial pivoting.

$$x_1 + x_2 + 2x_3 = 1$$
$$4x_1 + 2x_2 + x_3 = 2.5$$
$$2x_1 + 3x_2 + 4x_3 = 1$$

$x_1+x_2+2x_3$ - 1
$4x_1+2x_2+x_3$ =2.5
$2x_1+3x_2+4x_3$ =1

The coefficient of matrix is :

$$\begin{bmatrix} 1 & 1 & 2 \mathrm{I}\, 1 \\ 4 & 2 & 1 \mathrm{I} 2.5 \\ 2 & 3 & 4 \mathrm{I}\, 1 \end{bmatrix}$$

We do following operations for eliminating x_1 from II and III row.

$$R_2 - R_1 \times 4,\ R_3 - 2R_1$$

$$\begin{bmatrix} 1 & 1 & 2\ \mathrm{I}\ 1 \\ 4 & -2 & -7 \mathrm{I} 2.5 \\ 0 & 0 & 0\ \mathrm{I}\ 1 \end{bmatrix}$$

We do, $R_3 - \frac{1}{2}R_2$ for eliminating x_2 and R_3

$$\begin{bmatrix} 1 & 1 & 2 \text{ I } 1 \\ 4 & -2 & -7 \text{ I } 2.5 \\ 0 & 0 & 0 \text{ I } 1 \end{bmatrix}$$

By performing back substitution on the equations :

$$x_3 + x_2 + 2x_1 = 1$$

$$-2x_2 - 7x_1 = 2.5$$

$$-\frac{7}{2}x_1 = 2.5 \qquad \Rightarrow x_1 = -\frac{2}{7}$$

$$\therefore x_2 = \frac{2.5 + 7x_1}{-2} = \frac{2.5 + (-2)}{(-2)} = -\frac{0.5}{2} = -\frac{5}{20} = -\frac{1}{4}$$

$$\therefore x_3 = 1 - x_2 - 2x_1$$

$$= 1 - \left(-\frac{1}{4}\right) - 2 \times \left(-\frac{2}{7}\right)$$

$$= 1 + \frac{1}{4} + \frac{4}{7}$$

$$= \frac{28 + 7 + 16}{28}$$

$$x_3 = \frac{51}{28}$$

Therefore, the solutions of the equations are $x_1 = -\frac{2}{7}, x_2 = -\frac{1}{4}, x_3 = \frac{51}{28}$

Q4(a).If $f''(x_o)$ is approximated by

$$f''(x_o) = \frac{1}{12h^2}\left[-f(x_0 - 2h) + 16f(x_0 - h) + cf(x_0) + 16f(x_0 + h) - f(x_0 + 2h)\right]$$

find the value of c.

We have to find the value of 'c' when f'(x_o) is approximated by

$$f''(x_0) = \frac{1}{12h^2}[-f(x_0 - 2h) + 16f(x_0 - h) + cf(x_0) + 16(x_0 + h) - f(x_0 + 2h)] ----(i)$$

Taylor's Series Theorem is given by

$$f(x+h) = f(x) + hf'(x) + \frac{1}{2!}h^2 f''(x) + \frac{h^3}{3!} f'''(x) + --$$

Taking $x=x_0$, we get

$$f(x_0+h) = f(x_0) + hf'(x_0) + \frac{1}{2}h^2 f''(x_0) + \frac{1}{6}h^3 f'''(x_0) + ...(ii)$$

Replacing h by -h in eq^n (ii) we get

$$f(x_0-h) = f(x_0) - hf'(x_0) + \frac{1}{2}h^2 f''(x_0) - \frac{1}{6}h^3 f'''(x_0) + ...(iii)$$

Replacing h by 2h in eq^n (ii) we get

$$f(x_0+2h) = f(x_0) + 2hf'(x_0) + \frac{1}{2}(2h)^2 f''(x_0) + \frac{1}{6}(2h)^3 f'''(x_0) + --$$

$$f(x_0+2h) = f(x_0) + 2hf'(x_0) + 2h^2 f''(x_0) + \frac{4}{3} f'''(x0) + -- \qquad (iv)$$

Replacing h by –2h in eq^n we get

$$f(x_0-2h) = f(x_0) - 2hf'(x_0) + 2h^2 f''(x_0) - \frac{4}{3}h^3 f'''(x_0) + -- \qquad (v)$$

Adding eq^n (ii) and (iii) we get

$$f(x_0+h)+f(x_0-h)=2f(x_0)+h^2 f''(x_0) ---------- \qquad (vi)$$

Neglecting term containing h^3, h^4—

Adding eq^n (iv) and (v)

$$f(x_0+2h)+f(x_0-2h)=2f(x_0)+4h^2 f''(x_0) ------(vii)$$

Multiplying eq^n (vi) by 16, we get

$$16f(x_0+h)+16f(x_0-h)=32f(x_0)+16h^2 f''(x_0) ------(viii)$$

Subtracting eq^n (vii) from (viii), we get

$$16f(x_0+h)+16f(x_0-h)-f(x_0+2h)-f(x_0-2h)=30f(x_0)+12h^2 f''(x_0)$$

$$12h^2 f''(x_0)=16f(x_0+h)+16f(x_0-h)-f(x_0+2h)-f(x_0-2h)-30f(x_0).$$

$$f''(x_0) = \frac{1}{12h^2}[-f(x_0-2h)+16f(x_0-h)-30f(x_0)+16f(x_0-h)-f(x_0+2h)] ----(ix)$$

Equating eq^n (i) by (ix) we get

$$\boxed{c=-30}$$

(b) Solve the initial value problem

$$y^1 = \frac{2y-x}{2y+x}, y(0)=1$$

using Euler's method in [0, 0.3] with h = 0.1

We have given that : $y' = \frac{2y-x}{2y+x}, y(0)=1$ over the interval [0, 0.3]

h = 0.1

here x0=0

$$f(x,y) = \frac{2y-x}{2y+x}$$

The Euler method for the given problem is :

$$y\left(x_{j+1}\right) = y\left(\left(x_j\right) + h\left(\frac{2y-x_j}{2y+x_j}\right)\right)$$

For j = 0, we have

$$y\left(x_1\right) = y\left(x_0\right) + 0.1\left(\frac{2y-x_0}{2y+x_0}\right)$$

$$y\left(0.1\right) = 1 + 0.1\left(\frac{2y-0}{2y+0}\right) = 1 + 0.1\times 1 = 1.01$$

For (j=1) we have

$$y\left(0.2\right) = y(0.1)\left(\frac{2y-x_1}{2y+x_1}\right) = 1.01 + 0.1\times 1.01 = 1.01 + 0.101$$

y(0.2) = 1.111

$$y\left(0.3\right) = y(0.2) + 0.1\left(\frac{2y-x_2}{2y+x_2}\right) = 1.111 + 0.1\times 1.111 = 1.2221$$

y(0.3) = 1.2221

(c) Find the interpolation polynomial that fits the data f(0) = 1, f(2) = 25, f(3) = 82, f(4) = 193. Hence, find an approximation to f(1).

We have given that :

x	0	1	2	3
f(x)	1	25	82	193

The difference table is as under :

2	f(x)	$\Delta f(x)$	$\Delta^2 f(x)$	$\Delta^3 f(x)$
0	1			
2	25	24	33	
3	82	57	54	21
4	193	111		

Newton's Formula for interpolation is given as $f(a+mh)=f(a)+{}^{m}c_1\Delta f(a)+{}^{m}c_2\Delta^2 f(a)+{}^{m}c_3\Delta^3 f(a)+..........$

where a+mh=x, h = 1, a = 0

$$\therefore m=\frac{x}{h}=\frac{x}{1}=x$$

$$\therefore f(x)=1+{}^{x}c_1\times 24+{}^{x}c_2\times 33+{}^{x}c_3\times 21$$

$$=1+x\times 24+\frac{x(x-1)}{2!}\times 33+\frac{x(x-1)(x-2)}{3!}\times 21$$

$$=1+24x+\left(x^2-x\right)\frac{33}{2}+\frac{(x^2-x)(x-2)}{3\times 2}\times 21$$

$$=1+24x+\frac{33x^2-33x}{2}+\frac{(x^3-3x^2+2x)7}{2}$$

$$=\frac{2+48x+33x^2-33x+7x^3-21x^2+14x}{2}$$

$f(x)=\frac{1}{2}\left(7x^3+12x^2+29x+2\right)$ at x = 1

$f(1)=\frac{1}{2}(7+12+29+2)=\frac{50}{2}=25 \;=>\; f(1)=25$

Q5(a). Use the Runge-Kutta method of order 4 to evaluate y (1.1) for the IVP $\frac{dy}{dx}=x^2+y^2$, y (1) = 0.

We have given that $f(x)=\frac{dy}{dx}=x^2+y^2$

$x_0 = 1$, $y_0 = 0$, h = 0.1. $y = y_0 + K$.........(i) is the solution of given differential equation where $K=\frac{1}{6}\{(K_1+K_4)+2(K_2+K_3)\}$..........(2)

Now, $K_1 = h\,f(x_0,y_0)=0.1[1]=0.1$. $K_1 = 0.1$

$$K_2 = h\,f\left(x0+h, y0+K_1\right) = 0.1\left[\left(1+\frac{0.1}{2}\right)^2 + \left(0+\frac{0.1}{2}\right)^2\right]$$

$$K_2 = 0.1\left[(1.05)^2 + 0.0025\right] = 0.1[1.2125+0.0025] = 0.1 \times 1.21500$$

$$K_2 = 0.121500 = 122$$

$$K_3 = hf\left(x_0+\frac{h}{2}, y_0+\frac{K_2}{2}\right) = 0.1\left[\left(1+\frac{.01}{2}\right)^2 + \left(\frac{.122}{2}\right)^2\right]$$

$$= 0.1(1.2125+0.3721) = 0.1\times 1.5846 = 0.15846. \qquad K_3 = 0.158$$

$$K_4 = hf\left(x_0+\frac{h}{2}, y0+\frac{K_3}{2}\right) = 0.1\left[(1.05)^2 + \left(\frac{0.158}{2}\right)^2\right]$$

$$K_4 = 0.1[1.2125+0.6241] = 1.8366\times 0.1 = 0.18366. \qquad K_4 = 0.184$$

Now from (2)

$$K = \frac{1}{6}\left[(0.1+0.184)+2(0.122+0.158)\right]$$

$$= \frac{1}{6}\left[(0.284+0.760)\right] = \frac{1.004}{6} = 0.1673$$

K=0.1673 $\quad \therefore from(1) \quad y = y_0 + K = 0 + 0.1673. \quad y = 0.1673$

(b) Which of the following statement is true ? Give reasons for your answer. (i) 2.145 is the floating point representation of 21.45.

(ii) The round-off 4.50936 to 4 significant digits is 4.5094.

(iii) Numbers in 3-digit decimal arithmetic with rounding satisfy the distributive property of multiplication over addition.

(i) False, because the floating point representation of 21.45 be 0.2145E4 where E4 is used to represent 10^4

(ii) True, because in the round off method, the last retained significant digit is rounded by 1.

(iii) True

(c) Using inverse interpolation, find the value of x for y = 1, given the following data:

x	1	3	4
y	-3	0	3

$x: a_o 1,\ a_1 = 3,\ a_2 = 4$

$y = f(x): f(a_o) = -3,\ f(a_1) = 0,\ f(a_2) = 3$

we want x_1 when f(x) = 1,

using inverse interpolation formula:-

$$x = \frac{\left[(f(x)-f(a_1)\right]\left[f(x)-f(a_2)\right]}{\left[f(a_0)-f(a_1)\right]\left[f(a_0)-f(a_1)\right]} \times a_0$$

CS-71 : COMPUTER ORIENTED NUMERICAL TECHNIQUES
December, 2006

Note : Question no. 1 is **compulsory.** Answer any **three** questions from the rest. In total you have to answer **four** questions.

1.(a) Find the number of terms of the exponential series such that their sum gives the value of e^x correct to six decimal places at x = 1. *4*

Ans. We have that

$$e^x = 1 + x + \frac{x^2}{21} + \frac{x^3}{31} + \frac{x^4}{41} + \frac{x^5}{51} + \frac{x^6}{61} + \frac{x^7}{71} + \text{---------}$$

put x = 1

$$e = 1 + 1 + \frac{1}{21} + \frac{1}{31} + \frac{1}{41} + \frac{1}{51} + \frac{1}{61} + \frac{1}{71}$$

$$= 1 + 1 + 0.5 + \frac{1}{6} + \frac{1}{24} + \frac{1}{120} + \frac{1}{720} + \frac{1}{5040}$$

$= 2.5 + 16 + 0.41 + .0083 + .00138 + .000198$

$= 2.710878$

We see that there are 8 terms whose sum up to six decimal places of e^x at x =1 is 2.710878

(b) Estimate the error in evaluating $f(x, y) = x^2 + y^2$ for x =3.00 and y = 4.00 *4*

Ans. $f(x, y) = x^2 + y^2$

$= (3.00)^2 + (4.00)^2$

$= 9.0000 + 16.0000$

$= 25.0000$

$f(x, y) = x^2 + y^2$

$= (x + y)^2 - 2xy$

$= (3.00 + 4.00)^2 - 2 \times 3.00 \times 4.00$

$= (7.00)^2 - 24.0000$

$= 49.0000 - 24.0000$

$= 25.0000$

Error $= f(x, y) - f(x, y)$

$= 25.0000 - 25.0000$

$= 0$

No error occurred

(c) Derive Newton – Raphson formula using Taylor series expansion. *4*

Ans. Newton-Rapson Method : Newton-Rapson is a special example of fixed point. This method is generally used to improve the result obtained by one of the previous methods. Let x_0 be and approximate root of f (x)=0 and let $x_1 = x_0 + h$ be the correct root so that f (x_1)=0.

Expanding f $(x_0$+h) by Taylor's series then

$$f(x_0) + hf'(x_0) + \frac{h^2}{2!} f''(x_0) + ... = 0$$

Neglecting the second and higher order derivatives, we have

f (x_0) + hf^1 (x_0) = 0

which gives $h = -\frac{f(x_0)}{f'(x_0)}$

A better approximation than x_0 is therefore given by x_1 ,where

$$x_1 = x_0 - \frac{f(x_0)}{f^1(x_0)}$$

Successive approximations are given by $x_2, x_3, ..., x_{n+1}$, Where

$$x_{n+1} = x_n - \frac{f(x_n)}{f'(x_n)}$$

Which is the Newton Raphson Formula

(d) Evaluate

$$\Delta^{10}[(1-ax)(1-bx^2)(1-cx^3)(1-dx^4)]$$

(where $\Delta = \frac{d}{dx}$**)** *4*

Ans. We know by fundamental theorem of differential calculus that If f (x) be a polynomial of nth degree in x, then the nth difference of f(x) is constant and Δ^{n+1}f(x) = 0 and Δ^nf(x) =x^1h^n an i.e. Δ^rf(x) = 0 for x>n.

$\therefore \Delta^{10}[(1-ax)\ (1-bx^2)\ (1-cx^3)\ (1-dx^4)]$

$= \Delta^{10}(abcd\ x^{10})$

$= abcd\ \Delta^{10}x^{10}$

$= abcd(10!)$

(e) Find the cubic polynomial which takes the following (x, f(x)) set of the values. ***5***

x	0	1	2	3
f(x)	1	2	1	10

Ans.

x	f(x)
$x_0 = 0$	1
$x_1 = 1$	2
$x_2 = 2$	1
$x_3 = 3$	10

By Lagrange's interpolation formula we have

$$f(x) = \frac{(x-x_1)(x-x_2)(x-x_3)}{(x_0-x_1)(x_0-x_2)(x_0-x_3)} f(x_0) +$$

$$\frac{(x-x_0)(x-x_2)(x-x_3)}{(x_1-x_0)(x_1-x_2)(x_1-x_3)} f(x_1) +$$

$$\frac{(x-x_0)(x-x_1)(x-x_3)}{(x_2-x_0)(x_2-x_1)(x_2-x_3)} f(x_2) +$$

$$\frac{(x-x_0)(x-x_1)(x-x_2)}{(x_3-x_0)(x_3-x_1)(x_3-x_2)} f(x_3)$$

$$f(x) = \frac{(x-1)(x-2)(x-3)}{(0-1)(0-2)(0-3)} \times 1 +$$

$$\frac{(x-0)(x-2)(x-3)}{(1-0)(1-2)(1-3)} \times 2 +$$

$$\frac{(x-0)(x-1)(x-3)}{(2-0)(2-1)(2-3)} \times 1 +$$

$$\frac{(x-0)(x-1)(x-2)}{(3-0)(3-1)(3-2)} \times 10$$

$$= -6\,(x-1)\,(x-2)\,(x-3) + x(x-2)\,(x-3) - \frac{x(x-1)(x-3)}{2} + \frac{5x(x-1)(x-2)}{3}$$

$= -6\,[(x^2 - 2x - x + 2)\,(x - 3)] + x\,(x^2 - 3x - 2x + 6) -$

$$\frac{x(x^2 - 3x - x + 3)}{2} + \frac{5x\,(x^2 - 2x - x + 2)}{3}$$

$= -6\,[(x^2 - 3x + 2)\,(x - 3)] + x\,(x^2 - 5x + 6) -$

$$\frac{x(x^2 - 4x + 3)}{2} + \frac{5x(x^2 - 3x + 2)}{3}$$

$$\frac{-36\,[x^3 - 3x^2 - 3x^2 + 9x + 2x - 6] + 6[x^3 - 5x^2 + 6x] - 3[x^3 - 4x^2 + 3x] + 10[x^3 - 3x^2 + 2x]}{6}$$

$$= \frac{x^3\,[-36 + 6 - 3 + 10] + x^2\,[216 - 30 - 30] + x[-396 + 36 - 9 + 20] + (216)}{6}$$

$$= \frac{-23x^3 + 156x^2 - 349x + 216}{6}$$

$$= \frac{1}{6}(23x^3 - 156x^2 + 349x - 216)$$

(f) Find real roots of the equation $x^3 - x - 1 = 0$ using bisection method. Perform three iterations. ***5***

Ans. $f(x) = x^3 - x - 1$

$f(1) = 1 - 1 - 1 = -1$ (–ve)

$f(3) = 27 - 3 - 1 = 23$ (+ve)

$\therefore f(1) = -1$ (–ve) and $f(3) = 23$ (+ve) therefore root lies between 1 and 3. So we take

$$x_0 = \frac{1+3}{2} = 2$$

$f(x_0) = f(2) = 8 - 2 - 1 = 5$ (+ve)

$\therefore$ root lies between 1 and 2 $\therefore x_1 = \dfrac{1+2}{2} = 1.5$

$f(x_1) = f(1:5)$

$= (1.5)^3 - 1.5 - 1$

$= 3.375 - 2.5$

$= 0.875$

root lies between 1 and 1.5

$$\therefore x_2 = \frac{1+1.5}{2} = \frac{2.5}{2} = 1.25$$

$f(x_2) = f(1.25) = (1.25)^3 - 1.25 - 1$
$= 1.953125 - 2.25$
$= -0.296$ (- ve)

therefore x =1.25 is a root of equation

(g) Find the approximate value of $I = \int_0^1 \frac{dx}{1+x}$ using trapezoidal rule. Obtain the bound of errors. (Given I = In 2 = 0.693). *4*

Ans. divide the range of integration (0, 1) into four equal parts each of width

$$\frac{1-0}{4} = \frac{1}{4}$$

$\therefore h = \frac{1}{4}$ the value of y for each point of sub division are given below

x	$y = \frac{1}{1+x}$	
$x_0 = 0$	1	y_0
$x_0 + h = \frac{1}{4}$	$\frac{4}{5}$	y_1
$x_0 + 2h = \frac{1}{2}$	$\frac{2}{3}$	y_2
$x_0 + 3h = \frac{3}{4}$	$\frac{4}{7}$	y_3
$x_0 + 4h = 1$	$\frac{1}{2}$	y_4

using trapezoidal rule

$$\int_0^1 \frac{dx}{1+x} = h\left[\frac{1}{2}(y_0 + y_4) + (y_1 + y_2 + y_3)\right]$$

$$= \frac{1}{4}\left[\frac{1}{2}\left(1 + \frac{1}{2}\right) + \left(\frac{4}{5} + \frac{2}{3} + \frac{4}{7}\right)\right]$$

$$= \frac{1}{4}\left[\frac{3}{6} + \frac{214}{105}\right]$$

$$= \frac{1}{4}\left[\frac{533}{210}\right]$$

$$= \frac{533}{840}$$

$$= .63452$$

$$I=\int_0^1 \frac{dx}{1+x}$$

= [log (1 + x)]

= [log (1 + 1) – log (1 + 0)]

= log 2 –log1

=log 2

= .693

error = .693 – .63452

= 0.05848

$$\% \text{ error} = \frac{0.05848}{.693} \times 100 = 8.43$$

2.(a) Find the value of f(x) = $x^2 - 12$ correct to four decimal places using Newton Raphson method . ***5***

Ans. We have given that f(x) = $x^2 - 12$

It is evident that $x^2 - 12$ becomes negative for x =3. While it is positive for x = 3.5 Hence root of $x^2 - 12 = 0$ lies between 3 and 3.5.

Now let f(x) = $x^2 - 12$ so that the given equation is f(x) = 0.

Now let f `(x) = 2x

From Newton Raphson method,

We have

$$x_{n+1} = x_n - \frac{f(x_n)}{f'(x_n)}$$

when n = 0, $x_1 = x_0 - \frac{f(x_0)}{f'(x_0)} = 3.5 - \frac{f(3.5)}{f'(3.5)}$

= 3.1429

Again we have

when n = 1, $x_2 = x_1 - \frac{f(x_1)}{f'(x_1)}$

$$= 3.1429 - \frac{f(3.1429)}{f'(3.1429)}$$

= 3.4805

when n = 2, $x_3 = x_2 - \frac{f(x_2)}{f'(x_2)}$

$$= 3.4805 - \frac{f(3.4805)}{f'(3.4805)}$$

= 3.46414

when n = 3, $x_4 = x_3 - \frac{f(x_3)}{f'(x_3)}$

$= 3.46414 - \frac{f(3.46414)}{f'(3.46414)}$

= 3.46412

when n = 4, $x_5 = x_4 - \frac{f(x_4)}{f'(x_4)}$

$= 3.46412 - \frac{f(3.46412)}{f'(3.46412)}$

$x_5 = 3.46412$

We see that x_5 is just same as x_4 hence root is 3.46412

Or x = 3.46412

(b) If a,b, c,d are the arguments of f(x) = $\frac{1}{x}$, show that f(a,b,c,d) = $-\frac{1}{abcd}$ **5**

Ans. $f(x) = \frac{1}{x}$ arguments are a, b, c, d

The difference table is as follows

x	f(x)	Δf(x)	$\Delta^2 f(x)$	$\Delta^3 f(x)$
a	$\frac{1}{a}$	$\frac{\left(\frac{1}{b}-\frac{1}{a}\right)}{b-a} = -\frac{1}{ab}$	$\frac{-\frac{1}{bc}+\frac{1}{ab}}{c-a} = \frac{1}{abc}$	$\frac{\frac{1}{bcd}-\frac{1}{abc}}{d-a} = \frac{a-d}{abcd(d-a)}$ $= -\frac{1}{abcd}$
b	$\frac{1}{b}$	$\frac{\left(\frac{1}{c}-\frac{1}{b}\right)}{c-b} = -\frac{1}{bc}$	$\frac{-\frac{1}{dc}+\frac{1}{bc}}{d-b} = \frac{1}{bcd}$	
c	$\frac{1}{c}$	$\frac{\left(\frac{1}{d}-\frac{1}{c}\right)}{d-c} = -\frac{1}{dc}$		
d	$\frac{1}{d}$			

$\therefore f(a, b, c, d) = -\frac{1}{abcd}$

(c) The velocity v of a particle of distance s from a point on its path is given by

s.(ft)	0	10	20	30	40	50	60
v(ft/s)	47	58	64	65	61	52	38

Estimate time taken to travel 60 ft using Simpson's $\frac{3}{8}$ rule. *5*

Ans. Represent the distances along x–axis and velocity along y–axis then, y_0, y_1, y_2 ..... y_7 are the values given in table. Also here h = 10, using Simpson's $\frac{3}{8}$ rule, we have the approximate value of time.

$$= \int_0^{60} y\, dx =$$

$$= \frac{3}{8} h \left[(y_0 + y_6) + 3(y_1 + y_2 + y_4 + y_5) + 2(y_3) \right]$$

$$= \frac{3}{8} \times 10 \left[(47 + 38) + 3(10 + 20 + 40 + 50) + 2 \times 30 \right]$$

$$= \frac{30}{8} \left[85 + 120 + 60 \right]$$

$$= \frac{30}{8} \times 265$$

$$= \frac{7950}{8}$$

= 993.75 second

= 999 second

3.(a) Using Runge – Kutta method of fourth order solve for y(0.1) given that y` = xy + y^2,y(0) =1. *7*

Ans. $\frac{dy}{dx} = xy + y^2 \quad \therefore f(x, y) = xy + y^2$

y(0.1) = ? y(0) =1

we have given that x_0 =0, y_0 =1

Let h = 0.1

$p = f(x_0, y_0) = 0 \times 1 + 1^2 = 1$

$$p_1 = f\left(x_0 + \frac{h}{2}, y_0 + p\frac{h}{2} \right)$$

$$= \left(x_0 + \frac{h}{2}\right)\left(y_0 + p\frac{h}{2}\right) + \left(y_0 + p\frac{h}{2}\right)^2$$

$$= \left(0 + \frac{0.1}{2}\right)\left(1 + 1 \times \frac{0.1}{2}\right) + \left(1 + 1 \times \frac{0.1}{2}\right)^2$$

$= (0.05)\ (1.05) + (1.05)^2$

$= .0525 = 1.1025$

$p_1 = 1.155 = 1.2$

$$p_2 = f\left(x_0 + \frac{h}{2}, y_0 + p_1\frac{h}{2}\right)$$

$$= \left(x_0 + \frac{h}{2}\right)\left(y_0 + p_1\frac{h}{2}\right) + \left(y_0 + p_1\frac{h}{2}\right)^2$$

$= (0.5)\ (1{+}1.2 \times 0.5) + (1{+}1.2 \times 0.5)^2$

$= 3.5 + 49$

$= 52.5$

$p_3 = f(x_0 + h), (p_0 + p_2h)$

$= (x_0 + h)\ (p_0 + p_2h) + (p_0 + p_2h)^2$

$= (0 + 0.1)\ (1{+}1.2 \times 0.1) + (1{+}1.2 \times 0.1)^2$

$= 0.1 \times 0.012 + 0.000144$

$= 0.001344$

Now

$$\frac{dy}{dx} = y' = \frac{1}{6}h\{p + 2(p_1 + p_2) + p_3\}$$

$$= \frac{1}{6} \times 0.1\{1 + 2(1.2 + 52.5) + 0.01344\}$$

$$= \frac{0.1}{6}\{108.4 + 0.001344\}$$

$$= \frac{108.401344}{6} \times 0.1$$

$$= \frac{10.8401344}{6}$$

$= 1.806689067$

$= 1.81$

(b) Given $\sum_{1}^{10} f(x) = 500426,\ \sum_{4}^{10} f(x) = 329240,\ \sum_{7}^{10} f(x) = 175212,$ **f(10) = 40365, find f(1).** **5**

Ans. Let $f(1) = \sum^{10} f(x) = f(1) + f(2) + f(3) + f(4) + f(5) + \text{--------} + f(10)$

$$= f(1) + f(2) + f(3) + \sum^{10} f(x)$$

$500426 = f(1) + f(2) + f(3) + 329240$ ... (1)

$f(2) = \sum_{1}^{10} f(x) = f(1) + f(2) + f(3) + \text{-------------} + f(10)$

$$= f(1) + f(2) + f(3) + f(4) + f(5) + f(6) + \sum_{7}^{10} f(x)$$

$500426 = f(1) + f(2) + f(3) + f(4) + f(5) + f(6) + 175212$ ... (2)

from (1) $f(1) + f(2) + f(3) = 500426 - 329040$

$f(1) + f(2) + f(3) = 171386$ ... (3)

$\therefore f(1) = \overset{3}{\Sigma} f(x) = 171386$ ...(4)

from (3) put in (2)

$500426 - 171386 = f(4) + f(5) + f(6) + 175212$

$f(4) + f(5) + f(6) = 53828$

$f(4) = \sum_{4}^{6} f(x) = 53828$ ... (5)

$f(3) = \sum_{1}^{10} f(x) = f(1) + f(2) + \text{---------} + f(10)$

=> $f(1) = 58844$

(c) A civil engineer has measured the height of a 10-floor building as 2950 cm and the working height of each beam as 35 cm while the true values are 2945 cm and 30 cm. Compare absolute and relative error. ***3***

Ans. Floors = 10

Height $x^* = 2950$ cm

Height of beam $y^* = 35$

$x = 2945$

$y = 30$

Absolute errors :

Absolute errorin in height of building $= \frac{x - f(x)}{x}$

$= \frac{2950 - 2945}{2950} = \frac{5}{2950}$
= 0.001694915
= 0.002

Absolute error in height of beam $= \frac{35 - 30}{35}$

$= \frac{5}{35}$
= 0.142857142
= 0.1429

Relative errors :

relative error $= \frac{|2945 - 30 \times 10| - |2950 - 35 \times 10|}{|2950 - 2945|}$

$= \frac{|2945 - 300| - |2950 - 350|}{5}$

$= \frac{2645 - 2600}{5}$

$= \frac{45}{5}$
= 9
relative error = 9%

4.(a) Determine stepsize h to be used in the tabulation of f(x) = sin x in [1,3] so that the linear interpolation will be correct to four decimal places. ***3***

Ans. h = ?

$f(x) = \sin x\ ,\ x \in [1,3]$

x_0, x = 1, f(1) = sin(1) = 0.017452406 = 0.0175
x_1, x = 2, f(2) = sin 2 = 0.034899496 = 0.0349
x_2, x = 3, f(3) = sin 3 = 0.052335956 = 0.0523
h = 0.0349 - 0.0175 = 0.174
or
h = 0.0523 - 0.0349 = 0.174
h = 0.174
steps involved = 3

(b) From the table below, for what value of x, is y minimum? Also find the value of y . *7*

X	3	4	5	6	7	8
y	0.205	0.24	0.259	0.262	0.25	0.224

Ans. The difference table in this case is

x	y	Δy	$\Delta^2 y$	$\Delta^3 y$	$\Delta^4 y$
3	0.205	.035			
4	0.24	.019	– 0.016	0	
5	0.259	.003	– 0.016		– 0.013
6	0.262	– 0.012	– 0.015	– 0.013	
7	0.25	–0.026	– 0.028		
8	0.224				

We write polynomial of degree 4 by looking $\Delta^4 y$

$\therefore$ Let $y = ax^4 + bx^3 + cx^2 + dx + e$

where a, b, c, d, e are constants to be determined

Put x = x = 3, 4, 5, 6, 7, 8

$y_1 = 81a + 27b + 9c + 3d + e = 0.205$ ... (1)

$y_2 = 256a + 64b + 16c + 4d + e = 0.24$ ... (2)

$y_3 = 625a + 125b + 25c + 5d + e = 0.259$ ... (3)

$y_4 = 1296a + 216b + 36c + 6d + e = 0.262$ ... (4)

$y_5 = 2401a + 343b + 49c + 7d + e = 0.25$ ... (5)

$y_6 = 4096a + 512b + 64c + 8d + e = 0.224$ ... (6)

Subtracting above equations

(2) – (1) $175a + 37b + 7c + d = 0.035$ ... (7)

(3) – (2) $396a + 61b + 9c + d = 0.019$ ... (8)

(4) – (3) $671a + 91b + 11c + d = 0.003$ ... (9)

(5) – (4) $1105a + 127b + 13c + d = -0.012$ ... (10)

(6) –(5) $1695a + 169b + 15c + d = -0.026$ ... (11)

Again subtracting

(8) – (7) $194a + 24b + 2c = 0.016$ ... (12)

(9) – (8) $302a + 30b + 2c = -0.016$ ... (13)

(10) – (9) $434a + 36b + 2c = -0.015$ ... (14)

(11) – (10) $540a + 42b + 2c = -0.014$ ... (15)

Again subtracting

(13) – (12) 108a + 6b = 0 ... (16)

(14) – (13) 132a + 6b = 0.001 ... (17)

(15) – (14) 156a + 6b = 0.001 ... (18)

Again subtracting

(17) – (16) 24a = 0.001

$$a=\frac{0.001}{24}=0.000041666$$

a = 0.000042

put value of a in (16)

$$108\times 0.000042+6b=0$$

$$b=\frac{0.004526}{6}$$

b = 0.000756

put value of a and b in ...(12)

$$194\times 0.000042+24\times -0.00756+2c=-0.016$$

0.008148 – 18144 + 2c = – 0.016

–.1,73292 + 2c = – 0.016

2c = – 0.016 + .173292

2c = .157292

$$2c=\frac{.157292}{2}$$

c = 0.078646

Putting values of a, b, c in (7)

$$175\times 0.000042+37\times(-0.000756)+7\times(-0.079)+d=0.035$$

0.00735 – 0.27972 – 0.553 + d = 0.035

0.00735 – .83272 + d = 0.035

– 0.82537 + d = 0.035

d = 0.035 + 0.82537

d = 0.86037

Putting the value of a, b, c, d in (1)

$$81\times 0.000042+27\times -0.000756+9\times 0.079+3\times 0.861+e=0.205$$

0.003402 – 0.020412 + 0.711 + 2.583 + e = 0.205

3.27699 + e = .205

e = .205 – 3.27699

e = – 3.07199

Putting values of a, b, c, d and e in y

$$\therefore \boxed{y=0.000042x^4-0.000756x^3+0.78646x^2+0.86037x-3.07199}$$

(c) Solve he following system of equations with partial pivoting using gauss elimination method. ***5***

2x + y + z = 10

3x + 2y + 3z = 18

x + 4y + 9z = 16

Ans. (a) Gauss Method. In the first stage, the multipliers are -3/2 and -1/2. We multiply the first equation successively by -3/2 and -1/2 and add it to the second and third equations respectively to obtain the equations.

$$\frac{1}{2}y + \frac{3}{2}z = 3$$

and $$\frac{7}{2}y + \frac{17}{2}z = 11$$

The augmented matrix therefore becomes

$$\begin{bmatrix} 2 & 1 & 1 & 10 \\ 0 & \frac{1}{2} & \frac{3}{2} & 3 \\ 0 & \frac{7}{2} & \frac{17}{2} & 11 \end{bmatrix}$$

At the second stage, we eliminate y from the third equation by multiplying the second equation by -7 and adding it to the third. The resulting system will be upper triangular

$$2x + y + z = 10$$
$$\frac{1}{2}y + \frac{3}{2}z = 3$$
$$-2z = -10$$

Back substitution gives the solution :

$$x = 7,\ y = -9 \text{ and } z = 5.$$

5. (a) Derive the Gauss – Seidel method in matrix form for the solution of the system of equations Ax = b.

Hence, derive the matrix formulation of the Gauss – Seidel method for the following system of equations (no iteration are to be performed) :

$$\begin{bmatrix} -4 & 1 & 1 \\ 1 & -4 & -1 \\ 1 & 1 & -4 \end{bmatrix}\begin{bmatrix} x_1 \\ x_2 \\ x_3 \end{bmatrix} = \begin{bmatrix} -2 \\ -4 \\ -2 \end{bmatrix}$$

4

Ans. Gauss Seidel Method : Gauss Seidel method, we have written the

iterative scheme of the system of equation
Ax = b as follows: -

$a_{11}x_i^{(k+1)} = -a_{12}x_2^{(k)} - a_{13}x_3^{(k)} - .... - a_n x_n^{k} + b_1$

$a_{21}x_1^{(k+1)} + a_{22}x_2^{(k+1)} = -a_{23}x_3^{(k)} - ... - a_{2n}x_n^{(k)} + b_2$

....

$a_{n1}x_1^{(k+1)} + a_{n2}x_2^{(k+1)} .... + a_{nn}x_n^{(k+1)} = +b_n$

This iteration method is also know as the method of successive displacement. For computation point of view, we rewrite (Ax) as

$$x_i^{(k+1)} = -1/a_{ii} \left[\sum_{j=1}^{i-1} a_{ij}\, x_j^{(k-1)} \sum_{ij=j+1}^{n} a_{ij}\, x_j^{(k)} - b_i \right]$$

i = 1, 2, ... n.

Equations are : –

$-4x_1 + x_2 + x_3 = -2$ … (i)

$x_1 - 4x_2 - x_3 = -4$ … (ii)

$x_1 + x_2 - 4x_3 = -2$ … (iii)

from (i) $x_1 = \frac{-2 - x_2 - x_3}{-4}$

$= \frac{2 + x_2 + x_3}{4}$

from (ii) $x_2 = \frac{x_1 - x_3 + 4}{4}$

from (iii) $x_3 = \frac{x_1 + x_2 + 2}{4}$

initally take $x^o = \begin{bmatrix} 0 \\ 0 \\ 0 \end{bmatrix}$

Iteration

$x_1 = \frac{2+0+0}{4} = \frac{1}{2}$

$x_2 = \frac{4 + \frac{1}{2} - 0}{4}$

$x_2 = \frac{9}{16}$

$$x_3 = \frac{\frac{1}{2} + \frac{9}{16} + 2}{4}$$

$$= \frac{8 + 9 + 32}{64}$$

$$x_3 = \frac{49}{64}$$

therefore the values after on interation are

$$x_1 = \frac{1}{2} = 0.5$$

$$x_2 = \frac{9}{16} = 0.5625$$

$$x_3 = \frac{49}{64} = 0.765625$$

(b) Perform three iteration to find the root of the equation $x^2 - 25 = 0$ using methods of false position with initial values 2 and 7. *7*

Ans.

$f(x) \equiv x^2 - 25 = 0$ $\quad\quad x_0 = 2$

$x_1 = 7$

$$f(2) = 2^2 - 25 = -2$$

$$f(7) = 7^2 - 25 = 24$$

Also we know that iteration formula
formula of Regula-Falsi method is

$$x_{i+1} = x_{i-1} - \frac{(x_i - x_{i-1}) f(x_{i-1})}{f(x_i) - f(x_{i-1})} \quad ...(1)$$

for first iteration x_2 :

put i =1, $x_{i-1} = x_0 = 2$ and so x_1 =7

$$f(x_1) = f(7) = 24$$

$$f(x_{i-1}) = f(x_0) = f(2) = -21,\ x_1 = 7$$

$$x_2 = x_0 - \frac{(x_1 - x_0) f(x_0)}{f(x_1) - f(x_0)}$$

$$= 2 - \frac{(7-2)(-21)}{24 - (-21)}$$

$$= 2 - \frac{5 \times -21}{24 + 21}$$

$$= 2 + \frac{105}{45}$$

$$= 2 + 2.33$$

$= 4.33$

$$x_2 = 4.33$$

For second iteration

$$x_3 = x_1 - \frac{(x_2 - x_1)f(x_1)}{f(x_2) - f(x_1)}$$

now suppose $x_1 = 4.33$, $x_2 = 7$

$$x_2 = 4.33 - \frac{(7 - 4.33)f(4.33)}{f(x_2) - f(x_1)}$$

$$=4.33 - \frac{(2.67)(-6.2511)}{24 - (-6.2511)}$$

$$=4.33 + \frac{16.690437}{30.2511}$$

$= 4.33 + .55172992$

$= 4.881729921$

$= 4.88$

$x_3 = 4.88$

For third iteration

Let

$x_2 = 4.88$

$x_3 = 7$

$$x_4 = x_2 - \frac{(x_3 - x_2)f(x_2)}{f(x_3) - f(x_2)}$$

$$= 4.88 - \frac{(7 - 4.88) + f(4.88)}{f(7) - f(4.88)}$$

$f(4.88) = (4.88)^2 - 25 = -1.1856$

$$= 4.88 - \frac{2.12 \times -1.1856}{24 - (-1.1856)}$$

$$= 4.88 + \frac{2.513472}{25.1856}$$

$= 4.88 + 0.99797979$

$= 4.97979798$

$= x_4 = 4.98$

we get the values :

$x_0 = 2$
$x_1 = 7$
$x_2 = 4.33$
$x_3 = 4.88$
$x_4 = 4.98$

In spite of above values 4.88 and 4.98 are very close to each other
$\therefore$ Required root correct to 2 decimal places is 4.88

(c) Find the Second order polynomials for the following data using Lagrange's interpolation method. *4*

X	0	1	2
f(x)	1	3	55

Ans. Lagrange's Interpolation formula is

$$f(x)=\frac{(x-x_1)(x-x_2)}{(x_0-x_1)(x_0-x_2)}f(x_0)+$$

$$\frac{(x-x_0)(x-x_2)}{(x_1-x_0)(x_1-x_2)}f(x_1)+$$

$$\frac{(x-x_0)(x-x_1)}{(x_2-x_0)(x_2-x_1)}f(x_2)$$

putting values from table given

$$f(x)=\frac{(x-1)(x-2)}{(0-1)(0-2)}\times 1+\frac{(x-0)(x-2)}{(1-0)(1-2)}\times 3+\frac{(x-0)(x-1)}{(2-0)(2-1)}\times 55$$

$$=\frac{x^2-3x+2}{2}+\frac{(x^2-2x)}{1\times -1}\times 3+\frac{(x^2-x)}{2\times 1}\times 55$$

$$=\frac{x^2-3x+2}{2}-3(x^2-2x)+\frac{(x^2-x)}{2}\times 55$$

$$f(x)=\frac{x^2-3x+2-6x^2+12x+55x^2-55x}{2}$$

$$f(x)=\frac{(50x^2-46x+2)}{2}$$

$$f(x)=25x^2-23x+1$$

CS-71 : COMPUTER ORIENTED NUMERICAL TECHNIQUES
June, 2007

Note : Question no. 1 is **compulsory.** Answer any **three** questions from the rest. In total you have to answer **four** questions.

1. (a) If the number x* = 4.3 approximates the number x = 4.305 correct upto n significant decimal digits, then calculate the value of n. **5**

Ans. $x^* = 4.3$, $x = 4.305$

$x - x^* = 4.305 - 4.3$

$= 0.005$

$|x - x^*| = |0.005| = 0.005$

$$= \frac{0.005}{2} \times 2$$

$$= \frac{1}{2}(.010)$$

$$= \frac{1}{2} \times 10^{-2}$$

Hence x^x approximates x correct to 2 decimal places $\therefore n = 2$

(b) Let $f(x) = x^{1/10}$, and suppose that x approximates x* correct upto 12 significant digits. Then compute upto how many significant decimal digits f(x*) approximates f(x). **5**

Ans. $r_{f(x)} = r_x . \frac{xf(x^*)}{f(x)}$

$$= r_x . \frac{x . \frac{1}{10} x^{*\frac{9}{10}}}{x^{\frac{1}{10}}}$$

$$= r_x \left(\frac{1}{10}\right)$$

$$| r_{f(x)} | = \left(\frac{1}{10}\right) | r_x | \le \frac{1}{10} . \frac{1}{2} 10^{1-12} = \frac{1}{2} \times 10^{1-(12+1)}$$

Therefore f(x) approximates f(x) correct to (n+1) significant digits i.e - (12 + 1) = 13 digits.

(c) Give one example of an equation with "multiple roots". And justify your answer. Also, write a polynomial equation of degree three which has a double root 62 and a single root 0. **5**

If n is a positive integer then polynomial $p_0x^n + p_1x^{n-1} + p_2x^{n-2} + ------- p_{n-1}x + p_n = 0$ is called equation with multiple roots some of constants $p_1, p_2, ----p_n$ may be zero though p_0 is always taken non zero.
The degree of the highest degree term is an algebraic equation is called the degree of the equation

Theorem of multiple roots :

If r roots of f(x) = 0 are equal to α then r– roots of f(x) = 0 will be equal to α

Let $x^3 + px^2 + qx + r = 0$ ... (1)

be any equation of degree 3.

such that $\alpha + \beta = 62$,

r = 0

where α, β, r are the roots of the equation.

$$\alpha + \beta + r = \frac{-p}{1}$$

$$r = 0, \quad \alpha + \beta = 62$$

$$\therefore\ 62 = -p$$

$$p = -62$$

$$\alpha\beta + \beta r + r\alpha = \frac{q}{1}$$

$$\alpha\beta + \beta \times 0 + 0 \times \alpha = q$$

$$\alpha\beta = q \qquad \alpha^2 + \beta^2 + 2\alpha\beta$$

$$\alpha\beta \times r = -r$$

$$\alpha\beta \times 0 = -r$$

$$\therefore r = 0$$

$\because$ equation has double root

$$\therefore \alpha = \beta \qquad \alpha + \alpha = 62$$

$$\alpha = 31 = \beta$$

$$\therefore\ q = 31 \times 31 = 961$$

p = – 62, q = 961, r = 0 put in (1)

$\therefore x^3 - 62x^2 + 961x = 0$ be the required equation which has double root 62 and single root 0.

(d) Estimate the missing data entry (a) using Newton's divided difference method: **5**

x	1	2	a	4
f(x)	3	0	2	4

Ans. We have the table below

x	1	2	a	4
f(x)	3	0	2	4

and to find a = ?

x	f(x)	$\Delta f(x)$	$\Delta^2 f(x)$
1	3	$\frac{0-3}{2-1}=-3$	$\frac{\frac{2}{a-2}-(-3)}{a-1}=\frac{3a-4}{(a-2)(a-1)}$
2	0	$\frac{2-0}{a-2}=\frac{2}{a-2}$	$\frac{\frac{2}{4-a}-\frac{2}{a-2}}{4-2}=\frac{4a-12}{(4-a)^2(a-2)2}$ $=\frac{2a-6}{(4-a)(a-2)(a-2)}$
a	2	$\frac{4-2}{4-a}=\frac{2}{4-a}$	
4	4		

for a, we have

$$\frac{2}{(a-2)}=\frac{2a-6}{(4-a)(a-2)}$$

$$2=\frac{2a-6}{4-a}$$

$$2=\frac{2(a-3)}{4-a}$$

$$1=\frac{a-3}{4-a}$$

$$4-a=a-3$$

$$a+a=4+3$$

$$2a=7$$

$$a=\frac{7}{2}$$

(e) If $f(x) = x^3$, then prove that for a > 0, b > 0, c > 0, we do also have the divided difference f[a, b, c] > 0. **5**

Ans. $f(x)=x^3$

$$f(a,b)=\frac{f(b)-f(a)}{b-a}$$

$$= \frac{b^3 - a^3}{b - a}$$

$$= \frac{(b-a)(b^2 - a^2 + ab)}{(b-a)}$$

$$= b^2 + a^2 + ab$$

$$f(b, c) = \frac{f(b, c) - f(a, b)}{c - a}$$

$$= \frac{f(c) - f(b)}{c - b}$$

$$= \frac{c^3 - b^3}{(c - b)}$$

$$= \frac{(c-b)(c^2 + b^2 + bc)}{(c-b)}$$

$$= b^2 + c^2 + bc$$

$$\therefore \; f(a, b, c) = \frac{f(b, c) - f(a, b)}{c - a}$$

$$= \frac{b^2 + c^2 + bc - b^2 - ab - a^2}{c - a}$$

$$= \frac{(c-a)(c+a+b)}{(c-a)}$$

$= a + b + c > 0$

Proved $\because$ a>0, b>0, c>0

(f) Prove that hD $\equiv$ $\log_e$ E, where D stands for "$\frac{d}{dx}$" and E is the advance operator. ***5***

Ans. $E = \Delta + 1$ ... (1)

$E = (1 - \nabla)^{-1}$ ... (2)

In E =$\log_e$ E

By Taylor series we have

$f(x+h) = f(x) + hf^1(x) + h^2 f^{11}(x)$ +--------

$= \left[1 + hd + h^2 d^2 + \text{----}\right] f(x)$ ... (3)

when $\frac{d}{dx} = D$

$f(x+h) = e^{hd} f(x)$ ... (4)

i.e E(f(x) = f(x + h), we obtain from equation (4), the identify

$E = e^{hd}$

taking log on both sides

$\boxed{hd = \log_e E}$ Hence proved

2. (a) Find a real root correct upto three decimal places of the function $\phi(x) = x^3 - 2x - 5$ using

(i) Bisection method,

(ii) Newton Raphson method. ***5+5=10***

Ans. (i) Bisection method,

$f(x) = x^3 - 2x - 5$

$x=1, f(1) = 1^3 - 2\times1 - 5 = -2$ (−ve)

$x = 3, f(3) = 3^3 - 2\times3 - 5 = 16$ (+ve)

we see that $f(1)$ and $f(3)$ are of opposite sign. Therefore thus exist at least one root lies between 1 and 3.

i.e $x_0 = \frac{1+3}{2} = \frac{4}{2} = 2$

$f(x_0) = f(2) = 2^3 - 2\times2 - 5$

$= 8 - 4 - 5$

$= 8 - 9$

$= -1$ (−ve)

$\therefore$ root lies between 2 and 3

$\therefore\ x_1 = \frac{2+3}{2} = \frac{5}{2} = 2.5$

$f(x_1) = f(2.5) = (2.5)^3 - 2\times2.5 - 5$

$= 15 - 625 - 5 - 5$

$= 5.625$ (+ve)

$\therefore$ Root lies 2 and 2.5

$\therefore\ x_2 = \frac{2+2.5}{2} = \frac{4.5}{2} = 2.25$

$f(x_2)=(2.25)^3 - 2\times 2.25 - 5$

$= 1.890625 \quad (+ve)$

$\therefore$ root lies between 2.25 and 2.50

$$(x_3) = \frac{2.25 + 2.50}{2} = 2.375$$

$f(2.375) = (2.375)^3 - 2\times 2.375 - 5$

$= 3.46484376 \quad (+ve)$

$$x_4 = \frac{2.245 + 2.375}{2}$$

$x_4 = 2.3125$

$f(x_4) = (2.3125)^3 - 2\times 2.3125 - 5$

$= 2.74145$

we see that

$x_0 = 2$

$x_1 = 2.5$

$x_2 = 2.25$

$x_3 = 2.375$

$x_4 = 2.3125$

we see that 2.375 and 2.3125 are nearly similar therefore 2.3125 is root.

(ii) Newton Raphson method.

Ans. Newton Raphson method

$f(x) = x^3 - 2x - 5$

$f^1(x) = 3x^2 - 2$

$$x_{n+1} = x_n - \frac{f(x_n)}{f^1(x_n)}$$

$\therefore\ f(x_n) = x_n^3 - 2x_n - 5$

$f^1(x_n) = 3x_n^2 - 2$

$$\therefore\ x_{n+1} = x_n - \frac{x_n^3 - 2x_n - 5}{3x_n^2 - 2} \qquad \dots (1)$$

Let $x_0 = 2.3$

$$x_1 = 2.3 - \left[\frac{(2.3)^3 - 2(2.3) - 5}{3(2.3)^2 - 2}\right]$$

$$= 2.3 - \left[\frac{2.567}{13.87}\right]$$

$$= 2.3 - [0.18507503]$$

$$= 2.114924297$$

$$x_1 = 2.1149$$

$$x_2 = 2.1149 - \left[\frac{(2.1149)^3 - 2(2.1149) - 5}{3(2.1149)^2 - 2}\right]$$

$$= 2.1149 - \left[\frac{.229728971}{11.4184}\right]$$

$$= 2.1149 - .020119191$$

$$= 2.094780809$$

$$x_2 = 2.0949$$

$$x_3 = 2.0949 - \left[\frac{(2.0949)^3 - 2(2.0949) - 5}{3(2.0949)^2 - 2}\right]$$

$$= 2.0949 - \left[\frac{0.02389073}{11.16581803}\right]$$

$$= 2.0949 - 0.00213963$$

$$= 2.092760369$$

$$x_3 = 2.0928$$

$$x_4 = 2.0928 - \left[\frac{(2.0928)^3 - 2(2.0928) - 5}{3(2.0928)^2 - 2}\right]$$

$$= 2.0928 - \left[\frac{0.010470218}{11.13943552}\right]$$

$$= 2.0928 - .000939923$$

$$x_4 = 2.091860076$$

$$x_4 = 2.09186$$

we may proceed this in further steps
we have that

$x_1 = 2.1149$

$x_2 = 2.0949 = 2.095$

$x_3 = 2.0928 = 2.093$

$x_4 = 2.09186 = 2.092$

We see that x_3 and x_4 are nearly similar, so 2.092 is the root.

$\therefore$ root = 2.092

(b) Using Lagrange's interpolation formula, obtain the value of y(1) from the following table: ***5***

x	0	1	3	4
y(x)	2	0	1	2

Ans.

	x_0	x_1	x_2	x_3
x	0	1	3	4
y(x)	2	0	1	2
	$f(x_0)$	$f(x_1)$	$f(x_2)$	$f(x_3)$

By Lagrange's Interpolation formula we have

$$y(x)=f(x) = \frac{(x-x_1)(x-x_2)(x-x_3)}{(x_0-x_1)(x_0-x_2)(x_0-x_3)} f(x_0) +$$

$$\frac{(x-x_0)(x-x_1)(x-x_3)}{(x_1-x_0)(x_1-x_2)(x_1-x_3)} f(x_1) +$$

$$\frac{(x-x_1)(x-x_0)(x-x_3)}{(x_2-x_0)(x_2-x_1)(x_2-x_3)} f(x_2)+$$

$$\frac{(x-x_1)(x-x_0)(x-x_2)}{(x_3-x_0)(x_3-x_1)(x_3-x_2)} f(x_3)+$$

$$= \frac{(x-1)(x-3)(x-4)}{(0-1)(0-3)(0-4)} 2 + \frac{(x-0)(x-3)(x-4)}{(1-0)(1-3)(1-4)} \times 0 + \frac{(x-1)(x-0)(x-4)}{(3-0)(3-1)(3-4)} \times 1$$

$$+ \frac{(x-1)(x-0)(x-3)}{(4-0)(4-1)(4-3)} \times 2$$

$$= \frac{(x-1)(x-3)(x-4)}{12} \times 2 + 0 + \frac{(x-1)(x)(x-4)}{-6} + \frac{(x-1)(x)(x-3)}{12} \times 2$$

$$\frac{-2(x-1)(x-3)(x-4) - 2x(x-1)(x-4) + 2(x-1)x(x-3)}{12}$$

$$= \frac{2(x^2-4x+3)(x-4)-2(x^2-x)(x-4)+(2x^2-2x)(x-3)}{12}$$

$$= \frac{-2(x^3-4x^2-4x^2+16x+3x-12)-2(x^3-4x^2-x^2+4x)+(2x^3-6x^2-2x^2+6x)}{12}$$

$$= \frac{-2x^3+16x^2-38x+24-2x^3+10x^2-8x+2x^3-8x^2+6x}{12}$$

$$= \frac{-2x^3+18x^2-40x+24}{12}$$

$$= \frac{-x^3+9x^2-20x+12}{6}$$

$$y(x) = -\frac{1}{6}(x^3-9x^2+20x-12)$$

put x =1

$$y(1) = -\frac{1}{6}(1+9\times1^2+20\times1-12)$$

$$= -\frac{1}{6}(1-9+20-12) = 0$$

y(1) =0

3. (a) Solve the system of following equations using Gauss Elimination method: ***5***

$\mathbf{3x_1 + 2x_2 + x_3 = 3}$

$\mathbf{2x_1 + x_2 + x_3 = 0}$

$\mathbf{6x_1 + 2x_2 + 4x_3 = 6}$

Ans. $3x_1 + 2x_2 + x_3 = 3$ ... (i)

$2x_1 + x_2 + x_3 = 0$ ... (ii)

$6x_1 + 2x_2 + 4x_3 = 6$ ... (iii)

We see I element of (i) not equation i.e. $a_{11} \neq 0$

$$\therefore \text{ (i)} \times \frac{-1}{3} + \text{(ii)} \div 2$$

$$-x_1 - \frac{2x_2}{3} - \frac{x_3}{3} = -1$$

$$x_1 + \frac{x_2}{2} + \frac{x_3}{2} = 0$$

$$-\frac{1}{6}x_2 + \frac{1}{6}x_3 = -1$$

or $\frac{x_2}{3} - \frac{1}{3}x_3 = -2$ ... (iv)

Now ∴ (i) $\times \frac{-6}{3}$ + (iii)

$$\begin{array}{r} -6x_1 - 4x_2 - 2x_3 = -6 \\ 6x_1 + 2x_2 + 4x_3 = 6 \\ \hline -2x^2 + 2x_3 = 0 \end{array}$$ ... (v)

Now new equivalent system then becomes,

$3x_1 + 2x_2 + x_3 = 3$ ... (i)

$\frac{1}{3}x_2 + \frac{1}{3}x_3 = -2$ ... (iv)

$-2x_2 + 2x_3 = 0$ ... (v)

which may be written as

$$a_{11} \neq 0 \left[\begin{array}{ccc|c} 3 & 2 & 1 & 3 \\ 0 & \frac{1}{3} & -\frac{1}{3} & -2 \\ 0 & -2 & 2 & 0 \end{array}\right]$$

$$\text{where } |A| = \left[\begin{array}{ccc|c} 3 & 2 & 1 & 3 \\ 2 & 1 & -1 & 0 \\ 6 & -2 & 4 & 6 \end{array}\right]$$

i.e (iv) × (6) + (v)

$$\begin{array}{r} 2x_2 - 2x_3 = 12 \\ -2x_2 + 2x_3 = 0 \\ \hline 0 + \quad 0 = -12 \end{array}$$

$$a_{22} \neq 0 \left[\begin{array}{ccc|c} 3 & 2 & 1 & 3 \\ 0 & \frac{1}{2} & -\frac{1}{3} & -2 \\ 0 & -2 & 2 & 12 \end{array}\right]$$

Thus system has no solution since x_3 cannot be determined from the last equation. This system is said inconsistent.

(b) When is a matrix A said to be strictly diagonally dominant? Give an example of 3 × 3 matrix. A which is strictly diagonally dominant. 5

Ans. A matrix in which all the off–diagonal elements are zero i.e a = 0 for

$i \neq j$, is called diagonal matrix x or diagonal dominated matrix.

$$eg \begin{bmatrix} a_{11} & 0 & 0 \\ 0 & a_{12} & 0 \\ 0 & 0 & a_{23} \end{bmatrix} 3 \times 3$$

(c) Find the minimum number of intervals required to evaluate

$$\int_0^1 \frac{dx}{1+x}$$

with an accuracy of 10^{-5} using Simpson's $\frac{1}{3}$ rule. *5*

Ans. $I = \int_0^1 \frac{dx}{1+x}$

Let intervals are 8

$\therefore$ i.e $N = 8,\ h = \frac{1}{8}$

table is

x	f(x)	
0	1	f_0
1/8	8/9	f_1
2/8	8/10	f_2
3/8	8/11	f_3
4/8	8/12	f_4
5/8	8/13	f_5
6/8	8/14	f_6
7/8	8/15	f_7
8/8	8/16	f_8

By Simpson's $\frac{1}{3}$ rule

$$I_s\ (f) = \frac{1}{3} \times \frac{1}{8}[f_0 + f_8 + 4(f_1 + f_3 + f_5 + f_7) + 2(f_2 + f_4 + f_6)]$$

$$= \frac{1}{24}\left[1 + \frac{8}{16} + 4\left(\frac{8}{9} + \frac{8}{11} + \frac{8}{13} + \frac{8}{15}\right) + 2\left(\frac{8}{10} + \frac{8}{12} + \frac{8}{14}\right)\right]$$

$= 0.69314$

The exact value of the given integral correct 5 decimal places is log 2= 0.69314

$\therefore$ actual error = 0.000008 the observe that N = 8 gives (I.E–0.5) accuracy.

We shall now determine N from the theoretical error bound for Simpson's $\frac{1}{3}$

rule which gives I.E–0.5 accuracy

Now

$$|E_s[fI]| \leq \frac{(b-a)^4}{2880\, N^3}$$

where

$$M_4 = \underset{0\leq x<c1}{\text{Man}} \left|f^{iv}(x)\right.$$

$$= \underset{0\leq x<c1}{\text{Man}} \left|\frac{24}{(1+x)^4}\right| = 24$$

To obtain the required accuracy we should therefore have

$$\left|\frac{24}{2880\, N^3}\right| \leq 10^{-5} \text{or} \quad N^3 \geq \frac{24\times 10^5}{2880}$$

$= 833.3333$

$\therefore N \geq 9.5$

We find that we cannot take N = 9 since to make use of Simpson's rule we should have even number of intervals we therefore conclude that N = 10 should be the minimum number of subintervals to obtain the accuracy IE – 0.6 i.e. 10^{-5}.

4. (a) Find a solution of the system of linear equations: **5**

83x + 11y – 4z = 95

7x + 52y + 13z = 104

3x + 8y + 29z = 71

Ans. 83x + 11y – 4z = 95 ... (1)

7x + 52y + 13z = 104 ... (2)

3x + 8y + 29z = 71 ... (3)

equ $(1)\times 13$

equ $(2)\times 3$

$$1079x + 13y - 52z = 1235 \quad \text{... (4)}$$

$$\underline{\_28x +\_ 208y +\_ 52z =\_ 416} \quad \text{... (5)}$$

$$135x + 221y = 1651$$

135x + 221y = 1651 ... (6)

equ $(2)\times 29$

equ $(3)\times 13$

$$\begin{array}{l} 203x + 1508y + \ 377z = 3016 \quad \dots (7) \\ \underline{{}_{-}39x +_{-} 104y +_{-} 377z =_{-} 923} \quad \dots (8) \\ 164x + 1404y \qquad = 2093 \end{array}$$

$164x + 1404y = 2093$ ... (9)

equ $(6) \times 164$

equ $(9) \times 135$

$$\begin{array}{l} 22140x + 36244y = 270764 \quad \dots (7) \\ \underline{{}_{-}22140x +_{-} 189540y =_{-} 282555} \quad \dots (8) \\ \qquad -153296y \ = -11791 \end{array}$$

$y = \dfrac{11791}{153296}$

$y = 0.0769166$

Put the value of y in equation (6)

$135x + 221 \times 0.0769166 = 1651$

$135x + 16.998569 = 1651$

$135x = 1651 - 16.998569$

$135x = 1634.0014$

$x = \dfrac{1634.0014}{135}$

$x = 12.103714$

Put the value of x & y in equation (1)

$83x + 11y - 4z = 95$

$83 \times 12.103714 + 11 \times 0.0769166 - 4z = 95$

$1004.6083 + 0.8460826 - 4z = 95$

$1005.4544 - 4z = 95$

$-4z = 95 - 1005.4544$

$-4z = -910.4544$

$z = \dfrac{910.4544}{4}$

$z = 227.6136$

$x = 12.103714$

$y = 0.0769166$

$z = 227.6136$

(b) Given 1³ = 1, 2³ = 8 and 4³ = 64. Using numerical differentiation, compute the value of 3² from these data. **5**

Ans. We have given that

$1^3 = 1,\ 2^3 = 8,\ 4^3 = 64$

we have to find value of 3^2

$\therefore x = 3^2$

$f(x) = x - 3^2 = 0$ root lies between 8 and 10

f(8) = 8 – 9 = –1

f(10) = 10 – 9 = 1

Because f(8) and f(9) are negative and positive respectively

Regula falsi method :

$$x_{i+1} = x_{i-1} - \frac{(x_i - x_{i-1})(f(x_{i-1}))}{f(x_i) - f(x_{i-1})}$$

$x_0 = 8$

For first iteration

$x_1 = 10$

$i = 1$

$$x_2 = x_0 - \frac{(x_1 - x_0)(f(x_0))}{f(x_1) - f(x_0)}$$

$$= 8 - \frac{(10-8)(-1)}{1-8}$$

$$= 8 - \frac{(-2)}{-7}$$

$$= 8 - \frac{2}{7}$$

$= 8 - 0.285714285$

= 7.714285714

$x_2 = 7.7$

$x_2 = 10$

For second iteration i =2

$x_1 = 7.7$

$$x_3 = x_1 - \frac{(x_2 - x_1)(f(x_1))}{f(x_2) - f(x_1)}$$

$= 7.7 - \frac{(10 - 7.7)(-1.3)}{1 - (-1.3)}$

$= 7.7 - \frac{2.3 \times (-1.3)}{1 + 1.3}$

$= 7.7 + \frac{2.99}{2.3}$

$= 7.7 + 1.3$

$x_3 = 9$

$\therefore$ we can say that value of $x = 3^2 = 9$ i.e. $x_3 = 9$

(c) Evaluate $\int_0^1 \frac{dx}{1+x^2}$ with six subintervals using Trapezoidal rule. Hence find an approximate value of π. **5**

Ans. $\int_0^1 \frac{dx}{1+x^2}$

intervals $= 6 \therefore h = \frac{1}{6}$

table is

x	$f(x) = \frac{1}{1+x^2}$	Or	
0	1	1	f_0
$\frac{1}{6}$	$\frac{36}{37} =$	0.972973	f_1
$\frac{2}{6}$	$\frac{36}{40} =$	0.9	f_2
$\frac{3}{6}$	$\frac{36}{45} =$	0.8	f_3
$\frac{4}{6}$	$\frac{36}{52} =$	0.692308	f_4
$\frac{5}{6}$	$\frac{36}{61} =$	0.590167	f_5
$\frac{6}{6} = 1$	$\frac{1}{2} =$	0.5	f_6

By trapezoidal rule we have

$$I = \frac{h}{2}[(f_0 + f_6) + 2(f_1 + f_2 + f_3 + f_4 + f_5)]$$

$$I = \frac{1}{12}[(1 + 0.5) + 2(0.972973 + 0.8 + 0.9 + 0.692308 + 0.590167)]$$

$$I = 0.784241333 \qquad \text{... (1)}$$

$$I = \int_0^1 \frac{dx}{1+x^2} = \left[\tan^{-1} x\right]_0^1 = \frac{\pi}{4} \qquad \text{... (2)}$$

from (1) & (2)

$$\frac{\pi}{4} = 0.78441$$

$$\pi = 0.784241 \times 4$$

$$\pi = 3.136964$$

Real value of $\pi = 3.141593$

$$= 3.141593 - 3.136964$$
$$= 0.004629$$

5. (a) In RKM of second order or third order of fourth order, what is the significance of the term "order"? Explain it for all the above cases by taking one example of each order. **5**

Ans. Order of differential equation :

The order of differential equation is the order of the highest derivative involved in the differential equation

eq (1) $\left(\frac{dy}{dx}\right)^2 = 4\left(\frac{dy}{dx}\right) - 2y^2 + 4x$

first order differential equation

(2) $\left(\frac{d^2y}{d^2x}\right) = ky$(second order differential equation)

Runge Kutta Method (R.K.M) of IInd order :

Let the method is

$$y_{n+1} = y_n + w_1k_1 + w_2k_2$$

$$k_1 = h_f(t_n, y_n)$$

$$k_2 = hf(t_n + c_2h, y_n + a_2, k_1)$$

Where c_2, a_{21}, w_1 and w_2 are chosen to make y_{n+1} closer to $y(t_n = 1)$

R.K.M is given as

$$y_{n+1} = y_n + hf_n \frac{h^2}{2}\left(f_1 + f_n f_y\right) + \frac{c_2 h^3}{4}\left(f_n + 2f_n f_{yy} + f_n{}^2 f_{yy}\right) + ---$$

III order :

Let the method is defined as

$$y_{n+1} = y_n + w_1k_1 + w_2k_2 + w_3k_3$$

where $k_1 = hf(t_n, y_n)$

$$k_2 = hf(t_n + c_2h, y_n + a_{21}k_1)$$

and $w_1 + w_2 + w_3 = 1$

IV Order

consider the method as :

$$y_{n+1} = y_n + w_1k_1 + w_2k_2 + w_3k_3 + w_4k_4$$

where

$$k_1 = hf(t_n, y_n)$$

$$k_2 = hf(t_n + c_2h, y_n + a_{21}k_1)$$

$$k_3 = hf(t_n + c_3h, y_n + a_{31}k_1 + a_{32}k_2)$$

$$k_1 = hf(t_n, c_4h, y_n + a_{41}k_2 + a_{43}k_3)$$

We see that R.KM being single step methods are self starting methods. If we take general way. Then

$$k_i = f\left[t_n + c_ih, \sum_{i=1}^{j-1} a_{ij}\, k_j\right]$$

$i = 1, 2$------------m, $c_j = 0$

Here is the order of method the unknown c_i, a_{ij} and w_j are then obtained by expanding k_i's and y_{n+1} is Taylor series about the point (t_n, y_n) and compassing the coefficients of different powers of h.

(b) Solve the IVP: y' = y + x, y(0) = 1 with h = 0.1 in the interval [0, 0.2] using Euler's method. **5**

Ans. IVP → Initial Value Problem

$f(x, y) = x + y$

$h = 0.1$,

we have $y_{n+1} = y_n + hf_n$

$y(0.1) = y_1 = y_0 + (0.1)f_0$

$= 1 + (0.1)\,[1+0]$

$= 1 + 0.1 \times 1$

$= 1.1$

$$y(0,2) = y_2 = y_1 + h\,f(1)$$

$$y_2 = 1.1 + 0.1 \times (1.1 + .1)$$

$$y_2 = 1.1 + 0.1 \times 1.2$$

$$= 1.1 + 1.2$$

$$y_2 = 1.22$$

(c) If u = $\frac{4x^2y^3}{z^4}$ and errors in x, y, z be 0.001, compute the relative maximum error in u when x = y = z = 1. **5**

Ans. $u = \frac{4x^2y^3}{z^4}$

$x = 1,\ y = 1,\ z = 1$`

$x^* = 0.001$

$y^* = 0.001$

$z^* = 0.001$

$$\frac{4(x^*)^2(y^*)^3}{(z^*)^4} = \frac{4 \times (0.001)^2 \times (0.001)^3}{(0.001)^4}$$

$$= \frac{4 \times 1 \times 10^{-9}}{10^{-12}} = 4 \times 10^3$$

$$= \frac{4x^2y^3}{z^4} = 4$$

Relative error

$$= \frac{\frac{4x^2y^3}{z^4} - \left|\frac{4(x^*)^2(y^*)^3}{(z^*)^4}\right|}{4\frac{x^2y^3}{z^4}}$$

$$= \frac{4 - 4 \times 10^3}{4}$$

$$= 1 - 10^3 = 1 - 1000 = -999$$

$$= -.9 \times 10^3$$

$$= -9.0 \times 10^2$$

CS – 71: COMPUTER ORIENTED NUMERICAL TECHNIQUES
December, 2007

*Note: Question number 1 is **compulsory**. Attempt any **three** questions from the rest. In total you have to answer **four** questions.*

Q1. (a) Evaluate Relative error of the function $f = xy^2z^3$, if x = 37.1, y = 9.87, z = 6.052 and $\Delta x = 0.3$, $\Delta y = 0.11$, $\Delta z = 0.016$.

Ans. $x = 37.1 \pm 0.3$

$y = 9.87 \pm 0.11$

$z = 6.052 \pm 0.016$

$f = x y^2 z^3$

$r_{y^2} = \pm 2\dfrac{0.11}{9.87}, r_{z^3} = \pm 3\dfrac{0.016}{6.052}$

$r_x = \pm\dfrac{0.3}{37.1}$ $\qquad r_{xy^2z^3} = \pm\left(r_x + r_{y^2} + r_{z^3}\right)$

$= \pm\left(\dfrac{0.3}{37.1} + 2\dfrac{0.11}{9.87} + 3\dfrac{0.016}{6.052}\right) = \pm\left(0.008086 + 0.022289 + 0.007931\right)$

$= \pm 0.038297$

(b) Perform three iterations of the Newton – Raphson method to obtain the approximate value of $(17)^{1/3}$ starting with the initial approximation $x_0 = 2$.

Ans. Newton - Raphson

Let $x = (17)^{\frac{1}{3}}$

or $x^3 = 17$

or $x^3 - 17 = 0$

$f(x) = x^3 - 17$

$f'(x) = 3x^2$

Initial approximation $x_0 = 2$.

Ist Iteration

$$x_1 = x_0 - \frac{f(x_0)}{f'(x_0)} = 2 - \frac{2^3 - 17}{3 \times 2^2} = 2 - \frac{-9}{12}$$

$$x_1 = 2 + \frac{3}{4} = \frac{11}{4} = 2.75$$

IInd Iteration

$$x_2 = 2.75 - \frac{(2.75)^3 - 17}{3\times(2.75)^2} = 2.58$$

IIIrd Iteration

$$x_3 = 2.58 - \frac{(2.58)^3 - 17}{3\times(2.58)^2} = 2.5713$$

(c) (i) Prove that $\Delta\nabla = \Delta - \nabla$

Ans. Δ = forward difference operator

∇ = backward difference operator

E = shift operator

L.H.S. $\Delta\nabla = (E-1)\left(1-E^{-1}\right)$

$= (E-1)\left(1-\frac{1}{E}\right)$

$= E-1-1+\frac{1}{E}$

$= (E-1)-\left(1-\frac{1}{E}\right)$

$= (E-1)-\left(1-E^{-1}\right)$

$= \Delta - \nabla$ R.H.S

(ii) Evaluate $\frac{\Delta^2}{E}\left(x^3\right)$

Ans. $\frac{\Delta^2}{E}\left(x^3\right) = \Delta^2 E^{-1}\left(x^3\right)$

$= \Delta^2 (x-h)^3$

$= \Delta^2 \left(x^3 - 3h\,x^2 + 3h^2x - h^3\right)$

$= \Delta\left[\Delta x^3 - 3h\Delta x^2 + 3h^2\Delta x - \Delta h^3\right]$

$= \Delta\left[(x+h)^3 - x^3 - 3h\left((x+h)^2 - x^2\right) + 3h^2\left((x+h)-x\right) - h^3\right]$

$= \Delta\left[x^3 + 3x^2h + 3h^2x + h^3 - x^3 - 3h\left(x^2 + 2hx + h^2 - x^2\right) + 3h^3 - h^3\right]$

$= \Delta\left[3x^2h + 3h^2x + h^3 - 6h^2x - 3h^3 + 3h^3 - h^3\right]$

$$= \Delta\left[3x^2h - 3h^2x\right]$$
$$= 3\Delta\left[x^2h - h^2x\right]$$
$$= 3\left[h\Delta x^2 - h^2\Delta x\right]$$
$$= 3\left[h\left((x+h)^2 - x^2\right) - h^2\left((x+h) - x\right)\right]$$
$$= 3\left[h\left(x^2 + 2hx + h^2 - x^2\right) - h^2\ h\right]$$
$$= 3\left[2h^2x + h^3 - h^3\right]$$
$$= 3\left[2h^2x\right] = 6h^2x$$

(d) Use fixed point iteration method to evaluate $\sqrt[3]{48}$, correct to four decimal places.

Ans. Let $x = \sqrt[3]{48}$

$\Rightarrow x^3 = 48 \Rightarrow x^3 - 48 = 0$

$\therefore f(x) = x^3 - 48$

$f'(x) = 3x^2$

For function f(x)

x	2	3	4
f(x)	-40	-11	16

$\therefore$ Initial value $(x_0) = \dfrac{3+4}{2} = 3.5$

Newton – Raphson Method

$$x_{i+1} = x_1 - \frac{f(x_i)}{f'(x_i)}$$

Iteration 1:

$$x_1 = x_0 - \frac{f(x_0)}{f'(x_0)}$$

$$= 3.5 - \frac{f(3.5)}{f'(3.5)} = 3.6395$$

Iteration 2:

$$x_2 = x_1 - \frac{f(x_1)}{f'(x_1)} = 3.6342$$

Iteration 3:

$$x_3 = x_2 - \frac{f(x_2)}{f'(x_2)}$$

$$= 3.6342 - \frac{f(3.6342)}{f'(3.6342)} = 3.6342$$

(e) Find the root of the equation $xe^x = \cos x$ using the secant method, correct to four decimal places. Do three iterations.

Ans. $x\,e^x = \cos x$

$\cos x - x\,e^x = 0$

$f(x) = \cos x - x\,e^x$

For function f(x)

x	0	1
f(x)	1	-15.19

The root lies between 0 and 1

$x_0 = 0,\ x_1 = 1$

Ist Iteration

$$x_2 = \frac{x_0 f(x_1) - x_1 f(x_0)}{f(x_1) - f(x_0)} = \frac{0 \times (-15.19) - 1 \times 1}{-15.19 - 1} = 0.3146 \quad f(x_2) = 0.5198$$

IInd Iteration:

$$x_3 = \frac{x_1 f(x_2) - x_2 f(x_1)}{f(x_2) - f(x_1)} = 0.4467 \quad f(x_3) = 0.2036$$

IIIrd Iteration:

$$x_4 = \frac{x_2 f(x_3) - x_3 f(x_2)}{f(x_3) - f(x_2)} = 0.5317$$

(f) Using the data sin (0.1) = 0.09983 and sin (0.2) = 0.19867, find an approximate value of sin (0.15) by Lagrange interpolation. Obtain on the truncation error.

Ans. Lagrange interpolation

x	0.1	0.2
sin x	0.09983	0.19867

$$f(x) = \frac{x - 0.2}{0.1 - 0.2} 0.09983 + \frac{x - 0.1}{0.2 - 0.1} 0.19867$$

$$f(0.15) = \frac{0.15 - 0.2}{-0.1} \times 0.09983 + \frac{0.15 - 0.1}{0.1} \times 0.19867$$

$$= \frac{-0.05}{-0.1} \times 0.09983 + \frac{0.05}{0.1} \times 0.19867 = 0.0499 + 0.09933 = 0.1492$$

truncation error is given by

$$|\text{error}| \le \frac{|x_n - x_0|^{n+1}}{(n+1)!} \max\left|f^{n+1}(\xi)\right|$$

$$\le \frac{0.09884}{2} \times |\sin(0.19867)| = 0.04942 \times 0.19736 = 0.0097$$

Q2. (a) Given the values

$x:$	5	7	11	13	17
$f(x):$	150	392	1452	2366	5202

Evaluate f(9), using
(i) Lagrange's formula.

Ans.

$x:$	5	7	11	13	17
$f(x):$	150	392	1452	2366	5202

From Lagrange's Interpolation Formula

$$f(x) = y_1 \frac{(x-x_2)(x-x_3)(x-x_4)(x-x_5)}{(x_1-x_2)(x_1-x_3)(x_1-x_4)(x_1-x_5)}$$

$$+y_2 \frac{(x-x_1)(x-x_3)(x-x_4)(x-x_5)}{(x_2-x_1)(x_2-x_3)(x_2-x_4)(x_2-x_5)}$$

$$+y_3 \frac{(x-x_1)(x-x_2)(x-x_4)(x-x_5)}{(x_3-x_1)(x_3-x_2)(x_3-x_4)(x_3-x_5)}$$

$$+y_4 \frac{(x-x_1)(x-x_2)(x-x_3)(x-x_5)}{(x_4-x_1)(x_4-x_2)(x_4-x_3)(x_4-x_5)}$$

$$+y_5 \frac{(x-x_1)(x-x_2)(x-x_3)(x-x_4)}{(x_5-x_1)(x_5-x_2)(x_5-x_3)(x_5-x_4)}$$

$$\therefore f(9) = 150\frac{(9-7)(9-11)(9-13)(9-17)}{(5-7)(5-11)(5-13)(5-17)}$$

$$+392\frac{(9-5)(9-11)(9-13)(9-17)}{(7-5)(7-11)(7-13)(7-17)}$$

$$+1452\frac{(9-5)(9-7)(9-13)(9-17)}{(11-5)(11-7)(11-13)(11-17)}$$

$$+2366\frac{(9-5)(9-7)(9-11)(9-17)}{(13-5)(13-7)(13-11)(13-17)}$$

$$+5202\frac{(9-5)(9-7)(9-11)(9-13)}{(17-5)(17-7)(17-11)(17-13)}$$

$$=150\frac{.(2).(-2).(-4).(-8)}{(-2)(-6)(-8)(-12)}+392\frac{(4)(-2)(-4)(-8)}{(-2)(-4)(-6)(-10)}$$

$$+1452\frac{(4)(2)(-4)(-8)}{(6)(4)(-2)(-6)}.+2366\frac{(4)(2)(-2)(-8)}{(8)(6)(2)(-4)}$$

$$+5202\frac{(4)(2)(-2).(-4)}{.(11)(10)(6)(4)}$$

= -16.67 – 209.07 + 1290.67 – 788.67 + 126.11 = 402.37

(ii) Newton's dividend difference formula.

Ans.

x	f(x)	$\Delta_d f(x)$	$\Delta_d^2 f(x)$	$\Delta_d^3 f(x)$	$\Delta_d^4 f(x)$
5	150	$\frac{242}{2}=121$	$\frac{144}{6}=24$	$\frac{8}{8}=1$	
7	392	$\frac{1060}{4}=265$	$\frac{192}{6}=32$	$\frac{10}{10}=1$	0
11	1452	$\frac{914}{2}=457$	$\frac{252}{6}=42$		
17	5202				

where Δd is divide difference operator

From Newton's Divide difference formula

$$f(x)=y_1+\Delta_d f(x)(x-x_1)+\Delta_d^2 f(x)(x-x_1)(x-x_2)$$

$$+\Delta_d^3 f(x)(x-x_1)(x-x_2)(x-y)$$

$$f(9)=150+121(9-5)+24(9-5)(9-7)$$

$$+1.(9-5)(9-7)(9-11)$$

= 150 + 121.4 + 24.4.2 + 1.4.2 (-2)

= 150 + 484 + 192 – 16 = 826 – 16 = 810

(b) Solve the initial value problem

u^1 = - $2tu^2$, u(0) = 1

with h = 0.2 on the interval [0, 0.4] using the fourth order classical Runge – Kutta method. Compare with the exact solution.

Ans. We have x_0 = 1, u_0 = 1, h = 0.2

and f(t, u) = -2t u^2

for n = 0

k_1 = h f(f_0, u_0) = 0

$$k_2 = hf\left(t_0 + \frac{h}{2}, u_0 + \frac{1}{2}k_1\right) = -0.04$$

$$k_3 = hf\left(t_0 + \frac{h}{2}, u_0 + \frac{1}{2}k_2\right) = -0.0384$$

$$k_4 = hf\left(t_0 + h, u_0 + k_3\right) = -0.0739$$

$$u(0.2) \approx u_1 = 1 + \frac{1}{6}[0 - 0.08 - 0.07683 - 0.07397]$$

= 0.9615

for n = 1

$t_1 = 0.2$, $u_1 = 0.9615$

$k_1 = -0.0739$

$k_2 = -0.1025$

$k_3 = -0.09942$

$k_4 = -0.1189$

$$u(0.4) \approx u_2 = 0.9615 + \frac{1}{6}[-0.0739 - 0.20515 - 0.1988 - 0.1189] = 0.8620$$

Q3. (a) A real root of the equation f(x) = x³ – 5x + 1 = 0 lies in the interval (0, 1). Perform three iterations using Regula – Falsi method to obtain this root.

Ans. Regula – Falsi method

$f(x) = x^3 = 5x + 1$

$f(x_0) = f(0) = 0 - 0 + 1 = 1$

$f(x_1) = f(1) = 1 - 5 + 1 = -3$

$x_0 = 0$, $x_1 = 1$

$$x_2 = \frac{x_0 f(x_1) - x_1 f(x_0)}{f(x_1) - f(x_0)}$$

$$= \frac{0 \times (-3) - 1 \times 0}{-3 - 1}$$

$$= \frac{-1}{-4} = \frac{1}{4} = 0.25$$

$f(0.25) = -0.234$

Now root lies between 0 and 0.25

$x_1 = 0$

$x_2 = 0.25$

$$x_3 = \frac{0 \times (-0.234) - 0.25 \times 1}{-0.234 - 1} = \frac{-0.25}{-1.234} = 0.2025$$

$f(0.2025) = -0.00419$

Now root lies between 0 and 0.25

$x_2 = 0$
$x_3 = 0.2025$

$$x_4 = \frac{0\times(-0.00419)-0.2025\times1}{-0.00419-1} = \frac{-0.2025}{-1.00419} = 0.2016$$

(b) Apply Gauss – Seidel iteration method to solve the equations
20x + y – 2z = 17
3x + 20y – z = -18
2x – 3y + 20z = 25
Perform three iterations.

Ans. Gauss – Seidel Iteration Method

$$x = \frac{1}{20}(17 - y + 2z)$$

$$y = \frac{1}{20}(-18 - 3x + z)$$

$$z = \frac{1}{20}(25 - 2x + 3y)$$

Starting $x^{(0)} = (0, 0, 0)^T$

I^st^ Iteration:

$$x = \frac{17}{20} = 0.85$$

$$y = \frac{1}{20}(-18 - 3\times0.85 + 0) = -1.027$$

$$z = \frac{1}{20}(25 - 2\times0.85 + 3\times(-1.027)) = 1.0109$$

$x^{(1)} = (0.85, -1.027, 1.0109)^T$

IInd Iteration:

$$x = \frac{1}{20}(17 + 1.027 + 2\times1.0109) = 1.0024$$

$$y = \frac{1}{20}(-18 - 3\times1.0024 + 1.0109) = -0.9998$$

$$z = \frac{1}{20}(25 - 2\times1.0024 + 3\times(-0.9998)) = 0.9997$$

$x^{(2)} = (1.0024, -0.9998, 0.9997)^T$

IIIrd Iteration:

$$x = \frac{1}{20}(17 + 0.9998 + 2\times0.9997) = 0.9999$$

$$y = \frac{1}{20}(-18 - 3\times0.9999 + 0.9997) = -1$$

$$z = \frac{1}{20}\left(25 - 2 \times 0.9999 + 3 \times (-1)\right) = 0.95$$

$x^{(3)} = (0.9999, -1, 0.95)^T$

(c) Evaluate $\int_1^2 \log x \, dx$ by Trapezoidal rule.

Ans. Trapezoidal Rule

$$\int_1^2 \log x \, dx$$

We take h = 0.25

x	1	1.25	1.5	1.75	2
log x	0	0.0969	0.1760	0.2430	0.3010

$$\int_1^2 \log x \, dx = \frac{h}{2}\left[(0 + 0.3010) + 2(0.0969 + 0.1760 + 0.2430)\right]$$

$$= \frac{0.25}{2}[0.3010 + 1.0318] = \frac{0.25}{2} \times 1.3328 = 0.1666$$

Q4. (a) Find the cubic polynomial using Newton's forward interpolation formula, which takes the following values:

$$\begin{array}{lcccc} x: & 0 & 1 & 2 & 3 \\ f(x): & 1 & 2 & 1 & 10 \end{array}$$

Hence evaluate f(4).

Ans.
$$\begin{array}{lcccc} x: & 0 & 1 & 2 & 3 \\ f(x): & 1 & 2 & 1 & 10 \end{array}$$

x	f(x)	$\Delta f(x)$	$\Delta^2 f(x)$	$\Delta^3 f(x)$
0	1			
		1		
1	2		-2	
		-1		12
2	1		10	
		9		
3	10			

From Newton's Forward Interpolating Formula:

$$f(x) = f(x_1) + \frac{\Delta f(x_1)(x - x_1)}{h\underline{|1}} + \frac{\Delta^2 f(x_1)(x - x_1)(x - x_2)}{h^2 . \underline{|2}}$$

$$+ \frac{\Delta^3 f(x_1)(x - x_1)(x - x_2)(x - x_3)}{h^3 . \underline{|3}}$$

$$=1+\frac{1(x-0)}{1.1}+\frac{-2(x-0)(x-1)}{1.2}$$

$$+\frac{12(x-0)(x-1)(x-2)}{1.6}$$

$= 1 + x - x^2 + x + 2\,(x^2 - x)\,(x - 2)$

$= 1 + x - x^2 + x + 2x^3 - 4x^2 - 2x^2 + 4x$

$= 2x^3 - 7x^2 + 6x + 1$

Hence

$f(4) = 2.(4)^3 - 7.(4)^2 + 6.4 + 1 = 128 - 112 + 24 + 1 = 41$

(b) Use Simpson's $\frac{1}{3^{rd}}$ rule to find $\int_0^{0.5} e^{-x^2}dx$ by taking seven ordinates.

Ans. Let $I=\int_0^{0.6} e^{-x^2}dx$

x	0	0.1	0.2	0.3	0.4	0.5	0.6
$y=e^{-x^2}$	1	0.99	0.96	0.91	0.85	0.78	0.70

y_1 y_2 y_3 y_4 y_5 y_6 y_7

From Simpson's $\frac{1}{3}rd$ Rule

$$I=h/3\left[(y_1+y_7)+4(y_2+y_4+y_6)+2(y_3+y_5)\right]$$

$$=\frac{0.1}{3}\left[(1+0.70)+4(0.99+0.91+0.78)+2(0.96+0.85)\right]$$

$$=\frac{0.1}{3}\left[1.70+10.72+3.62\right] = 0.53$$

(c) Solve the following differential equation by Euler's method $\frac{dy}{dx}=\frac{y-x}{y+x}$, given y(0) = 1.

Find y approximately for x = 0.1 in five steps.

Ans. Given

$$\frac{dy}{dx}=\frac{y-x}{y+x}$$

y(0) = 1

h = 0.1

$$\therefore f(x,y)=\frac{y-x}{y+x}$$

$x_0 = 0$

$y_0 = 1$

From Euler's Method

$y_{i+1} = y_i + h\ f(x_i, y_i)$

Iteration 1:

If i = 0

$y_1 = y_0 + h\ f(x_0, y_0)$

$= 1 + (0.1)\ f(0, 1) = 1 + 0.1\ (+1) = 1 + 0.1 = 1.1$

Iteration 2:

If i = 1

$y_2 = y_1 + h\ f(x_1, y_1)$

$= 1.1 + (0.1) + (0.1, 1.1) \quad = 1.1 + (0.1)\left(\frac{1}{1.2}\right) = 1.1 + 0.08 = 1.18$

Iteration 3:

If i = 2

$y_3 = y_2 + h\ f(x_2, y_2)$

$= 1.18 + (0.1) + (0.2, 1.18) \quad = 1.18 + (0.1)\left(\frac{.98}{1.38}\right) = 1.25$

Iteration 4:

If i = 3

$x_4 = y_3 + h\ f(x_3, y_3)$

$= 1.25 + (0.1) + (0.3, 1.25) \quad = 1.25 + (0.1)\left(\frac{.95}{1.55}\right) = 1.31$

Iteration 5:

If i = 4

$y_5 = y_4 + h\ f(x_4, y_4)$

$= 1.31 + (0.1) + (0.4, 1.31) \quad = 1.31 + (0.1)\left(\frac{.91}{1.71}\right) = 1.36$

Q5. (a) Solve the equations:

$\mathbf{x_1 + x_2 + x_3 = 6}$

$\mathbf{3x_1 + 3x_2 + 4x_3 = 20}$

$\mathbf{2x_1 + x_2 + 3x_3 = 13}$

using Gauss – Elimination method with partial pivoting.

Ans. Taking in Matrix form

$$\left[\begin{array}{ccc|c} 1 & 1 & 1 & 6 \\ 3 & 3 & 4 & 20 \\ 2 & 1 & 3 & 13 \end{array}\right]$$

$R_1 \leftrightarrow R_2$ (for partial pivoting)

$$\left[\begin{array}{ccc|c} 3 & 3 & 4 & 20 \\ 1 & 1 & 1 & 6 \\ 2 & 1 & 3 & 13 \end{array}\right]$$

$$R_2 \rightarrow R_2 - \frac{1}{3}R_1, R_3 \rightarrow R_3 - \frac{2}{3}R_1$$

$$\left[\begin{array}{ccc|c} 3 & 3 & 4 & 20 \\ 0 & 0 & \frac{-1}{3} & \frac{-2}{3} \\ 0 & -1 & \frac{1}{3} & \frac{-1}{3} \end{array}\right]$$

$R_2 \leftrightarrow R_3$ (for partial pivoting)

$$\left[\begin{array}{ccc|c} 3 & 3 & 4 & 20 \\ 0 & -1 & \frac{1}{3} & \frac{-1}{3} \\ 0 & 0 & \frac{-1}{3} & \frac{-2}{3} \end{array}\right]$$

Now in equation format

$3x_1 + 3x_2 + 4x_3 = 20$ ... (1)

$-x_3 + \frac{1}{3}x_3 = \frac{-1}{3}$ ... (2)

$\frac{-1}{3}x_3 = \frac{-2}{3}$ ... (3)

From eq. (3) $x_3 = 2$

From eq. (2) $x_2 = -\left(\frac{-1}{3} - \frac{2}{3}\right) = 1$

From eq. (3) $x_1 = (20 - 3 \times 1 - 4 \times 2) = 3$

(b) By using the Bisection method, find an approximate root of the equation $\sin x = \frac{1}{x}$ that lies between x = 1 and x = 1.5 (measured in radians). Carry out computations upto the 3rd stage.

Ans. Bisection Method

$$f(x) = \sin x - \frac{1}{x}$$

$x_0 = 1$

$x_1 = 1.5$

f(1) = -0.158 (+ve)

f(1.5) = 0.3308 (+ve)

$$x_2 = \frac{1+1.5}{2} = 1.25$$

$$f(1.25) = \sin 1.25 - 1/1.25 = 0.1489 \text{ (+ve)}$$

$$x_3 = \frac{1+1.25}{2} = 1.125$$

f(1.125) = 0.133 (+ve)

$$x_4 = \frac{1+1.125}{2} = 1.0625$$

f(1.0625) = -0.0676 (+ve)

$$x_5 = \frac{1.0625+1.125}{2} = 1.09375$$

(c) Form a backward difference table for y = log x given that

x:	10	20	30	40	50
y:	1.0000	1.3010	1.4771	1.6021	1.6990

Also find $\nabla^3 y_{40}$.

Ans.

x	y	∇y	$\nabla^2 y$	$\nabla^3 y$	$\nabla^4 y$
10	1.0000				
		0.3010			
20	1.3010		-0.1249		
		0.1761		0.0738	
30	1.4771		-0.0511		-0.0508
		0.125		0.023	
40	1.6021		-0.0281		
		0.0969			
50	1.6990				

$$\nabla^3 y_{40} = 0.0738$$

CS-71 : COMPUTER ORIENTED NUMERICAL TECHNIQUES

June, 2008

Note : Question number is **compulsory.** Attempt any **three** questions from Q2 to Q5.

Q1. (a) If the number x* = 0.678 approximates the number x = 0.6775 correct upto n significant decimal digits, then calculate the value of n.

Ans. x = 0.6775

x* = 0.678

x – x* = 0.6775 – 0.678 = – 0.0005

$$|x - x^*| = 0.0005$$

$$\frac{|x - x^*|}{|x|} = \frac{0.0005}{0.6775}$$

$= 0.000738$

≤ 0.005

$= \frac{1}{2}(0.01)$

$= \frac{1}{2}(10^{-2})$

$= \frac{1}{2}10^{1-3}$

Hence x* approximate x correct to 3 significant decimal digits.

(b) Evaluate $f(x) = \frac{x^3}{x - \sin x}$ when x = 0.12 × 10^{-10} using two digit arithmetic.

Ans. $f(x) = \frac{x^3}{x - \sin x}$

$$= \frac{x^3}{x - \left(x - \frac{x^3}{3!} + \frac{x^5}{5!}\right)} = \frac{x^3}{\frac{x^3}{\underline{|3}} - \frac{x^5}{\underline{|5}} + \ldots\ldots}$$

$$= \frac{1}{\frac{1}{\underline{|3}} - \frac{x^2}{\underline{|5}} + \ldots\ldots\ldots}$$

Now putting $x = 0.12 \times 10^{-10}$

$$= \frac{1}{\frac{1}{\lfloor 3} - 0 + \ldots\ldots\ldots\ldots} = \frac{1}{\frac{1}{6}} = 6$$

(c) If $u = \frac{5xy^2}{z^3}$ and error in x, y, z is 0.001, compute the relative maximum error in u when
x = y = z = 1.

Ans. $x = 1 \pm 0.001$

$y = 1 \pm 0.001$

$z = 1 \pm 0.001$

$$u = \frac{5xy^2}{z^3}$$

$$r_{y2} = \pm 2 \frac{\Delta y}{y} = \pm 2 \frac{0.001}{1} = \pm 0.002$$

$$r_{xy2} = \pm\left(\gamma x + \gamma y^2\right) = \pm\left(\frac{0.001}{1} + 0.002\right) = 0.003$$

$$\gamma_{z3} = \pm 3.\frac{\Delta z}{z} = \pm 3.\frac{0.001}{1} = \pm 0.003$$

$$\frac{\gamma xy^3}{z^3} = \pm(0.003 + 0.003) = \pm 0.006$$

$$\frac{{}^{\gamma}xy^2}{z^3} = (0.003 + 0.003) = \pm 0.006$$

$$\frac{{}^{\gamma}5xy^2}{z^3} = \pm 0.006$$

(d) Prove that $e^{-hD} = 1 - \nabla$.

Ans. The relation between the backward difference operator ∇ and the shift operator E is :

$\nabla = 1 - E^{-1}$

or, $E^{-1} = 1 - \nabla$

or, $E = (1 - \nabla)^{-1}$

or, $e^{hD} = \frac{1}{1 - \nabla}$

or, $E^{-hD} = (1 - \nabla)$

(e) If a, b, c, d are arguments of $f(x)=\frac{1}{x}$, show that $f(a,b,c,d)=\frac{-1}{abcd}$.

Ans. $f[a,b]=\frac{\frac{1}{b}-\frac{1}{a}}{b-a}=\frac{-1}{ab}$

$f[b,c]=-\frac{1}{bc}$ and $f[c,d]=\frac{-1}{cd}$

$f[a,b,c]=\frac{1}{abc}, f[b,c,d]=\frac{1}{bcd}$

Now

$$f[a,b,c,d]=\frac{f[b,c,d]-f[a,b,c]}{d-a}=\frac{-1}{a,b,c,d}$$

(f) Use Lagrange's Interpolation formula to find the value of y when x = 10, if the value of x and y are given as below:

x	5	6	9	11
y	12	13	14	16

Ans. $L_0(x)=\frac{(x-6)(x-9)(x-11)}{(5-6)(5-9)(5-11)}$

$L_1(x)=\frac{(x-5)(x-9)(x-11)}{(6-5)(6-9)(6-11)}$

$L_2(x)=\frac{(x-5)(x-6)(x-11)}{(9-5)(9-6)(9-11)}$

$L_3(x)=\frac{(x-5)(x-6)(x-9)}{(11-5)(11-6)(11-9)}$

$$f(x)=12\frac{(x-6)(x-9)(x-11)}{(-1)\times(-4)\times(-6)}+13\frac{(x-5)(x-9)(x-11)}{1\times(-3)\times(-5)}$$

$$+14\frac{(x-5)(x-6)(x-11)}{4\times3\times(-2)}+\frac{(x-5)(x-6)(x-9)}{6\times5\times2}$$

$$f(10)=12\frac{4\times1\times(-1)}{(-1)\times(-4)\times(-6)}+13\frac{5\times1\times(-1)}{(-3)\times(-5)}+14\frac{5\times4\times(-1)}{4\times3\times(-2)}+\frac{5\times4\times1}{6\times5\times2}$$

$$=-2+\left(\frac{-13}{3}\right)+\frac{35}{3}+\frac{1}{3}\quad=-2-\frac{13}{3}+\frac{35}{3}+\frac{1}{3}$$

$$=\frac{-6-13+35+1}{3}=\frac{17}{3}$$

Q2. (a) For the following equation
x^4 - x - 10 = 0
determine initial approximation for finding the smallest positive root. Use these to find the roots correct to three decimal places with the following methods:
(i) Regula Falsi Method

Ans. Initial approximation 1 and 2.

1. Regula falsi method:

$x_0 = 1$ and $x_1 = 2$

$f(1) = 1^4 - 1 - 10 = -10$ $(-ve)$

$f(2) = 2^4 - 2 - 10 = 4$ $(+ve)$

$$\therefore x_2 = \frac{x_0 f(x_1) - x_1 f(x_0)}{f(x_1) - f(x_0)}$$

$$= \frac{1 \times (-10) - 2 \times 4}{-10 - 4} = \frac{-10 - 8}{-14} = \frac{18}{14} = \frac{9}{7} = 1.2857 = 1.28$$

Now $f(x_2) = (1.28)^4 - 1.28 - 10$

= -8.59

$\because f(x_0)$ and $f(x_2)$ have same sign

$\therefore x_1 = x_2$ $\therefore x_1 = 1.28$

Iteration II:

$x_0 = 1$ $f(x_0) = -10 = -ve$

$x_1 = 1.28$ $f(x_1) = -8.59 = -ve$

$$x_2 = \frac{x_0 + x_1}{2} = \frac{1 + 1.28}{2} = 1.14$$

$f(x_2) = -9.71$ $(-ve)$

$\because f(x_0)$ and $f(x_2)$ have same sign

$\therefore x_1 = x_2$

$x_1 = 1.14$

Iteration III :

$x_0 = 1$ $f(1) = -10(-ve)$

$x_1 = 1.14$ $f(1.14) = -9.71(-ve)$

$$x_2 = \frac{1 + 1.14}{2} = \frac{2.14}{3} = 1.7$$

$f(x_2) = -3.34$

$\therefore\ f(x_0)$ and $f(x_2)$ have same sign

$\therefore\ x_1 = x_2$

$\therefore\ x_1 = 1.2$

(ii) Newton Raphson Method

Ans. Newton Raphson Method

Initial value $x_0 = 1.5$

$f(x) = x^4 - x - 10$

$f(1.5) = (1.5)^4 - 1.5 - 10$

$f'(x) = 4x^3 - 1$

$$x_1 = x_0 - \frac{f(x_0)}{f'(x_0)}$$

$$= 1.5 - \frac{(-6.43)}{12.5} \quad = 1.5 + \frac{6.43}{12.5} = 2.01$$

$$x_2 = x_1 - \frac{f(x_1)}{f'(x_1)} = 2.01 - \frac{4.31}{31.48} = 1.87$$

$$x_3 = x_2 - \frac{f(x_2)}{f'(x_1)} = 1.87 - \frac{0.35}{25.15} = 1.85$$

Q2(b) Find cubic polynomial which takes the following values: y(0) = 1 y(1) = 0 y(2) = 1 y(3) = 10. Find y(4) using Newton's Difference Interpolation formula.

Ans.

x	y	Δ_d	Δ_d^2	Δ_d^3
0	1			
		−1		
1	0		1	
		1		1
2	1		4	
		9		
3	10			

$y(x) = 1 + (x-0)(-1) + (x-0)(x-1)1 + (x-0)(x-1)(x-2)$

$y(x) = 1 + 4\times(-1) + 4\times3\times1 + 4\times3\times2\times1$

$= 1 - 4 + 12 + 24 = 33$

Q3. (a) Find a real root of the equation $x^3 + x^2 - 1 = 0$ on interval [0, 1] with an accuracy of 10^{-4} using iteration method.

Ans. $x_0 = 0$

$x_1 = 1$

$f(0) = -1$

$f(1) = 1$

$$x_2 = \frac{x_0 f(x_1) - x_1 f(x_0)}{f(x_1) - f(x_0)} = \frac{0 \times 1 - 1 \times (-1)}{1-(-1)} = \frac{0+1}{2} = 0.5$$

$f(x_2) = -0.625$

$\because f(x_0)$ and $f(x_2)$ have same sign $x_1 = x_2$

$x_1 = 0.5$

Iteration II:

$x_0 = 0 \qquad f(0) = -1$

$x_1 = 0.5 \qquad f(0.5) = -0.625$

$$x_2 = \frac{0(-0.625) - 0.5(-1)}{2} = \frac{0+0.5}{2} = \frac{0.5}{2} = 0.25$$

$f(0.25) = -0.921$

$\because f(0)$ and $f(0.25)$ have same sign

$\therefore x_1 = x_2, \; x_1 = 0.25$

Iteration III:

$x_0 = 0 \qquad f(0) = -1$

$x_1 = 0.25 \; f(0.25) = -0.921$

$$x_2 = \frac{0 \times (-0.921) - 0.25(-1)}{2} = \frac{0.25}{2} = 0.125$$

$f(0.125) = -0.982$

Q3(b) Solve the system of following equations using Gauss Elimination method:

$4x_1 + x_2 + x_3 = 4$

$x_1 + 4x_2 - 2x_3 = 4$

$3x_1 + 2x_2 - 4x_3 = 6$

Ans.

$$\left[\begin{array}{ccc|c} 4 & 1 & 1 & 4 \\ 1 & 4 & -2 & 4 \\ 3 & 2 & -4 & 6 \end{array}\right]$$

$$= \left[\begin{array}{ccc|c} 4 & 1 & 1 & 4 \\ 0 & -15 & 9 & 12 \\ 0 & -5 & 19 & -12 \end{array}\right] \qquad \begin{array}{l} R_2 \rightarrow R_1 - 4R_2 \\ R_3 \rightarrow 3R_1 - 4R_2 \end{array}$$

$$= \begin{bmatrix} 4 & 1 & 1 & 4 \\ 0 & -15 & 9 & 12 \\ 0 & 0 & 48 & -48 \end{bmatrix} \qquad R_3 \rightarrow R_2 - 3R_3$$

Now :

$4x_1 + x_2 + x_3 = 4$ ... (i)

$-15x_2 + 9x_3 = 12$ ... (ii)

$48x_3 = -48$ ... (iii)

Equation (iii) $x_3 = -1$

Equation (ii) :

$-15x_2 - 9 = 12$

$-15x_2 = 21$

$x_2 = \frac{21}{-15} = -1.4$

Equation (i) :

$4x_1 + (-1.4) + (-1) = 4$

$4x_1 = 4 + 1.4 + 1$

$x_1 = \frac{6.4}{4} = 1.6$

$\therefore x_1 = 1.6$

$x_2 = -1.4$

$x_3 = -1$

Q3(c) By using Simpson's $\frac{1}{3}$rd rule, evaluate $\int_0^1 \frac{dx}{1+x^2}$. Divide the interval into six equal parts.

Ans. h = $\frac{1}{6}$

$f(x) = \frac{1}{1+x^2}$

from x = 0 to 1

x	0	1/6	2/6	3/6	4/6	5/6	1
f(x)	1	0.97	0.9	0.8	0.69	0.59	0.5

$$\int_0^1 \frac{1}{1+x^2}dx$$

$$=\frac{h}{3}\left[1+0.5+4(0.97+0.8+0.59)+2(0.9+0.69)\right] = 0.785$$

Q4. (a) Solve the Gauss-Seidal Method upto third iteration:
8x - 3y + 2z = 20
4x + 11y - z = 33
6x + 3y + 12z = 35

Ans. The equation can be written as :

$$x = \frac{1}{8}(20+3y-2z)$$

$$y = \frac{1}{11}(33-4x+z)$$

$$z = \frac{1}{12}(35-6x-3y)$$

Starting with

$X^{(0)} = (0,0,0)^T$

$x^1 = 2.5$

$y^1 = 2.09$

$z^1 = 1.14$

$X^1 = (2.5, 2.09, 1.14)^T$

Using this $(2.5, 2.09, 1.14)^T$

$x^{(2)}=2.99$

$y^{(2)}=2.01$

$z^{(2)}=0.919$

$X^2 = (2.99, 2.01, 0.919)^T$

Using this $(2.99, 2.01, 0.919)^T$

$x^{(3)}=3.024$

$y^{(3)}=1.983$

$z^{(3)}=0.908$

Thus, $X^3 = (3.024, 1.983, 0.908)^T$

Q4(b) Find $\int_1^7 f(x)dx$ using Trapezoidal Rule for the following:

x	y
1	2.105
2	2.808
3	3.614
4	4.604
5	5.857
6	7.451
7	9.467

Ans.

$$\int_1^7 f(x).dx = \frac{1}{2}[2.105 + 9.467 + 2(2.808 + 3.614 + 4.604 + 5.857 + 7.451)]$$

$= 3.012$

Q4(c) Solve y¹ = -y with y(0) = 1 for x = 0.04 and step length 0.01 using Euler's method.

Ans. $y' = -y = f(x_o . y_o)$

$x_o = 0$

$y_o = 1$

$h = 0.01$

$y(0.01) = y_o + hf(x_o\ y_o)$

$= 1 + 0.01 \times 1 = 1.01$

$y(0.02) = 1.01 + 0.01 \times \dfrac{2 \times 1.01}{1.01} = 1.03$

$y(0.03) = 1.03 + 0.01 \times \dfrac{2 \times 1.03}{1.02} = 1.05$

$y(0.04) = 1.05 + 0.01 \times \dfrac{2 \times 1.05}{1.03} = 1.07$

Q5. (a) Given $\dfrac{dy}{dx} = \sqrt{x+y}$ with y(0.4) = 0.41. Find y(0.6) with h = 0.2 using RKM of fourth order.

Ans. $f(x.y) = \sqrt{x+y}$

$x_o = 0.4$

$y_o = 0.41$

h = 0.2

$m_1 = f(x_o, y_o) = \sqrt{0.4+0.41}$ =0.9

$$m_2 = f\left(x_0 + \frac{h}{2}, y_0 + \frac{m_1 h}{2}\right)$$

f (10.5, 0.41+0.09)
f (0.5, 0.5)

$= \sqrt{0.5+0.5} = 1$

$$m_3 = f\left(x_o + \frac{h}{2}, y_0 + \frac{m_2 h}{2}\right)$$

$$= f\left(0.5, 0.41 + \frac{1 \times 0.2}{2}\right)$$

= f(0.5, 0.51)

$= \sqrt{0.5+0.51} = 1.004$

$m_4 = f(x_o + h,\ y_o + m_3 h)$

= f(0.6, 0.41 + 1.004 × 0.2) = f(0.6, 0.610)

$= \sqrt{0.6+0.610} = 1.10$

$$y(0.6) = y_{0.4} + \left(\frac{m_1 + 2m_2 + 2m_3 + m_4}{6}\right)h$$

= 0.41+0.1334 = 0.5434

Q5(b). Find a root of the equation x^3 - 2x - 5 = 0 using Bisection method in three iterations.

Ans. Initially approximation 2 and 3

$\therefore\ x_o = 2$ f(2) = –1

$x_1 = 3$ f(3) = 16

$$x_2 = \frac{x_o + x_1}{2} = \frac{2+3}{2} = \frac{5}{2} = 2.5$$

f(2.5) = 5.625

$\because$ f(2) and f(2.5) have opposite sign

$\therefore\ x_1 = x_2$

$x_1 = 2.5$ $f(2.5) = 5.625$

<u>Iteration II</u>:

$x_o = 2$ $\qquad f(2) = -1$

$x_1 = 2.5$ $\qquad f(2.5) = 5.625$

$$x_2 = \frac{2+2.5}{2} = 2.25$$

$f(2.25) = 1.890$

$\because$ f(2) and f(2.25) have opposite sign

$\therefore x_1 = x_2$ $\qquad x_1 = 2.25$

Iteration III:

$x_0 = 2$ $\qquad$ f(2) = –1

$x_1 = 2.25$ $\qquad$ f(2.25) = 1.890

$$x_2 = \frac{2+2.25}{2} = 2.125$$

f(2.125) = 0.3457

(c) If x* approximates x correct to 4 significant decimal digits then calculate how many significant decimal digits $ex^{*/100}$ approximates $e^{x/100}$.

Ans. We know that $f(x) = e^{x/100}$

$$f'(x) = \frac{1}{100} e^{x/100}$$

$$r_{f(x)} = r_x \left| \frac{x - f'(x^*)}{f(x)} \right|$$

$$r_{f(x)} = r_x \left| \frac{x \frac{1}{100} e^{x^*/100}}{e^{x/100}} \right|$$

$$= r_x \left| \frac{x}{100} \right|$$

$$r_{f(x)} \approx \frac{1}{100} |\gamma x|$$

$$\leq \frac{1}{100} \frac{1}{2} 10^{1-4}$$

$$= \frac{1}{2} 10^{1-6}$$

Therefore, $e^{x^*/100}$ approximates $e^{x/100}$ correct for 6 significant decimal digits.

CS-71 : COMPUTER ORIENTED NUMERICAL TECHNIQUES
Dec, 2008

***Note:** Question number **1** is **compulsory**. Attempt only **three** Questions from the rest. In total you have to answer **four** questions. Calculator is allowed.*

Q1. (a) Find the relative error in the number 834.123 correct to five significant figures.

Ans. Let x = 834.123

$\Rightarrow x = 0.834123 * 10^3$

with five decimal digit accuracy

$x^* = 0.83412 * 10^3$ while $x = 0.834123 * 10^3$

$$\text{Relative Error} = \left|\frac{x - x^*}{x}\right|$$

$$= \left|\frac{0.834123 * 10^3 - 0.83412 * 10^3}{0.834123 * 10^3}\right| = \left|\frac{0.000003}{0.834123 * 10^3}\right| = 3.60 * 10^{-9} \text{ Ans.}$$

(b) Prove that

(i) $\Delta = \Delta E^{-1}$

Ans. $\Delta = \Delta E^{-1}$, ∇ = backward difference operators

Δ = forward difference operator, E^{-1} = shift operator

LHS ∇

$$\Rightarrow \nabla = 1 - E^{-1} \Rightarrow 1 - \frac{1}{E} = \frac{E - 1}{E} = \frac{\Delta}{E} = \Delta E^{-1} \text{ RHS}$$

Hence LHS = RHS

(ii) $\mathbf{E = 1 + \Delta}$

Ans. $E = 1 + \Delta$

RHS $1 + \Delta = \cancel{1} + E - \cancel{1}$ $\qquad \therefore [\Delta = E - 1]$

= E LHS

LHS = RHS

(c) Solve the equation $3x^3 - 4x^2 + x + 88 = 0$, one root being $z + \sqrt{7}\,i$.

Ans. $3x^3 - 4x^2 + x + 88 = 0$. Let α, β, γ are three roots. One root $\alpha = z\sqrt{7}i$

Other roots = $z - \sqrt{7}i$ $\qquad \because \alpha + \beta + \gamma = \dfrac{4}{3}$ $\qquad z + \cancel{\sqrt{7}}i + z - \cancel{\sqrt{7}}i + \cancel{\gamma} = \dfrac{4}{3}$

$2z+\gamma=\frac{4}{3}$ $\boxed{\gamma=\frac{4}{3}-2z}$ $\boxed{\text{Roots are } z+\sqrt{7}i,\ z-\sqrt{7}i, \frac{4}{3}-2z}$

(d) Find the root of the equation $xe^x = \cos x$ using the secant method, correct to four decimal places with initial value $x_0 = 0$ and $x_1 = 1$.
Refer to Dec-2007, Q.No.-1(e)

(e) Use iteration method to evaluate $\sqrt[3]{48}$ correct to four decimal places.
Refer to Dec-2007, Q.No.-1(d)

(f) Apply Lagrange's formula to find f(5) given.

x:	1	3	4	6	10
f(x):	0	18	48	180	900

Ans.

$$L_0(x)=\frac{(x-3)(x-4)(x-6)(x-10)}{(1-3)(1-4)(1-6)(1-10)}$$

$$L_0(5)=\frac{(5-3)(5-4)(5-6)(5-10)}{-2*-3*-5*-9}=\frac{2*5}{6*45}=\frac{10}{270}=0.0370$$

$$L_1(x)=\frac{(x-1)(x-4)(x-6)(x-10)}{(3-1)(3-4)(3-6)(3-10)}$$

$$L_1(5)=\frac{(5-1)(5-4)(5-6)(5-10)}{4*-1*-3*-7}=\frac{-20}{42}=-0.4762$$

$$L_2(x)=\frac{(x-1)(x-3)(x-6)(x-10)}{(4-1)(4-3)(4-6)(4-10)}$$

$$L_2(5)=\frac{(5-1)(5-3)(5-6)(5-10)}{3*1*-2*-6}=\frac{40}{36}=1.1111$$

$$L_3(x)=\frac{(x-1)(x-3)(x-4)(x-10)}{(6-1)(6-3)(6-4)(6-10)}$$

$$L_3(5)=\frac{(5-1)(5-3)(5-4)(5-10)}{5*3*2*-4}=\frac{-40}{-120}=0.3333$$

$$L_4(x)=\frac{(x-1)(x-3)(x-6)(x-4)}{(10-1)(10-3)(10-6)(10-4)}$$

$$L_4(5)=\frac{(5-1)(5-3)(5-6)(5-4)}{9*7*4*6}=\frac{-8}{1512}=-0.0053$$

$$f_{(5)} = L_0(5)*f_0(x) + L_1(5)*f_1(x) + L_2(5)*f_2(x) + L_3(5)*f_3(x) + L_4(5) + f_4(x)$$

= 0.03704 * 0 + (-0.4762) * 18 + 1.1111 * 48 + 0.3333 * 180 + (-0.0053) *900

= 0 – 8.5716 + 53.3328 + 59.9940 – 4.7700 = 99.9852 Ans.

Q2. (a) Describe Regula-Falsi method for finding root of an equation.
Refer to June-2006, Q.No.-2(a)

(b) From the following table, estimate the number of students, who obtained marks between 40 and 45, using Newton's Forward interpolation formula.

Marks	30 – 40	40 – 50	50 – 60	60 – 70	70 – 80
No. of Students	31	42	51	35	31

Ans.

Marks	No. of Students
30 – 40	31
40 – 50	42
50 – 60	51
60 – 70	35
70 – 80	31

Mid point = upper limit + lower limit/2 $= \frac{40+30}{2} = \frac{70}{2} = 35$

(c) A civil engineer has measured the height of a 10 floor building as 2950 cm and the working height of each beam as 35 cm while the true values are 2945 cm and 30 cm respectively. Compare their absolute and relative errors.
Refer to Dec-2006, Q.No.-3(c)

Q3. (a) Use Newton-Raphson Method to find the root of the equation $x^3 - 4x + 1 = 0$ with $x_0 = 0$.
Refer to June-2001, Q.No.-3(a)

(b) Evaluate $\int_0^6 \frac{dx}{1+x^2}$, by using Trapezoidal Rule.

Ans. Decide the range of integration (0, 6) into 6 equal parts for h.

$h = \frac{6-0}{6} = \frac{6}{6} = 1$

The values of y for each point of subdivision are given below:

x	$y = \frac{1}{1+x^2}$	y
$x_0 = 0$	1.00	y_0
$x_0 + h = 1$	0.50	y_1
$x_0 + 2h = 2$	0.20	y_2
$x_0 + 3h = 3$	0.10	y_3
$x_0 + 4h = 4$	0.059	y_4
$x_0 + 5h = 5$	0.038	y_5
$x_0 + 6h = 6$	0.027	y_6

By using Trapezoidal Rule

$$\int_0^6 \frac{dx}{1+x^2} dx = \frac{h}{2}\left[(y_0 + y_b) + 2(y_1 + y_2 + y_3 + y_4 + y_5)\right]$$

$$= \frac{1}{2}\left[(1 + 0.027) + 2(0.50 + 0.20 + 0.10 + 0.059 + 0.038)\right]$$

$$= \frac{1}{2}\left[1.027 + 2(0.897)\right] = \frac{1}{2}(1.027 + 1.794) = \frac{2.821}{2} = 1.4105 \text{ Ans.}$$

(c) Solve, by Jacobi iteration method, the equations are:
20x + y – 2z = 17 3x + 20y – z = -18 2x – 3y + 20z = 25

Refer to June-2006, Q.No.-5(a)

Q4. (a) Given $\frac{dy}{dx} = x^2 + y^2, y(1)1.5$ **and h = 0.1. Find y(1.2) using Runge-Kutta method.**

Ans. Given $\frac{dy}{dx} = x^2 + y^2$ y(1) = 1.5 and h = 0.1 find y(1.2)

Using R-K Method $x_0 = 1$ $y_0 = 1.5$ $h = 0.1$

and $(x, y) = x^2 + y^2$

$k_1 = 0.1\ [1 + 1.5] = .1 * [2.5]$

$\boxed{k_1 = 0.25}$ $k_2 = (0.1)\left[\left(1 + \frac{0.1}{2}\right) + 1.5 + \left(\frac{1.5}{2}\right)\right]$

(0.1) [1.05 + 1.5 + 0.75]

$k_2 = 0.33$

$$k_3 = (0.1)\left[0 + \frac{0.1}{2} + \frac{0.33}{2}\right] = (0.1)[1 + 0.05 + 0.165]$$

= 0.1[1.05 + 0.165] = 0.1215

k_4 = (0.1) [1 + 0.1 + 1.5 + 0.1215] = 0.27215

$$k = \frac{1}{6}\left[(0.25 + 0.27215) + 2(0.33 + 0.1215)\right] = 0.237525$$

$y = y_0 + k$ = y = 1.5 + 0.237525 = 1.737525

(b) Solve the following system of equation by Gauss-Seidal iteration method, up-to two iteration.

27x + 6y – z = 85 6x + 15y + 2z = 72 x + y + 54z = 110

Ans. Gauss Seidal method, we consider the given equations

Assume to start with $x(0) = (0, 0, 0)^T$

$$27x = 85 - 6y + z \Rightarrow x = \frac{85}{27} - \frac{6}{27}y + \frac{1}{27}z \Rightarrow x = 3.15 = 0.22y + 0.04z$$

$$15y = 72 - 6x - 2z \Rightarrow y = \frac{72}{15} - \frac{6}{15}x - \frac{2}{15}z \Rightarrow y = 4.8 - 0.4x + 0.13z$$

$$54z = 110 - x - y \Rightarrow z = \frac{110}{54} - \frac{x}{54} - \frac{y}{54} \Rightarrow z = 2.04 - x - y$$

$$\sum_{i=1}^{n} \frac{aij}{aii} \leq 1 \quad (i = 1, 2, 3, \ldots n)$$

It can be verified that these equations satisfy the conditional given in:

The result are given in the tables below:

Iteration	x	y	z
0	0	0	0
1	3.15	3.54	-4.65
2	2.00	-3.32	-3.47

(c) Find the smaller root of the equation x^2 – 400x + 1 = 0, using four digit arithmetic.

Ans. $f(x) = x^2 - 400x + 1 = 0 \Rightarrow f'(x) = 2x - 400$

We have to find the value of root starting with $x_0 = 0$

$$x_0 = \frac{0 - (0)^2 - 400(0) + 1}{2(0) - 400} = \frac{1}{-400} = -0.0025$$

(by $x_1 = x_0 - \frac{f(x_0)}{f'(x_0)}$ using Newton Raphson Method x_1 = -0.0025

$$x_2 = x_1 - \frac{f(x_1)}{f'(x_1)} = -0.0025 - \frac{(-0.0025)^2 - 400*(-0.0025)+1}{2*(-0.0025)-400}$$

$$= -0.0025 - \frac{(-0.00000625)+1+1}{-0.005-400} = -0.0025 + \frac{1.99899}{-400.005}$$

$= -0.0025 - 0.005 \quad = \quad x_2 = -0.0075$

Q5. (a) Perform five iterations of the Bisection method to obtain the smallest Positive root of the equation
$f(x) = x^3 - 5x + 1 = 0$.

Refer to Dec-2001, Q.No.-6(b)

(b) Evaluate $\int_1^2 x^2 dx$ by Simpson's Rule with h = 0.2.

Ans. h = 0.2 $\quad f(x) = x^2 \quad x = 1$ to 2

x	$y = x^2$	y
$x_0 + n = 1$	1.00	y_0
$x_0 + h = 1.2$	1.44	y_1
$x_0 + 2h = 1.4$	1.96	y_2
$x_0 + 3h = 1.6$	2.56	y_3
$x_0 + 4h = 1.8$	3.24	y_4
$x_0 + 5h = 2$	4.00	y_5

Using Simpson's Rule

$$\int_1^2 x^2 dx = \frac{h}{3}\left[(y_0 + y_5) + 4(y_2 + y_4) + 2(y_1 + y_3)\right]$$

$$= \frac{0.2}{3}\left[(1.06 + 4.06) + 4(1.96 + 3.24) + 2(1.44 + 2.56)\right]$$

$$= \frac{0.2}{3}[5 + 4*5 - 20 + 2*4.00]$$

$$= \frac{0.2}{3}[5 + 20.8 + 8] = \frac{0.2}{3}*33.8 = \frac{6.76}{3} = 2.253333 \text{ Ans.}$$

(c) Apply Euler's method to find the solution $y^1 = y - \frac{2x}{y}$ on the interval [0, 1], with initial condition y(0) = 1 for h = 0.2

Ans. Given $\frac{dy}{dx} = y - \frac{2x}{y} \quad y(0) = 1 \quad h = 0.2$

interval [0 – 1] $\quad \therefore f(x,y) = y - \frac{2x}{y}$

From Euler's method $y_{i+1} = y_i + h\,\&\left(x_i, y_i\right)$

Iteration I : if i = 0

$y_1 = y_0 + h\,\&(x_0, y_0)$ $y_1 = y_0 + 0.2f(0, 1)$

$= 1 + 0.2\,[1 - 0] = 1 + 0.2 = 1.2$

Iteration II

if i = 1 $y_2 = y_1 + hf(x_1, y_1)$

$= 1.2 + 0.2f(0.2, 1.2)$ $= 1.2 + 0.2\left[1.2 - \frac{0.4}{1.2}\right]$ $= 1.37$

Iteration III : if i = 2 $y_3 = y_2 + hf(x_2, y_2)$ $= 1.37 + 0.2\,\&\,(0.4, 1.37)$

$= 1.37 + 0.2\,(1.37 - 0.58)$ $= 1.53$

Iteration IV : if i = 3 $y_4 = y_3 + hf(x_3, y_3)$ $= 1.53 + 0.2f(0.6, 1.53)$

$= 1.53 + 0.2\left(1.53 - \frac{1.2}{1.53}\right)$ $= 1.53 + 0.2\,(1.53 - 0.78)$

$= 1.53 + 0.2 * 0.75$ $= 1.53 + 0.15$ $= 1.68$

Iteration V : if i = 4 $y_5 = y_4 + hf(x_4, y_4)$

$= 1.68 + 0.2\left(1.68 - \frac{1.6}{1.68}\right)$ $= 1.68 + 0.2(1.68 - 0.95)$ $= 1.83$

Iteration VI : if i = 5 $y_6 = y_5 + hf(x_5, y_5)$

$= 1.83 + 0.2\left[1.83 - \frac{2}{1.83}\right]$ $= 1.83 + 0.2(1.83 - 1.09)$ $= 1.98$

CS-71 : COMPUTER ORIENTED NUMERICAL TECHNIQUES
June, 2009

Note: Question number 1 is ***compulsory****. Attempt only* ***three*** *Questions from the rest. In total you have to answer* ***four*** *questions. Calculator is allowed.*

Q1. (a) The solution of a problem is given as 3.436. It is known that absolute error in the solution is less than 0.01. Find the interval with in which the exact value must lie.

Ans. Let exact value = x* and * = 3.436. Absolute error = |x – x*|

Absolute error = 0.01

$\rightarrow |x - x^*| =< 0.01$ $\rightarrow (x - x^*) < +0.01$ $\rightarrow 3.436 - x^* < 0.01$

$\rightarrow x^* > 3.437 - 0.01$ $\rightarrow x^* > 3.427$ $\rightarrow x^* > 3.427$

again |x – x*| = 0.01 $\rightarrow (x - x^*) > -0.01$ $\rightarrow 3.437 - x^* > -0.01$

$\rightarrow x^* < 3.437 + 0.01$ $\rightarrow x^* < 3.447$. Hence x* lies between 3.427 to 3.447

(b) Show that,

(i) $\delta = \nabla(1-\nabla)^{-1/2}$

(ii) $E = e^{hD}$

Refer to Page No.-260

(c) Solve the equation $2x^3 + x^2 - 13x + 6 = 0$. One of the roots lies between 1 and 3.

Ans. $f(x) = 2x^3 + x^2 - 13x + 6 = 0$. Let a = 1 and b = 3

$f(1) = 2 \times (1)^3 + (1)^2 - 13 \times 1 + 6 = 2 + 1 - 13 + 6 = 9 - 13 = -4$

$f(3) = 2 \times (3)^3 + (3)^2 - 13 \times 3 + 6 = 2 \times 27 + 9 - 39 + 6 = 54 + 9 + 6 - 39$

= 69 – 39 = 30

x	1	3
f(x)	-4	30

$c = \frac{a+b}{2}$ $c = \frac{1+3}{2}$ $c = 2$

$f(2) = 2(2)^3 + (2)^2 - 13 \times 2 + 6 = 16 + 4 - 26 + 6 = 26 - 26 = 0$

When f(x) = 0 then x is the solution of function.

Therefore, x = 2 is the solution of $2x^3 + x^2 - 13x + 6$ lies between 1 and 3.

(d) Using Newton's iterative method, find the real root of $x \log_{10} x = 1.2$, correct to five decimal places.

Ans. $x \log_{10} x = 1.2$ $x \log_{10} x - 1.2 = 0$ at x = 1

$f(1) = 1 \times \log_{10} 1 - 1.2$ = -1.2 at x = +2

$f(2) = 2 \log_{10} 2 - 1.2 = -0.59794$ at $x = 3$, $f(3) = 3 \log_{10} 3 - 1.2 = 0.23136$
Solution lies between 2 and 3 let a number between 2 and 3

$x_1 = 2.5$ $\quad f'(x) = \cancel{x}.\frac{1}{\cancel{x}} + 1.\log_{10} x - 0 \quad$ $f'(x) = 1 + \log_{10} x$

Iteration I : $x_2 = x_1 - \frac{f(x_1)}{f'(x_1)} = 2.5 - \frac{2.5 \times \log_{10} 2.5 - 1.2}{1 + \log_{10} 2.5} = 2.5 + \frac{(-0.20515)}{1.39794}$
$= 2.5 + 0.14675 = 2.64675$

Iteration II : $x_3 = 2.64675 - \frac{2.64675 \times \log_{10} 2.64675 - 1.2}{1 + \log_{10} 2.64675}$

$= 2.64675 + \frac{0.08118}{1.42271} = 2.64675 + 0.05706 = 2.70381$

Iteration III: $x_4 = 2.70381 - \frac{2.70381 \times \log_{10} 2.70381 - 1.2}{1 + \log_{10} 2.70381}$

$= 2.70381 + \frac{0.03202}{1.43198}$. Hence, solution of $x \log_{10} x = 1.2$ is 2.72617

(e) The following table gives the population of a town during the last 6 censuses. Estimate the population for the year 1956, by using Newton's Backward formula.

Year:	**1921**	**1931**	**1941**	**1951**	**1961**	**1971**
Population ('000)	**20**	**24**	**30**	**39**	**45**	**50**

YEAR	POPULATION ('000)
1921	20
1931	24
1941	30
1951	39
1961	45
1971	50

x_i	y_i	$y_i = y_n - y_{n-1}$	$\nabla^2 y_i = \nabla y_n - \nabla y_{n-1}$	$\nabla^3 y_i = \nabla^2 y_n - \nabla^2 y_{n-1}$
1921	20			
1931	24	$\nabla y_2 = 4$		
1941	30	$\nabla y_3 = 6$	$\nabla^2 y_3 = 2$	
1951	39	$\nabla y_4 = 9$	$\nabla^2 y_4 = 3$	$\nabla^3 y_4 = 1$
1961	45	$\nabla y_5 = 6$	$\nabla^2 y_5 = -3$	$\nabla^3 y_5 = -6$
1971	50	$\nabla y_6 = 5$	$\nabla^2 y_6 = -1$	$\nabla^3 y_6 = 2$

Using formula of Newton backward

$$f(x) = y_n + \frac{\nabla y_n (x - x_n)}{1!h} + \frac{\nabla^2 y_n (x - x_n)(x - x_{n-1})}{2!h}$$

$$+ \frac{\nabla^3 y_n (x - x_n)(x - x_{n-1})(x - x_{n-2})}{3!h}. \text{ Where } h = 10$$

$$f(1956) = 50 + \frac{5 \times 10}{10} + \frac{(-1) \times 10 \times 20}{2 \times 10 \times 10} + 2 \times \frac{10 \times 20 \times 30}{6 \times 10 \times 10}$$

$= 50 + 5 - 10 + 2 = 50 + 5 - 1 + 2 = 57 - 1 = 56$

(f) From the table given below,
Determine the percentage of criminals 35 years of age, by applying Lagrange's method.

Age (years)	% of criminals
25	52.0
30	67.3
40	84.1
50	94.4

Ans. $f(x) = \frac{y_1 (x - x_2)(x - x_3)(x - x_4)}{(x_1 - x_2)(x_1 - x_3)(x_1 - x_4)} + \frac{y_2 (x - x_4)(x - x_3)(x - x_4)}{(x_2 - x_4)(x_2 - x_3)(x_2 - x_4)}$

$$+ \frac{y_3 (x - x_1)(x - x_2)(x - x_4)}{(x_3 - x_1)(x_3 - x_2)(x_3 - x_4)} + \frac{y_4 (x - x_1)(x - x_2)(x - x_3)}{(x_4 - x_4)(x_4 - x_2)(x_4 - x_3)}$$

$$f(35) = \frac{52(5)(-5)(-15)}{(-5)(-15)(+25)} + \frac{67.3(15)(-5)(-15)}{(5)(-10)(-20)}$$

$$+ \frac{84.1 \times 10 \times 5 \times (+15)}{15 \times 10 \times (-10)} + \frac{94.4 \times 15 \times 5 \times (-5)}{25 \times 20 \times 10}$$

$$f(35) = \frac{-52}{5} + 67.3 \times \frac{9}{8} + \frac{84.1}{2} - 94.4 \times \frac{3}{40}$$

$\Rightarrow -10.4 + 75.7125 + 42.05 - 37.08 = 70.2825$

Q2. (a) Perform four iterations of the Newton Raphson method to obtain the approximate value of $(17)^{1/3}$ starting with the initial approximation $x_0 = 2$.

Ans. $x = (17)^{1/3}$ $x^3 = 17$ $x^3 - 17 = 0$

$f(x) = x^3 - 17$ $f'(x) = 3x^2$

Iteration I : $x_0 = 2$ $x_1 = x_0 \frac{f(x_0)}{f'(x_0)}$

$x_1 = 2 - \frac{(2)^3 - 17}{(2)^2} \qquad = 2 + \frac{9}{4} \qquad = 2 + 2.25 \qquad = 4.25$

Iteration II : $x_1 = 4.25$ $\quad x_2 = 4.25 - \frac{(4.25)^3 - 17}{(4.25)^2} = 4.25 - \frac{76.7656 - 17}{18.0625}$

$\Rightarrow 4.25 - \frac{59.7656}{18.0625} \qquad \Rightarrow 4.25 - 3.3088 \qquad = 0.9412$

Iteration III : $x_2 = 0.9412$

$x_3 = 0.9412 - \frac{(0.9412)^3 - 17}{(0.9412)^2} = 0.9412 + \frac{1.611662}{0.8859} = 09412 + 1.8192$

$= 2.7604$. Hence solution of $(17)^{1/3} = (2.7604)$

(b) Describe Gauss elimination method to solve the system of linear equations. Refer to Page No.-19

(c) Explain Newton's forward difference interpolation formula.
Refer to Page No.-36 to 38

Q3. (a) By using the bisection method, find an approximate root of the equation $\sin x = \frac{1}{x}$ that lies between x = 1 and x = 1.5 (measured in radians). Carry out computation up to 3rd stage.

Ans. $\sin x = \frac{1}{x} \qquad \sin x - \frac{1}{x} = 0 \qquad f(x) = \sin x - \frac{1}{x}$

Iteration I : at x = 1 $\quad f(1) = \sin 1 - \frac{1}{1} = -.98255$

$f(1.5) = \sin 1.5 - \frac{1}{1.5} = -0.64048$

$x_3 = \frac{1 + 1.5}{2} = \frac{2.5}{2} = 1.25$

$f(1.25) = \sin(1.25) - \frac{1}{1.25} = -0.77818$

Sign of f(1) and (1.25) is same changes $\quad x_1 \to x_3 \;\; x_2 \to x_2$

New interval is 1.25 and 1.5

Iteration II : f(1.25) = -0.77818 $\qquad$ f(1.5) = -0.64048

$x_3 = \frac{1.25 + 1.5}{2} = 1.375$

$$f(1.375) = \sin(1.375) - \frac{1}{1.375} = -0.70328$$

Sign of f(1.25) and f(1.375) is same changes $x \rightarrow x_3$ $x_2 \rightarrow x_2$

New interval is 1.375 and 1.5

Iteration III:

f(1.375) = -0.70328 f(1.5) = -0.64048

$$x_3 = \frac{1.375 + 1.5}{2} = 1.4375$$

$$f(1.4375) = \sin(1.4375) - \frac{1}{1.4375} = -0.67056$$

An approximate root of equation $\sin x = \frac{1}{x}$ is 1.4375

(b) Describe Simpson's rule for integration.

Refer to Page No.-45

(c) Apply Gauss – Jordan method to solve the equation.
x + y + z = 9, 2x – 3y + 4z = 13,
and 3x + 4y + 5z = 40.

Ans. $x + y + z = 9$ $2x + (-3y) + 4z = 13$ $3x + 4y + 5z = 40$

$$x = 9 - y - z \quad \ldots (1)$$

$$y = \frac{-1}{3}(13 - 2x - 4z) \quad \ldots (2)$$

$$z = \frac{1}{5}(40 - 3x - 4y) \quad \ldots (3)$$

Iteration I: $x = 0, y = 0, z = 0$ $x_1 = 9 - 0 - 0 = 9$

$$y_1 = \frac{-1}{3}(13 - 0 - 0) = \frac{-13}{3} = -4.3 \qquad z_1 = \frac{1}{5}(40 - 0 - 0) = \frac{40}{5} = 8$$

Iteration II: $x_1 = 9, y_1 = -4.3, z_1 = 8$ $x_2 = 9 + 4.3 - 8$

$= +5.3$ $y_2 = \frac{-1}{3}(13 - 2 \times 9 - 4 \times 8) = 12.333$

$$z_2 = \frac{1}{5}(40 - 3 \times 9 + 4 \times 4.3) = 6.04$$

Iteration III:

$x_2 = 5.3, y_2 = 12.33, z_2 = 6.04$ $x_3 = 9 - 12.33 - 6.04 = -9.37$

$$y_3 = \frac{-1}{3}[13 - 2 \times 5.3 - 4 \times 6.04] = +7.2533$$

$$z_3 = +\frac{1}{5}[40 - 3 \times 5.3 - 4 \times 12.33]$$

= -5.044

Iteration IV : x_3 = -9.37 y_3 = 7.2533 z_3 = -5.044

$x_4 = 9 + 5.044 - 7.533 \Rightarrow 6.511$ $y_4 = -\frac{1}{3}[13 + 2 \times 9.37 + 4 \times 5.044]$

= -17.30533

$z_4 = \frac{1}{5}[40 + 3 \times 9.37 - 4 \times 7.2533] = \frac{1}{5} \times 39.0968 = 7.81936$

$[x^4, y^4, z^4] = [6.511, -17.3053, 7.81936]$

Q4. (a) A real root of the equation f(x) = x^3 – 5x + 1 = 0 lies in the interval (0, 1). Perform four iterations of the secant method to obtain this root.

Ans. f(x) = x^3 – 5x + 1 = 0

Iteration I : f(0) = $(0)^3$ – 5 × 0 + 1 = 1 $\rightarrow f(1) = (1)^3 - 5 \times 1 + 1$

= 1 – 5 + 1= -3 $x_3 = \frac{0+1}{2}$ x_3 = 0.5

$f(0.5) = (0.5)^3 - 5 \times 0.5 + 1$ = -1.375

f(a) and f(0.5) are opposite in sign. The new interval $x_2 \rightarrow x_3 \Rightarrow x_2 = 0.5$

$x_1 \rightarrow x_1 \Rightarrow x_1 = 0$

Iteration II : x_1 = 0.5 x_2 = 0 $x_3 = \frac{0.5+0}{2}$

$x_3 = \frac{0.5}{2} = 0.25$ f(0.25) = $(0.25)^3$ – 5 × (0.25) + 1 = -0.2344

f(0.25) and f(0) are opposite in direction.

Iteration III: x_1 = 0 x_2 = 0.25

$x_3 = \frac{0+0.25}{2} = 0.125$ f(0.125) = $(0.125)^3$ – 5 × (0.125) + 1 = 0.37695

Iteration IV: x_1 = 0.125 x_2 = 0.25

$x_3 = \frac{0.125+0.25}{2}$ $= \frac{0.15}{2}$ = 0.075

f(0.075) = $(0.075)^3$ – 5 × (0.075) + 1 f(0.075) = 0.6254

Hence solution of x^3 – 5x + 1 is x = 0.6254

(b) Apply Runge-Kutta method to find approximate value of y for x = 0.2, in steps of 0.1, if $\frac{dy}{dx} = x + y^2$, given that y = 1 where x = 0

Ans. $\frac{dy}{dx} = x + y^2$ where h = 0.1

$x = 0.2$ $y = ?$ $y_{n+1} = y_n + \frac{1}{2}(k_1 + k_2)$

where $k_1 = nf(x_n, y_n)$ $k_2 = nf(x_{n+n}, y_{n+h.k1})$

$y = 1$ $x = 0$

Iteration I : $y_{n+1} = y_n + \frac{1}{2}(k_1 + k_2)$ $k_1 = nf(x_1, y_1)$

$= 0.1 \times (x + y^2)$ $x = 0, y = 1$

$= 0.1 \times 1$ $= 0.1$

$k_2 = 0.1\ (x + y^2)$ $x = 0.1, y = 1.01$

$= 0.1 \times (0.1 + (1.01)^2)$ $= 0.11201$

$y_2 = 1 + \frac{1}{2}(0.1 + 0.11201)$ $y_2 = 1.106$

Iteration II : $y_{n+1} = y_n + \frac{1}{2}(k_1 + k_2)$ where $k_1 = nf(x_1, y_1)$

$= 0.1 \times \left(0.1 + (1.106)^2\right) = 0.1 \times (0.1 + 1.223)$ $x_1 = 0.1, y_1 = 1.106$

$= 0.1323$

$k_2 = 0.1 \times (0.2 + (0.1323)^2) = 0.1 \times 0.2175 = 0.0217$

$y_3 = y_2 + \frac{1}{2}(k_1 + k_2)$

$= 1.106 + \frac{1}{2}(0.1323 + 0.0217)$ $= 1.106 + 0.077 \Rightarrow 1.1830$. Hence when x = 0.2 then y = 1.18320

(c) Solve the system of equation
$2x_1 - x_2 + 0x_3 = 7$ $-x_1 + 2x_2 - x_3 = 1$ $0x_1 - x_2 + 2x_3 = 1$
using the Gauss-Seidel method.

Ans. $\begin{bmatrix} 2 & -1 & 0 \\ -1 & 2 & -1 \\ 0 & -1 & 2 \end{bmatrix} = \begin{bmatrix} x_1 \\ x_2 \\ x_3 \end{bmatrix} = \begin{bmatrix} 7 \\ 1 \\ 1 \end{bmatrix}$

$2x_1 - x_2 + 0x_3 = 7$

$-x_1 + 2x_2 - x_3 = 1$

$0x_1 - x_2 + 2x_3 = 1$

Iteration I: $x_1 = 0, x_2 = 0, x_3 = 0$

$x_1 = \frac{1}{2}[7 + 1x_2 - 0x_3] = \frac{1}{2}[7 + 1 \times 0 - 0 \times 0] = \frac{1}{2}[7 + 0 - 0] = \frac{7}{2} = 3.5$

$x_2 = \frac{1}{2}[1 + 1 \times 3.5 + 1 \times 0] = \frac{1}{2}[1 + 3.5] = \frac{1}{2}[4.5] = 2.25$ $x_3 = \frac{1}{2}[1 + 1 \times 2.25]$

$$= \frac{1}{2}[1+2.25] = \frac{1}{2}[3.35] = 1.675$$

Iteration II : $x_1 = 3.5$, $x_2 = 2.25$, $x_3 = 1.675$

$$x_1 = \frac{1}{2}[7+1\times 2.25 - 0\times 1.675] = \frac{1}{2}[7+2.25] = \frac{1}{2}[9.25] = 4.625$$

$$x_2 = \frac{1}{2}[1+4.625+1.675] = \frac{1}{2}[7.25] = 3.625$$

$$x_3 = \frac{1}{2}[1+3.625] = \frac{1}{2}[4.625] = 2.3125$$

Iteration III : $x_1 = 4.625$, $x_2 = 3.625$, $x_3 = 2.3125$

$$x_1 = \frac{1}{2}[7+3.625] = \frac{1}{2}[10.625] = 5.3125$$

$$x_2 = \frac{1}{2}[1+5.3125+2.3125] = \frac{1}{2}[8.625] = 4.3125$$

$$x_3 = \frac{1}{2}[1+4.3125] = \frac{1}{2}[5.3125] = 2.65625$$

Iteration IV : $x_1 = 5.3125$. $x_2 = 4.3125$, $x_3 = 2.65625$

$$x_1 = \frac{1}{2}[7+4.3125] = \frac{1}{2}[11.3125] = 5.65625$$

$$x_2 = \frac{1}{2}[1+5.65625+2.65625] = 4.65625$$

$$x_3 = \frac{1}{2}[1+4.65625] = 2.828125$$

Q5. (a) When a computer uses a number base 2, how many significant decimal digits are contained in the mantissa of floating numbers.

Ans. An n-digit floating point number in base β (a given natural no.) has the form. $x = \pm(d_1 d_2 \ldots d_n)_\beta \beta^e, 0 <= d_i < \beta,\ m \le e \le M;$ I = 1, 2, … n, $d_1 \ne 0$; where $(d_1 d_2 \ldots d_n)_\beta$ is a $\beta -$ fraction called Mantissa and its value is given by $\left(d_1 d_2 \ldots d_\beta = d_1 \times \frac{1}{\beta} + d_2 \times \frac{1}{\beta^2} + \ldots + d_n \times \frac{1}{\beta^n} \right)$; e is an integer called exponent.

The exponent e is also limited to range m < e < M, where m and M are integers varying from computer to computer. Usually M = -M.

In IBM 1130, M = -128 (in binary), -39 (decimal) and M = 127 (in binary), 38 (in decimal). For most of computer $\beta = 2$ (binary), on some computer $\beta = 16$ (hexadecimal) and in pocket calculators $\beta = 10$ (decimal).

(b) Given $\frac{dy}{dx} = \frac{y - x}{y + x}$ with initial condition, y = 1 at x = 0, find y for x = 0.1 by Euler's method.

Ans. $\frac{dy}{dx} = \frac{y-x}{y+x} = f(x.y)$ $x_1 = 0, y_1 = 1, h = 0.1.$

Euler's method $y_{i+1} = y_i + h + n_i, y_i$ $\quad 1 = 1$

$y_2 = y_1 + h + (x_1, y_1) = 1 + (0.1).F(0, 1) = 1 + (0.1)\left[\frac{1-0}{1+0}\right] = 1 + 0.1\ (1)$

$y_2 = 1 + 0.1 = 1.1$ $\qquad y(0.1) = 1.1$

(c) Prove with the usual notations, that $\Delta = \frac{1}{2}\delta^2 + \delta\sqrt{1 + \frac{\delta^2}{4}}$

Ans. $\frac{1}{2}\delta^2 + \delta\sqrt{(1 + \delta^2 + 4)}$

$$= \frac{1}{2}\left(E^{\frac{1}{2}} - E^{-\frac{1}{2}}\right)^2 + \left(E^{\frac{1}{2}} - E^{-\frac{1}{2}}\right)\sqrt{\left[1 + \left(E^{\frac{1}{2}} - E^{-\frac{1}{2}}\right)^2 / 4\right]}$$

$$= \frac{1}{2}\left(E + E^{-1} - 2\right) + \left(E^{\frac{1}{2}} - E^{-\frac{1}{2}}\right)\sqrt{\left(E + E^{-1} + 2\right)4}$$

$$= \frac{1}{2}\left(E + E^{-1} - 2\right) + \left(E^{\frac{1}{2}} - E^{-\frac{1}{2}}\right)\left(E^{\frac{1}{2}} + E^{-\frac{1}{2}}\right)/2 = \frac{1}{2}\left[\left(E + E^{-1} - 2\right) + \left(E - E^{-1}\right)\right]$$

$$= \frac{1}{2}(2E - 2) = \frac{1}{2} \times 2(E - 1) = E - 1 = \Delta \text{ Proved}$$

CS-71: COMPUTER ORIENTED NUMERICAL TECHNIQUES
December, 2009

Note: *Question number **1** is **compulsory**. Attempt only **three** questions from the rest. In total you have to answer **four** questions. Calculator is allowed.*

Q1. (a). Let x = 0.005998. Find the relative error, if x is rounded off to three decimal digits.

Ans. x = 0.005998 has 4 significant digits

So, $x = 0.5998 * 10^{-2}$

Now, fl (x) is the value of x, rounded off to three decimal digits.

Case I. $fl(0.5998 * 10^{-2}) = 0.599 * 10^{-2}$ (chopping)

$$\text{Relative Error} = = \frac{|x - fl(x)|}{x} = \frac{|0.5998 * 10^{-2} - 0.599 \times 10^{-2}|}{0.5998 \times 10^{-2}} = 0.00133378$$

Case II. $Fl(0.5998 * 10^{-2}) = 0.6 * 10^{-2}$ (rounding)

$$\text{Relative Error} = \frac{|x - fl(x)|}{x} = \frac{|0.5998 * 10^{-2} - 0.6 * 10^{-2}|}{0.5998 * 10^{-2}} = 0.000333444$$

(b) Prove that: (i) $\delta = E^{+\frac{1}{2}} - E^{-\frac{1}{2}}$

Ans. $\delta = \nabla(1-\nabla)^{-1/2} = (1-E^{-1})\left(1-(1-E^{-1})\right)^{\frac{-1}{2}}$

$= (1-E^{-1})(E^{-1})^{\frac{-1}{2}}$

$= (1-E^{-1})E^{\frac{1}{2}} = E^{\frac{1}{2}} - E^{-1}E^{\frac{1}{2}} \qquad = E^{\frac{1}{2}} - E^{\frac{-1}{2}}$

(ii) $\mu^2 = 1 + \frac{1}{4}\delta^2$

Ans. $\delta^2 = \left(E^{\frac{1}{2}} - E^{\frac{-1}{2}}\right)^2 = E + E^{-1} - 2 \qquad$ (i)

Now, $1 + \frac{1}{4}\delta^2 = 1 + \frac{1}{4}(E + E^{-1} - 2) \qquad = \frac{1}{4}(E + E^{-1} + 2)$

$= \left[\frac{1}{2}\left(E^{\frac{1}{2}} + E^{\frac{-1}{2}}\right)\right]^2 = \mu^2$

(c) Use the method of Regula – fabi method, to find the fourth root of 32 correct to three decimal places.

Ans. To find the fourth root of 32 correct to 3 decimal places.

$$f(x) = x - 32^{\frac{1}{4}}$$
$$= x - 2\sqrt[4]{2}$$

X	0	2	3
f(x)	-2.37841423	-1.37841423	0.62158577

Here, $x_0 = 1$ $\quad x_1 = 3$

$f(x_0) = -1.37841423$ $\quad f(x_1) = 0.62158577$

Iteration I.

$$x_2 = \frac{x_0 f(x_1) - x_1 f(x_0)}{f(x_1) - f(x_0)} = \frac{1(0.62158577) - 3(-1.37841423)}{0.62158577 - (-1.37841423)}$$
$$=2.387006335$$

$f(x_2) = .008592105$

Iteration 2.

$$x_3 = \frac{x_1 f(x_2) - x_2 f(x_1)}{f(x_2) - f(x_1)}$$
$$= \frac{3(0.008592105) - 2.387006335(0.62158577)}{0.008592105 - 0.62158577}$$
$$= 2.37841423$$

(d) Solve the equation $x^4 - 2x^3 + 4x^2 + 6x - 21 = 0$, given that the sum of two its roots is zero.

Ans. $x^4 - 2x^3 + 4x^2 + 6x - 21 = 0$ is equation of degree 4. And, the sum of two of its root is zero. So, expected roots are $\mathcal{L}, -\mathcal{L}, \beta, \gamma$

$$(x - \mathcal{L})(x - (-\mathcal{L}))(x - \beta)(x - \gamma) = x^4 - 2x^3 + 4x^2 + 6x - 21$$
$$(x^2 - \mathcal{L}^2)(x - \beta)(x - \gamma) = x^4 - 2x^3 + 4x^2 + 6x - 21 \qquad (1)$$
$$x_4 - (\beta + \gamma)x^3 + (\beta\gamma - \mathcal{L}^2)x^2 + (\mathcal{L}^2\beta + \mathcal{L}^2\gamma)x - \mathcal{L}^2\beta\gamma$$
$$= x^4 - 2x^3 + 4x^2 + 6x - 21$$
$$\beta + \gamma = 2 \qquad \text{....(2)}$$
$$\beta\gamma - \mathcal{L}^2 = 4 \qquad \text{....(3)}$$
$$\mathcal{L}^2(\beta + \gamma) = 6 \qquad \text{....(4)}$$

$\mathcal{L}^2\beta\gamma = 21 \qquad \ldots.(5)$

$(4)\ \&\ (2) \Rightarrow \mathcal{L}^2(\beta+\gamma) = \mathcal{L}^2(2) = 6$

$\Rightarrow \mathcal{L}^2 = 3 \Rightarrow \mathcal{L} = \mp\sqrt{3}$

$(5) \Rightarrow \mathcal{L}^2\beta\gamma = 21 \qquad 3(\beta\gamma) = 21$

$\beta\gamma = 7$

Dividing eq by $(x^2 - 3)$

$g(x) = -x^2 + 2x - 7$

X	0	1	2
g(x)	-7	-6	1

$g'(x) = -2x + 2$

$x_0 = 1.5 \qquad g(x_0) = -6.25$

$g'(x_0) = -7.25 \qquad x_1 = x_0 - \frac{g(x_0)}{g'(x_0)}$

$= 1.5 - \left(\frac{-6.55}{-7.25}\right) = 0.637931034$

(e) Apply Runge – Kutta fourth order method to find an approximate value of y when x = 0.2 given that $\frac{dy}{dx} = x + y$ and y = 1 when x = 0.

Ans. $\frac{dy}{dx} = y' = x + y$

$x_0 = 0, \qquad y = 1, \ h = x_1 - x_0 = 0.2$

Now, $K_1 = hf(x_0, y_0) \qquad = 0.2(x_0 + y_0) = 0.2(0+1) = 0.2$

$K_2 = hf\left(x_0 + \frac{h}{2}, y_0 + \frac{K_1}{2}\right) \qquad = 0.2\left(\left(0 + \frac{0.2}{2}\right) + \left(1 + \frac{0.2}{2}\right)\right)$

$= 0.2(0.1 + 1.1) = 0.24$

$K_3 = hf\left(x_0 + \frac{h}{2}, \ y_0 + \frac{K_2}{2}\right) \qquad = (0.2)\left(\left(0 + \frac{0.2}{2}\right) + \left(1 + \frac{0.24}{2}\right)\right)$

$= 0.2\ (0.1 + 1.12) = 0.244$

$K_4 = hf(x_0 + h, y_0 + K_3) \qquad = 0.2((0 + 0.1) + (1 + 0.244))$

$= 0.2(0.1 + 1.244) = 0.2688$

$$y_1 = y_0 + \frac{1}{6}(K_1 + 2K_2 + 2K_3 + K_4)$$

$$= 1 + \frac{1}{6}(0.2 + 0.48 + 0.488 + 0.2688) \qquad = 1 + \frac{1}{6}(1.4368) = 1 + 0.23946667$$

$y_1 = 1.23946667$ at $x_1 = 0.2$

(f) The observed values of a function are respectively 168, 120, 72 and 63 at the four positions 3, 7, 9 and 10 of the independent variable. What is the best estimate you can give of the value of the function at the position 6 of the independent variable?

Ans.

$y_0 = 168$ at $x_0 = 3$

$y_1 = 120$ at $x_1 = 7$

$y_2 = 72$ at $x_2 = 9$

$y_3 = 63$ at $x_3 = 10$

Table of Divided Difference

x	y = f[.]	f[. , .]	f[. , . , .]	F[. , . , . , .]
3	168			
7	120	-12	-5.33333333	
9	72	-.44	11.66666667	2.428571429
10	63	-9		

$$P_4(x) = f[x_0] + (x - x_0) f[x_0, x_1] + (x - x_0)(x - x_1) f[x_0, x_1, x_2] + (x - x_0)$$
$$(x - x_1)(x - x_2)\, f[x_0, x_1, x_2, x_3]$$

=168 + (x-3) (-12) + (x-3) (x-7) (-5.33333333) + (x-3) (x-7) (x-9) (2.428571429)

At x = 6,

$$P_4(6) = 168 + (6-3)(-12) + (6-3)(6-7)(-5.33333333) + (6-3)(6-7)$$
$$(6-9)(2.428571429)$$

=168 -36 + 15.99999999 + 21.857142861

y(x = 6)=169.857142851

Q2. (a) Using Newton's iteration method, find the real root of the equation 3x = cos x +1.

Ans. $f(x) = \cos x - 3x + 1$ $\qquad f'(x) = -\sin x - 3$

Let

$x_0 = 0$ $\qquad f(x_0) = 2$

$f'(x_0) = -3$

$$x_1 = x_0 - \frac{f(x_0)}{f'(x_0)} = 0 - \frac{2}{-3} = 0.66666667$$

$$f(x_1) = -0.214112751$$

$$f'(x_1) = -3.618369806$$

$$x_2 = x_1 - \frac{f(x_1)}{f'(x_1)} = 0.66666667 - \frac{-0.214112751}{-3.618369806}$$

$$x_2 = 0.607492853$$

$f(x_2) = -0.001396856$ $\quad f'(x_2) = -3.570810684$

$$x_3 = x_2 - \frac{f(x_2)}{f'(x_2)} = 0.607492853 - \frac{-0.001396856}{-3.570810684}$$

$$= 0.607101666$$

$f(x_3) = -0.000000064$ $\quad f'(x_3) = -3.570489444$

$$x_4 = x_3 - \frac{f(x_3)}{f'(x_3)} = 0.607101666 - \frac{-0.000000064}{-3.570489444}$$

$$= 0.607101648$$

$$f(x_4) = 0$$

The real root of the equation is 0.607101648

(b) Use Simpson's $\frac{1}{3^{rd}}$ rule to find $\int_0^{0.6} e^{-x^2}\,dx$ by taking seven ordinates.

Ans. The values of the function $f(x) = e^{-x^2}$ is

x	f(x)
0	1
0.1	0.990049834
0.2	0.960789439
0.3	0.91391185
0.4	0.852143789
0.5	0.778800783
0.6	0.697676326

Here, h = 0.1

Applying composite Simpson's $\frac{1}{3}$ rule,

$$I=\int_0^{0.6} f(x)\,dx=\int_0^{0.2} f(x)\,dx+\int_{0.2}^{0.4} f(x)\,dx+\int_{0.4}^{0.6} f(x)\,dx$$

$$=\frac{h}{3}\left[f_0+4f_1+f_2\right]+\frac{h}{3}\left[f_2+4f_3+f_4\right]+\frac{h}{3}\left[f_4+4f_5+f_6\right]$$

$$=\frac{h}{3}\left[(f_0+f_6)+4\left(f_1+f_3+f_5\right)+2\left(f_2+f_4\right)\right]$$

$$=\frac{0.1}{3}\begin{bmatrix}(1+0.697676326)+4(0.990049834+0.91391185+0.778800783)\\ +2(0.960789439+0.8521436789)\end{bmatrix}$$

$$I = 0.535153088$$

(c) In the table below, the values of y are consecutive terms of a series of which 23.6 is the 6th term. Using Newton forward interpolation formula find the first term of the series.

x:	3	4	5	6	7	8	9
y	4.8	8.4	14.5	23.6	36.2	52.8	73.9

Ans.

x	y	Δy	$\Delta^2 y$	$\Delta^3 y$	$\Delta^4 y$	$\Delta^5 y$	$\Delta^6 y$
3	4.8						
		3.6					
4	8.4		2.5				
		6.1		0.5			
5	14.5		3.0		0.0		
		9.1		0.5		0.0	
6	23.6		3.5		0.0		1.0
		12.6		0.5		1.0	
7	36.2		4.0		1.0		
		16.6		1.5			
8	52.8		5.5				
		21.1					
9	73.9						

Here h = 1

Newton Forward Interpolation Formula

$$y=y_0+\frac{(x-x_0)}{h}\Delta y_0+\frac{(x-x_0)(x-x_1)}{h^2\,2!}\Delta^2 y_0+\frac{(x-x_0)(x-x_1)(x-x_2)}{h^3\,3!}$$

$$\Delta^3 y_0+\frac{(x-x_0)(x-x_1)(x-x_2)(x-x_3)}{h^4\,4!}\Delta^4 y_0+\frac{(x-x_0)(x-x_1)(x-x_2)(x-x_3)(x-x_4)}{h^5\,5!}$$

$$\Delta^5 y_0+\frac{(x-x_0)(x-x_1)(x-x_2)(x-x_3)(x-x_4)(x-x_5)}{h^6\,6!}\Delta^6 y_0$$

$$=4.8+(x-3)(3.6)+(x-3)(x-4)\left(\frac{2.5}{2}\right)+(x-3)(x-4)(x-5)\left(\frac{0.5}{6}\right)+0+0$$

$$+(x-3)(x-4)(x-5)(x-6)(x-7)(x-8)\left(\frac{1}{6!}\right)$$

The first term of series,

$$y(x=1)=4.8+3.6(1-3)+(1-3)(1-4)\left(\frac{2.5}{2}\right)+(1-3)(1-4)(1-5)\left(\frac{0.5}{6}\right)+(1-3)$$

$$(1-4)(1-5)(1-6)(1-7)(1-8)\left(\frac{1}{720}\right)$$

= - 3.9

Q3. (a) Find the root of the equation $xe^x = \cos x$ using the secant method, correct to four decimal places.

Ans. $xe^x = \cos x$

$f(x) = \cos x - xe^x$

x	0	1	2
f(x)	1	0.540302306	-0.416146837

$x_0 = 1 \qquad f(x_0) = 0.540302306$

$x_1 = 2 \qquad f(x_1) = -0.416146837$

$$x_2 = \frac{x_0 f(x_1) - x_1 f(x_0)}{f(x_1) - f(x_0)}$$

$$= \frac{1(-0.416146837) - 2(0.540302306)}{-0.416146837 - 0.540302306} \qquad =1.564904376$$

$f(x_2) = -7.477821363$

$$x_3 = \frac{x_1 f(x_2) - x_2 f(x_1)}{f(x_2) - f(x_1)} \qquad =2.02564033$$

$f(x_3) = -15.795628012$

$$x_4 = \frac{x_2 f(x_3) - x_3 f(x_2)}{f(x_3) - f(x_2)} \qquad =0.411252785$$

$f(x_4) = 0.296160905$

$$x_5 = \frac{x_3 f(x_4) - x_4 f(x_3)}{f(x_4) - f(x_3)} = -0.457816481$$

$f(x_5) = 1.18666354$

$$x_6 = \frac{x_4 f(x_5) - x_5 f(x_4)}{f(x_5) - f(x_4)} \qquad =0.420552838$$

$f(x_6) = 0.272444174$

$$x_7 = \frac{x_5 f(x_6) - x_6 f(x_5)}{f(x_6) - f(x_5)} = 0.682313431$$

$$f(x_7) = -0.573806661$$

$$x_8 = \frac{x_6 f(x_7) - x_7 f(x_6)}{f(x_7) - f(x_6)} = 0.504824718$$

$$f(x_8) = 0.038918624$$

$$x_9 = \frac{x_7 f(x_8) - x_8 f(x_7)}{f(x_8) - f(x_7)} = 0.517834718$$

$$f(x_9) = \cos(0.517834718) - 0.517834718 e^{0.517834718}$$
$$= 0.000002163$$

(b) Evaluate $\int_1^2 \log x \, dx$ by Trapezoidal rule.

Ans. $f(x) = \log x$

f(1) = 0 at x = 1

f(2) = 0.693147181 at x = 2

Trapezoidal rule

$$I = \int_{x_0}^{x_1} f(x)\,dx = \frac{h}{2}[f_0 + f_1]$$

$$I = \int_1^2 \log x \, dx = \int_1^2 f(x).dx = \frac{h}{2}[f(1) + f(2)]$$

Here h = 2 – 1 = 1

$$I = \frac{1}{2}[0 + 0.693147181] = 0.34657359$$

(c) Solve, by Gauss-Seidel iteration method, the equations:

$$20x + y - 2z = 17$$
$$3x + 20y - z = -18$$
$$2x - 3y + 20z = 25$$

Ans.

$$20x + y - 2z = 17 \quad --(1)$$
$$3x + 20y - z = -18 \quad --(2)$$
$$2x - 3y + 20z = 25 \quad --(3)$$

$$(1) \Rightarrow x = \frac{1}{20}(17 - y + 2z) \quad (2) \Rightarrow y = \frac{1}{20}(18 - 3x + z)$$

$$(3) \Rightarrow z = \frac{1}{20}(25 - 2x + 3y) \qquad \text{Let} \quad (x, y, z)^0 = (0, 0, 0)$$

Iteration I

$$x = \frac{1}{20}(17 - 0 + 0) = 0.85 \quad y = \frac{1}{20}(-18 - 2.55 + 0) = -1.0275$$

$$z = \frac{1}{20}(25 - 1.7 - 3.0825) = 1.010875$$

Iteration II

$$x = \frac{1}{20}(17 - 1.0275 - 2.02175) = 0.6975375$$

$$y = \frac{1}{20}(-18 - 2.0926125 + 1.010875) = -0.954086875$$

$$z = \frac{1}{20}(25 - 1.395075 - 2.862260625) = 1.037133219$$

Iteration III

$$x = \frac{1}{20}(17 - 0.954086875 - 2.074266438) = 0.698582334$$

$$y = \frac{1}{20}(-18 - 2.095747003 + 1.037133219) = -0.952930689$$

$$z = \frac{1}{20}(25 - 1.397164668 - 2.858792068) = 1.037202163$$

Q4. (a) Find the root of the equation $x^3 - 4x - 9 = 0$, using the bisection method, correct to three decimal places.

Ans. $x^3 - 4x - 9 = 0$

$f(x) = x^3 - 4x - 9$

x	0	1	2	3
f(x)	-9	-12	-9	6

a = 2 f(a) = -9

b = 3 f(b) = 6

$$c = \frac{a+b}{2} = \frac{2+3}{2} = 2.5$$

$$f(c) = (2.5)^3 - 4(2.5) - 9 \qquad = 15.625 - 10 - 9 = -3.375$$

$f(a)\,f(c) < 0$	$f(c)\,f(b) < 0$
$(-9)\,(-3.375) \not< 0$	$(-3.375)\,(6) < 0$

$a = 2.5$ $f(a) = -3.375$

$b = 3$ $f(b) = 6$

$$c = \frac{a+b}{2} = \frac{2.5+3}{2} = \frac{5.5}{2} = 2.75$$

$$f(c) = (2.75)^3 - 4(2.75) - 9 \quad = 20.796875 - 11 - 9 = 0.796875$$

$f(a)\, f(c) < 0$	$f(c)\, f(b) < 0$
$(-3.375)(0.796875) < 0$	$(0.796875)(6) \not< 0$

$a = 2.5$ $f(a) = -3.375$

$b = 2.75$ $f(b) = 0.796875$

$$c = \frac{a+b}{2} = \frac{2.5+2.75}{2} = 2.625$$

$$f(c) = (2.625)^3 - 4(2.625) - 9 \quad = 18.087890625 - 10.5 - 9$$

$$= -1.412109375$$

$f(a)\, f(c) < 0$	$f(c)\, f(b) < 0$
$(-3.375)(-1.412109375) \not< 0$	$(-1.412109375)(0.796875) < 0$

$a = 2.625$ $f(a) = -1.412109375$

$b = 2.75$ $f(b) = 0.796875$

$$c = \frac{a+b}{2} = \frac{2.625+2.75}{2} = 2.6875$$

$$f(c) = (2.6875)^3 - 4(2.6875) - 9 \quad = 19.410888671875 - 10.75 - 9$$

$$= 0.339111328125$$

$f(a)\, f(c) < 0$	$f(c)\, f(b) < 0$
$(-1.412109375)(0.339111328125) < 0$	$(0.339111328125)(0.796875) \not< 0$

$a = 2.625$ $f(a) = -1.412109375$

$b = 2.6825$ $f(b) = 0.339111328125$

$$c = \frac{2.625+2.6825}{2} = 2.65375$$

$$f(c) = (2.65375)^3 - 4(2.65375) - 9$$

$$= 18.688739974609375 - 10.615 - 9$$

$$= -0.926260025$$

$f(a)\, f(c) < 0$	$f(c)\, f(b) < 0$
$(-1.412109375)(-0.926260025) \not< 0$	$(-0.926260025)(0.339111328125) < 0$

$a = 2.65375$ $f(a) = -0.926260025$

b = 2.6825 f(b) = 0.339111328125

c = 2.668125

f(c) = -0.678408909

$$f(a)\,f(c) < 0 \qquad\Bigg|\qquad f(c)\,f(b) < 0$$

$$(-0.92626005)(-0.678408909) \not< 0 \;\Big|\; (0-678408909)(0.339111328125) < 0$$

a = 2.668125 f(a) = -0.678408909

b = 2.6825 f(b) = 0.339111328125

c = 2. 6753125

f(c) = - 0.553243943

(b) Compare Direct methods and iterative methods for solving system of linear equations.

Refer to Dec–2001, Q.No.-1(b)(ii), Page No.-143

(c) Use the Euler method to solve numerically the initial value problem $v' = -2tv^2$, v(0)=1 with h=0.2 and 0.1 on the interval [0, 1].

Ans. $v_k' = f(t_k, v_k) = -2t_k v_k^{\,2}$

Euler Method

$v_{k+1} = v_k + h f_k(t, y)$

Starting with

$t_0 = 0, \qquad v_0 = 1$.

At h = 0.2

t	v
0	1
0.2	0.92
0.4	0.852288
0.6	0.78458
0.8	0.63684
1.0	0.50706

At $h = 0.1$

t	v
0	1
0.1	1
0.2	0.98
0.3	0.94158
0.4	0.88839
0.5	0.82525
0.6	0.75715
0.7	0.68835
0.8	0.62202
0.9	0.56011
1.0	0.50364

Q5. (a) Find the truncation error in the result of the following function for $x = \frac{1}{5}$, when we use:

(i) First three terms

(ii) $e^x = 1 + x + \frac{x^2}{2!} + \frac{x^3}{3!} + \frac{x^4}{4!} + \frac{x^5}{5!} + ...$

Ans. Let y = Real Root for e^x at $x = \frac{1}{5}$

$y = e^{1/5} = 1.221402758$ $\qquad$ $y^* = \text{Approximate value of } y.$

using $e^x = 1 + x + \frac{x^2}{2!}$

$$e^{1/5} = 1 + \frac{1}{5} + \frac{(1/5)^2}{2!} = 1 + \frac{1}{5} + \frac{1}{50} = \frac{61}{50} \qquad = 1.22$$

$$\text{Truncation Error} = |y - y^x| \qquad = |1.221402758 - 1.22|$$
$$= 0.001402758 \qquad \text{(Absolute)}$$

$$\text{Truncation Error} = \frac{|y - y^x|}{y} \qquad = \frac{|1.221402758 - 1.22|}{1.221402758}$$

$$= 0.001148481 \ (\text{Relative})$$

(b) Solve the system of equations:

$$4x_1 + x_2 + x_3 = 2$$

$$x_1 + 5x_2 + 2x_3 = -6$$

$$x_1 + 2x_2 + 3x_3 = -4$$

Using the Jocobi iteration method.

Ans. Here

$$x_1 = \frac{1}{4}(2 - x_2 - x_3) \qquad --(1)$$

$$x_2 = \frac{1}{5}(-6 - x_1 - 2x_3) \quad --(2)$$

$$x_3 = \frac{1}{3}(-4 - x_1 - 2x_2) \quad --(3)$$

Now, let $(x_1, x_2, x_3)^0 = (0,0,0)$

Then,

Iteration I

$$x_1 = \frac{2}{4} = 0.5 \quad x_2 = \frac{-6}{5} = -1.2 \qquad x_3 = \frac{-4}{3} = -1.33333333$$

Iteration II

$$x_1 = \frac{1}{4}(2 + 1.2 + 1.33333333) = \frac{4.53333333}{4} = 1.13333333$$

$$x_2 = \frac{1}{5}(-6 - 0.5 + 2.66666666) = -0.76666666$$

$$x_3 = \frac{1}{3}(-4 - 0.5) + 2.4) = -0.7$$

Iteration III

$$x_1 = \frac{1}{4}(2 + 0.76666666 + 0.7) = 0.86666665$$

$$x_2 = \frac{1}{5}(-6 - 1.13333333 + 1.4) = -1.14666666$$

$$x_3 = \frac{1}{3}(-4 - 1.13333333 - 1.53333332) = -1.2$$

(c) Compute the population of 1941 from the following table:

Year	Population (in millions)
1921	253
1931	287
1941	?
1951	315
1961	319

Ans. Using Newton interpolation of Divided Difference

x	f(.)	f(., .)	f(., ., .)	f(., ., ., .)
1921	253			
		3.4		
1931	287		-0.06666667	
		1.4		-0.00666667
1951	315		-0.3333333	
		0.4		
1961	319			

$$y = f(x_0) + (x - x_0) f(x_0, x_1) + (x - x_0)(x, x_1) f(x_0, x_1, x_2) + (x - x_0) f(x, x_1)$$
$$(x - x_2) f(x_0, x_1, x_2, x_3)$$

y (x =1941)=253+(1941-1921) (3.4) + (1941-1921) (1941-1931) (-0.06666667) + (1941-1921) (1941 – 1931) (1941-1951) (-0.00666667)

= 253 + 68 – 13.333334+ 13.33334

= 321 millions (app.)

CS-71: COMPUTER ORIENTED NUMERICAL TECHNIQUES
June, 2010

Note: *Question number **1** is **compulsory**. Attempt only **three** questions from the rest. In total you have to answer **four** questions. Calculator is allowed.*

Q1. (a) Write the following numbers in floating point form: 48.61416, 2.3748, 0.0436, 1.03092.
Round these numbers to:
(i) 4 significant digits, (ii) 2 significant digits.

Ans. The numbers are: 48.61416, 2.3748, 0.0436, 1.03092

(i) Rounded numbers upto 4 digits

Number	Rounding	Chopping
48.61416	$.4861*10^2$	$.4861*10^2$
2.3748	$.2375*10^1$	$.2374*10^1$
0.0436	$.436*10^{-1}$	$.436*10^{-1}$
1.03092	$.1031*10^1$	$.1030*10^1$

(ii) Rounded numbers upto 2 digits.

Number	Rounding	Chopping
48.61416	$.49\ *10^2$	$.48\ *10^2$
2.3748	$.24\ *10^1$	$.23\ *10^1$
0.0436	$.44\ *10^{-1}$	$.43*10^{-1}$
1.03092	$.10\ *10^1$	$.10\ *10^1$

(b) An approximate value of $\sqrt{2} = 1.414214 \cdots\cdots$ is given by 1.414. Find the absolute error and the relative error in the approximation.

Ans. Actual value of $\sqrt{2} = 1.414214 \cdots\cdot$

Approximate value = 1.414

Absoluter Error $= |\text{Actual Value -App. Value}|$

$= |1.414214... - 1.414|$ $\qquad = 0.000214...$

$$\text{Relative Error} = \frac{|\text{Actual Value - App. Value}|}{\text{Actual Value}}$$

$$= \frac{|1.414214 - 1.414|}{1.414214}$$

=0.00015132

(c) Prove the following relations:

(i) $\Delta\left(\frac{1}{f_i}\right) = -\frac{\Delta f_i}{f_i f_{i+1}}$

Ans. $\Delta\left(\frac{1}{f_i}\right) = \frac{1}{f_{i+1}} - \frac{1}{f_i} \quad = \frac{f_i - f_{i+1}}{f_i f_{i+1}} = \frac{-(f_{i+1} - f_i)}{f_i f_{i+1}} = \frac{-\Delta f_i}{f_i f_{i+1}}$

(ii) $\Delta\left(f_i^2\right) = \left(f_i + f_{i+1}\right)\Delta f_i$

Ans. $\Delta(f_i^2) = f^2{}_{i+1} - f_i^2 \qquad = \left(f_{i+1} + f_i\right)\left(f_{i+1} - f_i\right)$

$= \left(f_i + f_{i+1}\right)\Delta f_i$

Hence Proved

(d) Solve the following equations by Jocobi's iteration method.

$20x + y - 2z = 17$

$3x + 20y - z = -18$

$2x - 3y + 20z = 25$

Ans. Here, $x = \frac{1}{20}(17 - y - 2z)$

$y = \frac{1}{20}(-18 - 3x + z) \qquad z = \frac{1}{20}(25 - 2x + 3y)$

Let, the initial values are $(x, y, z)^0 = (0, 0, 0)$

<u>**Iteration I**</u>

$x = \frac{1}{20}(17 - 0 + 0) = .85 \qquad y = \frac{1}{20}(-18 - 0 + 0) = -0.9$

$z = \frac{1}{20}(25 - 0 + 0) = 1.25$

<u>**Iteration II**</u>

$x = \frac{1}{20}(17 + 0.9 + 2.5) = 1.02 \qquad y = \frac{1}{20}(-18 - 25.5 + 1.25) = -2.115$

$z = \frac{1}{20}(25 - 17 - 2.7) = 0.265$

Iteration III

$$x = \frac{1}{20}(17 + 2.115 + 0.53) = 0.98225$$

$$y = \frac{1}{20}(-18 - 3.06 + 0.265) = -1.03975$$

$$z = \frac{1}{20}(20 - 2.04 - 6.345) = 0.58075$$

(e) Find the Lagrange interpolating polynomial that fits the following data values:

x	2.5	3.5
f(x)	6	8

Determine the approximate value of f(3).

Ans. Lagrange's Interpolating Polynomial

$$P_2(x) = \frac{(x - x_1)}{(x_0 - x_1)} y_o + \frac{(x - x_0)}{(x_1 - x_0)} y_1 = \frac{(x - 3.5)}{2.5 - 3.5} 6 + \frac{(x - 2.5)}{3.5 - 2.5} 8$$

$$= -(x - 3.5)6 + (x - 2.5)8 = (3.5 - x)6 + (x - 2.5)8$$

$$= 21 - 6x + 8x - 20 = 2x + 1$$

Now,

$$f(3) = P_2(3) = 2 \times 3 + 1 = 7$$

(f) Find the cube root of 41, using Newton – Raphson Method.

Ans. Let

$$f(x) = x - (41)^{1/3} = x - 3.44821724$$

$$f'(x) = 1$$

x	3	4
f(x)	-0.44821724	0.55178276

Let $x_0 = 3.5$

$$f(x_0) = 0.05178276$$

Iteration

$$x_1 = x_0 - \frac{f(x_0)}{f'(x_0)} = 3.5 - \frac{0.05178276}{1}$$

$$= 3.44821724$$

$$f(x_1) = 0$$

So, cube root of 41 is 3.44821724

Q2. Perform four iterations of the Gauss - Seidal Method to solve the following system of equations:

$4x - y + z = 4$

$-x + 4y - z = 2$

$x - y + 4z = 4$

Take initial approximation $(x_0, y_0, z_0) = (0,0,0)$.

Ans.

$4x - y + z = 4 \quad --(1)$

$-x + 4y - z = 2 \quad --(2)$

$x - y + 4z = 4 \quad --(3)$

And $(x_0, y_o, z_0) = (0,0,0)$

$(1) \Rightarrow x = \frac{1}{4}(4 + y - z)$ $\qquad (2) \Rightarrow y = \frac{1}{4}(2 + x + z)$

$(3) \Rightarrow z = \frac{1}{4}(4 - x + y)$

Iteration I

$x = \frac{1}{4}(4 + 0 - 0) = 1$ $\qquad y = \frac{1}{4}(2 + 1 + 0) = 0.75$

$z = \frac{1}{4}(4 - 1 + 0.75) = 0.9375$

Iteration II

$x = \frac{1}{4}(4 + 0.75 - 0.9375) = 0.953125$

$y = \frac{1}{4}(2 + 0.953125 + 0.9375) = 0.97265625$

$z = \frac{1}{4}(4 - 0.953125 + 0.97265625) = 1.004882813$

Iteration III

$x = \frac{1}{4}(4 + 0.97265625 - 1.004882813) = 0.991943359$

$y = \frac{1}{4}(2 + 0.991943359 + 1.004882813) = 0.999206543$

$z = \frac{1}{4}(4 - 0.991943359 + 0.999206543) = 1.001815796$

(b) Solve the following equations by Gauss- Elimination Method:

$54x + y + z = 110$

$2x + 15y + 6z = 72$

$-x + 6y + 27z = 85.$

Ans.

$54x + y + z = 110$

$2x + 15y + 6z = 72$

$-x + 6y + 27z = 85.$

In matrix format

$$\begin{matrix} A & X & = & B \end{matrix}$$

$$\begin{bmatrix} 54 & 1 & 1 \\ 2 & 15 & 6 \\ -1 & 6 & 27 \end{bmatrix} \begin{bmatrix} x \\ y \\ z \end{bmatrix} = \begin{bmatrix} 110 \\ 72 \\ 85 \end{bmatrix}$$

Matrix $[A|B]$

$$= \left[\begin{array}{ccc|c} 54 & 1 & 1 & 110 \\ 2 & 15 & 6 & 72 \\ -1 & 6 & 27 & 85 \end{array}\right]$$

$R_2 \leftarrow R_2 - (R_1/27)$

$$= \left[\begin{array}{ccc|c} 54 & 1 & 1 & 110 \\ 0 & 14.666667 & 5.66667 & 67.925925926 \\ -1 & 6 & 27 & 85 \end{array}\right]$$

$R_3 \leftarrow R_3 + R_1/54$

$$= \left[\begin{array}{ccc|c} 54 & 1 & 1 & 110 \\ 0 & 14.666666667 & 5.666666667 & 67.925925926 \\ 0 & 6.018518519 & 27.018518519 & 87.037037037 \end{array}\right]$$

$R_3 \leftarrow R_3 - \dfrac{6.018518519}{14.666666667} R_2$

$$= \left[\begin{array}{ccc|c} 54 & 1 & 1 & 110 \\ 0 & 14.666666667 & 5.666666667 & 67.925925926 \\ 0 & 0 & 24.693181818 & 59.16339319 \end{array}\right]$$

In Equation Format

$54x + y + z = 110 \quad --(1)$

14.666666667y+5.666666667z=67.925925926 —(2)

24.693181818z=59.16339319 —(3)

$(3) \Rightarrow z = 2.395940451$

$(2) \Rightarrow y = 3.705608866$

$(1) \Rightarrow x = 1.924045383$

(c) Construct the forward difference table for the data:

x	-4	-2	0	2	4	6
f(x)	-139	-21	1	23	141	451

Determine the corresponding interpolating polynomial. Also compute the approximate value of f(3).

Ans. Forward Difference Table

x	y	Δ y	Δ^2 y	Δ^3 y	Δ^4 y	Δ^5 y
-4	-138					
		118				
-2	-21		-96			
		22		96		
0	1		0		0	
		22		96		0
2	23		96		0	
		118		96		
4	141		192			
		310				
6	451					

Corresponding Interpolating Polynomial

$$P_5(x) = y_0 + \frac{(x-x_0)}{1!h^1}\Delta y_0 + \frac{(x-x_0)(x-x_1)}{2!h^2}\Delta^2 y_0 + \frac{(x-x_0)(x-x_1)(x-x_2)}{3!h^3}\Delta^3 y_0$$
$$+ \frac{(x-x_0)(x-x_1)(x-x_2)(x-x_3)}{4!h^4}\Delta^4 y_0 + \frac{(x-x_0)(x-x_1)(x-x_2)(x-x_3)(x-x_4)}{5!h^5}\Delta^5 y_0$$

Here, h = 2

App. Value of f(3)

$$f(3) = -139 + \frac{(3-(-4))}{2}(118) + \frac{(3-(-4))(3-(-2))}{2\ .\ 4}(-96) + \frac{(3-(-4))(3-(-2))(3-0)}{6\ .\ 8}(96)$$
$$+0+0$$

= -139 + 413 – 420 + 210 + 0 + 0

f(3) = 64

Q3. (a) Solve the following equations by Jocobi's method:

$2x + y + z = 10$

$3x + 2y + 3z = 18$

$x + 4y + 9z = 16.$

Ans.

$$2x+y+z=10$$
$$3x+2y+3z=18$$
$$x+4y+9z=16.$$

$$x=\frac{1}{2}(10-y-z) \quad y=\frac{1}{2}(18-3x-3z)=\frac{3}{2}(6-x-z)$$

$$z=\frac{1}{9}(16-x-4y)$$

Let Initial Approximation is $(x_0, y_0, z_0)=(0,0,0)$

Iteration I

$$x=\frac{1}{2}(10-0-0)=5 \qquad y=\frac{3}{2}(6-0-0)=9$$

$$z=\frac{1}{9}(16-0-0)=1.777778$$

Iteration 2

$$x=\frac{1}{2}(10-9-1.777778)=-0.388889$$

$$y=\frac{3}{2}(6-5-1.777778)=-1.166667$$

$$z=\frac{1}{9}(16-5-36)=-2.777778$$

Iteration 3

$$x=\frac{1}{2}(10+1.166667+2.777778)=6.9722225$$

$$y=\frac{3}{2}(6+0.388889+2.777778)=13.7500005$$

$$z=\frac{1}{9}(16+0.388889+4.666668)=2.339506$$

(b) Find the Lagrange's interpolating polynomial that fits the following data values:

x	1	2	4
f(x)	1	7	61

Determine the approximate value of f(3).

Ans. Lagrange's Interpolating Polynomials

$$P_3(x) = \frac{(x-x_1)(x-x_2)}{(x_0-x_1)(x_0-x_2)} f_0 + \frac{(x-x_0)(x-x_2)}{(x_1-x_0)(x_1-x_2)} f_1 + \frac{(x-x_0)(x-x_1)}{(x_2-x_0)(x_2-x_1)} f_2$$

$$= \frac{(x-2)(x-4)}{(1-2)(1-4)}(1) + \frac{(x-1)(x-4)}{(2-1)(2-4)}(7) + \frac{(x-1)(x-2)}{(4-1)(4-2)}(61)$$

$$= \frac{(x-2)(x-4)}{3} - \frac{7(x-1)(x-4)}{3} + \frac{61(x-1)(x-2)}{6}$$

$$f(3) = \frac{(3-2)(3-4)}{3} - \frac{7(3-1)(3-4)}{3} + \frac{61(3-1)(3-2)}{6}$$

$$= \frac{1}{3}[-1+14+61] = \frac{74}{3} \qquad f(3) = 24.666667$$

(c) Find a real root of the equation $x\log_{10} x = 1.2$ by Regular-Falsi method correct to four decimal places.

Ans. $f(x) = x\log_{10} x - 1.2$

x	1	2
f(x)	-1.2	0.597940009

$x_0 = 1 \qquad f(x_0) = -1.2$

$x_1 = 2 \qquad f(x_1) = 0.597940009$

$$x_2 = \frac{x_0 f(x_1) - x_1 f(x_0)}{f(x_1) - f(x_0)}$$

$$= \frac{1(0.59794009) - 2(-1.2)}{0.59794009 + 1.2} = 1.667430425$$

$f(x_2) = -0.829750873$

$$x_3 = \frac{x_1 f(x_2) - x_2 f(x_1)}{f(x_2) - f(x_1)}$$

$$= \frac{2(-0.829750873) - (1.667430425)(0.597940009)}{(-0.829750873) - (0.597940009)} = 1.860714489$$

$f(x_3) = -0.698203002$

$$x_4 = \frac{x_2 f(x_3) - x_3 f(x_2)}{f(x_3) - f(x_2)} = 2.886588285$$

$f(x_4) = 0.128941499$

$$x_5 = \frac{x_3 f(x_4) - x_4 f(x_3)}{f(x_4) - f(x_3)} \qquad = 2.72666737$$

$$f(x_5) = -0.012176001$$

$$x_6 = \frac{x_4 f(x_5) - x_5 f(x_4)}{f(x_5) - f(x_4)} \qquad = 2.740465781$$

$$f(x_6) = -0.000157259$$

$$x_7 = \frac{x_5 f(x_6) - x_6 f(x_5)}{f(x_6) - f(x_5)} \qquad = 2.740646326$$

$$f(x_7) = 0.000000201$$

Q4. (a) Using Runge – Kutta method of order 4, find y (0.2) for the equation:

$$\frac{dy}{dx} = \frac{y-x}{y+x},$$

y (0) = 1. Take h = 0.2.

Ans. $f(x,y) = y' = \dfrac{y-x}{y+x}$

$$y(0) = 1, \qquad h = 0.2$$

$$y_{n+1} = y_n + \frac{1}{6}(K_1 + 2K_2 + 2K_3 + K_4)$$

$$x_0 = 0, \qquad y_0 = 1$$

$$x_1 = x_0 + h = 0 + 0.2 = 0.2$$

$$K_1 = h.f(x_0, y_0) = (0.2) . f(0,1) = 0.2$$

$$K_2 = h . f\left(x_0 + \frac{h}{2}, y_0 + \frac{K_1}{2}\right) = (0.2) f(0.1, 1.1) = 0.166667$$

$$K_3 = h . f\left(x_0 + \frac{h}{2}, y_0 + \frac{K_2}{2}\right) = (0.2) f(0.1, 1.08333) = 0.166197$$

$$K_4 = h. f(x_0 + h, y_0 + K_3) = (0.2) f(0.2, 1.166197) = 0.141443$$

$$y_1 = y_0 + \frac{1}{6}(K_1 + 2K_2 + 2K_3 + K_4)$$

$$= 1 + \frac{1}{6}(0.2 + 0.333334 + 0.332394 + 0.141443) = 1.167862$$

(b) Perform three iterations of the Regula – Falsi method to obtain the smallest positive root of:

$x^3 - 5x + 1 = 0.$

Ans. $f(x) = x^3 - 5x + 1$

x	0	1
f(x)	1	-3

$x_0 = 0 \qquad f(x_0) = 1$

$x_1 = 1 \qquad f(x_1) = -3$

Iteration I

$$x_2 = \frac{x_0 f(x_1) - x_1 f(x_0)}{f(x_1) - f(x_0)} = \frac{(0)(-3) - (1)(1)}{-3-1} = 0.25$$

$f(x_2) = (0.25)^3 - 5(0.25) + 1$

$= 0.015625 - 1.25 + 1 \qquad = -0.234375$

Iteration II

$$x_3 = \frac{x_1 f(x_2) - x_2 f(x_1)}{f(x_2) - f(x_1)} = \frac{1(-0.234375) - (0.25)(-3)}{(-0.234375) - (-3)}$$

$$= \frac{-0.234375 + 0.75}{-0.234375 + 3} = \frac{0.515625}{2.765625} = 0.186441$$

$f(x_3) = (0.186441)^3 - 5(0.186441) + 1$

$= 0.006481 - 0.9322034 + 1 \qquad = 0.0742776$

Iteration III

$$x_4 = \frac{x_2 f(x_3) - x_3 f(x_2)}{f(x_3) - f(x_2)} = \frac{(0.25)(0.0742776) - 0.186441(-0.234375)}{0.0742776 + 0.234375}$$

$= 0.201737$

$f(x_4) = (0.201737)^3 - 5(0.201737) + 1$

$= 0.01208813 - 1.008685 + 1$

$= 0.0034031$

(c) Evaluate: $\int_0^2 \frac{x^2}{1+x^3}$ **using, the Simpson's** $\frac{1}{3}$ **rule with** $h = \frac{1}{4}$.

Ans. $\int_0^2 \frac{x^2}{1+x^3} dx \ , \quad h = \frac{1}{3}.$

Here $f(x)=\dfrac{x^2}{1+x^3}$ $\quad f(0)=0$

$$f(0.25)=\frac{(0.25)^2}{1+(0.25)^3}=\frac{0.0625}{1+0.015625}=0.061538$$

$$f(0.50)=\frac{(0.5)^2}{1+(0.5)^3}=\frac{0.25}{1+0.125}=0.222222$$

$$f(.75)=\frac{(0.75)^2}{1+(0.75)^3}=\frac{0.5625}{1+0.421875}=0.395604$$

$$f(1)=\frac{1^2}{1+1^3}=0.5$$

$$f(1.25)=\frac{1.5625}{1+1.953125}=0.529101$$

$$f(1.5)=\frac{2.25}{1+3.375}=0.514286$$

$$f(1.75)=\frac{3.0625}{1+5.359375}=0.481572$$

$$f(2)=\frac{4}{1+8}=0.444444$$

Now, $\displaystyle\int_0^2 \frac{x^2}{1+x^3}dx=\int_{x_0}^{x_2} f(x)dx+\int_{x_2}^{x_4} f(x)dx+\int_{x_4}^{x_6} f(x)dx+\int_{x_6}^{x_8} f(x)dx$

$$=\frac{0.25}{3}[0.+0.246152+0.222222]+\frac{0.25}{3}[0.222222+1.582416+0.5]$$

$$+\frac{0.25}{3}[0.5+2.116404+0.514286]+\frac{0.25}{3}[0.514286+1.926288+0.444444]$$

$=0.732393$

Q5. (a) Find a root of the equation: $x^3-4x-9=0$, using the Bisection methods in four stages.

Ans. $f(x)=x^3-4x-9$

x	0	1	2	3
f(x)	-9	-13	-9	6

Stage I

$a_1=2\ f(a_1)=-9$ $\quad b_1=3$ $\quad f(b_1)=6$

$c_1 = \frac{a_1 + b_1}{2} = 2.5$ $f(c_1) = (2.5)^3 - 4(2.5) - 9$

= -3.375

Stage II

Since $f(a_1)$ & $f(c_1)$ *both* $(-ive)$

$a_2 = 2.5$ $f(a_2) = -3.375$

$b_2 = 3$ $f(b_2) = 6$ $c_2 = \frac{a_2 + b_2}{2} = 2.75$

$f(c_2) = (2.75)^3 - 4(2.75) - 9$ = 0.796875

Stage III

Since $f(b_2)$ & $f(c_2)$ *both* $(+ive)$

$a_3 = 2.5$ $f(a_3) = -3.375$ $b_3 = 2.75$ $f(b_3) = 0.796875$

$c_3 = \frac{a_3 + b_3}{2} = 2.625$

$f(c_3) = (2.625)^3 - 4(2.625) - 9$ = -1.412109375

Stage IV

$f(a_3)$ & $f(c_3)$ *both* $(-ive)$

$a_4 = 2.625$ $f(a_3) = -1.412109375$ $b_4 = 2.75$

$f(b_3) = 0.796875$

$c_4 = \frac{a_4 + b_4}{2} = 2.6875$ $f(c_4) = (2.6875)^3 - 4(2.6875) - 9$

$= -0.339111328$

(b) Perform three iteration of the Newton – Raphson method to find a root of the equation:

$xe^x - 1 = 0,$

which is close to 0.5.

Ans.

$xe^x - 1 = 0,$ $f(x) = xe^x - 1$

$f'(x) = e^x(1 + x)$ Here $x_0 = 0.5$

$f(x_0) = 0.5e^{0.5} - 1 = -0.175639365$ $f'(x_0) = e^{0.5}(1 + 0.5) = 2.473081906$

Iteration I

$$x_1 = x_0 - \frac{f(x_1)}{f'(x_2)} \quad = 0.5 + \frac{0.175639365}{2.473081906} \quad = 0.57102044$$

$f(x_1) = 0.010747511$

$f'(x_1) = 2.78089894$

Iteration II

$$x_2 = x_1 - \frac{f(x_1)}{f'(x_1)} \quad = 0.567155569$$

$f(x_2) = 0.000033928 \qquad f'(x_2) = 2.763278413$

Iteration III

$$x_3 = x_2 - \frac{f(x_2)}{f'(x_2)} \quad = 0.567143291$$

$f(x_3) = 0.000000001 \qquad f'(x_3) = 2.763222837$

(c) For the data:

x	1	1.1	1.2	1.3	1.4
f(x)	7.0	8.093	9.384	10.891	12.632

find an approximation of f(1.35) and f(1.25).

Ans. Using Newton's Forward Difference Interpolating Polynomial

Forward Difference Table

x	f	Δf	Δ²f	Δ³f	Δ⁴f
1	7.0				
		1.093			
1.1	8.093		0.198		
		1.291		0.018	
1.2	9.384		0.216		0.000
		1.507		0.018	
1.3	10.891		0.234		
		1.741			
1.4	12.632				

Here h = 0.1

Interpolating Polynomial

$$f_4(x) = f_0 + \frac{(x-x_0)}{1!\,h^1}\Delta f_0 + \frac{(x-x_0)(x-x_1)}{2!h^2}\Delta^2 f_0 + \frac{(x-x_0)(x-x_1)(x-x_2)}{3!h^3}\Delta^3 f_0$$

$$+ \frac{(x-x_0)(x-x_1)(x-x_2)(x-x_3)}{4!h^4}\Delta^4 f_0$$

$$= 7.0 + \frac{(x-1)}{0.1}(1.093) + \frac{(x-1)(x-1.1)}{2(0.1)^2}0.198 + \frac{(x-1)(x-1.1)(x-1.2)}{6\,(0.1)^3}0.018 + 0$$

Now,

$$f(1.35)=7.0+(0.35)(0.1093)+\frac{(0.35)(0.25)(0.00198)}{2}+\frac{(0.35)(0.25)(0.15)(0.000018)}{6}$$

$= 7.038341664$

$$f(1.25)=7.0+(0.25)(0.1093)+\frac{(0.25)(0.15)(0.00198)}{2}+\frac{(0.25)(0.15)(0.05)(0.000018)}{6}$$

$= 7.027362131$

CS-71: COMPUTER ORIENTED NUMERICAL TECHNIQUES
December, 2010

*Note: Question number **1** is **compulsory.** Attempt any **three** questions from the rest. In total you have to answer **four** questions. Calculator is allowed.*

Q1. (a) (i) The approximations to the number $2/3$ are given as 0.6, 0.66, and 0.67. Which of these is the best approximation and why?

Ans. Let $x = 0.67, x^* = \frac{2}{3} = 0.66$

$\therefore x - x^* = 0.67 - 0.66 = 0.01 \Rightarrow |x - x^*| = 0.01$

$$\frac{|x-x^*|}{x} = \frac{0.01}{0.67} = 0.01492$$

$$\leq 0.005 = \frac{1}{2}(0.01) = \frac{1}{2}(10)^{-2} = \frac{1}{2}(10)^{1-3}$$

Hence x* approximated x correct to 3 significant digits.

(ii) Find up to how many significant digits is the value $355/113$, an accurate approximation to π = 3.14159265....

Ans. $\frac{355}{113}$ =3.14159292, $\pi = 3.14159265$

$\therefore$ 6 significant digits of the given value is accurate.

(b) If x= 0.178693 x 10^1, y= 0.178693 are accurate to six significant digits, then find the number of significant digits in $z = x - y$

Ans. Given x = 0.178693

y = 0.178693

$\therefore z = x - y$

= 0.178693-0.178693

= 0

$\therefore$ there is no significant digit.

(c) Prove the following relations:

(i) $\Delta\left(\frac{f_i}{g_i}\right) = \frac{g_i \Delta f_i - f_i \Delta g_i}{g_i g_{i+1}}$

Ans. $$\text{L.H.S} = \Delta\left(\frac{f_i}{g_i}\right) = \frac{f_{i+1}}{g_{i+1}} - \frac{f_i}{g_i} = \frac{g_i \cdot f_{i+1} - f_i \cdot g_{i+1}}{g_i \cdot g_{i+1}} = \frac{g_i \cdot \Delta f_i - f_i \cdot \Delta g_i}{g_i \cdot g_{i+1}}$$

(ii) $\Delta+\nabla=\frac{\Delta}{\nabla}-\frac{\nabla}{\Delta}$

Ans. L.H.S= $=\Delta+\nabla$

$$=(E-1)+(1-E^{-1})=(E-1)+(1-\frac{1}{E})=E-1+1-\frac{1}{E}=E-\frac{1}{E}=\frac{E^2-1}{E}$$

$$=\frac{(E+1)(E-1)}{E}=\frac{(E-1)}{E.(E+1)}-\frac{(E+1)}{(E-1)}=\frac{\Delta}{\nabla}-\frac{\nabla}{\Delta}$$

(d) Solve the following equations by Gauss – Seidal iteration method:

$20x+y-2z=17,\ 3x+20y-z=-18,\ 2x-3y+20z=25$.

Start with the approximation $x_0=y_0=z_0=0$.

Refer to Page No.-282, Point(b)

(e) Find the Lagrange interpolating polynomial that fits the following data:

x	-2	1	0	2
$f(x)$	3	-3	1	-1

Also compute the approximate value of *f*(1.5)

Ans. The given data is

x_0 = -2	$f(x_0)$ = 3
x_1 = 1	$f(x_1)$ = -3
x_2 = 0	$f(x_2)$ = 1
x_3 = 2	$f(x_3)$ = -1

Lagrange's Interpolating Polynomial is

$$=\frac{(x-x_1)(x-x_2)(x-x_3)}{(x_0-x_1)(x_0-x_2)(x_0-x_3)}.f(x_0)+\frac{(x-x_0)(x-x_2)(x-x_3)}{(x_1-x_0)(x_1-x_2)(x_1-x_3)}.f(x_1)$$

$$+\frac{(x-x_1)(x-x_2)(x-x_3)}{(x_2-x_0)(x_2-x_1)(x_2-x_3)}.f(x_2)+\frac{(x-x_0)(x-x_1)(x-x_2)}{(x_3-x_0)(x_3-x_1)(x_3-x_2)}.f(x_3)$$

$$f(x)=\frac{(x-1)(x-0)(x-2)}{(-3)(-2)(-4)}.(3)+\frac{(x+2)(x-0)(x-2)}{(3)(1)(-1)}.(-3)$$

$$+\frac{(x+2)(x-1)(x-2)}{(2)(-1)(-2)}.(1)+\frac{(x+2)(x-1)(x-0)}{(4)(1)(2)}.(-1)$$

$$f(x)=\frac{-(x^3-3x^2+2x)}{8}+(x^3-4x)+\frac{(x^3-x^2-4x+4)}{4}-\frac{(x^2+x+2)}{8}$$

$$f(x)=-x^3+3x^2-2x+8x^3-32x+2x^3-2x^2-8x+8-x^2-x-2$$

$$f(x)=9x^3-43x+6$$

$$f(1.5)=9.(1.5)^3-43(1.5)+6=9.(3.375)-6.45+6=30.375-64.5+6=28.1$$

(f) Compute the cube root of 24 by using Newton – Raphson method.
Ans.

Let $x = \sqrt[3]{24} \therefore x^3 = 24$

$f(x) = x^3 - 24 = 0, f'(x) = 3x^2$

New by Newton-Raphson method, we have

$$x_{n+1} = x_n - \frac{f(x)}{f'(x)} \qquad for\, n = 0,1,2..........$$

Starting from $x_0 = 0,1$

$$x_1 = 1 - \frac{-23}{3} = 7.666 \Rightarrow x_1 = 7.666$$

$f(x_1) = f(7.666) = 406.942, f'(x_1) = f'(7.666) = 176.302$

$$x_2 = 7.666 - \frac{406.942}{176.302} = 7.666 - 2.308 .\therefore x_2 = 5.357$$

$f(x_2) = f(5.357) = 129.732, f'(x_2) = f'(5.357) = 86.092$

$$x_3 = 5.357 - \frac{129.732}{86.92} = 5.357 - 1.506, \therefore x_3 = 3.850$$

$f(x_3) = f(3.850) = 33.066$

$f'(x_3) = f(3.850) = 44.467$

$$x_4 = 3.850 - \frac{33.066}{44.467} = 3.850 - 0.743, \therefore x_4 = 3.106$$

So the real cube root of 24 are (7.666, 5.357, 3.850, 3.106)

Q2. (a) Solve the following equations by Jacobi's method:
$5x + 2y + z = 12,\ x + 4y + 2z = 15,\ x + 2y + 5z = 20.$

Ans. Solution from *(i)* $x = \frac{1}{5}(12 - 2y - 3)$

from (ii), $y = \frac{1}{4}(15 - x - 23)$

from(iii), $z = \frac{1}{5}(20 - x - 2y)$

Starting with $x^{(0)} = (0,0,0)^T$

$$\therefore x = x^{(1)} = \frac{12}{5}, y = y^{(1)} = \frac{15}{4}, z = z^{(1)} = 4,$$

$$\therefore x^{(1)} = \left[\frac{12}{5}, \frac{15}{4}, 4\right] = [2.4, 3.75, 4]$$

$$x^{(2)} = \frac{1}{5}\left(12 - 2\left(\frac{15}{4}\right) - 4\right),\ y^{(2)} = \frac{1}{4}(15 - (2.4) - 2.(4)), z^{(2)} = [20 - (12.4) - 2(3.75)]$$

$$x^{(2)} = [0.1, 1.15, 2.02]$$

$$x^{(3)} = \frac{1}{5}(12 - 2(1.15) - 2.02), y^{(3)} = \frac{1}{4}(15 - (0.1) - 2.(2.02)), z^{(3)} = \frac{1}{5}[20 - 0.1 - 2(1.15)]$$

$$\therefore x^{(3)} = [1.536, 2.715, 3.52]$$

(b) Find the real root of the equation $3x = \cos x + 1$ by Newton – Raphson method.

Refer to December-2009, Q.No.-2(a), Page No.-318

(c) Using Newton's interpolation formula, find the value of *f*(1.6) if

x	1	1.4	1.8	2.2
$f(x)$	3.49	4.82	5.96	6.5

Ans. According to given table:

x	$f(x)$	$\Delta df(x)$	$\Delta^2 df(x)$	$\Delta^3 df(x)$	$\Delta^4 df(x)$
1	3.49	3.33	1.2	6.37	
1.4	4.82	2.85	3.75		
1.8	5.96	1.35			
2.2	6.5				

Where Δd is divide difference operator. From, Newton's divide difference interpolation formula

$$f(x) = y_1 + \Delta df(x)(x - x_1) + \Delta^2 df(x)(x - x_1)(x - x_2)$$

$$+\Delta^3 df(x)(x - x_1)(x - x_2)(x - y)$$

$$f(1.6) = 3.49 + 3.33(1.6 - 1) + (1.2)(1.6 - 1)(1.6 - 1.4)$$

$$+3.49 + 1.998 + 0.144 - 0.152$$

$$f(1.6) = 5.48$$

Q3. (a) Solve the following equations by Guass – Elimination method:

$2x_1 + 4x_2 + x_3 = 3,\ 3x_1 + 2x_2 - 2x_3 = -2,\ x_1 - x_2 + x_3 = 6$

Ans. By Guass-Elimination method, The Coefficient matrix is

$$\begin{pmatrix} 2 & 4 & 1 \\ 3 & 2 & -2 \\ 1 & -1 & 1 \end{pmatrix}\begin{pmatrix} 3 \\ -2 \\ 6 \end{pmatrix}$$

Reduce the coefficient of x_1 from 2nd and 3rd equation to zero by performing operation.

$$R_2 \to R_2 - 3R_3, R_1 \to R_1 - 2R_2$$

$$\begin{pmatrix} 0 & 6 & -1 \\ 0 & 5 & -5 \\ 1 & -1 & 1 \end{pmatrix}\begin{pmatrix} -9 \\ -20 \\ 6 \end{pmatrix}$$

Now Reduce the x_2 coefficient to zero by performing the operation

$R_3 \rightarrow R_3 + R_1$

$$\begin{pmatrix} 0 & 6 & -1 \\ 0 & 5 & -5 \\ 1 & +5 & 0 \end{pmatrix}\begin{pmatrix} -9 \\ -20 \\ -3 \end{pmatrix}$$

By Performing Back substitution method an equation

$6x_2 - x_3 = -9 \quad 5x_2 - 5x_3 = -20 \quad x_1 - 5x_2 = -3$

After solving these equations, Solutions is-

$x_1 = 2,\ x_2 = -1, x_3 = 3$

(b) If $p = \frac{5xy^3}{3}$ and error inx, y, z is 0.001, compute the relative maximum error in p when $x = y = z = 1$.

Ans.

$x = 1 \pm 0.001, \quad y = 1 \pm 0.001, \quad z = 1 \pm 0.001$

$p = \frac{5xy^3}{3}$

$r_{y^3} = \pm 3.\frac{\Delta y}{y} = \pm.3.\frac{0.001}{1} = \pm 0.003$

$r_{xy^3} = \pm(\gamma x + \gamma y^3) = \pm\left[\frac{0.001}{1} + 0.003\right] = 0.004$

$\gamma_3 = \pm 0.003 \qquad \frac{\gamma xy^3}{3} = \pm 0.007$

(c) Find the real root of the equation $x^3 - 2x - 5 = 0$ by the Regula – Falsi method correct to three decimal places.

Refer to Dec-2003, Q.No.-5(b), Page No.-96

Q4. (a) Using Runge – Kutta method of order four, find y(0.2) given that $\frac{dy}{dx} = 3x + \frac{y}{2}$, $y(0)$, taking h=0.1.

Ans. Given $\frac{dy}{dx} = 3x + \frac{y}{2}$,

$x_0 = 0, y = 1, h = x_1 - x_0 = 0.2$

Now $K_1 = hf(x_0 - y_0) = 0.2(x_0 + y_0) = 0.2(0+1) = 0.2$

$$K_2 = hf\left(x_0+\frac{h}{2}, y_0+\frac{K_1}{2}\right) = 0.2\left(\left(0+\frac{0.2}{2}\right)+\left(1+\frac{0.2}{2}\right)\right) = 0.2(0.1+1.1) = 0.24$$

$$K_3 = hf\left(x_0+\frac{h}{2}, y_0+\frac{K_2}{2}\right) = 0.2\left(\left(0+\frac{0.2}{2}\right)+\left(1+\frac{0.24}{2}\right)\right) = 0.2(0.1+1.12) = 0.244$$

$$K_4 = hf\left(x_0+h, y_0+K_3\right) = 0.2\left((0.01)+(1+0.244)\right) = 0.2(0.1+1.244) = 0.2688$$

$$y_1 = y_0+\frac{1}{6}(K_1+2K_2+2K_3+K_4) = 1+\frac{1}{6}(0.2+0.48+0.488+0.2688)$$

$$=1+\frac{1}{6}(1.4368) = 1+0.23946667\; y_1 = 1.23946667, x_1 = 0.2$$

(b) A root of the equation $xe^x - 1 = 0$ lies in the interval (0.5, 1.0). Determine this root correct to three decimal places using Regula – falsi method.

Refer to June-2010, Q.No.-5(b), Page No,-340

(c) Evaluate $\int_0^2 \frac{dx}{x^2+2x+10}$ Using the Simpson's $\frac{1}{3}$ rule with $h = \frac{1}{4}$

Ans. $\int_0^2 \frac{dx}{x^2+2x+10}$

$$h = \frac{1}{4} = 0.25, f(x) = \frac{1}{x^2+2x+10}, x = 0\, to\, 2$$

i	x_i	$y_i = \frac{1}{x_i^2+2x_i+10}$
0	$x_0 = 0$	$y_0 = \frac{1}{0^2+2.0+10} = 0.1$
1	$x_1 = x_0+h = 0+0.25 = 0.25$	$y_1 = \frac{1}{(.25)^2+0.5+10} = \frac{1}{11.1}$
2	$x_2 = x_0+2h = 0.5$	$y_2 = \frac{1}{(15)^2+1+10} = \frac{1}{11.25}$
3	$x_2 = x_0+3h = .75$	$y_3 = \frac{1}{(.75)^2+(1.5)+10} = \frac{1}{12.06}$
4	$x_4 = x_0+4h = 1$	$y_4 = \frac{1}{(1)^2+2+10} = \frac{1}{13}$

by Simpson Rule- $\int_a^b f(x)dx = \frac{h}{3}[(y_0+y_n)+4(y_1+y_3+...)+2(y_2+y_4+...)]$

$$\int_a^b \frac{dx}{x^2+2x+10} = \frac{h}{3}[(y_0+y_4)+4(y_1+y_3)+2(y_2+y_4)]$$

$$= \frac{1}{4\times 3}[(0.1+0.07+4(0.09+0.08)+2(0.08+0.07))] = \frac{1}{12}[0.17+0.68+0.3] = 0.0958$$

Q5. (a) Find a real root of the equation $x^4 - x - 10 = 0$. Using the bisection method correct to three decimal places.

Ans.

Given $f(x) = x^4 - x - 10$

$f(1) = 1 - 1 - 10 = -10(-ve)$

$f(2) = 16 - 2 - 10 = 4(+ve)$

$\because f(1) = -10(-ve) and\ f(2) = 4(+ve)$

therefore root lies between 1 and 2. So we take $x_0 = \dfrac{1+2}{2} = 1.5$

$f(x_0) = (1.5)^4 - (1.5) - 10 = 5.0625 - 1.5 - 10 = -6.4375$

$\therefore$ root lies between 1.5 and 2

$$\therefore x_1 = \frac{1.5+2}{2} = 1.75$$

$f(x_1) = (1.75)^4 - 1.75 - 10 = 9.378 - 1.75 - 10 = -2.37(-ve)$

therefore x=1.75 is a root of equation

(b) Using Newton – Raphson method obtain a root of the equation $x^3 - 5x + 1 = 0$ correct to three decimal places. Assume $x_0 = 0.0$

Ans. The given equation is $x^3 - 5x + 1 = 0$

We have to find its root to 3 decimal places.

Let $f(x) = x^3 - 5x + 1$

$f'(x) = 3x^2 - 5$

we get,

$f(0) = 0^3 - 5 \times 0 + 1 = 0 - 0 + 1 = 1$

$f(1) = 1^3 - 5 \times 1 + 1 = 1 - 5 + 1 = -3$

$f'(0) = 3 \times 0^2 - 5 = -5$

Hence, the root lies between x=0 and 1. Let $x_0 = 0$

$$\therefore x_1 = x_0 - \frac{f(x_0)}{f'(x_0)} = 0 - \frac{1}{5} = .20$$

$x_1 = 0.20$

$$\text{Now } x_2 = x_1 - \frac{f(x_1)}{f'(x_1)}$$

$$x_2 = 0.20 - \frac{(0.20)^3 - 5(0.20) + 1}{3(0.20)^2 - 5}$$

$$x_2 = 0.20 - \frac{.008 - 1 + 1}{.12 - 5} = 0.20 - \frac{0.008}{-4.88}$$

$x_2 = 0.20 + 0.0016393 = 0.2016393$

Since x_1 and x_2 are very much closed to the required root is 0.2016

(c) For the data

x	0	0.2	0.4	0.6	0.8	1.0
$f(x)$	7.0	6.008	5.064	4.216	3.512	3.0

Find approximation to $f(0.1)$ and $f(0.3)$ by using Newton's Forward difference formula.

Ans.Newton's Forward difference formula is

x	$f(x)$	$\Delta f(x)$	$\Delta^2 f(x)$	$\Delta^3 f(x)$	$\Delta^4 f(x)$	$\Delta^5 f(x)$
0	7.0					
		-0.912				
0.2	6.088		-0.112			
		-1.024		0.288		
0.4	5.064		0.176		-0.356	
		-0.848		-0.068		0.508
0.6	4.216		0.108		0.152	
		-0.704		0.084		
0.8	3.512		0.192			
		-0.512				
1.0	3.0					

$$f(a+mh) = f(a) + m.\Delta f(a) + \frac{m(m-1)}{2!}\Delta^2 f(a) + \frac{m(m-1)(m-2)}{3!}.\Delta^3 f(a) + ...$$

Here $a = 0, h = 0.2, m = \frac{0.1-0}{0}$ and $\frac{0.3-0}{0} = 0$

for the given values *f(0.1) and f(0.3)*.

$\therefore$ *f(0.1)=f(0)*=7.0

and *f(0.3) = f(0)*=7.0

●●●

CS-71: COMPUTER ORIENTED NUMERICAL TECHNIQUES
June, 2011

Note: *Question number **1** is **compulsory.** Attempt any **three** questions from the rest. In total you have to answer **four** questions. Calculator is allowed.*

Q1. (a) Explain the loss of significant digits in subtraction of two nearly equal numbers.

Ans. Loss of significant is an undesirable effect in calculations using floating point arithmetic. It occurs when an operation on two numbers increases relative error substantially more than it increases absolute error, for example in subtracting two large and nearly equal numbers. The effect is that number of accurate digits in the result is reduced unacceptably.

(b) Prove that $\mu^2 = 1 + \frac{1}{4}\delta^2$

Refer to Dec–2009, Q.No.-1(b)(ii), Page No.-315

(c) Evaluate $\int_0^1 \frac{1}{1+x^2}dx$ Using Simpson's $\frac{1}{3^{rd}}$ rule taking h = $\frac{1}{4}$.

Refer to June–2005, Q.No.-4(b), Page No.-197

(d) Find a root of the equation $x^3 - x - 11 = 0$ correct to 4 decimals using bisection method.

Ans. Given equation is

$x^3 - x - 11 = 0$

$\therefore f(x) = x^3 - x - 11$

$f(2) = 8 - 2 - 11 = -5(-ve)$

$f(3) = 27 - 3 - 11 = 13(+ve)$

$\because f(2) = -5(-ve)$ and $f(3) = 13(+ve)$,

therefore root lies between 2 and 3. So we take , $x_0 = \frac{2+3}{2} = 2.5$

$f(x_0) = f(2.5) = 15.625 - 2.5 - 11 = 2.125(+ve), \therefore$ not lies between 2 and 2.5

$\therefore x_1 = \frac{2+2.5}{2} = 2.25$

$f(x_1) = f(2.25) = 11.39 - 2.25 - 11 = -1.1859(-ve)$

root lies between 2.25 and 2.5

$x_2 = \frac{2.25+2.5}{2} = 2.375, \therefore f(x_2) = 13.3964 - 2.375 - 11 = 0.02148(+ve)$

Root lies between 2.375 and 2.250.

(e) Find a root of the equation $x^3 - 3x^2 + 7x - 8 = 0$ correct to three decimals using Newton Rapson's method.

Ans. The given equation is $x^3 - 3x^2 + 7x - 8 = 0$

we have to find its root to 3 significant digits

Let $f(x) = x^3 - 3x^2 + 7x - 8 = 0$, $f'(x) = 3x^2 - 6x + 7$

we get, $f(0) = 0^3 - 3\times 0^2 + 7\times 0 - 8 = -8, f(1) = 1^3 - 3\times 1^2 + 7\times 1 - 8 = -3,$

$f(2) = 2^3 - 3\times 2^2 + 7\times 2 - 8 = 2$

Hence the root lies between x=1 and 2.

$$x_0 = 1, \therefore x_1 = x_0 - \frac{f(x_0)}{f'(x_0)} = -3 - \frac{(-8)}{7} = -3 + \frac{8}{7} = -1.857$$

$\therefore x_1 = (-1.857)$

Now

$$x_2 = x_1 - \frac{f(x_1)}{f'(x_1)} = -1.857 - \frac{(-1.857)^3 - 3.(1.857)^2 + 7.(1.857) - 8}{3.(1.857)^2 - 6.(1.857) + 7}$$

$$= -1.857 - \frac{9.852 - 3.(3.448) + 12.999 - 8}{3.(3.448) - 11.142 + 7}$$

$$= -1.857 - \frac{4.507}{6.202} = -1.857 - 726$$

$x_2 = -1.1302$

Root lies between 1.857 and 1.130

(f) Solve the equation $3x^3 - 4x^2 + x + 88 = 0$, one root being $2 + \sqrt{7}i$

Refer to Dec–2008, Q.No.-1(c), Page No.-299

Q2. (a) Using Newton's forward interpolation formula, find y at x =8 from the following table:

x :	0	5	10	15	20	25
y:	7	11	14	18	24	32

Ans. Newton's forward difference polynomial is:

x	$f(x)$	$\Delta f(x)$	$\Delta^2 f(x)$	$\Delta^3 f(x)$	$\Delta^4 f(x)$	$\Delta^5 f(x)$
$x_0 = 0$	7					
		4				
$x_1 = 5$	11		-1			
		3		2		
$x_2 = 10$	14		1			
		4			-1	
$x_3 = 15$	18		2	1		-2
		6				
$x_4 = 70$	24		0	-2	-3	
		6				
$x_5 = 25$	32					

$$f(x) = f(x_0) + (x-1)\Delta f(x_0) + \frac{(x-1)(x-2)}{\angle 2}\Delta^2 f(x_0) + \frac{(x-1)(x-2)(x-3)}{\angle 3}\Delta^3 f(x_0)$$
$$+ \frac{(x-1)(x-2)(x-3)(x-4)}{\angle 4}\Delta^4 f(x_0) + \frac{(x-1)(x-2)(x-3)(x-4)(x-5)}{\angle 5}\Delta^5 f(0)$$

$$= 7 + 4(x-1) + \left(\frac{-1}{2}\right)(x-1)(x-2) + \frac{1}{3}(x-1)(x-2)(x-3) +$$
$$\left(\frac{-1}{24}\right)(x-1)(x-2)(x-3)(x-4) + \left(\frac{-1}{60}\right)(x-1)(x-2)(x-3)(x-4) + (x-5)$$

on simplification it gives.

$$f(x) = \frac{7}{30}x^5 - \frac{11}{3}x^4 + 24x^3 - \frac{208}{3}x^2 + \frac{2963}{30}x - 41$$

for f at $x = 8$

$$f(7) = \frac{7}{30}(7)^5 - \frac{11}{3}(7)^4 + 24(7)^3 - \frac{208}{3}(7)^2 + \frac{2963}{30}(7) - 41 = 103.1307$$

(b) Find the root of the equation $x^3 - 4x - 9 = 0$, correct to three decimals using Regula Falsi method.

Ans. Given equation is $x^3 - 4x - 9 = 0,$

Regula Falsi method

$$f(x) = x^3 - 4x - 9, \quad f(2) = 2^3 - 4.2 - 9 = -9, \quad f(3) = 3^3 - 4.3 - 9 = 6$$

Root lies between 2 and 3

$x_0 = 2, x_1 = 3$

$$x_2 = \frac{x_0 f(x_1) - x_1 f(x_0)}{f(x_1) - f(x_0)}$$

$$= \frac{2.(6) - 3.(2)}{6-3} = \frac{12-6}{3} = 2$$

$x_2 = 2$

roots lies between 2 and 3. Therefore root will be 2.

(c) Solve the equation $x^3 - 7x^2 + 36 = 0$, given that one root is double of another.

Ans. Given equation is $x^3 - 7x^2 + 36 = 0,$

$$f(2) = 8 - 28 + 36 = 16, \; f(3) = 27 - 63 + 36 = 0, f(4) = 64 - 112 + 36 = -12$$

$x_0 = 2 \;\&\; x_1 = 4$

Iteration-I:

$$x_2 = \frac{x_0 f(x_1) - x_1 f(x_0)}{f(x_1) - f(x_0)} = \frac{2\times(-12) - 4\times(16)}{-12-16}$$

$$\frac{-24-64}{-28} = 3.14$$

$$x_0 = 3.14 \ \& \ x_1 = 4$$

Iteration-II:

$$x_2 = \frac{3.14\times(-12) - 4\times(-2.06)}{-12+2.06} = \frac{-37.68+8.24}{-9.94}$$

$$x_2 = 2.96$$

Iteration-III:

$$\therefore x_0 = 2.96, x_1 = 3.14$$

$$x_2 = \frac{2.96\times(-2.06) - 3.14\times(-0.59)}{-2.06-(-0.59)} = \frac{-6.09+1.85}{-9.94}$$

$$x_2 = 2.88 \therefore \text{root is } 2.88$$

Q3. (a) Find the cube root of 41, using Newton-Raphson's method.

Refer to Q.No.-5(a), Page No.-95

(b) Apply Runge – Kutta fourth order method, to find an approximate value of y when x=0.2 given that $\frac{dy}{dx} = x + y$ and y=1, when x=0.

Refer to Q.No.-5(a), Page No.-219

(c) Use Langrange's interpolation formula to find y when x=5 from the following data:

x :	0	1	3	8
y :	1	3	13	123

Ans. As shown in the given table, we will be giving the table as:

x	value	$f(x)$	value
x_0	0	$f(x_0)$	1
x_1	1	$f(x_1)$	3
x_2	3	$f(x_2)$	13
x_3	8	$f(x_3)$	123

The lagrange's interpolation polynomial is given by:

$$f(x) = \frac{(x-x_1)(x-x_2)(x-x_3)}{(x_0-x_1)(x_0-x_2)(x_0-x_3)} f(x_0) + \frac{(x-x_0)(x-x_2)(x-x_3)}{(x_1-x_0)(x_1-x_2)(x_1-x_3)} f(x_1)$$

$$+\frac{(x-x_0)(x-x_1)(x-x_3)}{(x_2-x_0)(x_2-x_1)(x_2-x_3)}-f(x_2)+\frac{(x-x_0)(x-x_1)(x-x_2)}{(x_3-x_0)(x_3-x_1)(x_3-x_2)}f(x_3)$$

here x=5, putting the values from table in the above equation, we get

$$f(5)=\frac{(5-1).(5-3).(5-8)}{(0-1)(0-3)(0-8)}.(1)+\frac{(5-0)(5-3)(5-8)}{(1-0)(1-3)(1-8)}.(3)$$

$$+\frac{(5-0)(5-1)(5-8)}{(3-0)(3-1)(0-8)}.(13)+\frac{(5-0)(5-1)(5-3)}{(8-0)(8-1)(8-3)}.(123)$$

$$+\frac{(-24)}{(-24)}.(1)+\frac{(-30)}{(14)}.(3)+\frac{(-60)}{-30}.(13)+\frac{(40)}{(280)}.(123)$$

=1- 6.42 + 26 + 17.57

f(5)=38.15

Q4. (a) Given the values

$x:$	5	7	11	13	17
$f(x):$	1 50	392	145 2	2366	520 2

Evaluate *f*(9) using Newton's divided difference formula.

Refer to Q.No.-2(a)(ii), Page No.-280

(b) Find the root of the equation $x^3 - 5x - 11 = 0$, correct to three decimals using iteration method.

Ans. Given Equation is $x^3-5x-11=0$,

Initially approximation 2 and 3

<u>Iteration -I:</u>

$\therefore x_0=2, f(2),=8-10-11=-13$

$\therefore x_1=3, f(3),=27-15-11=1$

$$x_2=\frac{x_0+x_1}{2}=\frac{2+3}{2}=\frac{5}{2}=2.5$$

$f(2.5)=15.625-12.5-11=-7.875$

$\because f(2.5)$ and $f(3)$ have opposite sign . $\therefore x_0=x_1$

<u>Iteration -II:</u>

$\therefore x_0=2.5, f(2.5),=-7.875$

$\therefore x_1=3.0, f(3),=1$

$$x_2=\frac{2.5+3}{2}=2.75$$

$f(2.75)=20.79-13.75-11=-3.96$

$\because f(2.75)$ and $f(3)$ have opposite sign.. $\therefore x_0 = x_1$

Iteration -III:

$\therefore x_0 = 2.75, f(2.75), = -3.96$

$\therefore x_1 = 3, f(3), = 1$

$$x_2 = \frac{2.75+3}{2} = 2.875$$

$f(2.875) = 23.76 - 143.75 - 11 = -1.615$

(c) Solve the following system of linear equations by Jacobi's iteration method.

2x + y + z = 4, x + 2y + z = 4, x + y + 2z = 4

by Jacobi's iteration method.

Ans. From the given equations

solution from (i)

$$x = \frac{1}{2}(4 - y - z)$$

solution from (ii)

$$y = \frac{1}{2}(4 - x - z)$$

solution from (iii)

$$z = \frac{1}{2}(4 - x - y)$$

Starting with $x^{(0)} = (0,0,0)^T$

$$\therefore x = x^{(1)} = \frac{4}{2} = 2, y = y^{(1)} = \frac{4}{2}, z = z^{(1)} = \frac{4}{2}, = 2$$

$\therefore x^{(1)} = [2,2,2,]$

$x^{(2)} = -4, y^{(2)} = -4, z^{(2)} = -4,$

$x^{(2)} = [-4,-4,-4]$

Similarly,

$x^{(3)} = [-6,-6,-6]$

Q5. (a) Solve the following equations by Gauss- Seidel method.

2x + y + 6z = 9, 8x + 3y + 2z = 13, x + 5y + z = 7.

Ans. Using Gauss-Seidel iteration Scheme

$$x = \frac{9 - y - 6z}{2}, \; y = \frac{13 - 8x - 2z}{3}, \; z = \frac{7 - x - 5y}{1}$$

initially we take

$$x^0 = \begin{bmatrix} 0 \\ 0 \\ 0 \end{bmatrix}$$

Iteration -I:

$$x = \frac{9-0-0}{2} = 4.5, y = \frac{13-8(4.5)-2(0)}{3} = -7.66, z = \frac{7-4.5-5.(-7.66)}{1} = -5.16$$

$$x^1 = \begin{bmatrix} 4.5 \\ -7.66 \\ -5.16 \end{bmatrix}$$

Iteration -II:

$$x = \frac{9-(-7.66)-6(-1.72)}{2} = 13.49$$

$$y = \frac{13-8.(4.5)-2(-1.72)}{3} = -6.52$$

$$z = \frac{7-4.5-5.(-7.66)}{1} = -5.16$$

$$x^2 = \begin{bmatrix} 13.49 \\ -6.52 \\ -5.16 \end{bmatrix}$$

Iteration -III:

$$x = \frac{9-(-6.52)-6(-5.16)}{2} = 23.24$$

$$y = \frac{13-8.(13.49)-2(-5.16)}{3} = -28.2$$

$$z = \frac{7-13.49-5.(-6.52)}{1} = 26.11$$

Hence the values after three iterations are x=23.24, y=-28.2, z=26.11

(b) Solve the system of equations

3x + y - z = 3, 2x - 8y + z = -5, x - 2y + 9z = 8

using Gauss- elimination method.

Ans.

$$A = \begin{pmatrix} 3 & 1 & -1 \\ 2 & -8 & 1 \\ 1 & -2 & 9 \end{pmatrix}, B = \begin{bmatrix} 3 \\ -5 \\ 8 \end{bmatrix}, [A|B] = \begin{pmatrix} 3 & 1 & -1 & | & 3 \\ 2 & -8 & 1 & | & -5 \\ 1 & -2 & 9 & | & 8 \end{pmatrix}$$

$$R_1 \to R_1 + R_2 = \begin{pmatrix} 5 & -7 & 0 & | & -2 \\ 2 & -8 & 1 & | & -5 \\ 1 & -2 & 9 & | & 8 \end{pmatrix}, \quad R_2 \to R_2\text{-}2R_3 = \begin{pmatrix} 5 & -7 & 0 & | & -2 \\ 2 & -4 & -7 & | & -21 \\ 1 & -2 & 9 & | & 8 \end{pmatrix}$$

$$R_3 \to R_3\text{-}\frac{1}{2}R_2 = \begin{pmatrix} 5 & -7 & 0 & | & -2 \\ 0 & -4 & -7 & | & -21 \\ 1 & -0 & 5.5 & | & 18.5 \end{pmatrix}$$

Using backward substitution,

$5x - 7y = -2$

$-4y - 7z = -21$

$x + 5.5z = 18.5$

by solving these equations x=-0.86, y=-0.32, z=3.52

(c) The velocity v (km\min) of a moped which starts from a rest id given at fixed intervals of time t (min) as follows:

t:	2	4	6	8	10	12	14	16	18	20
v:	10	18	25	29	32	20	11	5	2	0

Estimate approximately the distance covered in 20 minutes.

Ans. Represent the time along x-axis and velocity along y-axis. Then y_0, y_1, y_2............. y_9 are the values given in table. Also here h=10, using simpson's $\frac{3}{8}$ rule we have the approximate distance.

$$= \int_0^{20} y\, dx$$

$$= \frac{3}{8} h\left[(y_0 + y_9) + 3(y_1 + y_2 + y_3 + y_6 + y_7 + y_8) + 2(y_4 + y_5)\right]$$

$$= \frac{3}{8} \times 10\left[(10+0) + 3(18+25+29+11+5+2) + 2(32+20)\right]$$

$$= \frac{30}{8}\left[10+270+104\right] = \frac{30}{8}\left[384\right] = 1440\,\text{Km.}$$

CS-71: COMPUTER ORIENTED NUMERICAL TECHNIQUES
December, 2011

*Note: Question number **1** is **compulsory.** Attempt only **three** questions from the rest. In total, you have to answer **four** questions. Use of Calculator is permitted.*

Q1. (a) Prove that $\delta = \sqrt{E} - \frac{1}{\sqrt{E}}$

Ans. The first order central difference of f at x_k, denoted by δf_k, is defined as

$\delta f = f(x + h/2) - f(x - h/2) = f_{k+1/2} - f_{k-1/2}$

Operating with δ, we obtain the higher order central differences as

$$\delta^s f = \delta^{s-1}(\delta f) = \delta^{s-1} f_{k+1/2} - \delta^{s-1} f_{k-1/2} \qquad ...(1)$$

with $\delta^s f_k = f_k$ when s = 0.

The second order central difference is given by,

$$\delta^2 f_k = \delta[f_{k+1/2} - f_{k+1/2}] = \delta[f_{k+1/2}] - \delta[f_{k-1/2}] = f_{k+1} - f_k - f_k + f_{k-1}$$
$$= f_{k+1} - 2f_k + f_{k-1}$$

Similarly,

$$\delta^3 f_k = f_{k+3/2} - 3f_{k+1/2} + 3f_{k-1/2} - f_{k-3/2}$$

and $\delta^4 f_k = f_{k+2} - 4f_{k+1} + 6f_k - 4f_{k-1} + f_{k-2}$.

We can see that the even order differences at a tabular value x_k are expressed in terms of tabular values of f and odd order differences at a tabular value x_k are expressed in terms of non-tabular value of f. Also, we can see that the coefficients of $\delta^s f_k$ are the same as those of the binomial expansion of $(1-x)^s, s = 1,2,3,.........$

Since, $\delta f_k = f_{k+1/2} - f_{k-1/2} = (E^{1/2} - E^{-1/2}) f_k$

$\therefore$ We have the operation relation $\delta = E^{1/2} - E^{-1/2}$ or $\sqrt{E} - \frac{1}{\sqrt{E}}$.

(b) Prove that $\delta^2 = 4(\mu^2 - 1)$

Ans. Since, $\delta^2 = \left(\sqrt{E} - \frac{1}{\sqrt{E}}\right)^2$

$$= E + \frac{1}{E} - 2 \qquad ...(1)$$

Now, $4(\mu^2 - 1) = 4\left(\left(\frac{1}{2}\left[\sqrt{E} + \frac{1}{\sqrt{E}}\right]\right)^2 - 1\right) \qquad \left[\mu = \frac{1}{2}\left[\sqrt{E} + \frac{1}{\sqrt{E}}\right]\right]$

$$= 4\left(\frac{1}{4}\left(E + \frac{1}{E} + 2\right) - 1\right)$$

$$= E + \frac{1}{E} - 2 \qquad \ldots(2)$$

Hence, from equation (1) and (2), we can say that $\delta^2 = 4(\mu^2 - 1)$

(c) The speed v metres per second of a car t seconds after it starts is shown in the following table:

t :	**0**	**12**	**24**	**36**	**48**	**60**	**72**	**84**	**96**	**108**	**120**
v :	**0**	**3.60**	**10.08**	**18.90**	**21.60**	**18.54**	**10.26**	**5.40**	**4.50**	**5.40**	**9.00**

Using Simpson's one-third rule, find the distance travelled by the car in 2 minutes.

Ans. We have,

	v_0	v_1	v_2	v_3	v_4	v_5	v_6	v_7	v_8	v_9	v_{10}
t :	0	12	24	36	48	60	72	84	96	108	120
v :	0	3.60	10.08	18.90	21.60	18.54	10.26	5.40	4.50	5.40	9.00

If s metres is the distance covered in t seconds,

Then, $\frac{ds}{dt} = v$

$$\therefore \left[s \right]_{t=0}^{t=120} = \int_0^{120} v dt$$

Since, the number of sub-intervals is 10 (even).

Hence, by using Simpson's $\frac{1}{3^{rd}}$ rule,

$$\int_0^{120} v dt = \frac{h}{3}[(v_0 + v_{10}) + 4(v_1 + v_3 + v_5 + v_7 + v_9) + 2(v_2 + v_4 + v_6 + v_8)]$$

Since, h=12

$$\therefore \int_0^{120} vdt = \frac{12}{3}[(0+9) + 4(3.60 + 18.90 + 18.54 + 5.40 + 5.40) + 2(10.08 + 21.60 + 10.26 + 4.50)]$$

$$= 4[9 + 4(51.84) + 2(46.44)] = 4[309.24] = 1236.96$$

$\therefore$ The distance travelled by the car in 120 seconds i.e., 2 minutes is 1236.96 m.

(d) Find a root of the equation $x^3 - 4x - 15 = 0$ correct to 3 decimal places using Bisection method.

Ans. Here, $f(x) = x^3 - 4x - 15 = 0$

Now, we can see that

$f(2) = -15$; $\quad f(3) = 0$; $\quad f(4) = 33$

$\therefore f(2)f(4) < 0$.

Hence, there exist a root lies in interval]2,4[.

Now, we apply bisection method.

Here, the following results are shown in table.

No. of Bisection	Bisected value	$f(x_i)$	Improved Interval
1.	3	0	]2 , 3 [
2.	2.5	– 9.375	]2.5, 3 [
3.	2.75	– 5.2031	]2.75, 3 [
4.	2.875	– 2.736	]2.875, 3 [
5.	2.9375	– 1.4025	]2.9375, 3 [
6.	2.96875	– 0.7099	]2.96875, 3 [
7.	2.984375	– 0.35718	]2.984375, 3 [
8.	2.9921875	– 0.17913866	]2.9921875, 3 [
9.	2.99606375	– 0.089706481	]2.99609375, 3 [
10.	2.998046875	– 0.04488755	]2.999023438, 3 [

After 10th Bisection, the width of the interval is 0.000976562. Therefore, the root lies in]2.999023438, 3[

Hence, the required root correct to 3 decimal places is 2.999.

(e) Find a root of the equation $x^3 - 5x + 3 = 0$ correct to 3 decimals using Newton Raphson's method.

Ans. Given, $f(x) = x^3 - 5x + 3 = 0$

Since, f(x) being an algebraic function and $f'(x) = 3x^2 - 5$ also being an algebraic function.

Thus, f(x) satisfies all the conditions for applying Newton Raphson method. Now, we choose $x_0 = 1$ as the initial approximation to the root.

The iterated formula is $x_i = x_{i-1} - \dfrac{f(x_{i-1})}{f'(x_{i-1})}$, $i = 1, 2, 3.........$

Here, $x_0 = 1$. Then $f(x_0) = f(1) = -1$

and $f'(x_0) = f'(1) = 3 - 5 = -2$

$$\therefore x_1 = 1 - \frac{(-1)}{(-2)} = 1 - \frac{1}{2} = 0.5$$

for i=2, we get

$$x_2 = 0.5 - \frac{f(0.5)}{f'(0.5)} = 0.5 - \frac{(0.5)^3 - 5(0.5) + 3}{3(0.5)^2 - 5} = 0.5 - \frac{0.125 - 2.5 + 3}{0.75 - 5}$$

$$= 0.5 - \frac{0.625}{-4.25} = 0.5 + 0.147058824 = 0.647058824$$

for i=3, we get

$$x_3 = 0.647058824 - \frac{f(0.647058824)}{f'(0.647058824)} = 0.647058824 - \frac{0.0035619782}{-3.743944635}$$

$$= 0.647058824 + 0.000951397 = 0.648010221$$

for i=4, we get

$$x_4 = 0.648010221 - \frac{f(0.648010221)}{f'(0.648010221)} = 0.648010221 - \frac{0.032059563}{-3.740248260}$$

$$= 0.648010221 + 0.008571507 = 0.656581728$$

for i=5, we get

$$x_5 = 0.656620430$$

Since, x_4 and x_5 are same upto three decimal places. Hence, we stop the iteration process here.

Now, the root correct to three decimal places is 0.656.

(f) A civil engineer has measured the height of a 10 floor building as 2950 cm and the working height of each beam as 35 cm while the true values are 2945 cm and 30 cm respectively. Compare their absolute and relative errors.

Refer to Dec-2006, Q.No.-3(c), Page No.-248

Q2. (a) Given: sin45⁰=0.7071, sin50⁰=0.7660, sin55⁰=0.8192, sin60⁰=0.8660, find sin 52⁰, using Newton's forward interpolation formula.

Ans. We form the table of forward differences of f(x) as:

x	f(x) = Sinx	Δf	Δ²f	Δ³f
45	0.7071			
		0.0589		
50	0.7660		−0.0057	
		0.0532		−0.0007
55	0.8192		−0.0064	
		0.0468		
60	0.8660			

Here, the step length is h = 5.

Now, the Newton's forward interpolating polynomial is,

$$P_n(x) = f_0 + \frac{(x - x_0)}{1!}\frac{\Delta f_0}{h} + \frac{(x - x_0)(x - x_1)}{2!}\frac{\Delta^2 f_0}{h^2} + \ldots\ldots + \frac{(x - x_0)\ldots\ldots(x - x_{n-1})\Delta^n f_0}{n!h^n}$$

$$\therefore f(52) \simeq P(52) = 0.7071 + \frac{(52-45)(0.0589)}{1\times 5} + \frac{(52-45)(52-50)(-0.0057)}{2\times 25}$$

$$+ \frac{(52-45)(52-50)(52-55)(-0.0007)}{3\times 2\times 125}$$

$$= 0.7071 + 0.08246 + (-0.001596) + 0.000039200 = 0.7880032$$

Thus, $\sin 52^\circ$ =0.788 correct upto 3 decimal places.

(b) Find a root of the equation $x\log_{10} x = 1.2$ correct to three decimal places using Regula Falsi method.

Ans. Let $f(x) = x\log_{10} x - 1.2 = 0$

Now, we have to first find two numbers a and b such that f(a) f(b)<0. Since the function $\log_{10} x$ is defined only for positive values of x, Hence, we consider only positive numbers x. Let we take x = 1, 2, 3,........ Then, using a calculator,

$f(1) = 1(\log_{10} 1) - 1.2 = -1.2 < 0$

$f(2) = 2(\log_{10} 2) - 1.2 = 2(.30103) - 1.2 = -.59794 < 0$

$f(3) = 3(\log_{10} 3) - 1.2 = 3(.47712) - 1.2 = .23136 > 0$

This shows that f(2)f(3)<0 and therefore a root lies in]2,3[. Now put a=2 and b=3. Then, the first approximation of the root by using Regula Falsi method is,

$$x_1 = \frac{af(b) - bf(a)}{f(b) - f(a)} = \frac{2(.23136) - 3(-.59794)}{.23136 + .59794} = 2.72102$$

Now, f(2.72102)=2.72102($\log_{10} 2.72102$)–1.2 = –0.017086 < 0. Since f(2.72102)f(3)<0, a root lies in the interval]2.72102,3[.

Hence, the second approximation is,

$$x_2 = \frac{2.72102f(3) - 3f(2.72102)}{f(3) - f(2.72102)} = \frac{2.72102(.23136) - 3(-0.017086)}{.23136 - (-0.017086)} = 2.7402$$

We find $f(x_2) = -0.0004 < 0$

Therefore, the root lies in the interval]2.7402, 3[.

Now, the third approximation is obtained as,

$$x_3 = \frac{2.7402f(3) - 3f(2.7402)}{f(3) - f(2.7402)} = \frac{2.7402(.23136) - 3(-0.0004)}{.23136 - (-0.0004)} = 2.7406$$

Since x_2 and x_3 rounded off to three decimal places are the same. Therefore, we stop the process here. Hence, the desired approximate value of the root rounded off to three decimal places is 2.740.

(c) Compute the real root of the equation $3x^3 - 4x^2 + 3x - 4 = 0$. Correct to three decimals using Secant method.

Ans. Given, $f(x) = 3x^3 - 4x^2 + 3x - 4 = 0$

Here, f(0) = -4, f(1) = –2, f(2) = 10

Since, f(1) f(2)<0

Therefore, the root lies in interval]1, 2[.

Now, the iteration using secant method are defined as,

$$x_2 = \frac{x_0 f(x_1) - x_1 f(x_0)}{f(x_1) - f(x_0)}$$

i.e., $x_2 = \frac{1(10) - 2(-2)}{10 - (-2)} = \frac{10 + 4}{12} = \frac{14}{12} = 1.1667$

and $f(x_2) = 3(1.1667)^3 - 4(1.1667)^2 + 3(1.1667) - 4 = -1.1804$

Since, $f(x_2)f(2) < 0$.

Therefore, the root lies in interval]1.1667, 2[
Hence, the third approximation is,

$$x_3 = \frac{1.1667(10) - 2(-1.1804)}{10 - (-1.1804)} = 1.2547$$

and $f(x_3) = -0.6073$

Since, $f(x_3)f(2) < 0$

Therefore, the root lies in interval]1.2547,2[
Hence, the fourth approximation is,

$$x_4 = \frac{1.2547(10) - 2(-0.6073)}{10 - (-0.6073)} = 1.2974$$

and $f(x_4) = -0.2895$

Since, $f(x_4)f(2) < 0$

Therefore, the root lies in interval]1.2974, 2[.
Hence, the fifth approximation is,

$$x_5 = \frac{1.2974(10) - 2(-0.2895)}{10 - (-0.2895)} = 1.3172$$

and $f(x_5) = -0.1324$

Since, $f(x_5)f(2) < 0$

Therefore, the root lies in interval]1.3172, 2[
Hence, the sixth approximation is,

$$x_6 = \frac{1.3172(10) - 2(-0.1324)}{10 - (-0.1324)} = 1.3261$$

and $f(x_6) = -0.0122$

Since, $f(x_6)f(2) < 0$

Therefore, the root lies in interval]1.3261, 2[
Hence, the seventh approximation is,

$$x_7 = \frac{1.3261(10) - 2(-0.0122)}{10 - (-0.0122)} = 1.326$$

Since, x_6 and x_7 are same upto three decimal places. So, we stop the process. Therefore, the required root correct upto three decimal places is 1.326.

Q3. (a) Find the cube root of 47, using Newton-Raphson's method.

Ans. Let $x = \sqrt[3]{47}$

Then, we have $x^3 = 47$ i.e., $x^3 - 47 = 0$

Let $f(x) = x^3 - 47$

$\therefore f'(x) = 3x^2$

Here f(x) and f'(x), being an algebraic function, satisfies all the conditions for applying Newton – Raphson method.

Now, we choose $x_0 = 3.5$, This is because we know that $\sqrt{47}$ lies between $\sqrt{27}$ and $\sqrt{64}$.

Now, the iterated formula is:

$$x_i = x_{i-1} - \frac{f(x_i - 1)}{f'(x_i - 1)}, \; i = 1, 2, 3, \ldots\ldots$$

Here, $x_0 = 3.5$, Then $f(x_0) = -4.125$ and $f'(x_0) = 36.75$

$$\therefore x_1 = 3.5 - \frac{-4.125}{36.75} = 3.6122$$

for i=2, we get,

$$x_2 = 3.6122 - \frac{\left((3.6122)^3 - 47\right)}{3(3.6122)^2} = 3.6122 - \frac{0.13194}{39.1440} = 3.608829368$$

for i= 3, we get,

$$x_3 = 3.608829368 - \frac{\left((3.608829368)^3 - 47\right)}{3(3.608829368)^2} = 3.608829368 - \frac{0.000128460}{39.07094822}$$

$$= 3.608829368 - 0.000003288 = 3.608826080$$

Since, x_2 and x_3 are same upto 5 decimal places.

Hence, we stop the iteration process here.

Therefore, the cube root of 47, using Newton-Raphson's method, is 3.608826080.

(b) Apply Runge-Kutta method to find an approximate value of y for x=0.2 in steps of 0.1, if $\frac{dy}{dx} = x + y^2$, given that y=1, where x=0.

Ans. Here, the classical Runge–Kutta Method is,

$$y_{n+1} = y_n + \frac{1}{6}(K_1 + 2K_2 + 2K_3 + K_4)$$

Here, $t_0 = 0, y_0 = 1, h = 0.1$

$$K_1 = hf(t_0, y_0) = (0.1)(0,1) = (0.1)(1) = (0.1)$$

$$K_2 = hf\left(t_0 + \frac{h}{2}, y_0 + \frac{K_1}{2}\right) = (0.1)(0.05, 1.05) = (0.1)(1.1525) = 0.11525$$

$$K_3 = hf\left(t_0 + \frac{h}{2}, y_0 + \frac{K_2}{2}\right) = (0.1)(0.05, 1.057625) = (0.1)(1.168570641) = 0.116857064$$

$$K_4 = hf(t_0 + h, y_0 + K_3) = (0.1)(0.1, 1.1168570641) = (0.1)(1.347369701) = 0.134736970$$

$$\therefore \quad y(0.1) = 1 + \frac{1}{6}(0.1 + 2 \times 0.11525 + 2 \times 0.116857064 + 0.134736970)$$

$$= 1 + \frac{1}{6}(0.698951098) = 1.116491850$$

Now, taking $t_1 = 0.1, y_1 = 1.116491850$

We repeat the process and obtain,

$$K_1 = hf(t_1, y_1) = 0.1(0.1, 1.116491850) = (0.1)(1.346554051) = 0.134655405$$

$$K_2 = hf\left(t_1 + \frac{h}{2}, y_1 + \frac{K_1}{2}\right) = (0.1)(0.1 + 0.05, 1.116491850 + 0.067327703)$$

$$= (0.1)(0.15,1.183819553) = (0.1)(1.551428734) = 0.1551428734$$

$$K_3 = hf\left(t_1 + \frac{h}{2}, y_1 + \frac{K_2}{2}\right) = (0.1)\left(0.1 + 0.05, 1.116491850 + \frac{0.1551428734}{2}\right)$$

$$= (0.1)(0.15,1.194063287) = (0.1)(1.575787133) = 0.157578713$$

$$K_4 = hf(t_1 + h, y_1 + K_3) = (0.1)(0.1 + 0.1, 1.116491850 + 0.157578713)$$

$$= (0.1)(0.2,1.274070563) = (0.1)(1.8232558) = 0.18232558$$

$$\therefore y(0.2) = y(0.1) + \frac{1}{6}(K_1 + 2K_2 + 2K_3 + K_4)$$

$$= 1.116491850 + \frac{1}{6}(0.134655405 + 2 \times 0.1551428734 + 2 \times 0.157578713 + 0.18232558)$$

$$= 1.116491850 + \frac{1}{6}(0.942424158) = 1.273562543$$

$$\therefore \quad y(0.2) = 1.273562543$$

(c) Use Lagrange's interpolation formula to find the value of y when x =10, if the following table of x and y is given.

x :	5	6	9	11
y :	12	13	14	16

Ans. Here, the Lagrange's interpolating polynomial is,

$$L_0(x) = \frac{(x-6)(x-9)(x-11)}{(5-6)(5-9)(5-11)}; \qquad L_1(x) = \frac{(x-5)(x-9)(x-11)}{(6-5)(6-9)(6-11)};$$

$$L_2(x) = \frac{(x-5)(x-6)(x-11)}{(9-5)(9-6)(9-11)}; \qquad L_3(x) = \frac{(x-5)(x-6)(x-9)}{(11-5)(11-6)(11-9)}$$

$$\therefore f(x) = 12\frac{(x-6)(x-9)(x-11)}{(-1)\times(-4)\times(-6)} + 13\frac{(x-5)(x-6)(x-11)}{(1)\times(-3)\times(-5)}$$

$$+14\frac{(x-5)(x-6)(x-11)}{(4)(3)(-2)} + 16\frac{(x-5)(x-6)(x-9)}{(6)\times(5)\times(2)}$$

$$\Rightarrow f(10) = 12\times\frac{(10-6)(10-9)(10-11)}{-24} + 13\times\frac{(10-5)(10-9)(10-11)}{15}$$

$$+14\times\frac{(10-5)(10-6)(10-11)}{-24} + 16\times\frac{(10-5)(10-6)(10-9)}{60}$$

$$= \frac{4\times1\times-1}{-2} + \frac{13\times5\times1\times-1}{15} + \frac{14\times5\times4\times-1}{-24} + \frac{16\times5\times4\times1}{60}$$

$$= 2 - \frac{13}{3} + \frac{35}{3} + \frac{16}{3} = \frac{44}{3}$$

$$\therefore \quad f(10) = y(10) = \frac{44}{3}$$

Q4. (a) Using Newton's divided difference formula, evaluate f(8) and f(15), given:

$x:$	4	5	7	10	11	13
$f(x):$	48	100	294	900	1210	2028

Ans. The Newton's divided difference table is as follows:

x	f(x)	Δf(x)	Δ^2f(x)	Δ^3f(x)
4	48			
		$\underset{5}{\Delta} f(4)=\frac{100-48}{5-4}=52$		
5	100		$\underset{5,7}{\Delta^2} f(4)=\frac{97-52}{7-4}=15$	
		$\underset{7}{\Delta} f(5)=\frac{294-100}{7-5}=97$		$\underset{5,7,10}{\Delta^3} f(4)=\frac{21-15}{10-4}=1$
7	294		$\underset{7,10}{\Delta^2} f(5)=\frac{202-97}{10-5}=21$	
		$\underset{10}{\Delta} f(7)=\frac{900-294}{10-7}=202$		$\underset{7,10,11}{\Delta^3} f(5)=\frac{27-21}{11-5}=1$
10	900		$\underset{10,11}{\Delta^2} f(7)=\frac{310-202}{11-7}=27$	
		$\underset{11}{\Delta} f(10)=\frac{1210-900}{11-10}=310$		$\underset{10,11,13}{\Delta^3} f(7)=\frac{33-27}{13-7}=1$
11	1210		$\underset{11,13}{\Delta^2} f(10)=\frac{409-310}{13-10}=33$	
		$\underset{13}{\Delta} f(11)=\frac{2028-1210}{13-11}=409$		
13	2028			

$\therefore$ Newton's divided difference formula is:

$$f(x)=f(4)+(x-4)\underset{5}{\Delta}f(4)+(x-4)(x-5)\underset{5,7}{\Delta^2}f(4)+(x-4)(x-5)(x-7)\underset{5,7,10}{\Delta^3}f(4) \quad \text{...........(1)}$$

Putting x = 8 in (1),

We get f(8) = 48 + (8-4)×52 + (8-4) (8-5)×15 + (8-4) (8-5) (8-7)×1

$$= 48+208+180+12=448$$

Putting x = 15 in (1),

we get $f(15)=48+(15-4)\times 52+(15-4)(15-5)\times 15+(15-4)(15-5)(15-7)\times 1$

$$= 48+572+1650+880=3150.$$

(b) Find a real root of the equation $3x-6=x^2$ correct to three decimals using any iteration method.

Ans. Here, $f(x)=x^2-3x+6$

We find that the equation can be written as,

$x = 3 - \frac{6}{x} \Rightarrow g(x) = 3 - \frac{6}{x}$

Here, $g'(x) = \frac{6}{x^2}$

Now, at x = 3

$|g'(x)| = 0.667 < 1$

Hence, our assumption is satisfied for g(x).

Now, using the initial approximation at $x_0 = 3$.

We get the successive iteration are given by

$x_1 = g(3) = 1$; $x_2 = g(1) = -3$; $x_3 = g(-3) = 5$;

$x_4 = g(5) = 2.25$; $x_5 = g(2.25) = 0.333$; $x_6 = g(0.333) = -15.018$;

$x_7 = g(-15.018) = 3.340$; $x_8 = g(3.340) = 1.204$; $x_9 = g(1.204) = -1.985$;

$x_{10} = g(-1.985) = 6.022$; $x_{11} = g(6.022) = 2.004$; $x_{12} = g(2.004) = 0.005$;

$x_{13} = g(0.005) = -1197$; $x_{14} = g(-1197) = 3.005$; $x_{15} = g(3.005) = 1.003$;

$x_{16} = g(1.003) = -2.980$; $x_{17} = g(-2.980) = 5.013$;

: : :

: : :

After so many iterations, we reach to the result that there is no such root such that $|x_i - x_{i-1}| < 10^{-3}$

$\therefore$ The given equation does not contain any real root, it contain an imaginary root which can be calculated by quadratic formula as,

$$x = \frac{-(-3) \pm \sqrt{(-3)^2 - 4 \times 6}}{2} = \frac{3 \pm \sqrt{9 - 24}}{2} = \frac{3 \pm 3.873i}{2}$$

(c) Solve the following equations.

5x + 2y + z = 12

x + 4y + 2z = 15

x + 2y + 5z = 20

by using Jacobi's iteration method.

Ans. Given,

$5x + 2y + z = 12$ ...(1)

$x + 4y + 2z = 15$ ...(2)

$x + 2y + 5z = 20$ ...(3)

The matrix form of given equation are as,

$$\begin{bmatrix} 5 & 2 & 1 \\ 1 & 4 & 2 \\ 1 & 2 & 5 \end{bmatrix} \begin{bmatrix} x \\ y \\ z \end{bmatrix} = \begin{bmatrix} 12 \\ 15 \\ 20 \end{bmatrix}$$

The Jacobi method when applied to the given system of equations, becomes,

$$\left.\begin{array}{l} x^{(k+1)} = -\frac{1}{5}\left[2y^{(k)} + z^{(k)} - 12\right] = \frac{1}{5}\left[12 - 2y^{(k)} - z^{(k)}\right] \\ y^{(k+1)} = \frac{1}{4}\left[15 - x^{(k)} - 2z^{(k)}\right] \\ z^{(k+1)} = \frac{1}{5}\left[20 - x^{(k)} - 2y^{(k)}\right] \end{array}\right] \quad ....(4)$$

Starting with the initial approximation $x^{(0)} = y^{(0)} = z^{(0)} = \left[0\ 0\ 0\right]^T$, we obtain from the equation (4), the following result:

$k = 0$

$x^{(1)} = \frac{1}{5}[12 - 2\times0 - 0] = 2.4$; $y^{(1)} = \frac{1}{4}[15 - 0 - 2\times0] = 3.75$; $z^{(1)} = \frac{1}{5}[20 - 0 - 2\times0] = 4$

$k = 1$

$x^{(2)} = \frac{1}{5}[12\text{-}2\times3.75\text{-}4] = 0.1$; $y^{(2)} = \frac{1}{4}[15\text{-}2.4\text{-}2\times4] = 1.15$;

$z^{(2)} = \frac{1}{5}[20\text{-}2.4\text{-}2\times3.75] = 2.02$

$k = 2$

$x^{(3)} = \frac{1}{5}[12\text{-}2\times1.15\text{-}2.02] = 1.536$; $y^{(3)} = \frac{1}{4}[15 - 0.1 - 2\times2.02] = 2.715$;

$z^{(3)} = \frac{1}{5}[20\text{-}0.1\text{-}2\times1.15] = 3.52$

$k = 3$

$x^{(4)} = \frac{1}{5}[12 - 2\times2.715 - 3.52] = 0.61$; $y^{(4)} = \frac{1}{4}[15 - 1.536 - 2\times3.52] = 1.606$

$z^{(4)} = \frac{1}{5}[20 - 1.536 - 2\times2.715] = 2.607$

$k = 4$

$$\left.\begin{array}{l} x^{(5)} = \frac{1}{5}[12\text{-}2\times1.606\text{-}2.607] = 1.2362 \\ y^{(5)} = \frac{1}{4}[15\text{-}0.61\text{-}2\times2.607] = 2.294 \\ z^{(5)} = \frac{1}{5}[20\text{-}0.61\text{-}2\times1.606] = 3.2356 \end{array}\right] \quad ....(5)$$

Thus, after five iterations, we get the solution as given in equation (5), we find that after each iteration, we get better approximation to the exact solution

$[x\ y\ z] = [1\ 2\ 3]^T$

Q5. (a) Solve the following equations.

20x + y – 2z = 17

3x + 20y – z = -18

2x – 3y + 20z = 25

By applying Gauss-Seidal iteration method.

Ans. Refer to Dec-2007, Q.No.-3(b), Page No.-282
Thus, after three iterations, we can see that after each iterations, we get better approximation to the exact solution $[x\ y\ z] = [1 -1\ 1]^T$

(b) Solve the following equations.
3x + 4y – z = 8
-2x + y + z = 3
x + 2y – z = 2
by applying Gauss – Elimination method.
Ans. Given,

$$3x + 4y - z = 8 \quad \ldots(1)$$
$$-2x + y + z = 3 \quad \ldots(2)$$
$$x + 2y - z = 2 \quad \ldots(3)$$

To eliminate x from the second and third equation of system of equations, we add $= \frac{2}{3}$ times the first equation to the second equation and add $= \frac{-1}{3}$ times the first equation to the third equation. We obtain the new system as,

$$\left.\begin{array}{l} 3x + 4y - z = 8 \\ \frac{11}{3}y + \frac{1}{3}z = \frac{25}{3} \\ \frac{2}{3}y - \frac{2}{3}z = \frac{-2}{3} \end{array}\right] \quad \ldots.(4)$$

In the second stage, we eliminate y from the third equation of system (4).
Adding $= \frac{-2}{11}$ times the second equation to the third equation. We obtain the new system as,

$$\left.\begin{array}{l} 3x + 4y - z = 8 \\ \frac{11}{3}y + \frac{1}{3}z = \frac{25}{3} \\ \frac{-8}{11}z = \frac{-24}{11} \end{array}\right] \quad \ldots.(5)$$

Now, the system (5) is in upper triangular form and its solution is,
$x = 1, y = 2, z = 3$.

(c) If $u = \frac{4x^2y^3}{z^4}$ and errors in x, y and z be 0.001. Compute the relative maximum error in u when x = y = z = 1.
Refer to June-2007, Q.No.-5(c), Page No.-274

●●●

CS-71: COMPUTER ORIENTED NUMERICAL TECHNIQUES
June, 2012

*Note: Question number 1 is **compulsory.** Attempt only **three** questions from the rest. In total, you have to answer **four** questions. Use of Calculator is permitted.*

Q1. (a) Solve the quadratic equation. $x^2+9.9x-1=0$ using two decimal digit floating arithmetic with rounding.

Ans. Solving the quadratic equation, we have,

$$x_1 = \frac{-b+\sqrt{b^2-4ac}}{2a} = \frac{-9.9+\sqrt{(9.9)^2-4.1.(-1)}}{2} = \frac{-9.9+\sqrt{102}}{2} = \frac{-9.9+10}{2} = \frac{0.1}{2} = .05$$

While, the true solutions are -10 and 0.1.

Now, if rationalize the expression $x_1 = \frac{-b+\sqrt{b^2-4ac}}{2a}$

$$= \frac{-b+\sqrt{b^2-4ac}}{2a} \times \frac{b+\sqrt{b^2-4ac}}{b+\sqrt{b^2-4ac}} = \frac{\left(\sqrt{b^2-4ac}\right)^2 - b^2}{2a\left(b+\sqrt{b^2-4ac}\right)}$$

$$= \frac{b^2-4ac-b^2}{2a\left(b+\sqrt{b^2-4ac}\right)} = \frac{-4ac}{2a\left(b+\sqrt{b^2-4ac}\right)} = \frac{-2c}{\left(b+\sqrt{b^2-4ac}\right)} = \frac{2}{9.9+\sqrt{102}}$$

$$= \frac{2}{9.9+10} = \frac{2}{19.9} \simeq \frac{2}{20} = 0.1,(0.1000024)$$

Which is one of the true solutions.

(b) Evaluate $f(x) = \frac{x^3}{x-\sin x}$ when $x = .12\times 10^{-10}$ using two digit arithmetic.

Refer to June - 2008, Q.No.-1 (b), Page No.-288

(c) Perform three iterations using Gauss Seidal for following system of equation rounded to 4 decimal,

$$\begin{bmatrix} -8 & 1 & 1 \\ 1 & -5 & -1 \\ 1 & 1 & -4 \end{bmatrix} \begin{bmatrix} x_1 \\ x_2 \\ x_3 \end{bmatrix} = \begin{bmatrix} 1 \\ 16 \\ 7 \end{bmatrix}$$

Ans. The Gauss-Seidal method when applied to the system of given equations becomes,

$$x_1^{(k+1)} = \frac{1}{8}\left[x_2^{(k)} + x_3^{(k)} - 1\right]$$

$$x_2^{(k+1)} = \frac{1}{5}\left[x_1^{(k+1)} - x_3^{(k)} - 16\right]$$

$$x_3^{(k+1)} = \frac{1}{4}\left[x_1^{(k+1)} + x_2^{(k+1)} - 7\right], k = 0,1,...$$

Taking $x^{(0)} = 0$, we obtain the following iterations.

First iteration:

$$x_1^{(1)} = \frac{1}{8}[0+0-1] = -0.125$$

$$x_2^{(1)} = \frac{1}{5}[-0.125-0-16] = -3.225$$

$$x_3^{(1)} = \frac{1}{4}[-0.125-3.225-7] = -2.5875$$

Second iteration:

$$x_1^{(2)} = \frac{1}{8}[-3.225-2.5875-1] = -0.8516$$

$$x_2^{(2)} = \frac{1}{5}[-0.8516+2.5875-16] = -2.8528$$

$$x_3^{(2)} = \frac{1}{4}[-0.8516-2.8528-7] = -2.6761$$

Third iteration:

$$x_1^{(3)} = \frac{1}{8}[-2.8528-2.6761-1] = -0.8161$$

$$x_2^{(3)} = \frac{1}{5}[-0.8161+2.6761-16] = -2.8280$$

$$x_3^{(3)} = \frac{1}{4}[-0.8161-2.828-7] = -2.6610$$

Hence, the result obtained after three iterations by Gauss-Seidal method was,

$$x^{(3)} = [-0.8161 - 2.8280 - 2.6610]^T$$

(d) Find f'(x), given f_0, f_1, f_2 at x_0, x_1, x_2 respectively. Using Lagrange interpolation.

Ans. We know that,

By Lagrange's interpolation formula $f(x) \approx P_2(x) = L_0(x)f_0 + L_1(x)f_1 + L_2(x)f_2$

Where,

$$L_0(x) = \frac{(x-x_1)(x-x_2)}{(x_0-x_1)(x_0-x_2)} \; ; L_0'(x) = \frac{2x-x_1-x_2}{(x_0-x_1)(x_0-x_2)}$$

$$L_1(x) = \frac{(x-x_0)(x-x_2)}{(x_1-x_0)(x_1-x_2)} \; ; L_1'(x) = \frac{2x-x_0-x_2}{(x_1-x_0)(x_1-x_2)}$$

$$L_2(x) = \frac{(x-x_0)(x-x_1)}{(x_2-x_0)(x_2-x_1)} \; ; L_2'(x) = \frac{2x-x_0-x_1}{(x_2-x_0)(x_2-x_1)}$$

Hence,

$$f'(x) \approx P_2'(x) = L_0'(x)f_0 + L_1'(x)f_1 + L_2'(x)f_2$$

$$= \frac{2x-x_1-x_2}{(x_0-x_1)(x_0-x_2)} \times (f_0) + \frac{2x-x_0-x_2}{(x_0-x_1)(x_0-x_2)} \times (f_1) + \frac{2x-x_0-x_1}{(x_2-x_0)(x_2-x_1)} \times (f_3)$$

(e) Evaluate $\int_{0.2}^{0.4} (\sin x - \ln x + e^x)\, dx$ using Trapezoidal rule, h=0.1.

Ans. Let $f(x) = \sin x - \ln x + e^x$

Now, f (0.2) = 3.02951; f (0.3) = 2.84935; f (0.4) = 2.797534
and h = 0.1 (given)
Since,

$$I_T[f]=\left(\frac{h}{2}\right)[\text{First ordinate + Last ordinate +2(sum of the remaining ordinates)}]$$

$$=\left(\frac{0.1}{2}\right)\left[f(0.2)+f(0.4)+2f(0.3)\right]$$

$$=\left(\frac{0.1}{2}\right)\left[3.02951+2.797534+2(2.84935)\right]=\left(\frac{0.1}{2}\right)[11.525744]=0.57629$$

(f) Perform three iterations to find root of the equation $x^3-3x-5=0$ by Newton Raphson method.

Ans. Let $f(x)=x^3-3x-5=0$

Since, f(x) being an algebraic function and $f'(x)=3x^2-3$ also being an algebraic function.

Thus, f(x) satisfies all the conditions for applying Newton Raphson method. Now, we choose x_0=2 as the initial approximation to the root.

The iterated formula is,

$$x_i=x_{i-1}-\frac{f(x_{i-1})}{f'(x_{i-1})},\ i=1,2,...$$

Then, f (x_0) = f (2)= -3

and $f'(x_0)=f'(1)=9$

$$\therefore x_1=x_0-\frac{f(x_0)}{f'(x_0)} \Rightarrow 2-\frac{(-3)}{9}=2.333$$

for i = 2, we get,

$$x_2=x_1-\frac{f(x_1)}{f'(x_1)}$$

$$\Rightarrow 2.333-\frac{f(2.333)}{f'(2.333)} \Rightarrow 2.333-\frac{0.6992}{13.3287} \Rightarrow 2.333-0.05246=2.28054$$

for i=3, we get,

$$x_3=x_2-\frac{f(x_2)}{f'(x_2)}$$

$$=2.28054-\frac{f(2.28054)}{f'(2.28054)}=2.28054-\frac{0.019155}{12.60259}=2.28054-0.00152=2.279$$

Hence, after three iterations of the Newton Raphson method, the required root of the given equation is 2.279

Q2. (a) Find real root of the equation $f(x)=x^3-x-1=0$ using Bisection Method in 4 iterations.

Ans. Here, f (x) = x^3–x–1 = 0

Now, we can see that,

$f(1) = -1; \qquad f(2) = 5$

$\therefore \; f(1)\,f(2) < 0$

Hence, there exists a root lies in interval $]1,2[$.

Now, we apply bisection method.

Here, the following result are shown in table.

No. of iterations	Bisected value	$f(x_i)$	Improved interval
(1)	1.5	0.875	]1,1.5[
(2)	1.25	-0.296875	]1.25,1.5[
(3)	1.375	0.22460	]1.25,1.375[
(4)	1.3125	-0.05151	]1.3125,1.375[

After 4 iterations, the root lies in] 1.3125, 1.375[.

Therefore, the required root of the given equation using bisection method is 1.3125.

(b) Solve the following system of equation by Gauss Elimination method,

$4x_1 + x_2 + x_3 = 4$; $\qquad x_1 + 4x_2 - 2x_3 = 4$; $\qquad 3x_1 + 2x_2 - 4x_3 = 6$

Ans. Given,

$4x_1 + x_2 + x_3 = 4 \qquad \ldots (1)$

$x_1 + 4x_2 - 2x_3 = 4 \qquad \ldots (2)$

$3x_1 + 2x_2 - 4x_3 = 6 \qquad \ldots (3)$

To eliminate x_1 from the second and third equations, we add $= -\frac{1}{4}$ times the first equation to the second equation and add $= -\frac{3}{4}$ times the first equation to the third equation.

We obtain the new system as,

$$\left.\begin{array}{l} 4x_1 + x_2 + x_3 = 4 \\ \frac{15}{4}x_2 - \frac{9}{4}x_3 = 3 \\ \frac{5}{4}x_2 - \frac{19}{4}x_3 = 3 \end{array}\right\} \qquad \ldots.(4)$$

In the second stage, we eliminate x_2 from the third equation. For this, we add $= -\frac{1}{3}$ times the second equation to the third equation.

We obtain the new system as,

$$\left.\begin{array}{l} 4x_1 + x_2 + x_3 = 4 \\ \frac{15}{4}x_2 - \frac{9}{4}x_3 = 3 \\ \qquad -4x_3 = 3 \end{array}\right\} \qquad \ldots.(5)$$

Now, system (5) is an upper triangular form, and its solution is,

$x_1 = 1, \; x_2 = \frac{1}{2}, \; x_3 = -\frac{1}{2}$

(c) Find Lagrange Interpolating polynomial for the following data:

x	1/4	1/3	1
f(x)	-1	2	7

Ans. We have,

$x_0 = 1/4,\ x_1 = 1/3,\ x_2 = 1 \text{ and } f_0 = -1,\ f_1 = 2, f_3 = 7$

Now, the Lagrange's interpolation polynomial is given by

$$P(x) = L_0(x)f_0 + L_1(x)f_1 + L_2(x)f_2 \qquad .....(1)$$

where

$$L_0(x) = \frac{(x-x_1)(x-x_2)}{(x_0-x_1)(x_0-x_2)} = \frac{\left(x-\frac{1}{3}\right)(x-1)}{\left(\frac{1}{4}-\frac{1}{3}\right)\left(\frac{1}{4}-1\right)} = \frac{16}{3}(3x-1)(x-1),$$

$$L_1(x) = \frac{(x-x_0)(x-x_2)}{(x_1-x_0)(x_1-x_2)} = \frac{\left(x-\frac{1}{4}\right)(x-1)}{\left(\frac{1}{3}-\frac{1}{4}\right)\left(\frac{1}{3}-1\right)} = -\frac{9}{2}(4x-1)(x-1),$$

$$L_2(x) = \frac{(x-x_0)(x-x_1)}{(x_2-x_0)(x_2-x_1)} = \frac{\left(x-\frac{1}{4}\right)\left(x-\frac{1}{3}\right)}{\left(1-\frac{1}{4}\right)\left(1-\frac{1}{3}\right)} = \frac{1}{6}(4x-1)(3x-1).$$

Substituting these values in equation (1), we get

$$P(x) = \frac{16}{3}(3x-1)(x-1)\times(-1) - \frac{9}{2}(4x-1)(x-1)\times(2) + \frac{1}{6}(4x-1)(3x-1)\times(7)$$

$$\Rightarrow \frac{-16}{3}(3x-1)(x-1) - 9(4x-1)(x-1) + \frac{7}{6}(4x-1)(3x-1)$$

$$\Rightarrow \frac{-32(3x^2-4x+1) - 54(4x^2-5x+1) + 7(12x^2-7x+1)}{6}$$

$$\Rightarrow \frac{-96x^2+128x-32-216x^2+270x-54+84x^2-49x+7}{6} \Rightarrow \frac{-228x^2+349x-79}{6}$$

$\therefore$ The required Lagrange's interpolating polynomial for given data is:

$$P(x) = \frac{-1}{6}(228x^2-349x+79)$$

Q3. (a) Find root of the equation $f(x) = x^3 - 2x - 5 = 0$ using Regula Falsi method correct to 2 decimal places.

Ans. Here, $f(x) = x^3 - 2x - 5 = 0$

Now, we can see that,

$f(2) = 2^3 - 2\times 2 - 5 = -1;$ $\qquad f(3) = 3^3 - 2\times 3 - 5 = 16$

Since, f(2) f(3)< 0, Therefore, a root lies in]2, 3[

Now, put a = 2, b = 3

So, first approximation of the root is,

$$x_1 = \frac{a(f(b)) - b(f(a))}{f(b) - f(a)} = \frac{2(f(3)) - 3(f(2))}{f(3) - f(2)} = \frac{2(16) - 3(-1)}{16 - (-1)} = \frac{32 + 3}{17} = 2.05882$$

and, f(2.05882) = -0.390837 < 0

Since, f(2.05882) f(3) < 0.

Therefore, the root lies in]2.05882,3[

Now, second approximation of the root is

$$x_2 = \frac{2.05882(16) - 3(-0.390837)}{16 - (-0.390837)} = \frac{32.94112 + 1.172511}{16.390837} = 2.081262$$

and, f(2.081262) = - 0.147222 < 0

Since, f(2.081262) f(3) < 0

Therefore, the root lies in]2.081262, 3[

Now, third approximation of the root is,

$$x_3 = \frac{2.081262(16) - 3(-0.147222)}{16 - (-0.147222)} = \frac{33.300192 + 0.441666}{16.147222} = 2.089638$$

and $f(2.089638) = -0.05468$

Since, f(2.089638) f(3) < 0

Therefore, the root lies in]2.089638, 3[

Now, fourth approximation of the root is,

$$x_4 = \frac{2.089638(16) - 3(-0.05468)}{16 - (-0.05468)} = \frac{33.598248}{16.05468} = 2.092738$$

Since, x_4 and x_3 are rounded off to two decimal places are same, so we stop the process here. Hence, the desired approximative value of the root using Regula Falsi method correct to two decimal places is 2.09.

(b) Perform three iteration of Jacobi method for following system of equation.

$$\begin{bmatrix} 5 & -1 & -1 & -1 \\ -1 & 10 & -1 & -1 \\ -1 & -1 & 5 & 1 \\ -1 & -1 & -1 & 10 \end{bmatrix} \begin{bmatrix} x_1 \\ x_2 \\ x_3 \\ x_4 \end{bmatrix} = \begin{bmatrix} -4 \\ 12 \\ 8 \\ 34 \end{bmatrix}$$

Starting with X = (0,0,0,0).

Ans. When Jacobi method is applied to given system of equations becomes,

$$x_1^{(k+1)} = \frac{-1}{5}[-x_2^{(k)} - x_3^{(k)} - x_4^{(k)} + 4] = \frac{1}{5}[x_2^{(k)} + x_3^{(k)} + x_4^{(k)} - 4]$$

$$x_2^{(k+1)} = \frac{-1}{10}[-x_1^{(k)} - x_3^{(k)} - x_4^{(k)} - 12] = \frac{1}{10}[x_1^{(k)} + x_3^{(k)} + x_4^{(k)} + 12]$$

$$x_3^{(k+1)} = \frac{-1}{5}[-x_1^{(k)} - x_2^{(k)} + x_4^{(k)} - 8] = \frac{1}{5}[x_1^{(k)} + x_2^{(k)} - x_4^{(k)} + 8]$$

$$x_4^{(k+1)} = \frac{-1}{10}[-x_1^{(k)} - x_2^{(k)} - x_3^{(k)} - 34] = \frac{1}{10}[x_1^{(k)} + x_2^{(k)} + x_3^{(k)} + 34]$$

Now, starting with X = (0, 0, 0, 0), we get,

First Iteration:

$x_1^{(1)} = \frac{1}{5}[0+0+0-4] = -0.8$; $x_2^{(1)} = \frac{1}{10}[0+0+0+12] = 1.2$

$x_3^{(1)} = \frac{1}{5}[0+0-0+8] = 1.6$; $x_4^{(1)} = \frac{1}{10}[0+0+0+34] = 3.4$

Second Iteration

$x_1^{(2)} = \frac{1}{5}[1.2+1.6+3.4-4] = 0.44$; $x_2^{(2)} = \frac{1}{10}[-0.8+1.6+3.4+12] = 1.62$

$x_3^{(2)} = \frac{1}{5}[-0.8+1.2-3.4+8] = 1$; $x_4^{(2)} = \frac{1}{10}[-0.8+1.2+1.6+34] = 3.6$

Third iteration:

$x_1^{(3)} = \frac{1}{5}[1.62+1+3.6-4] = 0.44$; $x_2^{(3)} = \frac{1}{10}[0.44+1+3.6+12] = 1.704$

$x_3^{(3)} = \frac{1}{5}[0.44+1.62-3.6+8] = 1.292$; $x_4^{(3)} = \frac{1}{10}[0.44+1.62+1+34] = 3.706$

Thus, after three iterations, we get the solution as $[0.44\ 1.704\ 1.292\ 3.706]^T$

(c) Solve $\int_0^1 \frac{dx}{1+x}$ using Simpson $\frac{1}{3}$ rule, $h = \frac{1}{2}$.

Ans. Here $x_0 = 0, x_1 = 0.5, x_2 = 1$ and $h = \frac{1}{2}$

Using Simpson's $\frac{1}{3}$ rule, we have,

$$I_s[f] = \frac{h}{3}[f(0) + 4f(0.5) + f(1)] = \frac{1}{6}\left[1 + \frac{8}{3} + 0.5\right] = 0.694445$$

Q4. (a) Use Taylor Series method recursively to solve $y' = x^2 + y^2, y(0) = 0$ for the interval (0, 0.4) Using subinterval of size 0.2.

Ans. We have h = 0.2 and we wish to find y (0.4)

Now, we know that Taylor Series method of $o(h^3)$ is

$$y_{k+1} = y_k + hy'_k + \frac{h^2 y''_k}{2} + \frac{h^3}{6} y'''k$$

Now, with y(0) = 0

$y' = x^2 + y^2$; $y'(0) = 0$

$y'' = 2x + 2yy'$; $y''(0) = 0$

$y''' = 2 + 2yy'' + 2(y')^2$; $y'''(0) = 2$

Hence, $y(0.2) = 0 + 0 + 0 + \frac{(0.2)^3}{6} \times 2 = 0.002667$

Now,

$$y'(0.2) = (0.2)^2 + (0.002667)^2 = 0.04001$$

$$y''(0.2) = 2\times 0.2 + 2(0.002667)(0.04001) = 0.4002$$

$$y'''(0.2) = 2 + 2(0.002667)(0.4002) + 2(0.04001)^2 = 2.005336267$$

Hence,

$$y(0.4) = 0.002667 + (0.2)(0.04001) + \frac{(0.2)^2(0.4002)}{2} + \frac{(0.2)^3(2.005336267)}{6}$$

$$= 0.002667 + 0.008 + 0.008 + 0.002673 = 0.02134$$

(b) Find cubic polynomial which takes y(0) =1, y(1) = 0, y(2) = 1, y(3) = 10 and hence find y(4) by Newton Forward Difference for Interpolation.

Ans. We form a table of Newton forward differences for interpolation as:

x	y	Δy	$\Delta^2 y$	$\Delta^3 y$
0	1			
		-1		
1	0		1	
		1		1
2	1		4	
		9		
3	10			

$\therefore$ The required cubic polynomial is,

$$P(x) = 1 + (x-0)\times(-1) + (x-0)(x-1)\times(1) + (x-0)(x-1)(x-2)\times(1)$$

$$= 1 - x + x^2 - x + x^3 - 3x^2 + 2x$$

$$= x^3 - 2x^2 + 1$$

Now, $y(4) = p(4) = (4)^3 - 2(4)^2 + 1$

$$= 64 - 32 + 1 = 33$$

(c) Perform two iteration of Newton Raphson method on the quadration equation $x^4 - 4x^2 + 4 = 0$, $x_0 = 1.5$. It has double root.

Ans. Consider, $f(x) = x^2 - 4x^2 + 4 = 0$ which can be written as $(x^2-2)^2$, hence it contain double roots.

Now, f(x) and f'x which is equal to $4x^3 - 8x$, being an algebraic function.

Thus, f(x) satisfies all the conditions for applying Newton Raphson method.

Now, we choose $x_0 = 1.5$ (given) as the initial approximation to the root

The iterated formula is,

$$x_i = x_{i-1} - \frac{f(x_{i-1})}{f'(x_{i-1})}, i = 1.2..$$

Here, $x_0 = 1.5$

Then $f(x_0)=f(1.5)=0.0625$

and $f'(x_0)=f'(1.5)=1.5$

$\therefore\ x_1=1.5-\dfrac{0.0625}{1.5}=1.4583$

For i = 2, we get

$$x_2=1.4583-\frac{f(1.4583)}{f'(1.4583)}=1.4583-\frac{0.0160374}{0.73870}=1.436589698$$

Thus, after two iteration of Newton Raphson method, we get the required root as 1.436589698.

Q5. (a) Evaluate $\int_1^5 f(x)dx$ using Simpson $\frac{1}{3}$ rule on following data.

1	2	3	4	5
13	15	70	80	100

Ans. We have, h = 1

and $x_0=1,\ x_1=2,\ x_2=3,\ x_3=4,\ x_4=5,\ f_0=13, f_1=15, f_2=70, f_3=80, f_4=100$

Now, using Simpson's $\frac{1}{3}$ rule, we have,

$$I_s[f]=\frac{h}{3}\left[f_0+f_4+2(f_2)+4(f_1+f_3)\right]$$

$$=\frac{1}{3}\left[13+100+2(70)+4(15+80)\right]=\frac{1}{3}[633]=211$$

(b) Given $\frac{dy}{dx}=y-x, y(0)=2$. Find y(0.1) and y(0.2) using Runge Kutta method of second order, correct to 4 decimal places.

Ans. Here, the optimal Runge Kutta method of second order is:

$$y_{n+1}=y_n+\frac{1}{4}(k_1+3k_2)$$

Now, here, $t_0=0,\ y_0=2,\ h=0.1$

$k_1=hf(t_0,y_0)=(0.1)(2-0)=0.2$

$$k_2=hf\left(t_0+\frac{2h}{3},\ y_0+\frac{2k_1}{3}\right)=(0.1)\left(0+\frac{2\times0.1}{3},2+\frac{2\times0.2}{3}\right)=(0.1)\ (0.067,\ 2.133)$$

= (0.1) (2.133-0.067) = (0.1) (2.0663) = 0.20663

$$\therefore\ y(0.1)=2+\frac{1}{4}(0.2+3\times0.20663)=2+\frac{1}{4}(0.81989)=2.2049725$$

Now, taking t = 0.1, $y_1=2.2049725$

We repeat the process and obtain,

$k_1=hf(t_1,y_1)=(0.1)(0.1,\ 2.2049725)=(0.1)(2.2049725-0.1)$

$$=(0.1)(2.1049725)=0.21049725$$

$$k_2=hf\left(t_1+\frac{2h}{3},y_1+\frac{2k_1}{3}\right)=(0.1)\left(0.1+\frac{2\times0.1}{3},2.2049725+\frac{2\times0.21049725}{3}\right)$$

$$=(0.1)(0.1667,2.345304)=(0.1)(2.345304-0.1667)$$

$$=(0.1)(2.178604)=0.2178604$$

$$\therefore\ y(0.2)=2.2049725+\frac{1}{4}(0.21049725+3\times0.2178604)$$

$$= 2.2049725 + 0.216019613 \quad = 2.420992113$$

$\therefore y(0.1) = 2.2050$ and $y(0.2) = 2.4210$ are the values correct to 4 decimal places.

(c) Solve y' = -y with y(0) = 1 for x = 0.04 and step length = 0.01 using Euler's Method.

Ans. Euler's Method is,

$$y_{k+1}=h+y_k+hy_k^2$$

Now starting with $t_0=0$, and $y_0=1$, we have the following tables of values,

t	y(t)
0.01	1.02
0.02	1.0404040
0.03	1.061228405
0.04	1.081840689

Table : h =0.01

$\therefore$ y(0.04) = 1.081840689

●●●